Large Body and Plus size Croquis Fashion Design Sketchbook

Large Body and Plus size Croquis Fashion Design Sketchbook

By R. S. Fair

Copyright © 2020 by R. S. Fair

All rights reserved.

For Kevin and Markas

This Book Belongs to

_____

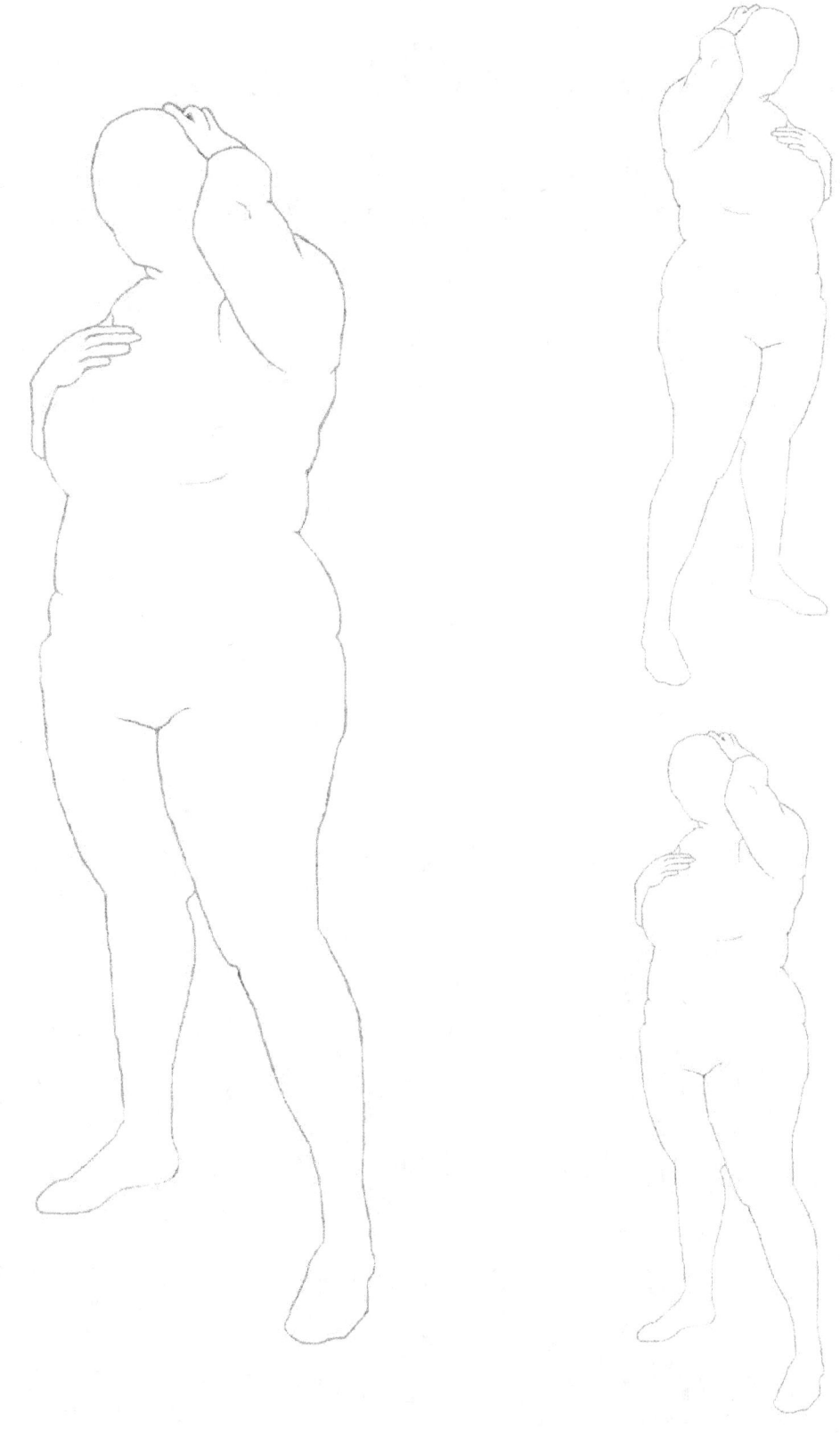

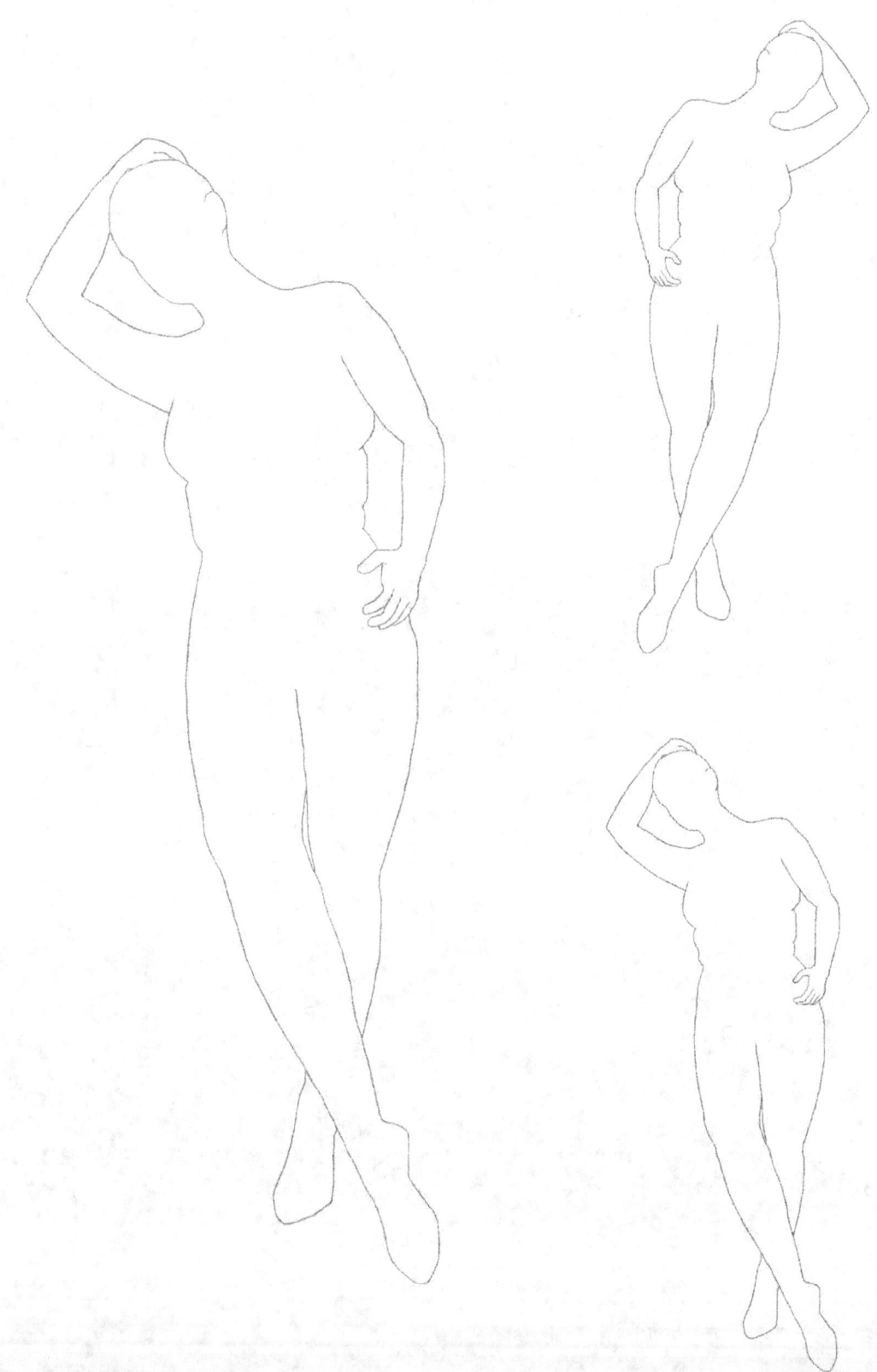

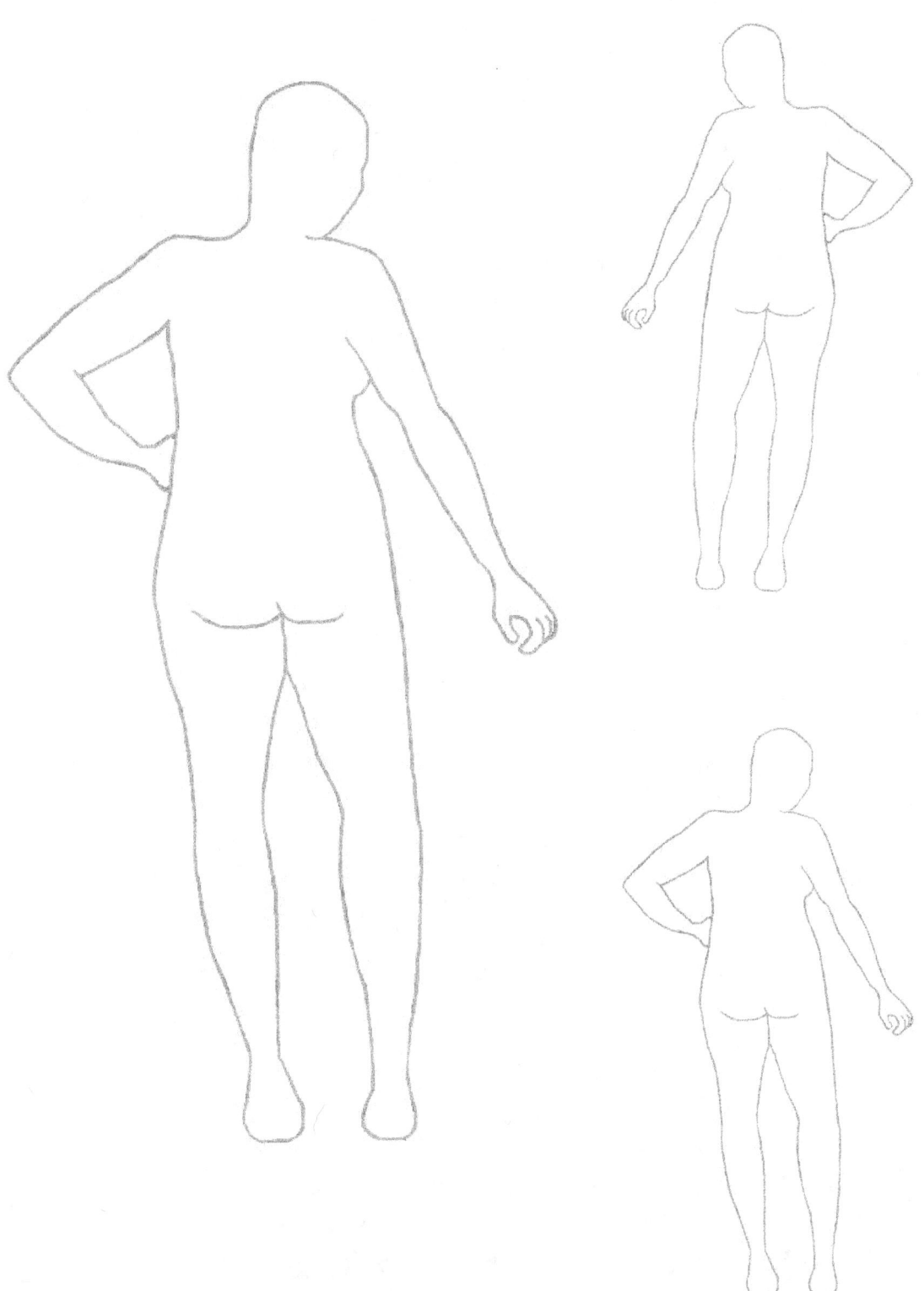

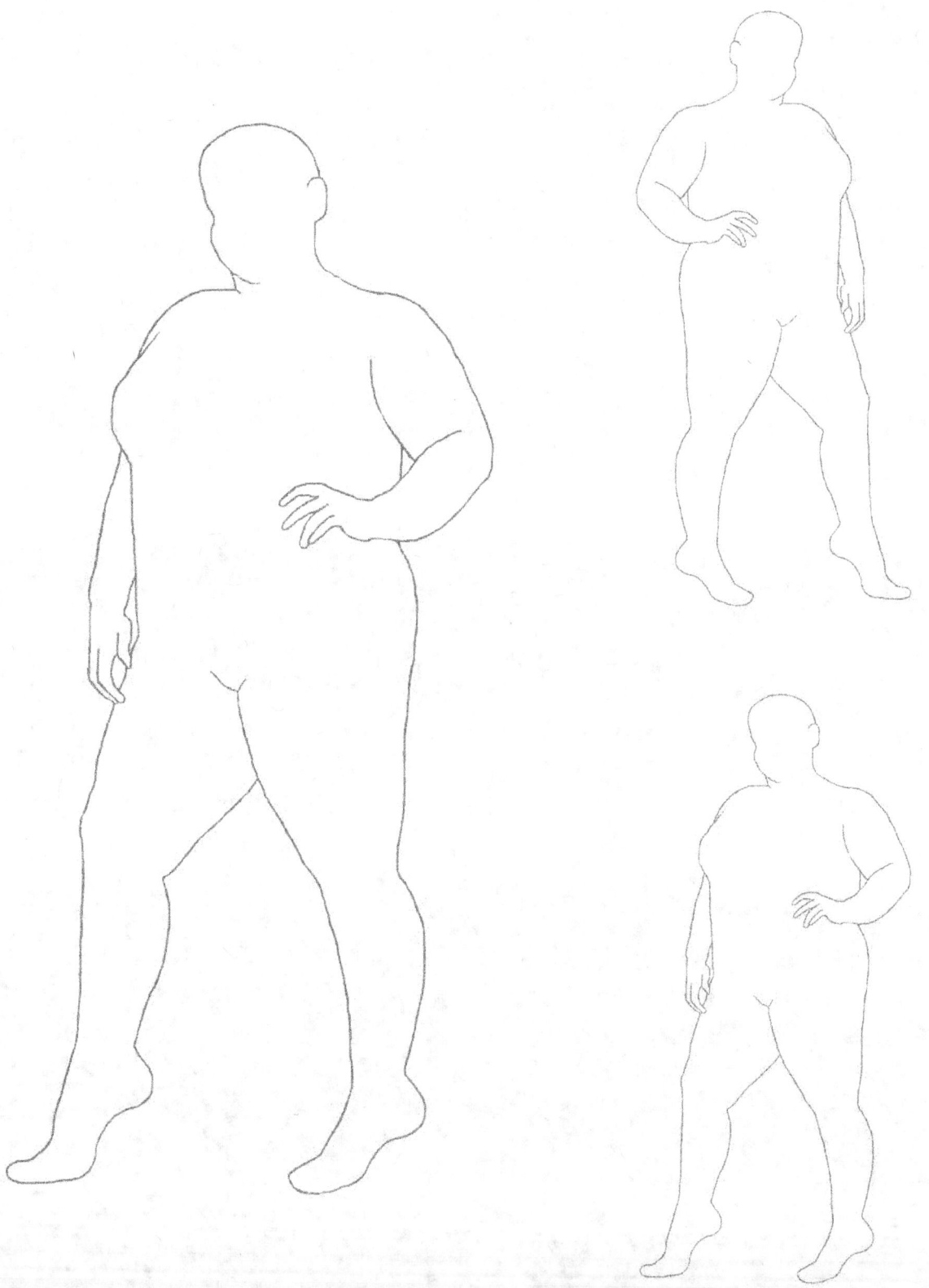

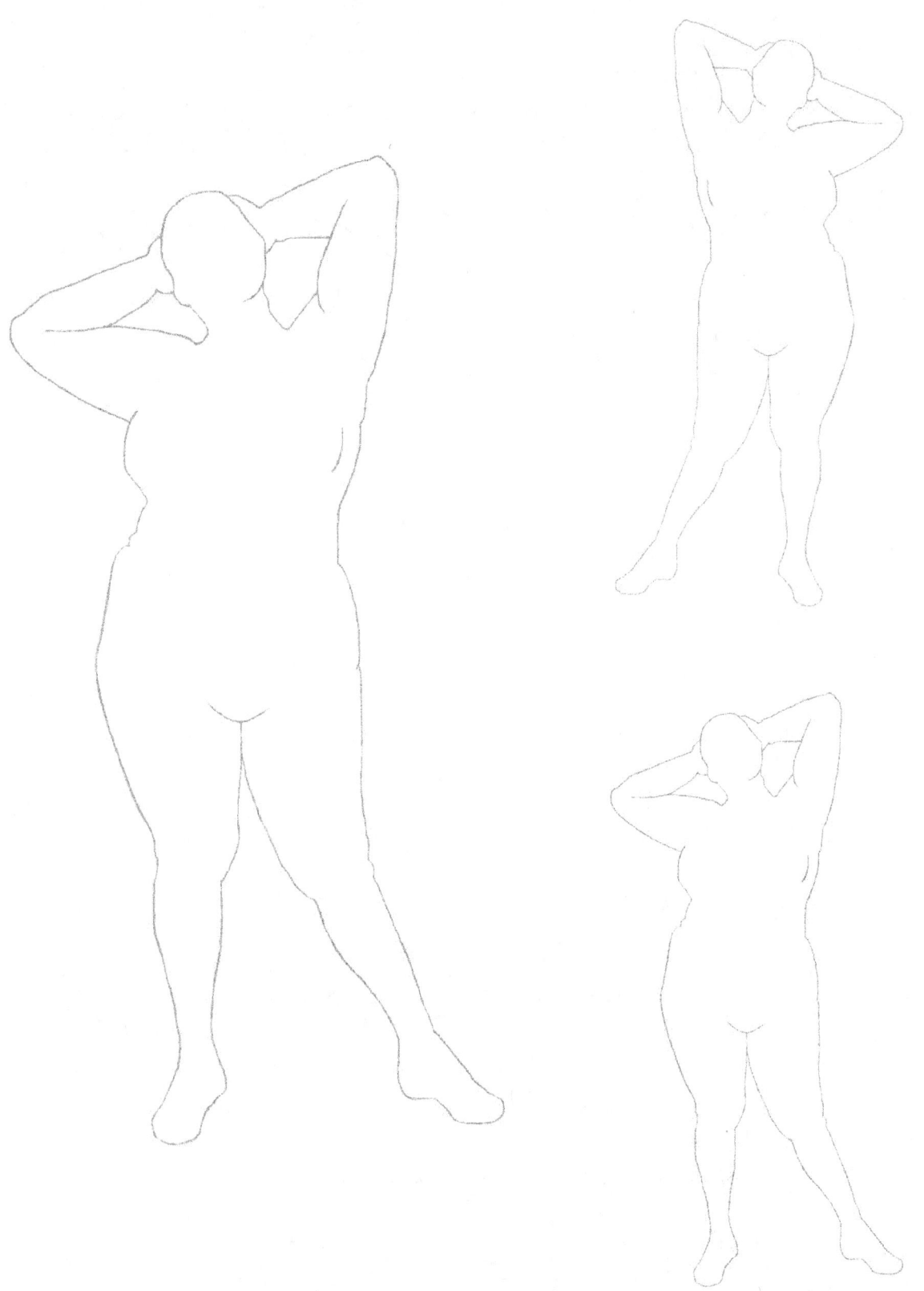

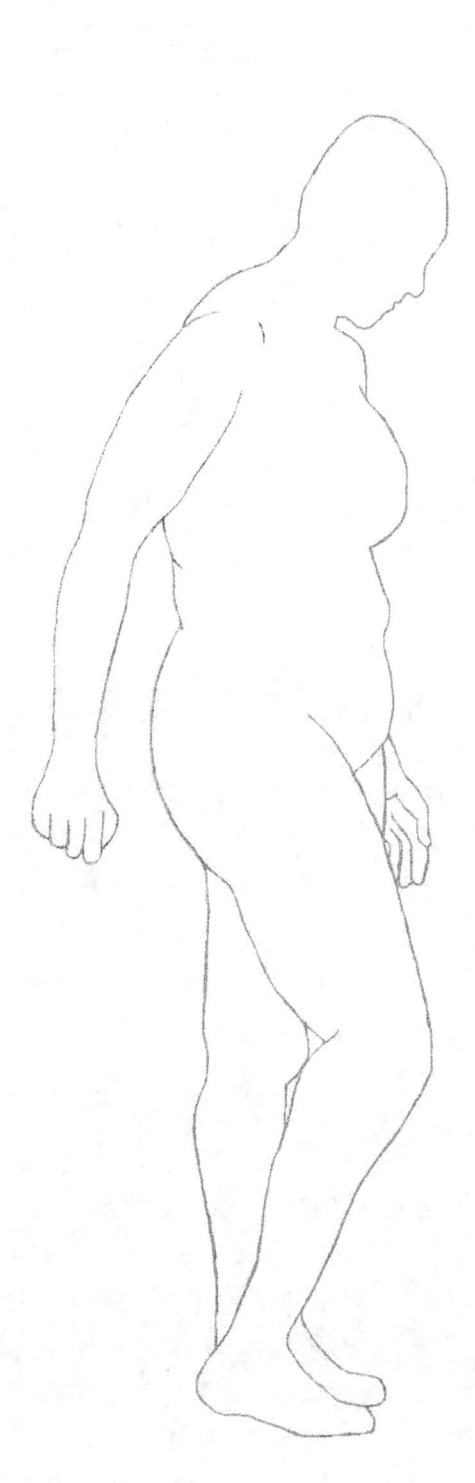
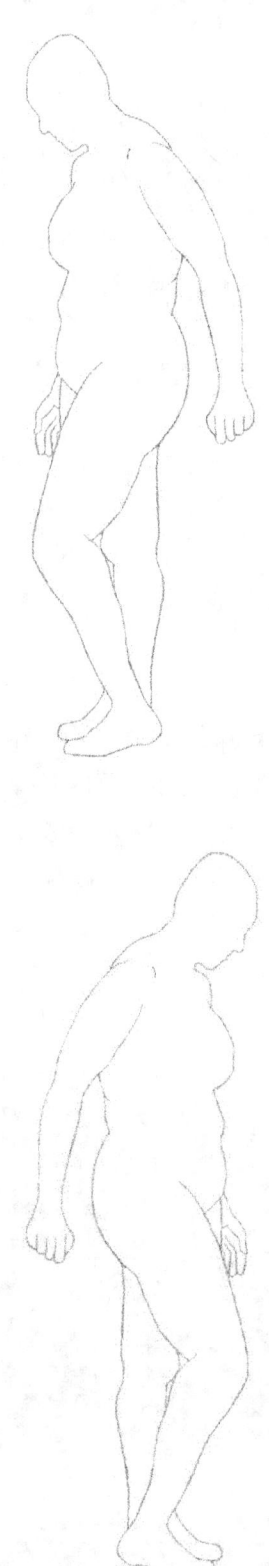

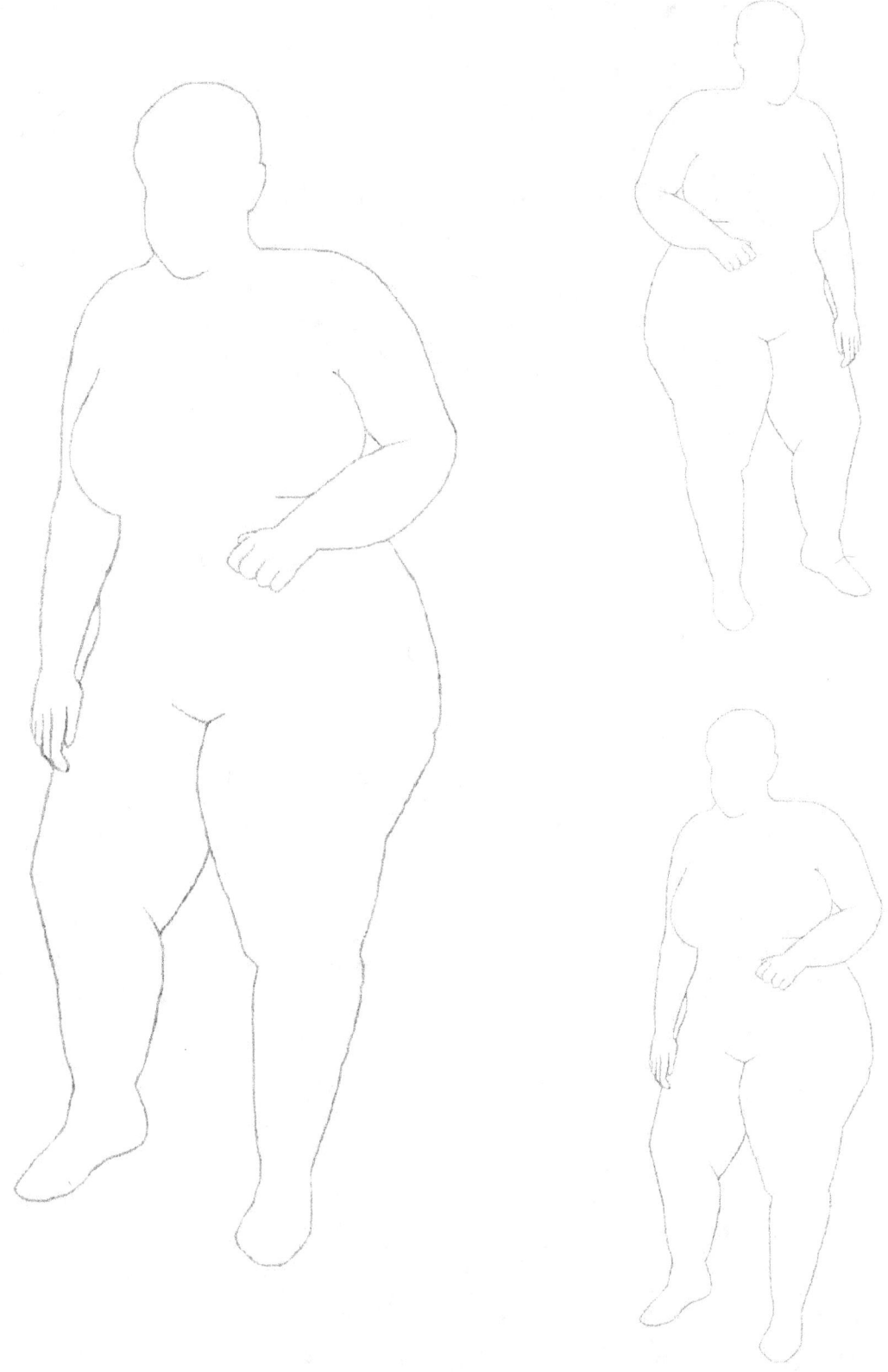

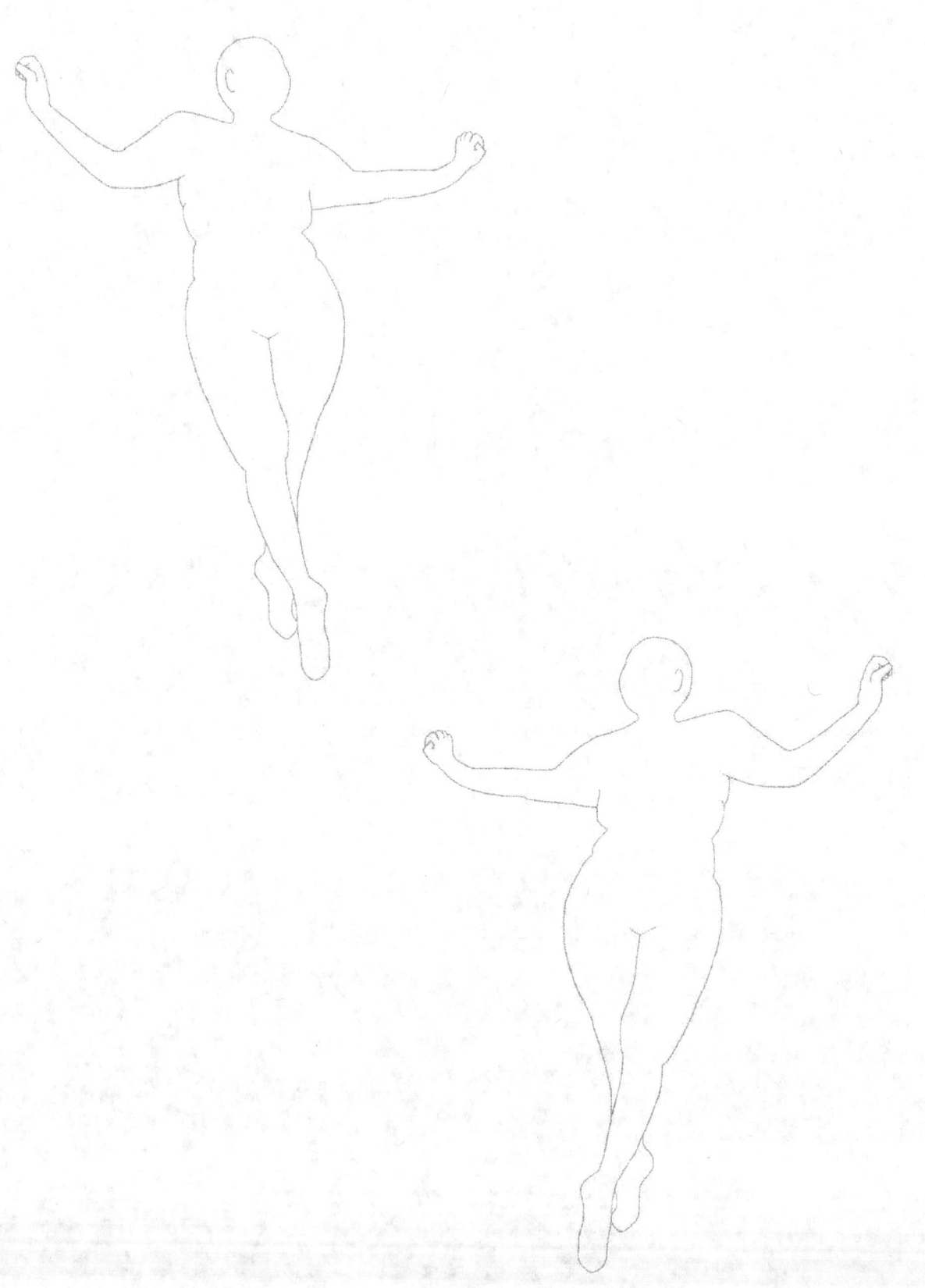

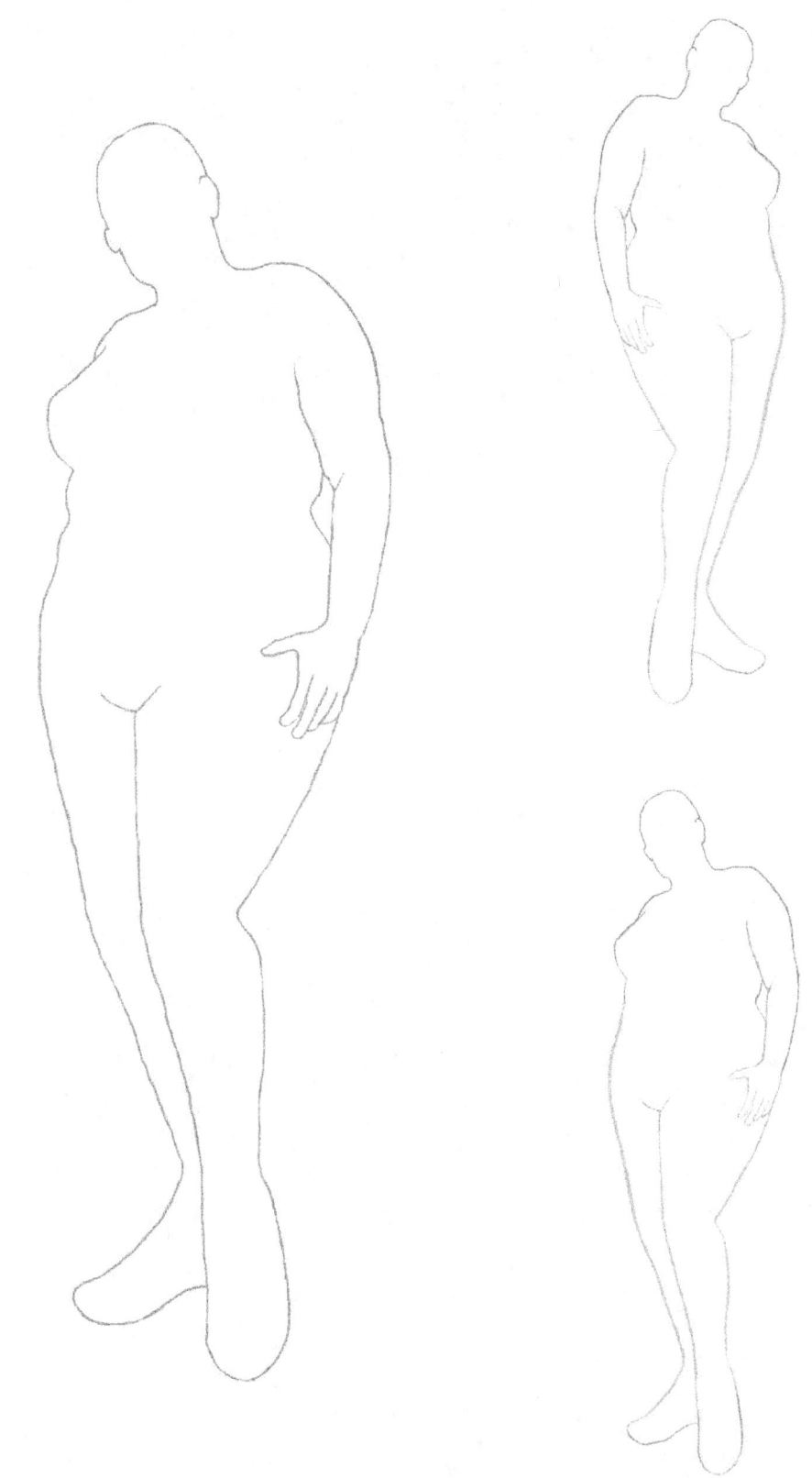

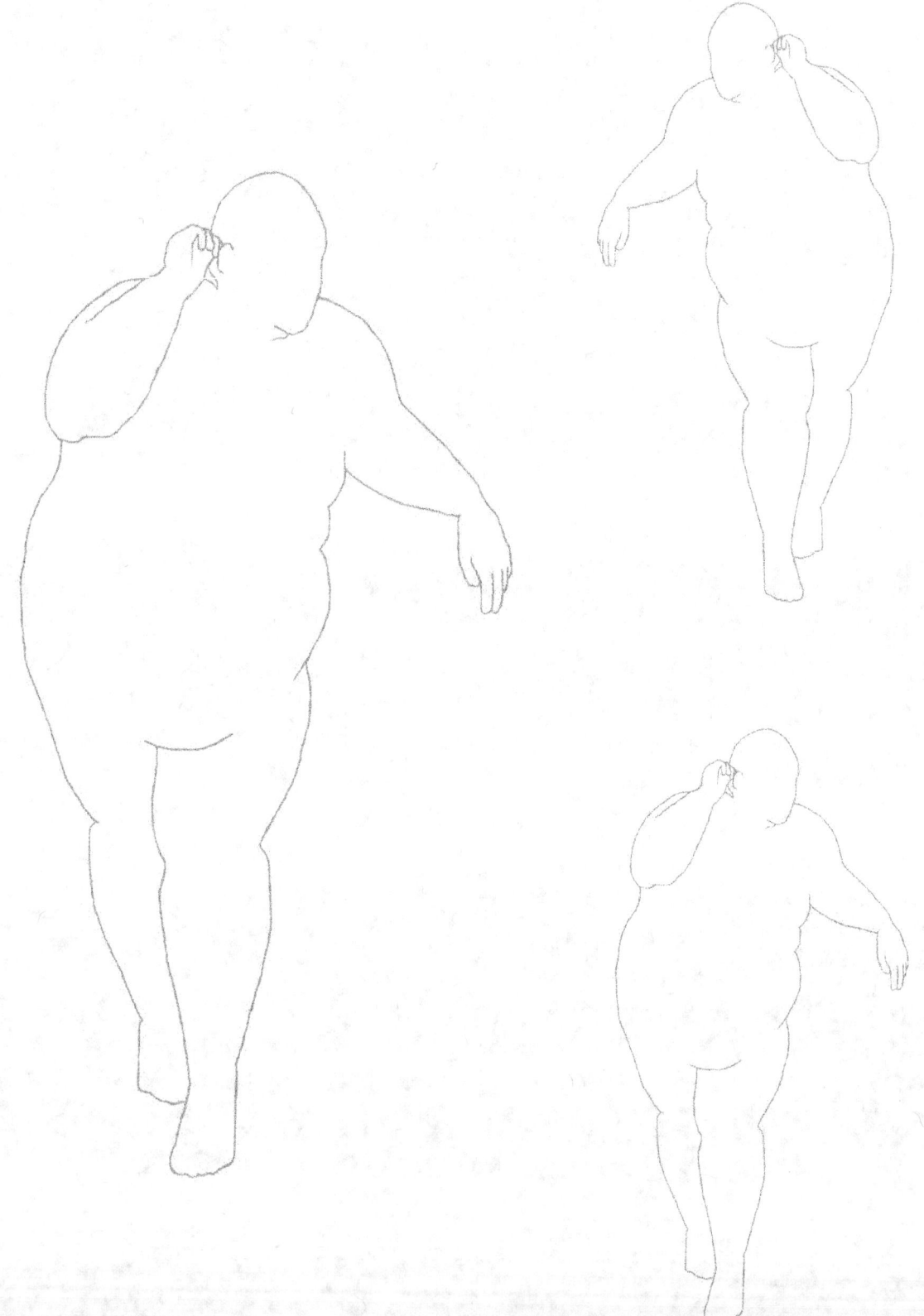

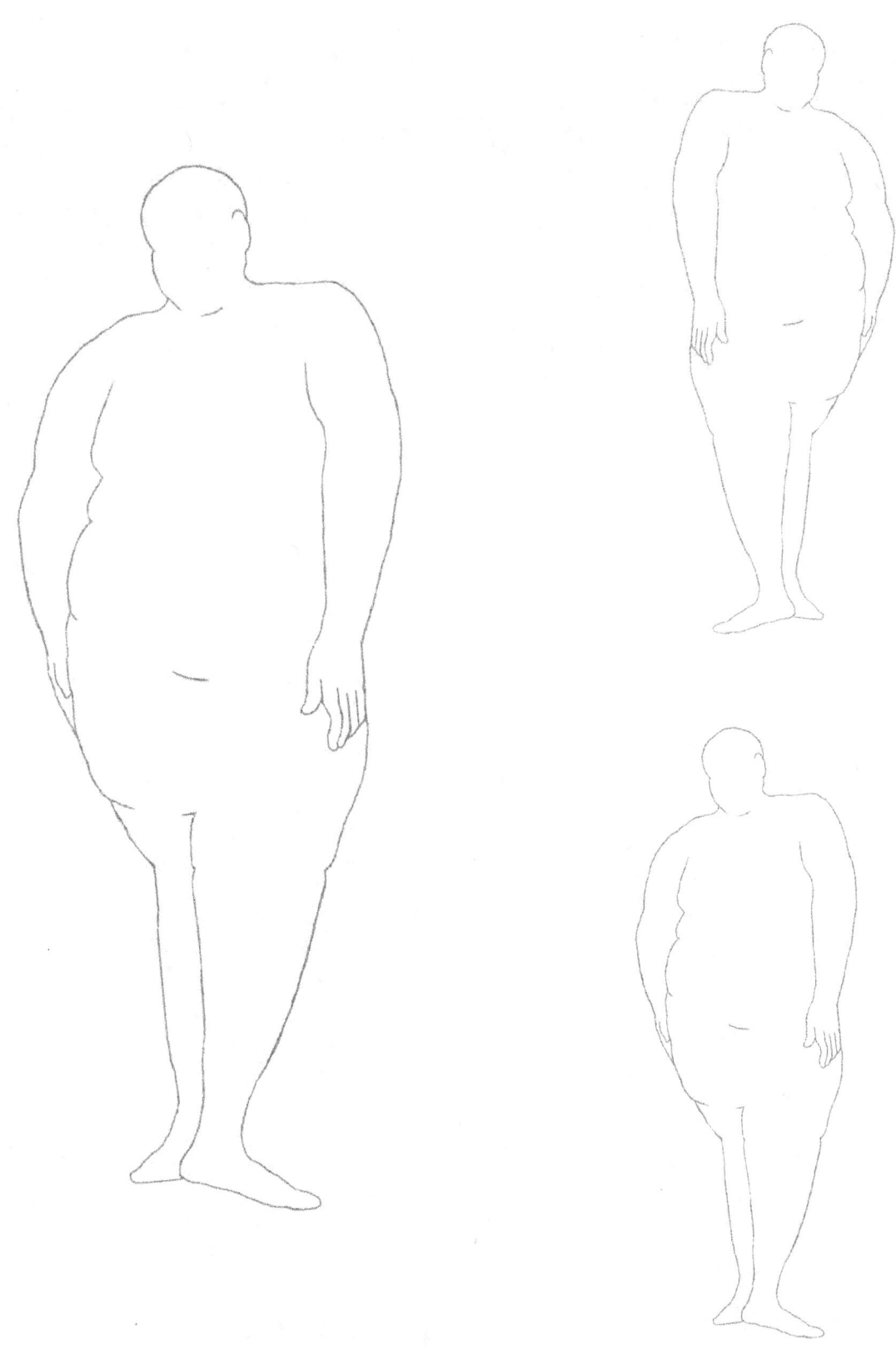

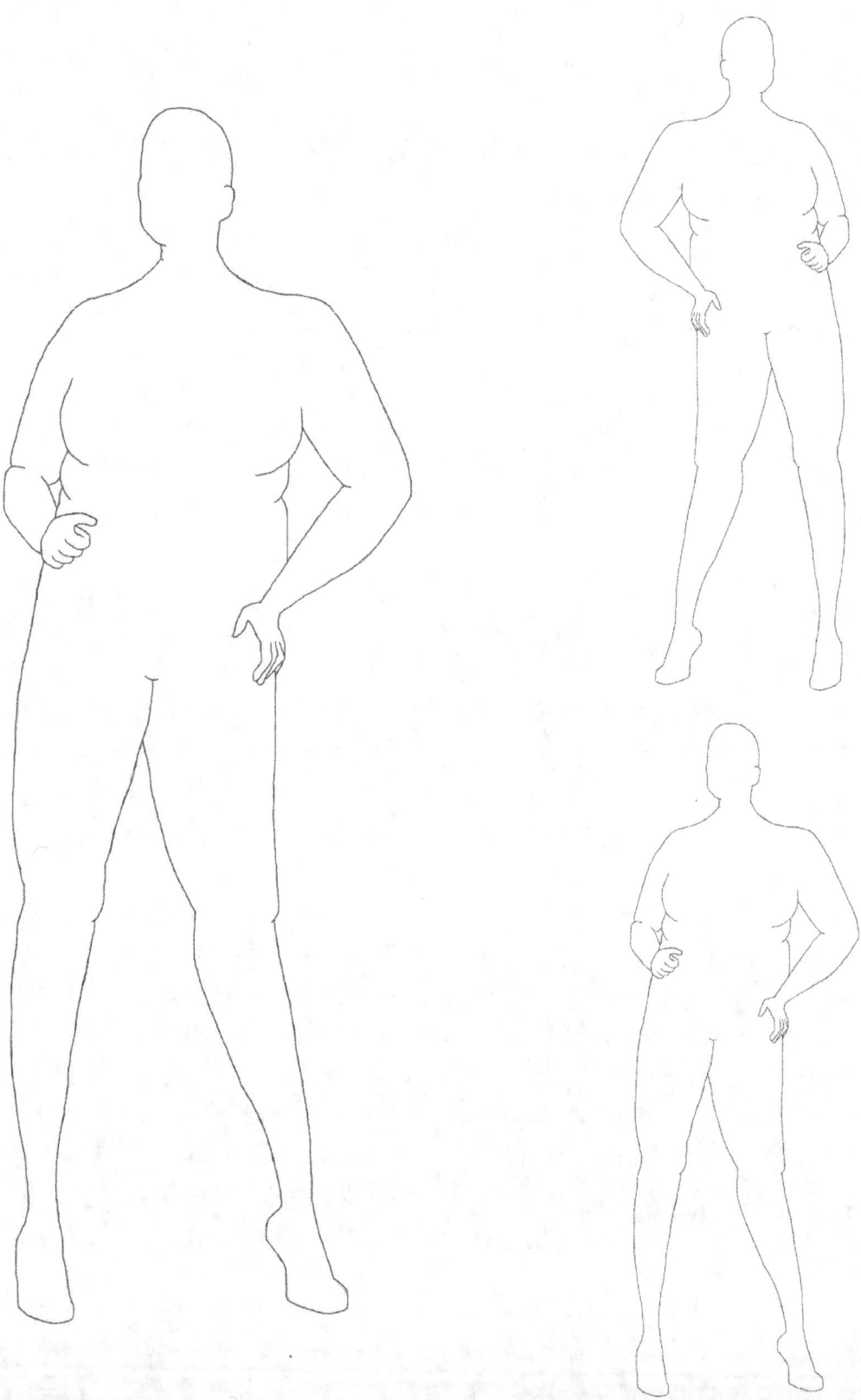

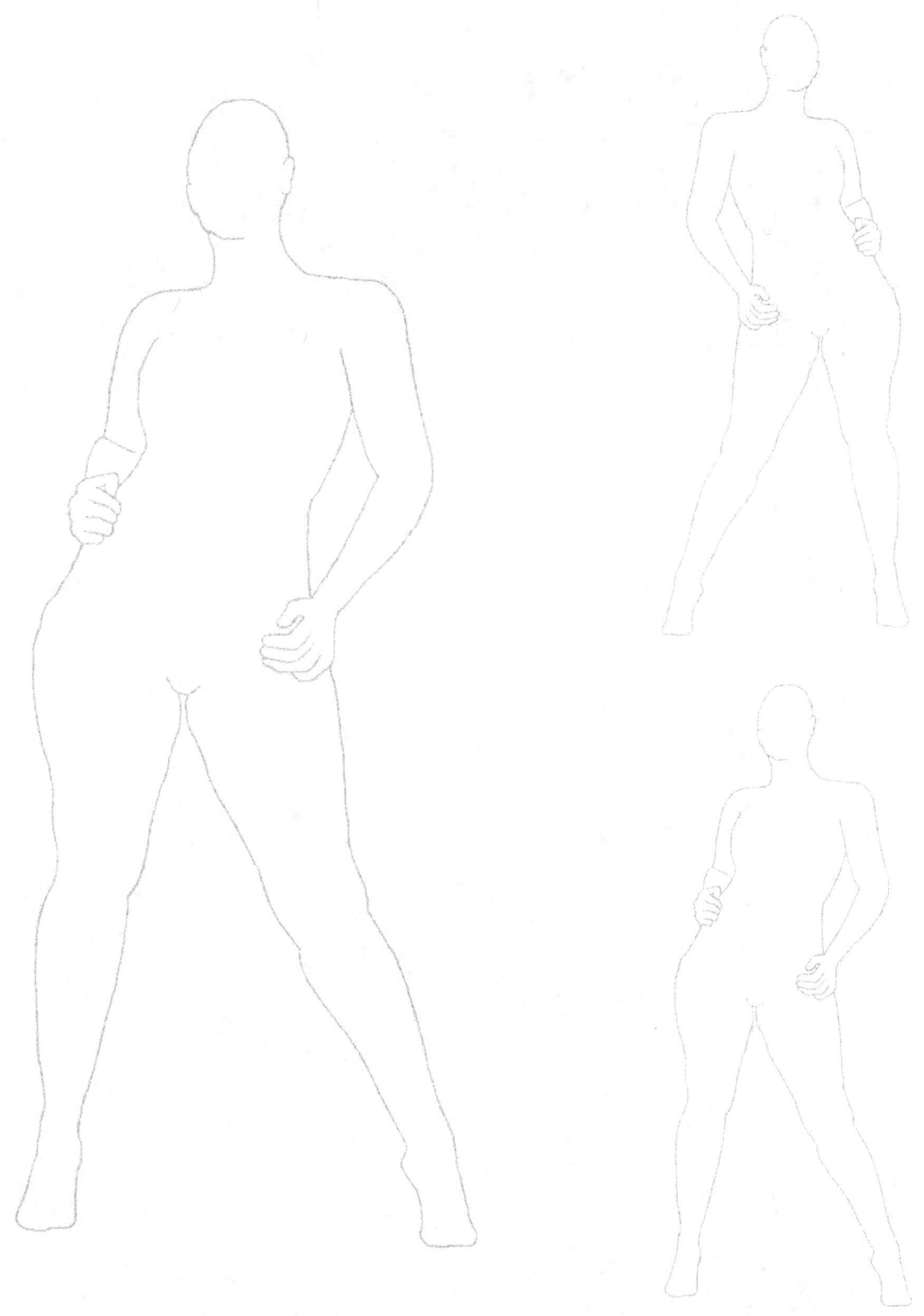

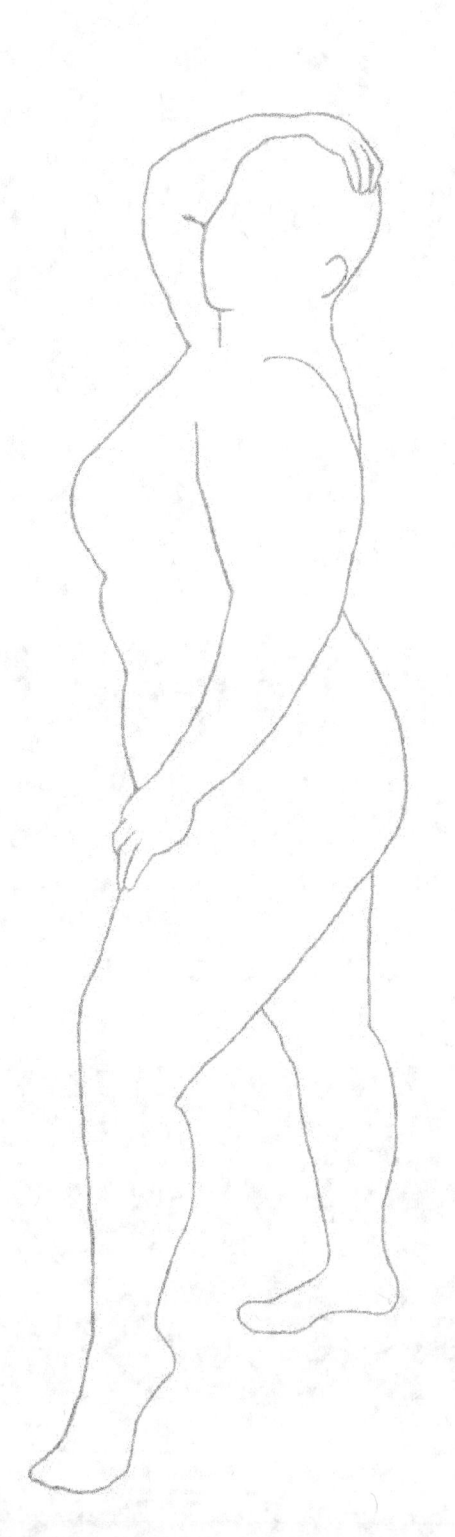
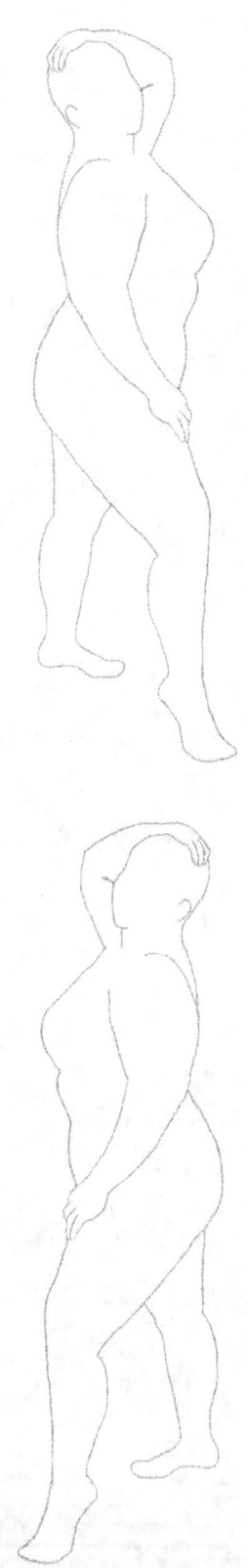

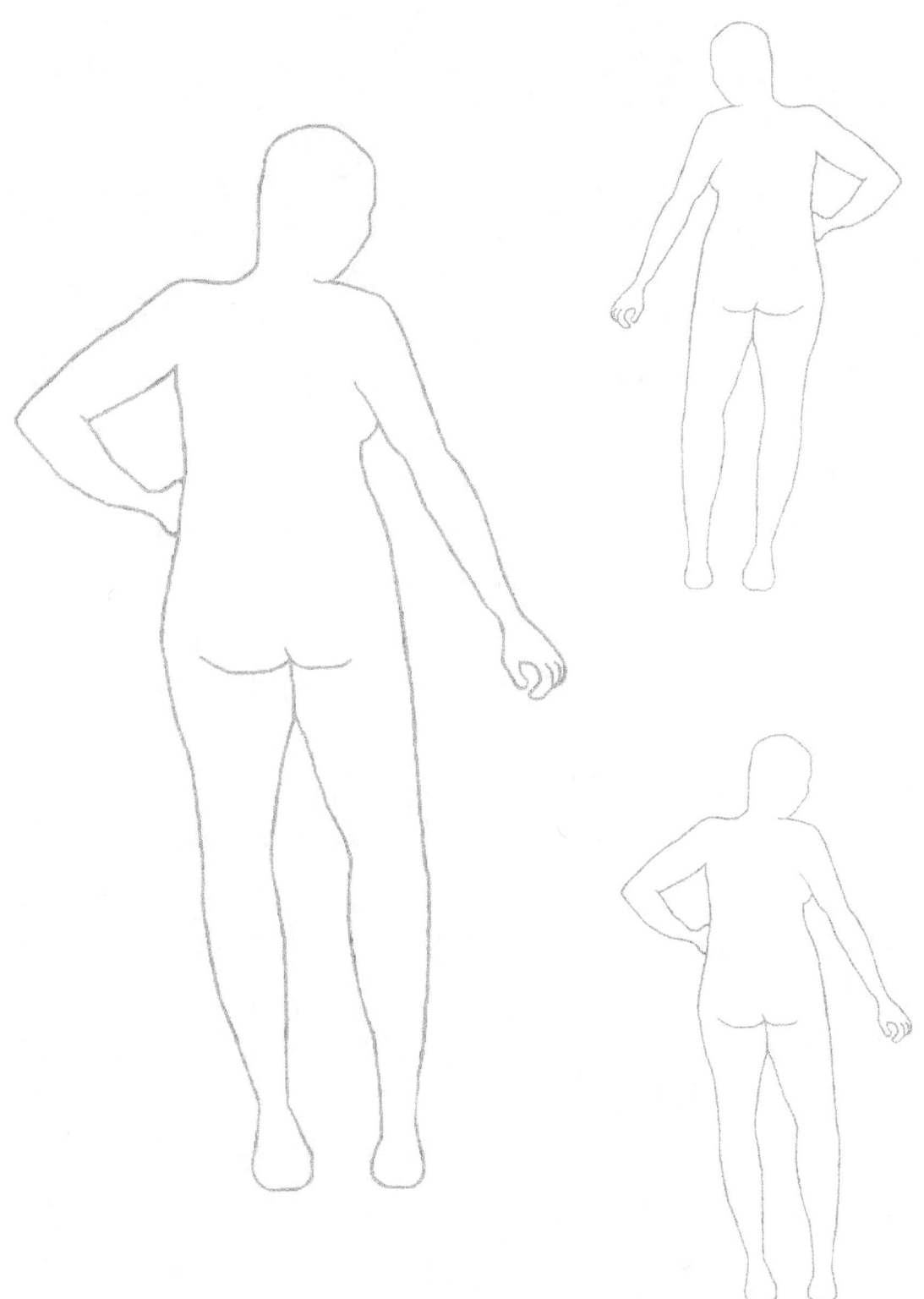

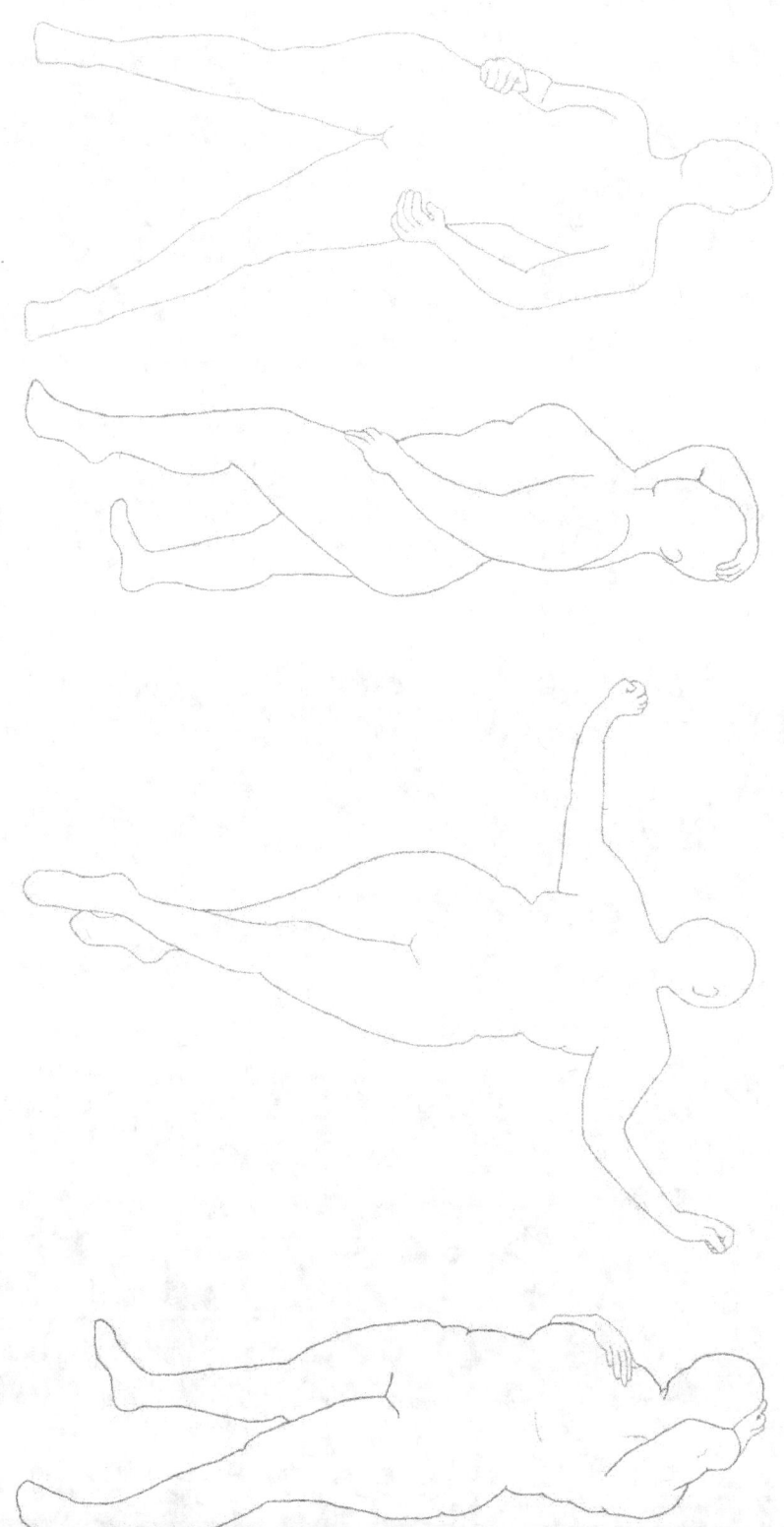

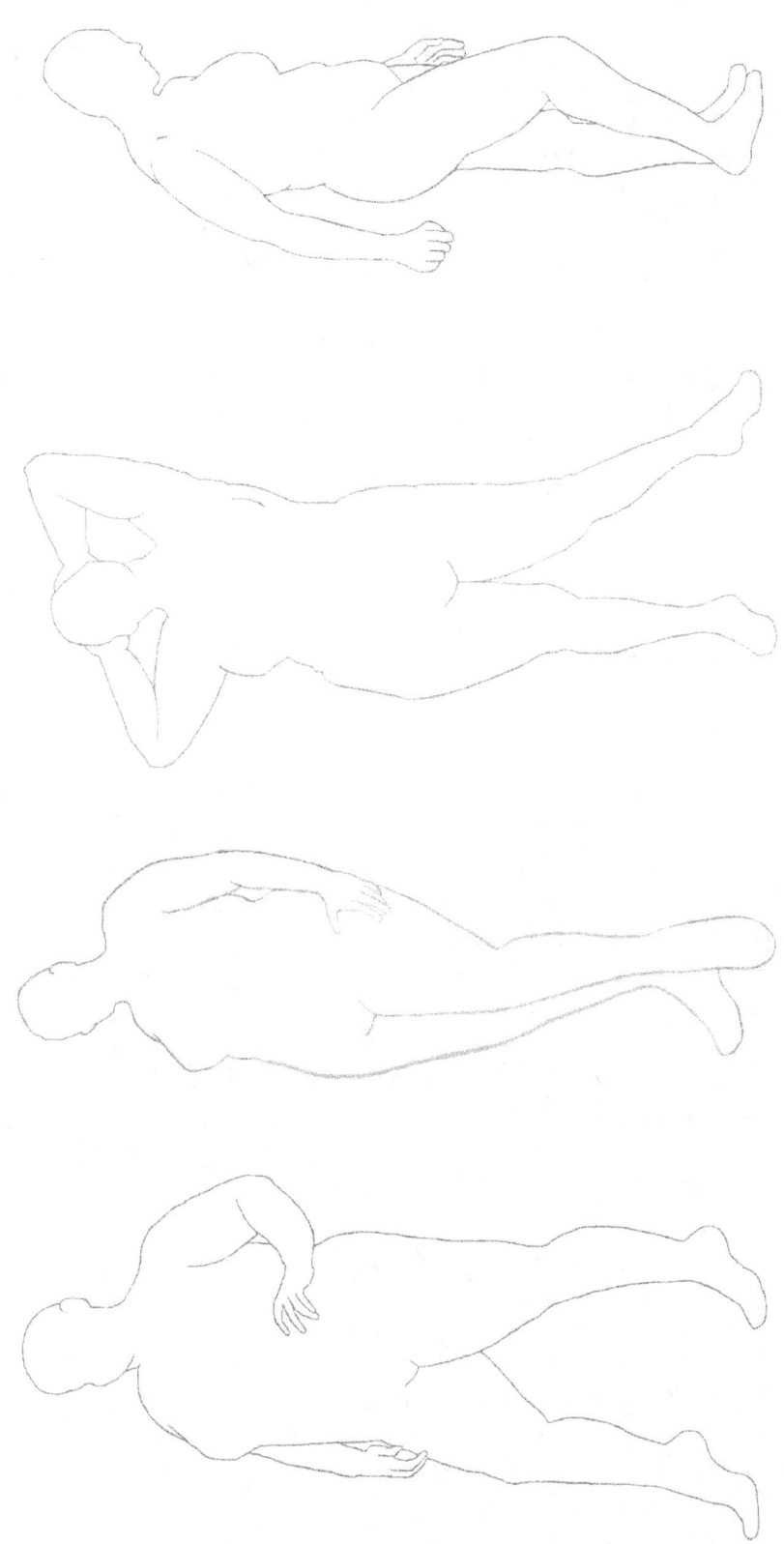

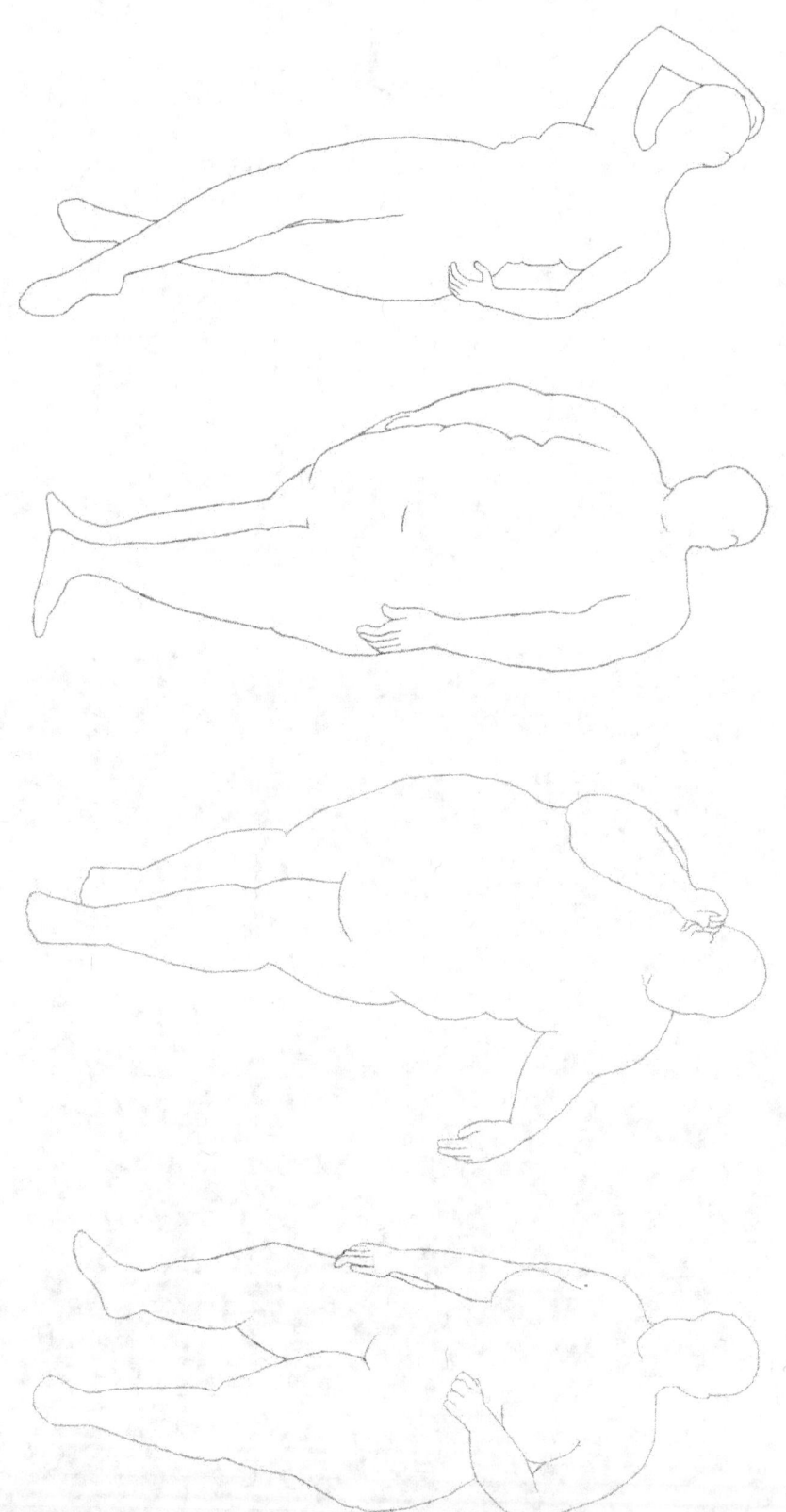

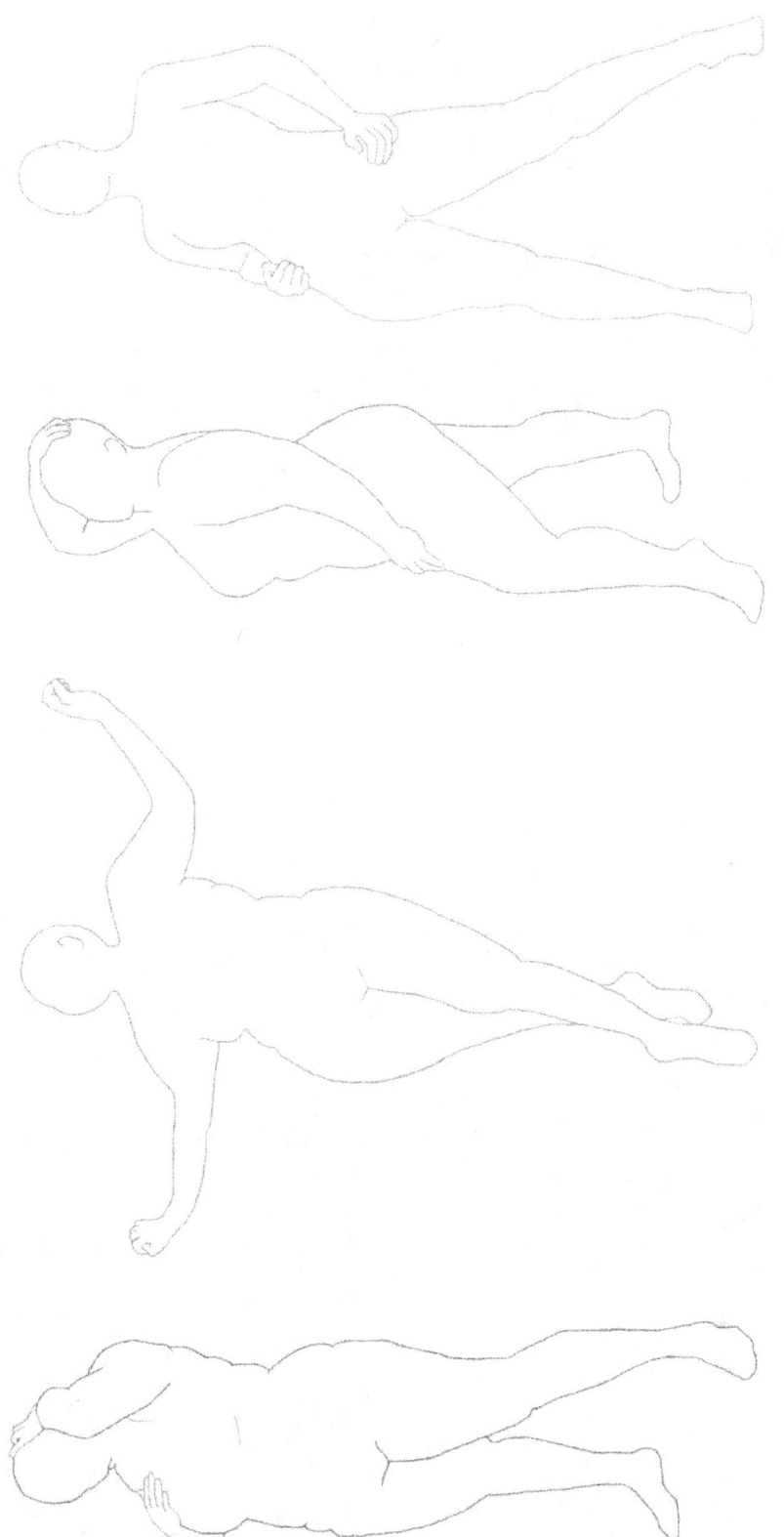

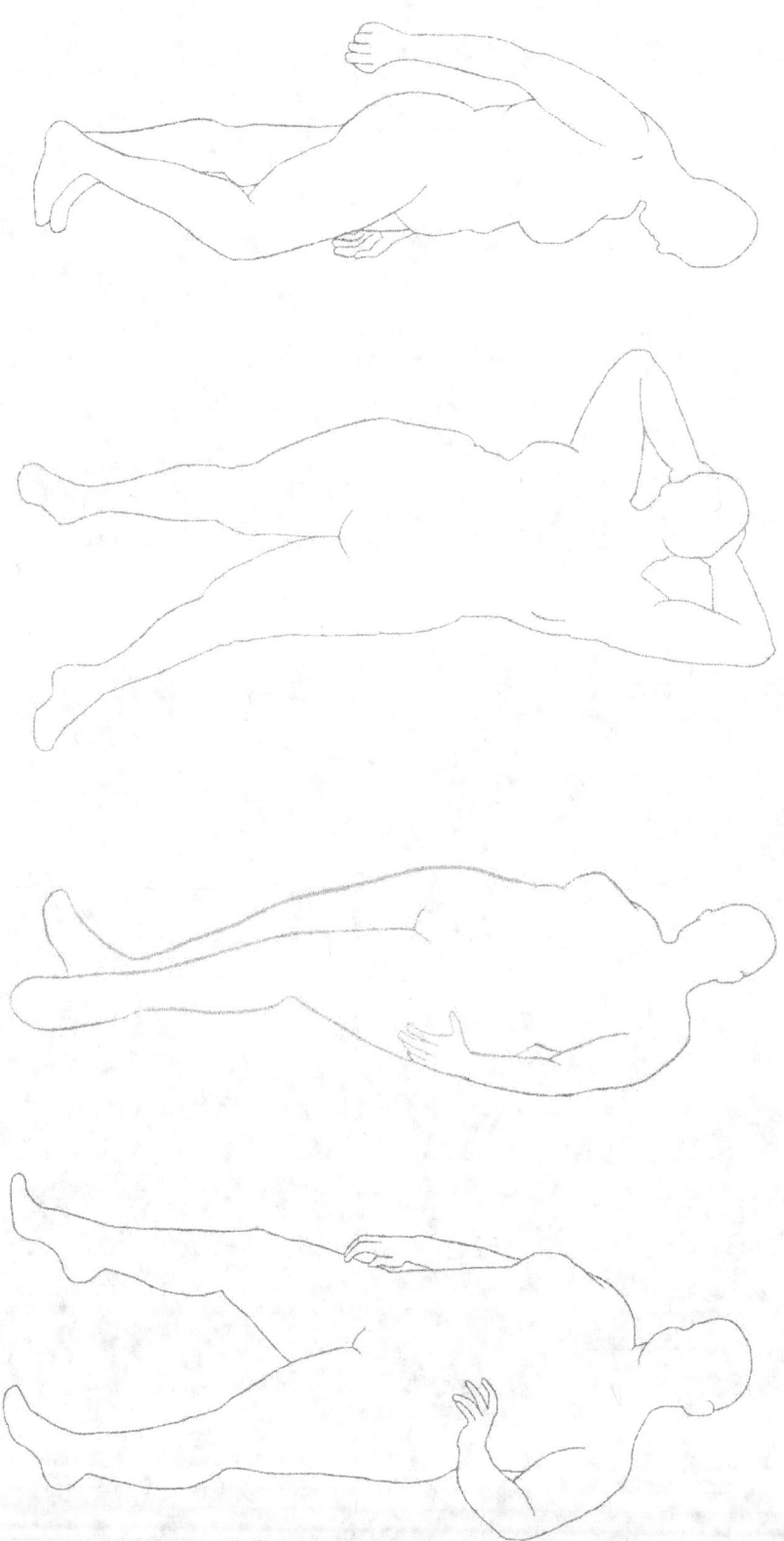

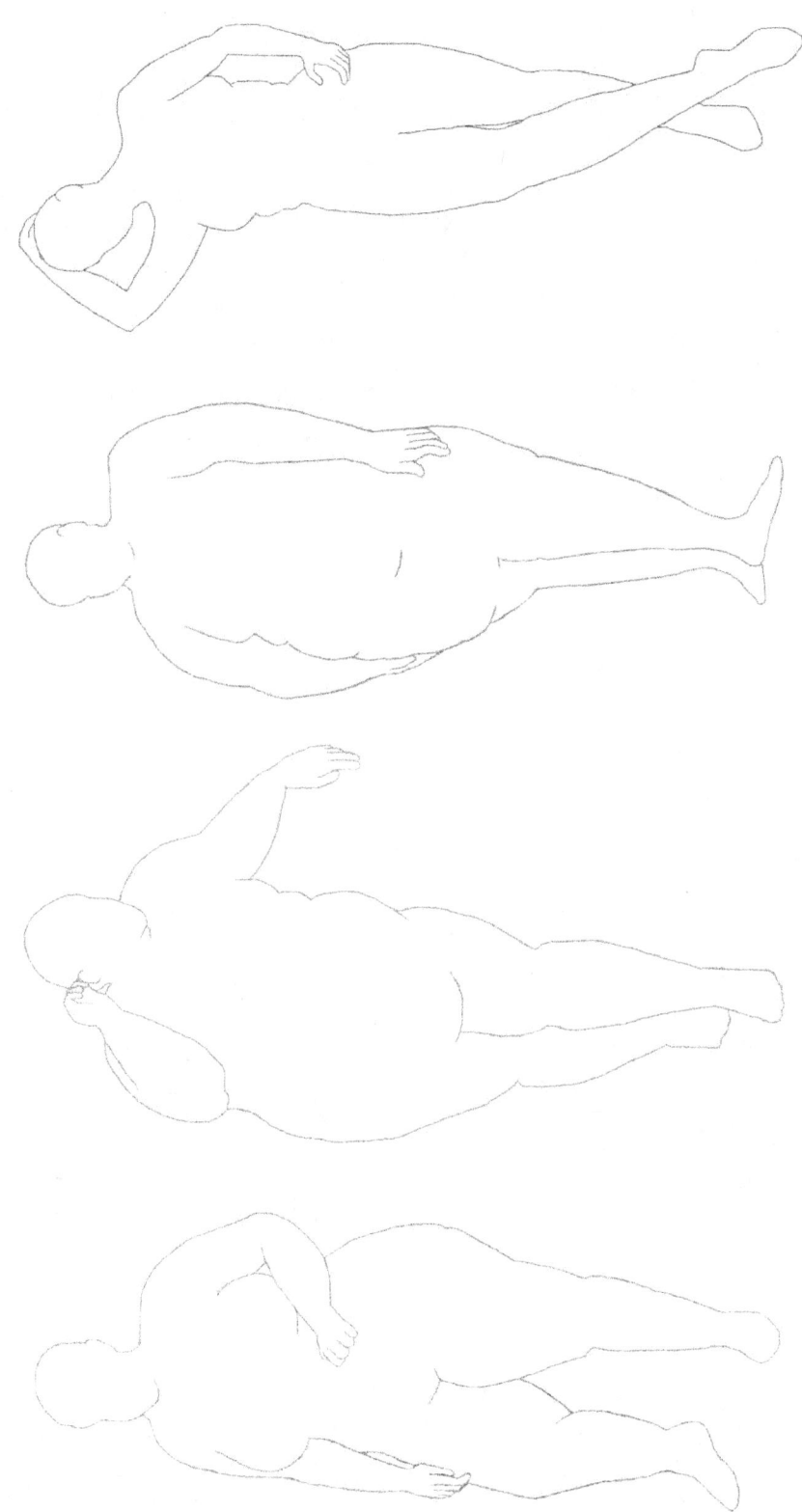

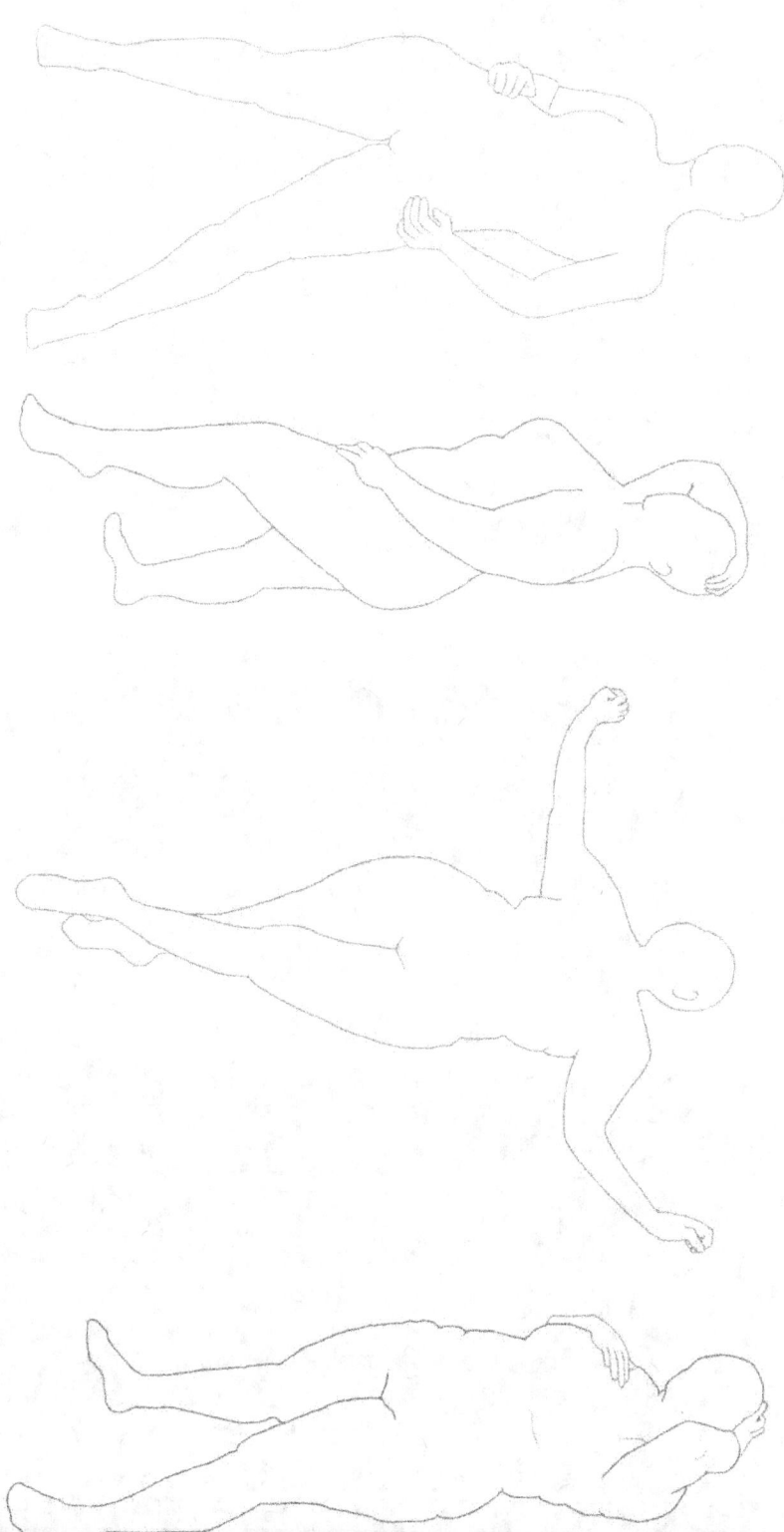

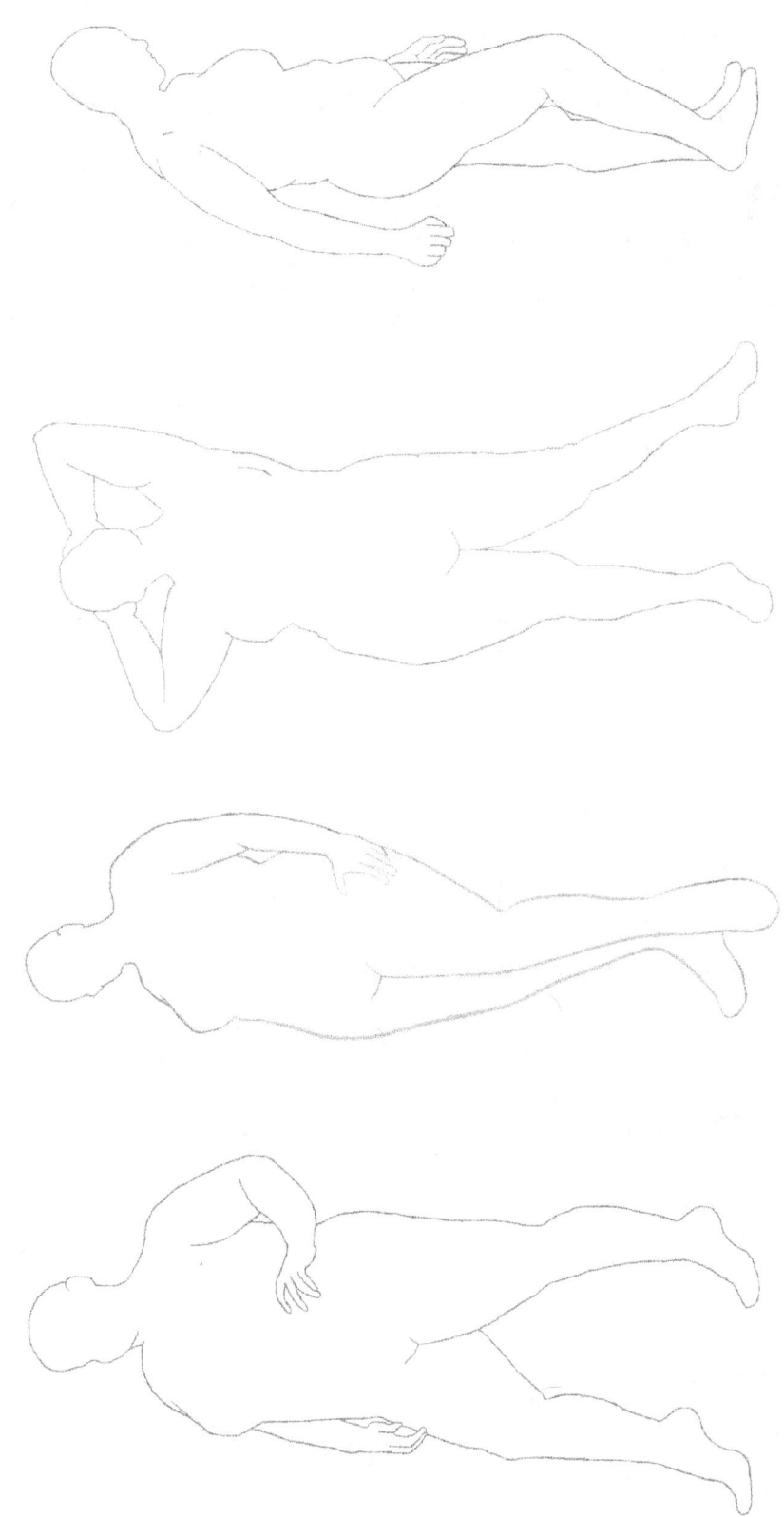

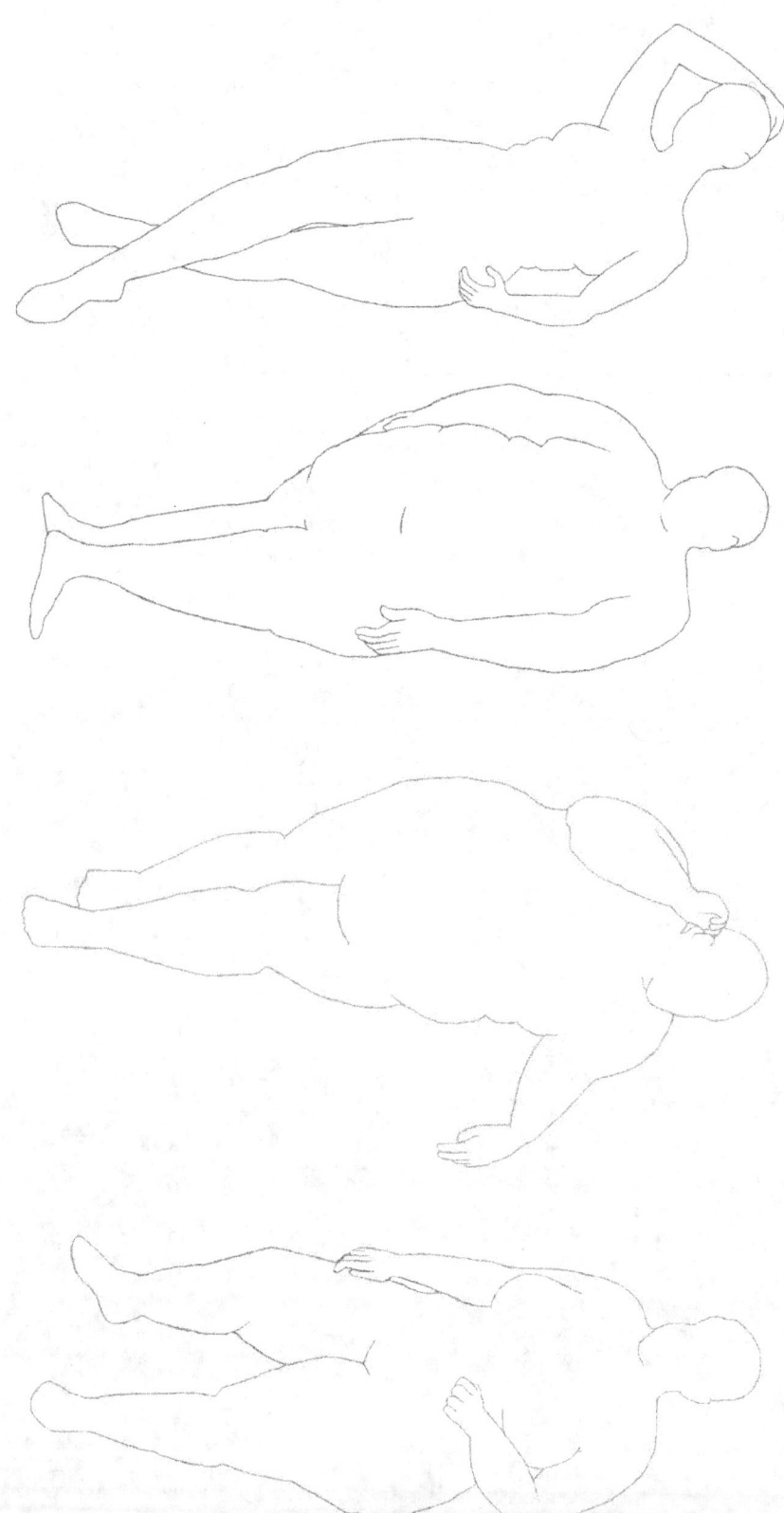

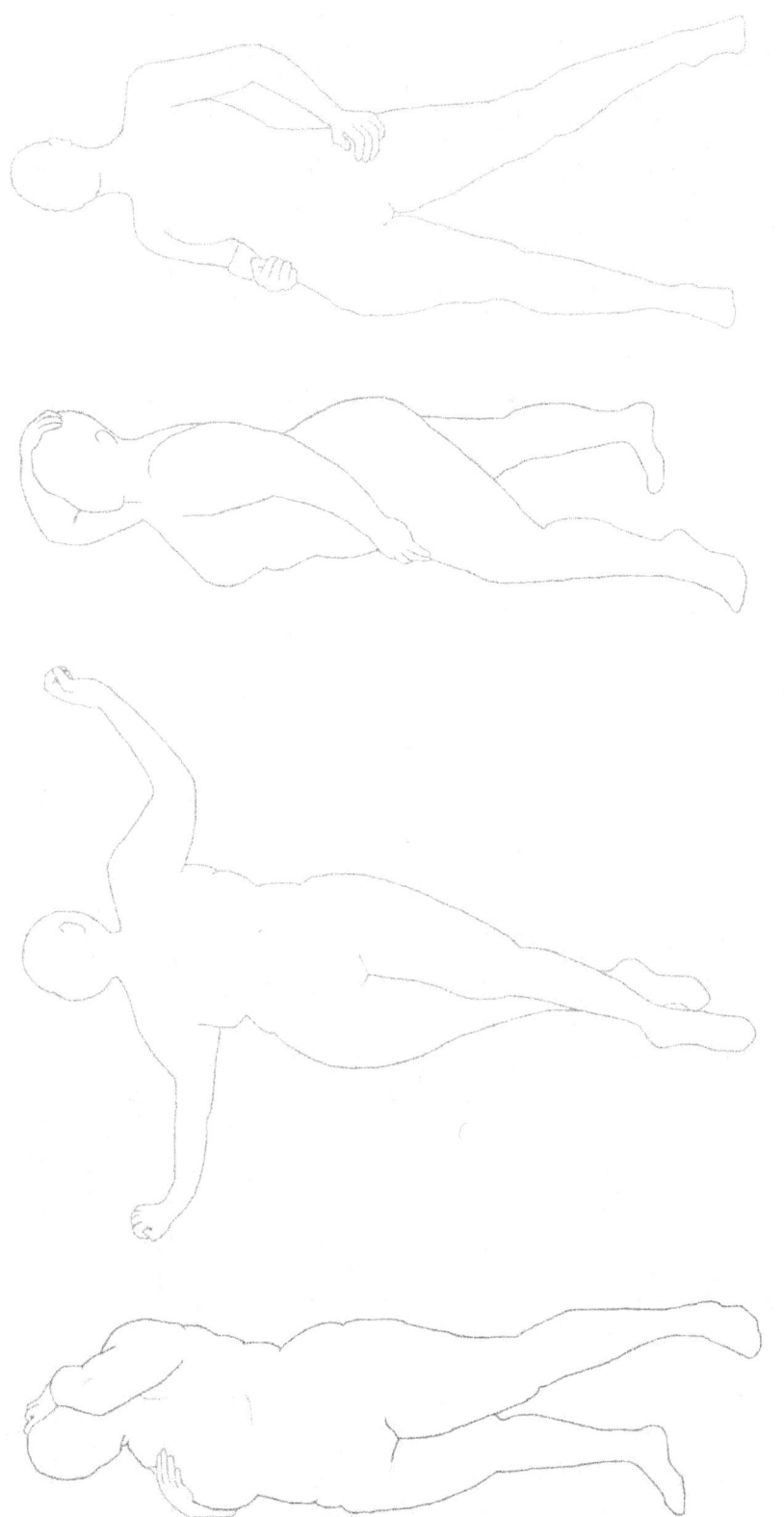

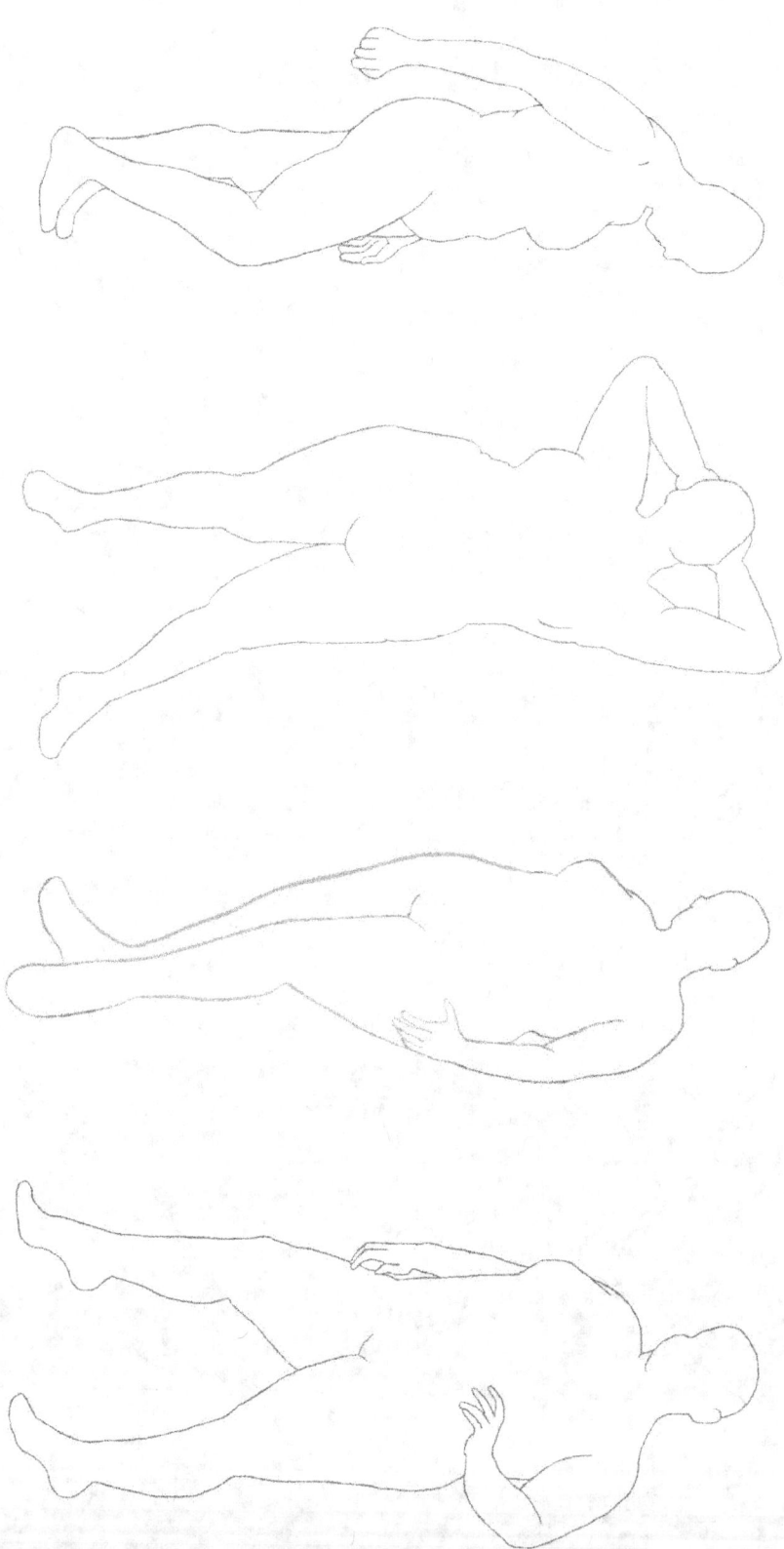

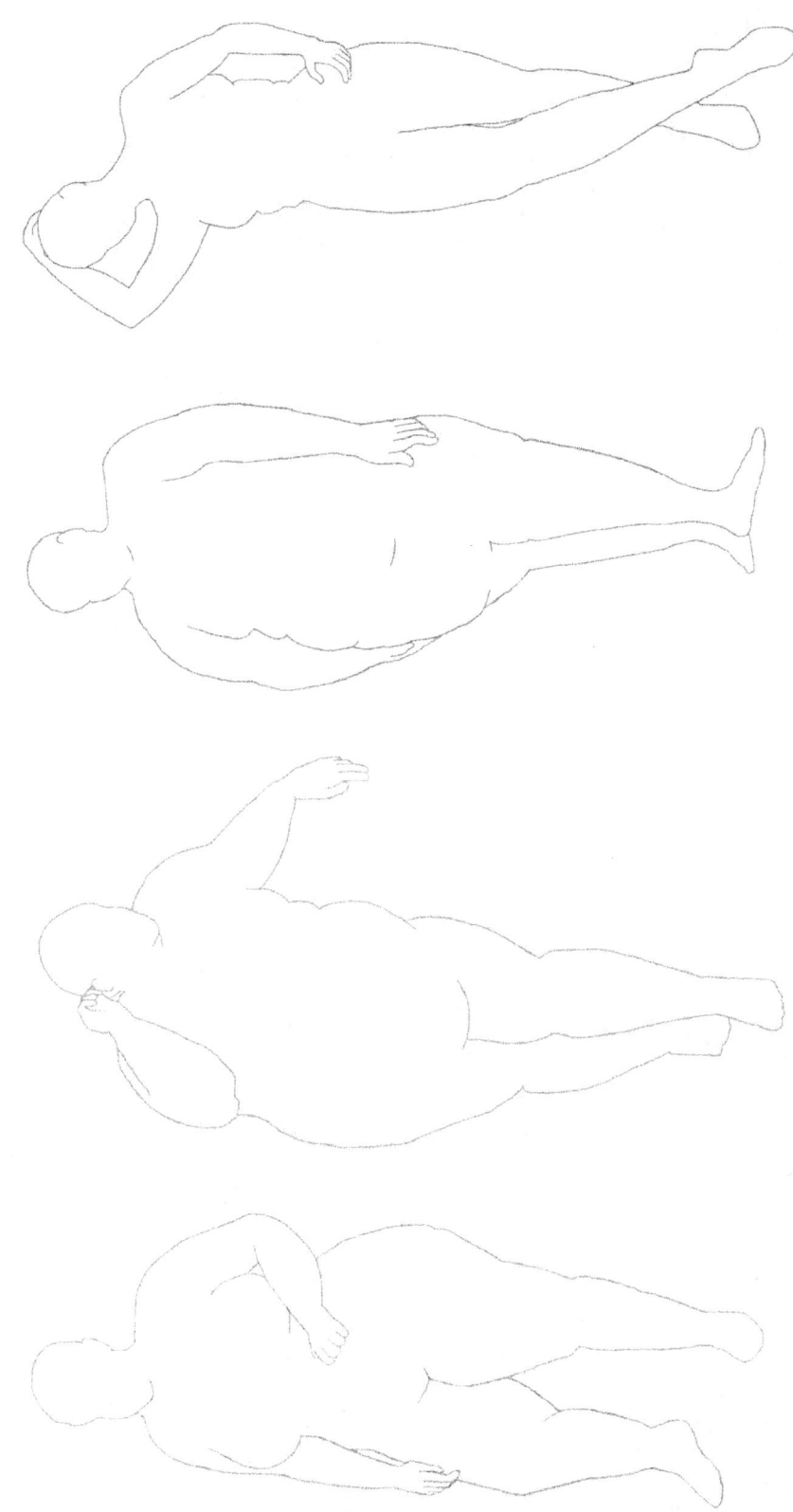

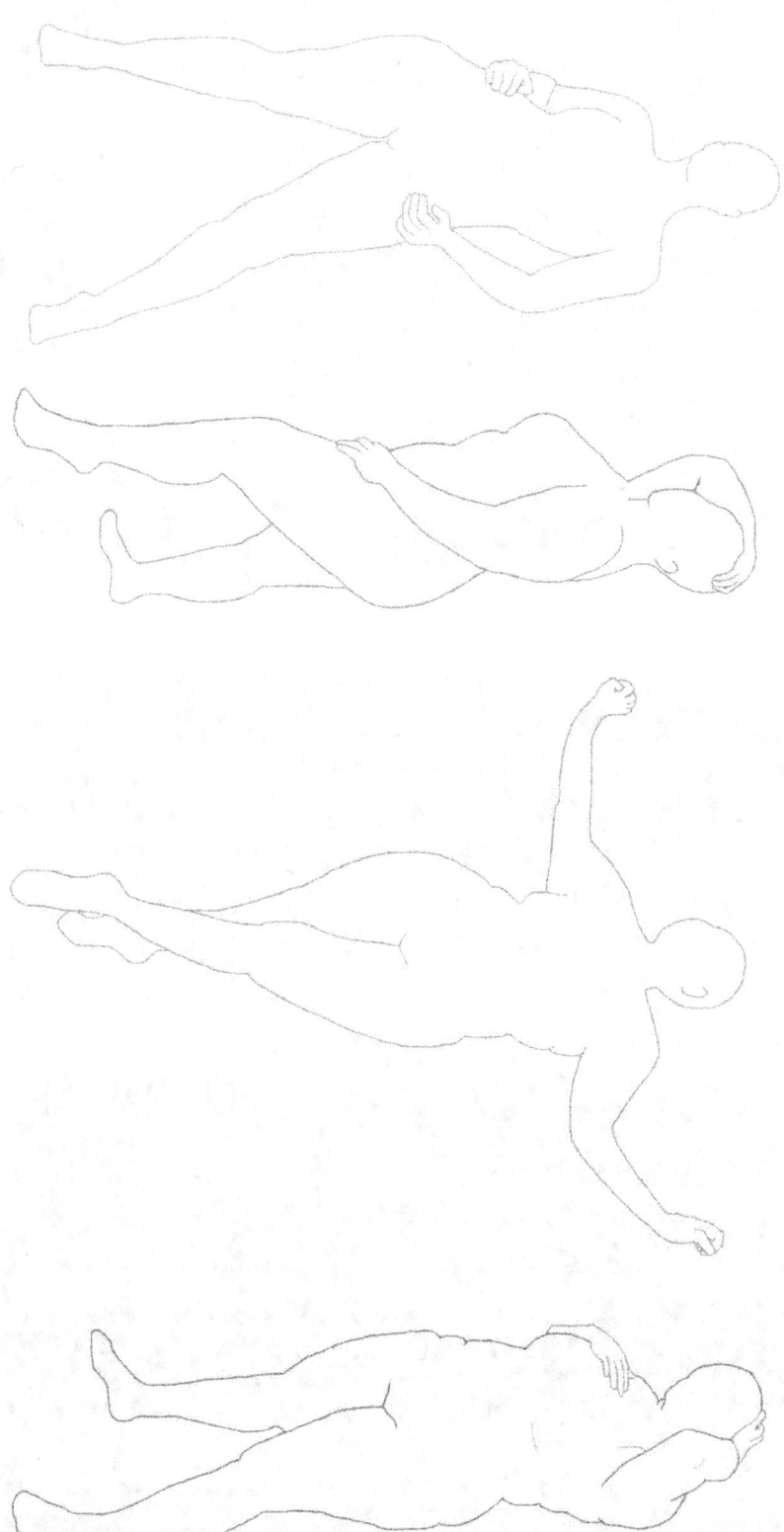

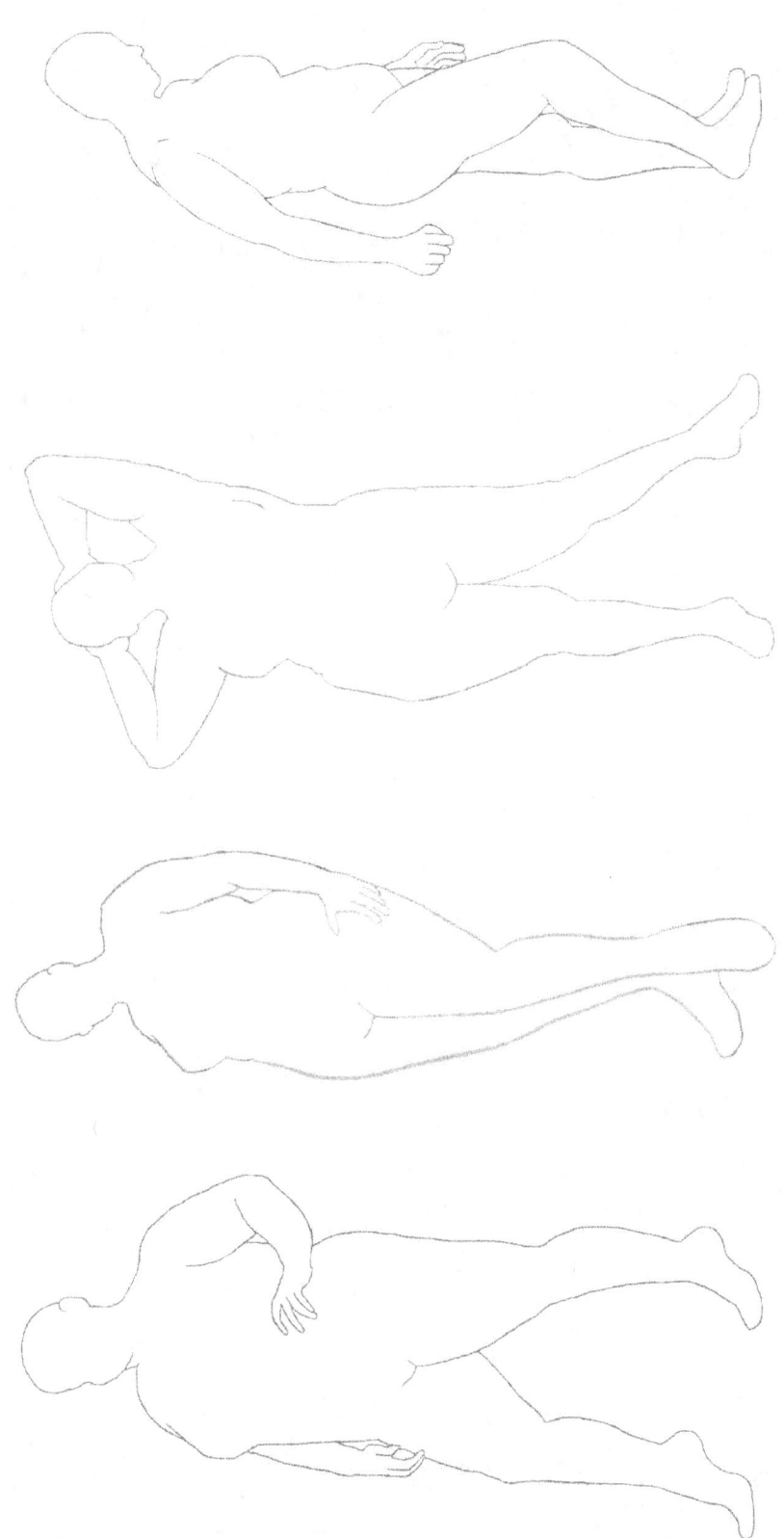

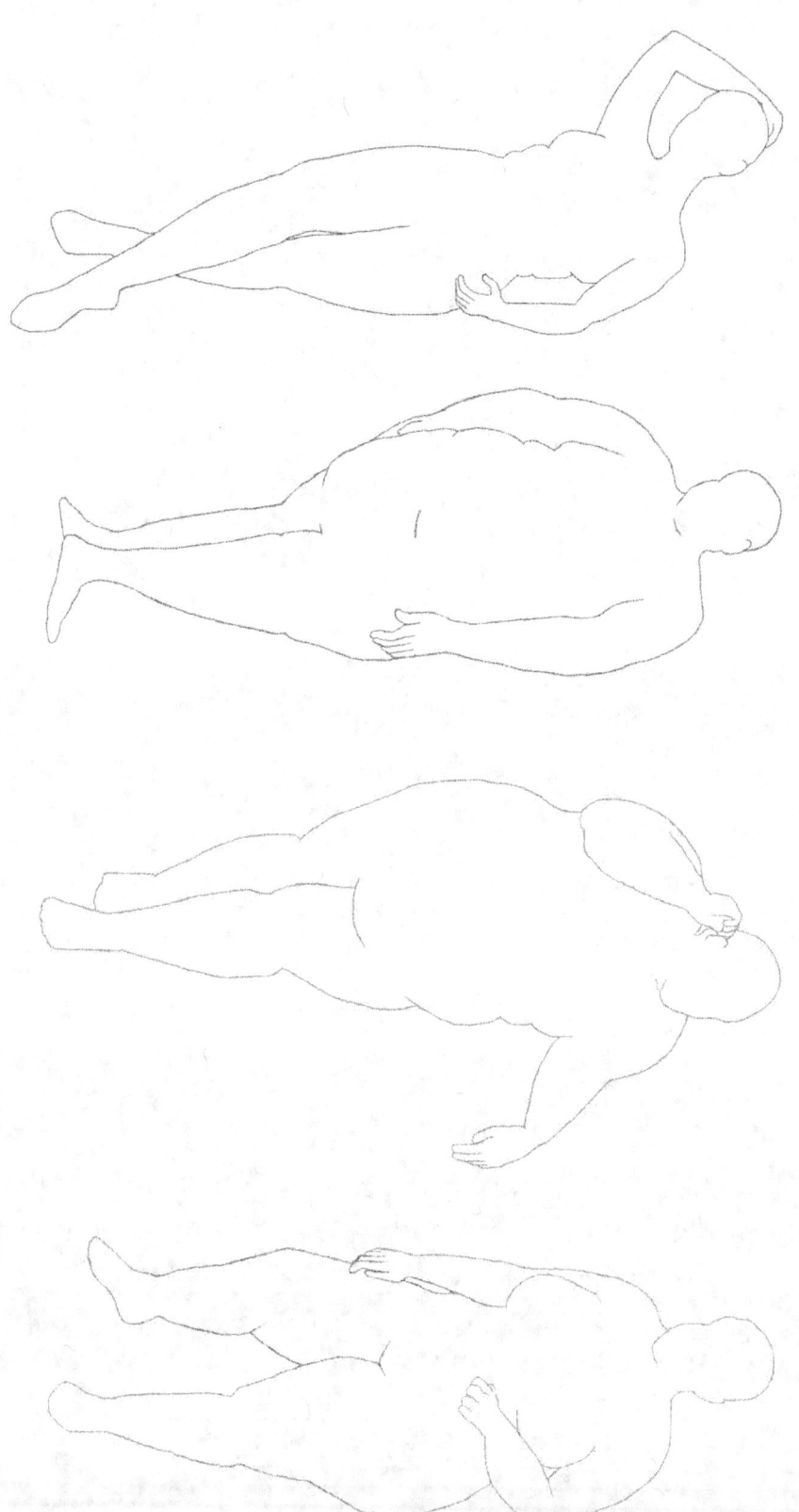

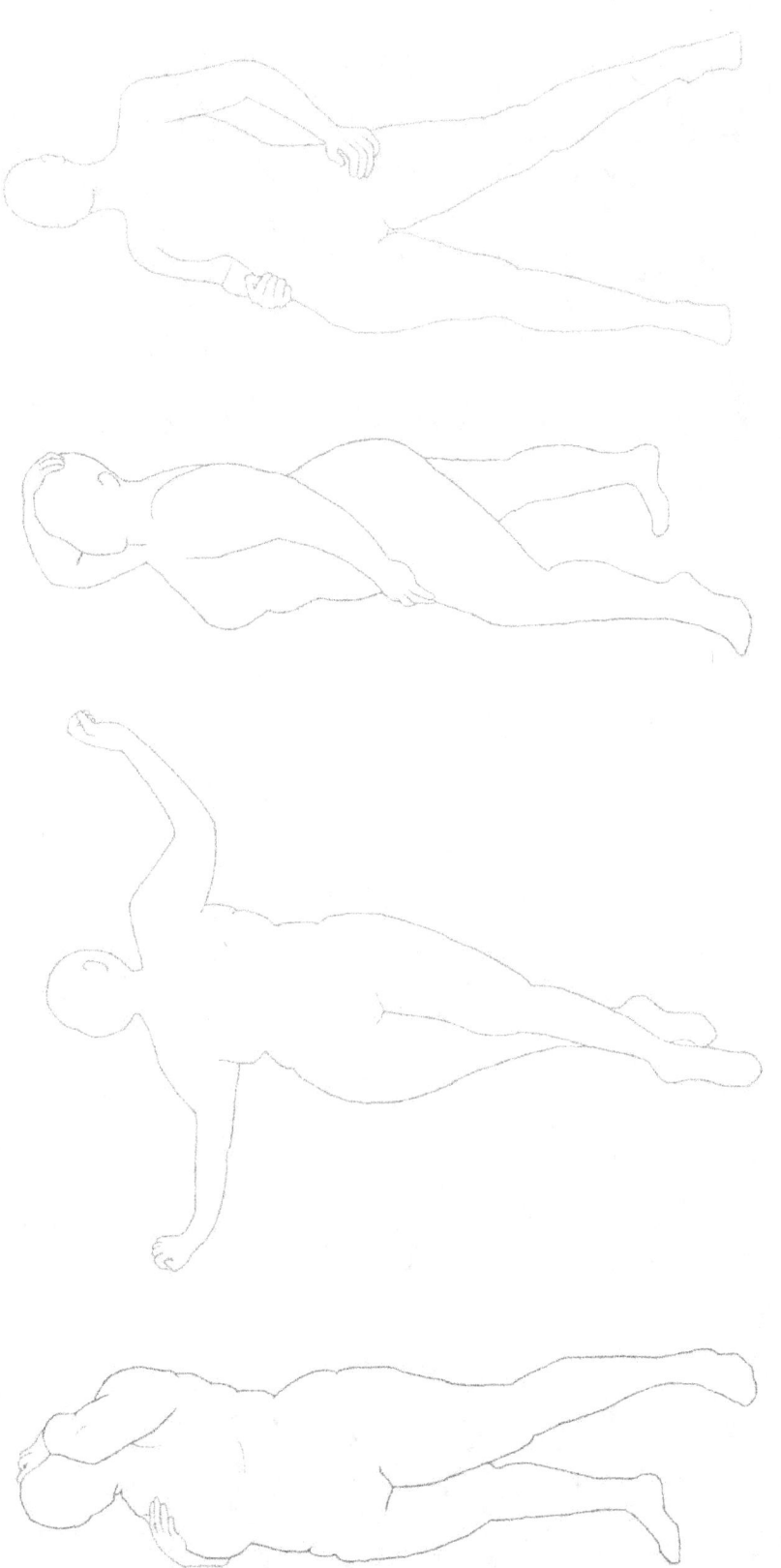

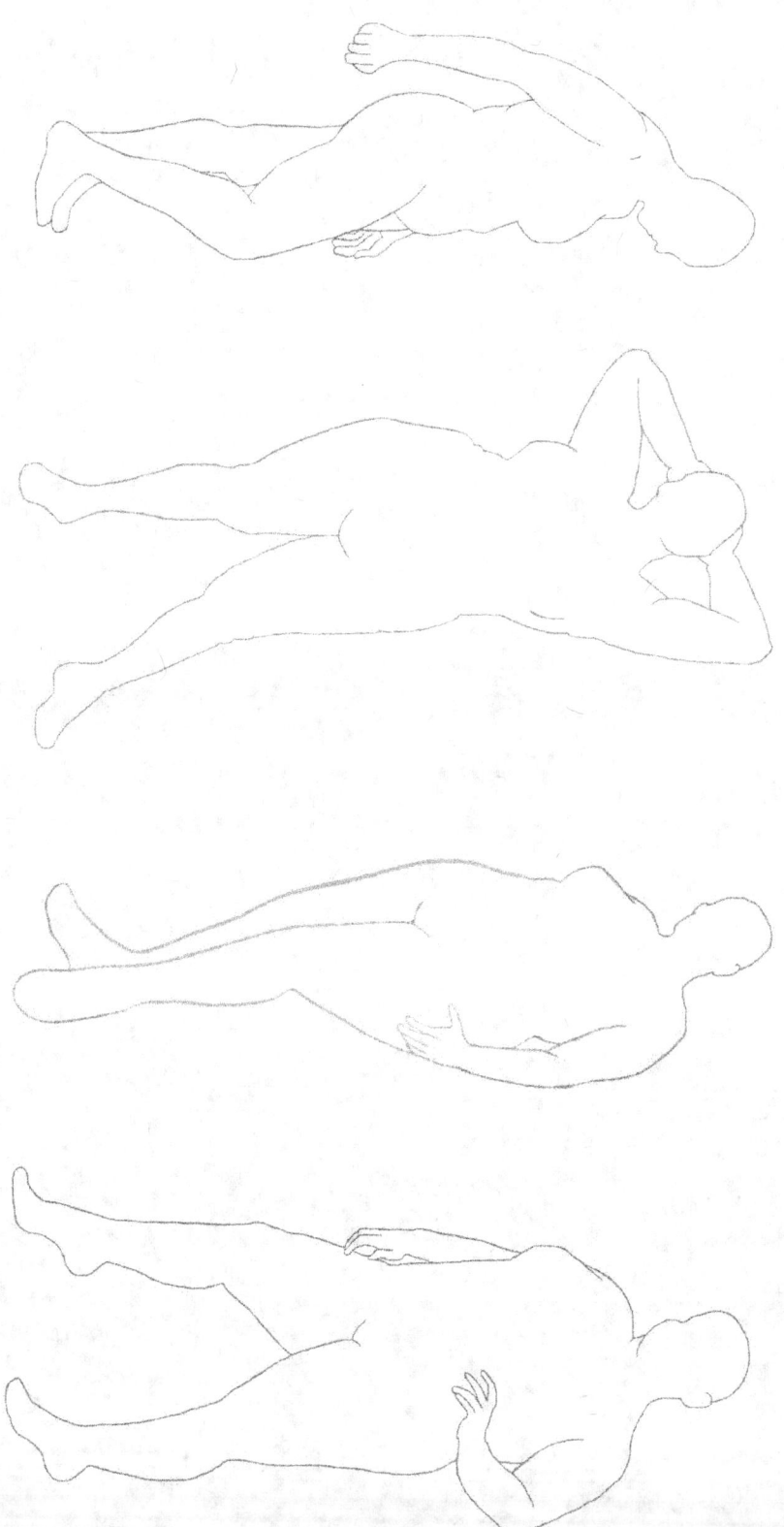

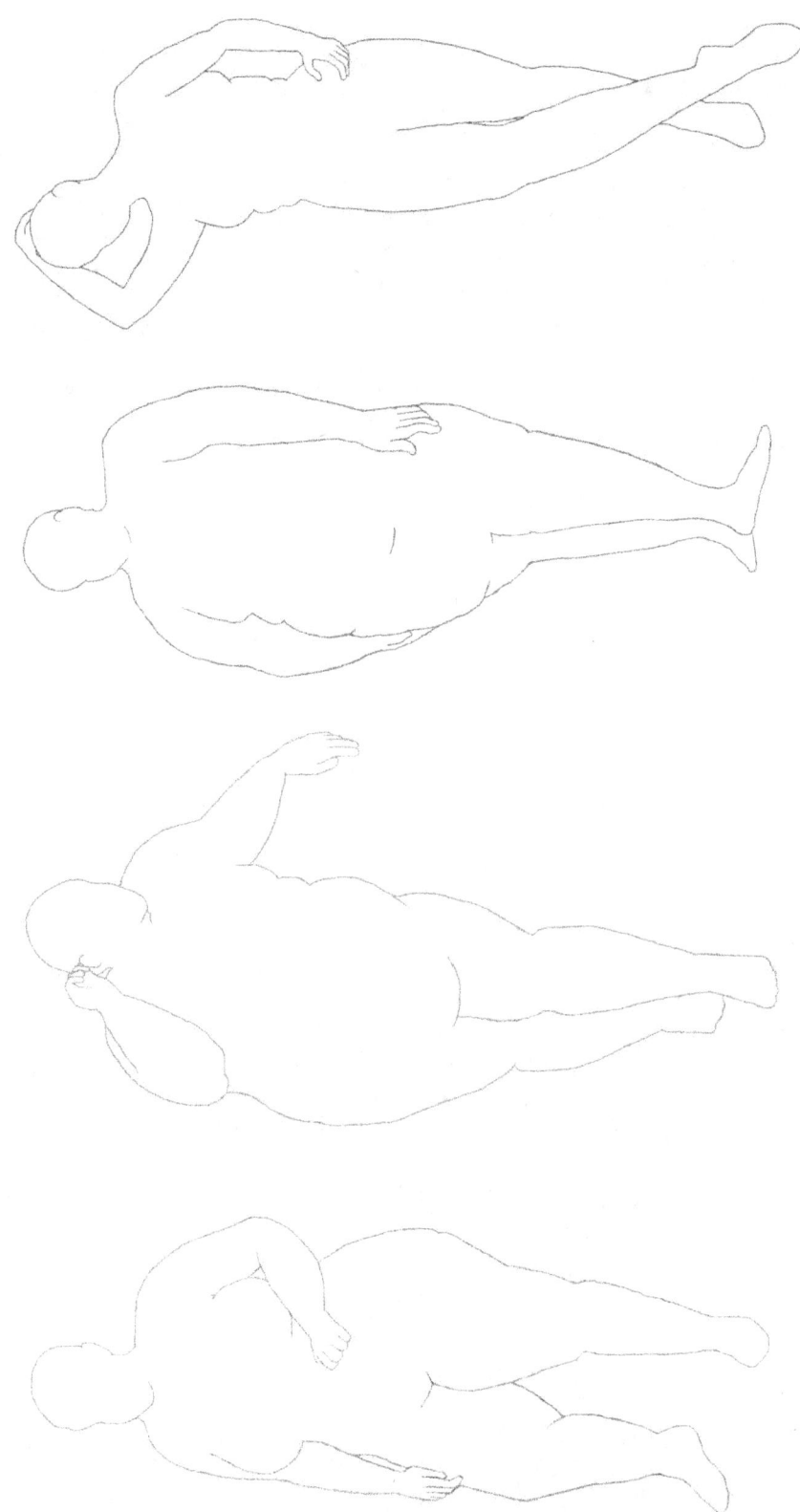

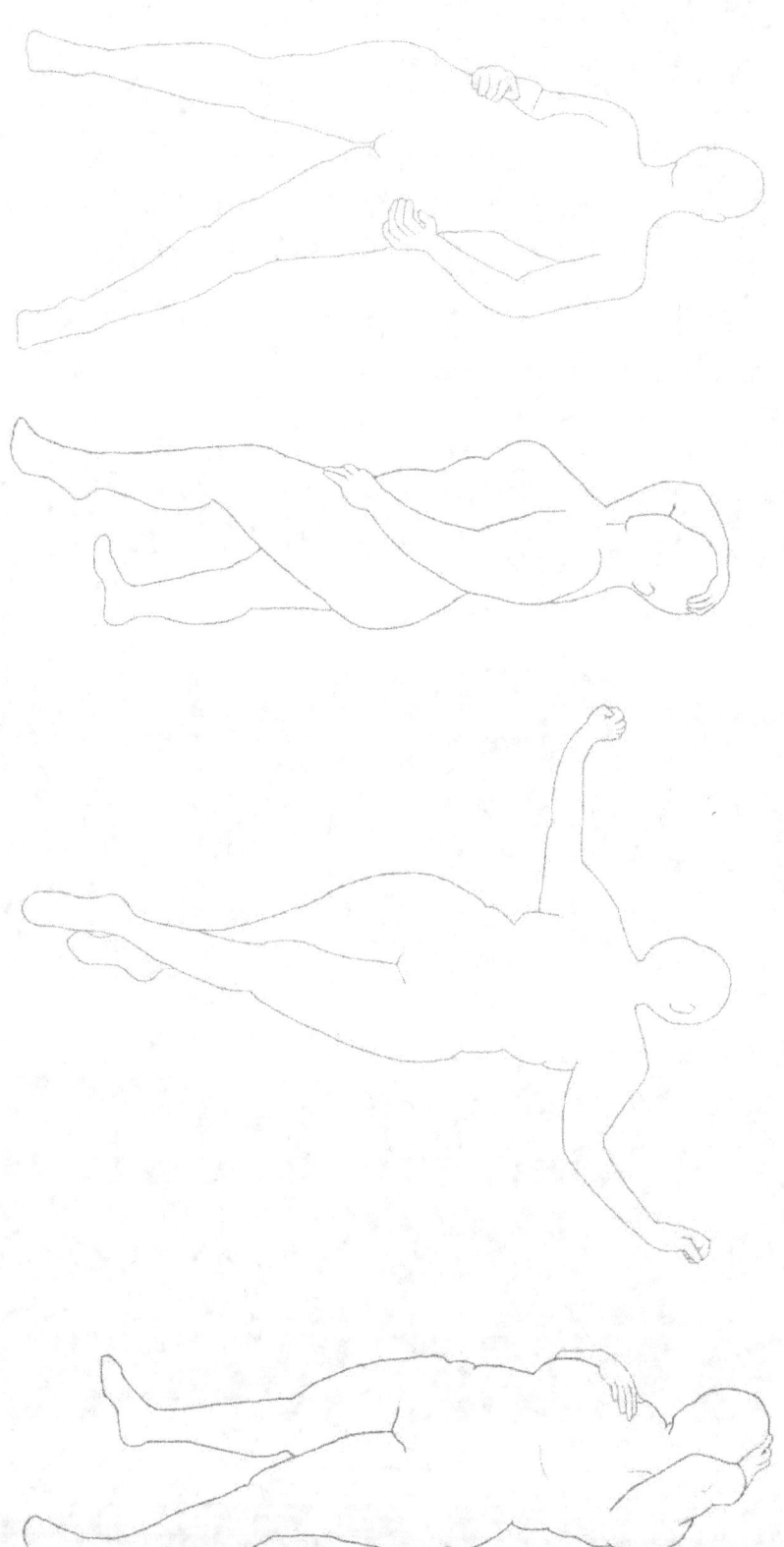

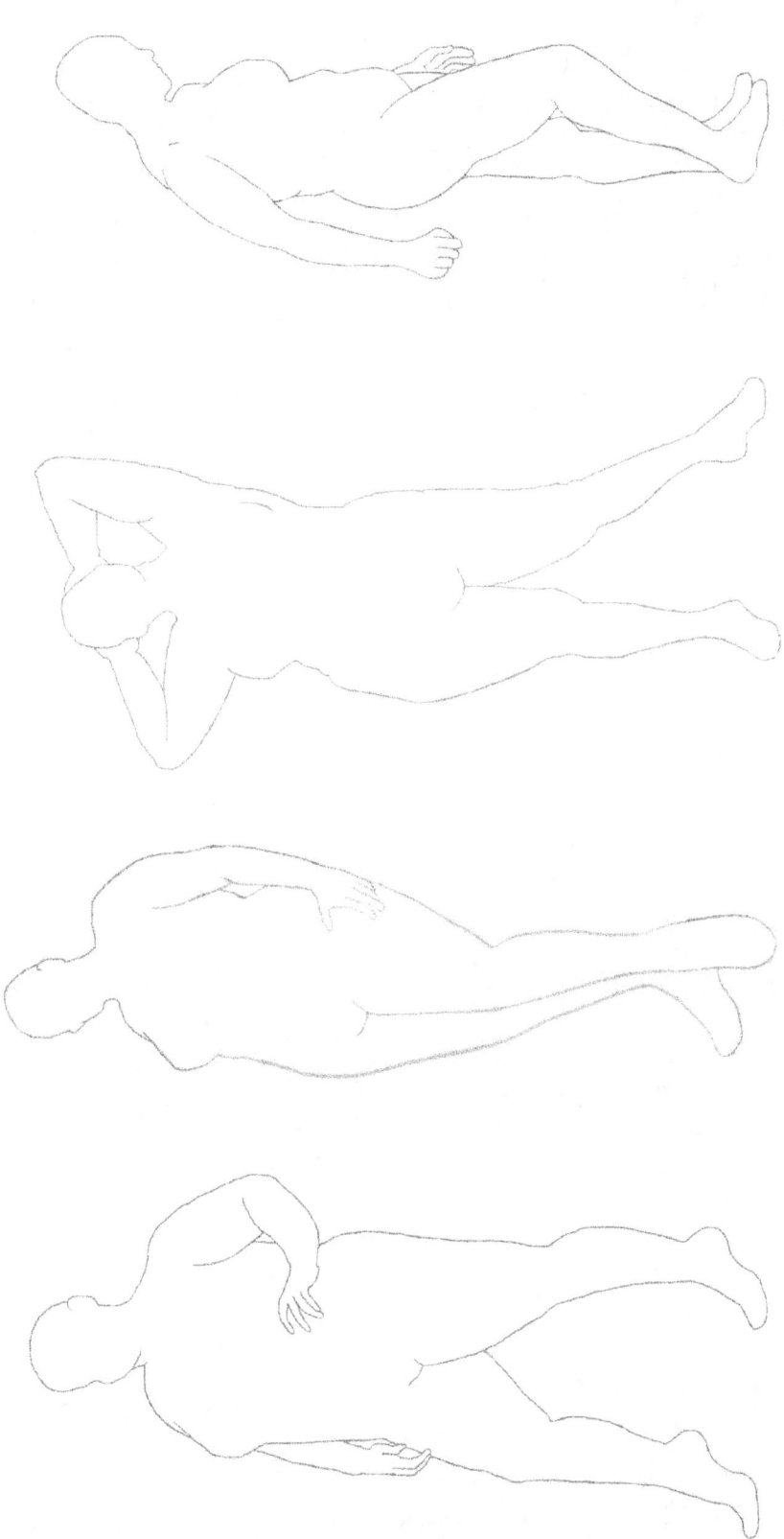

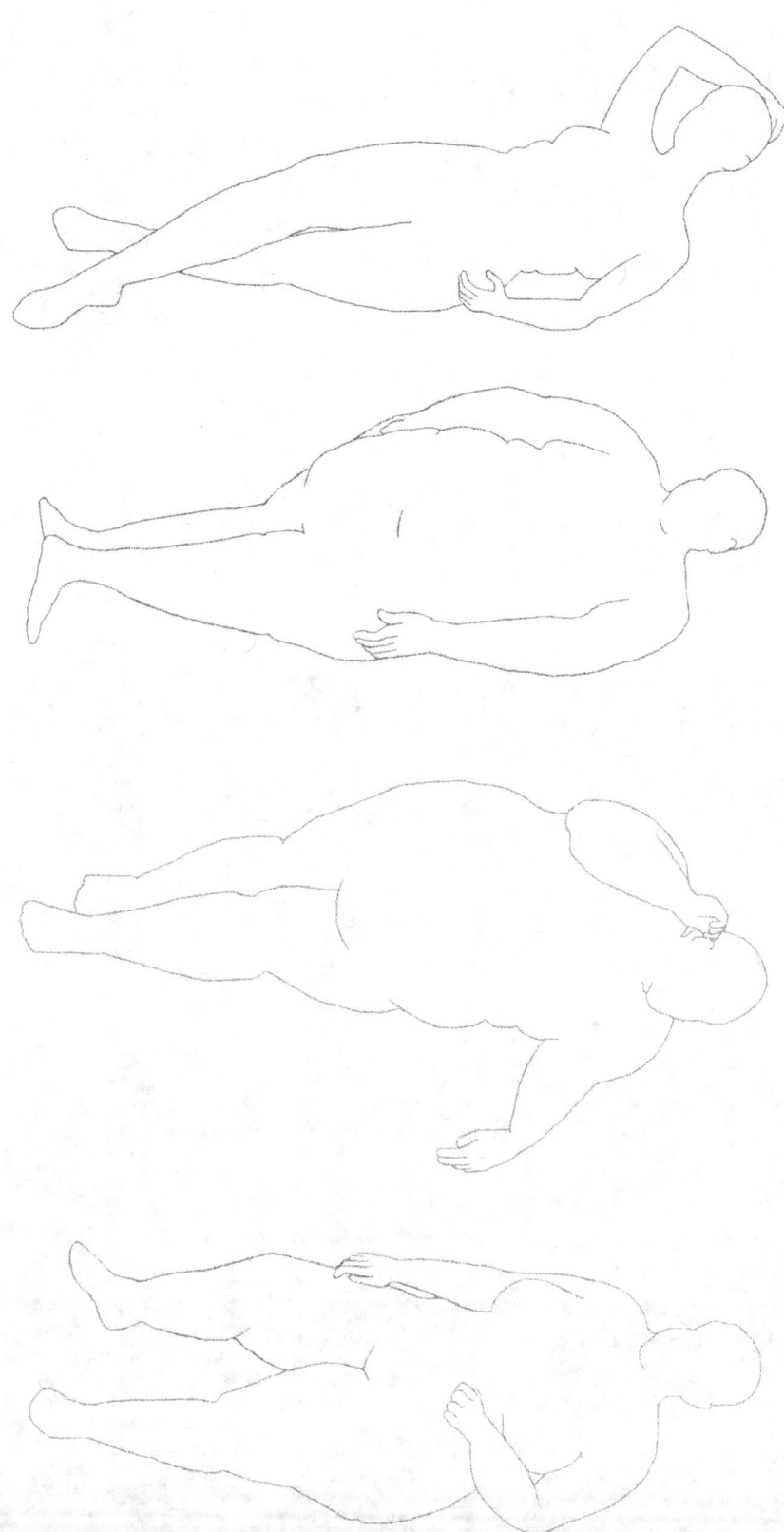

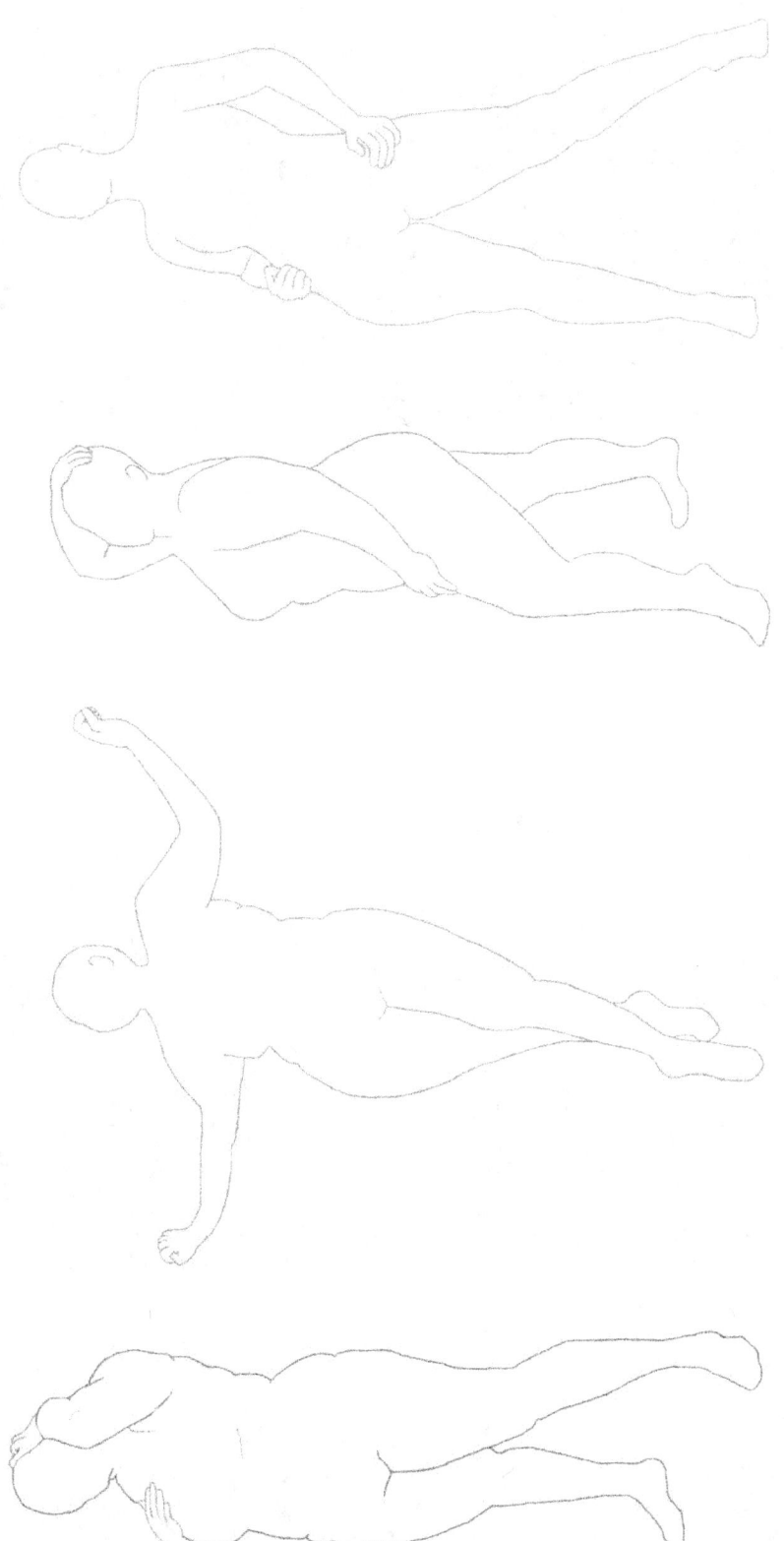

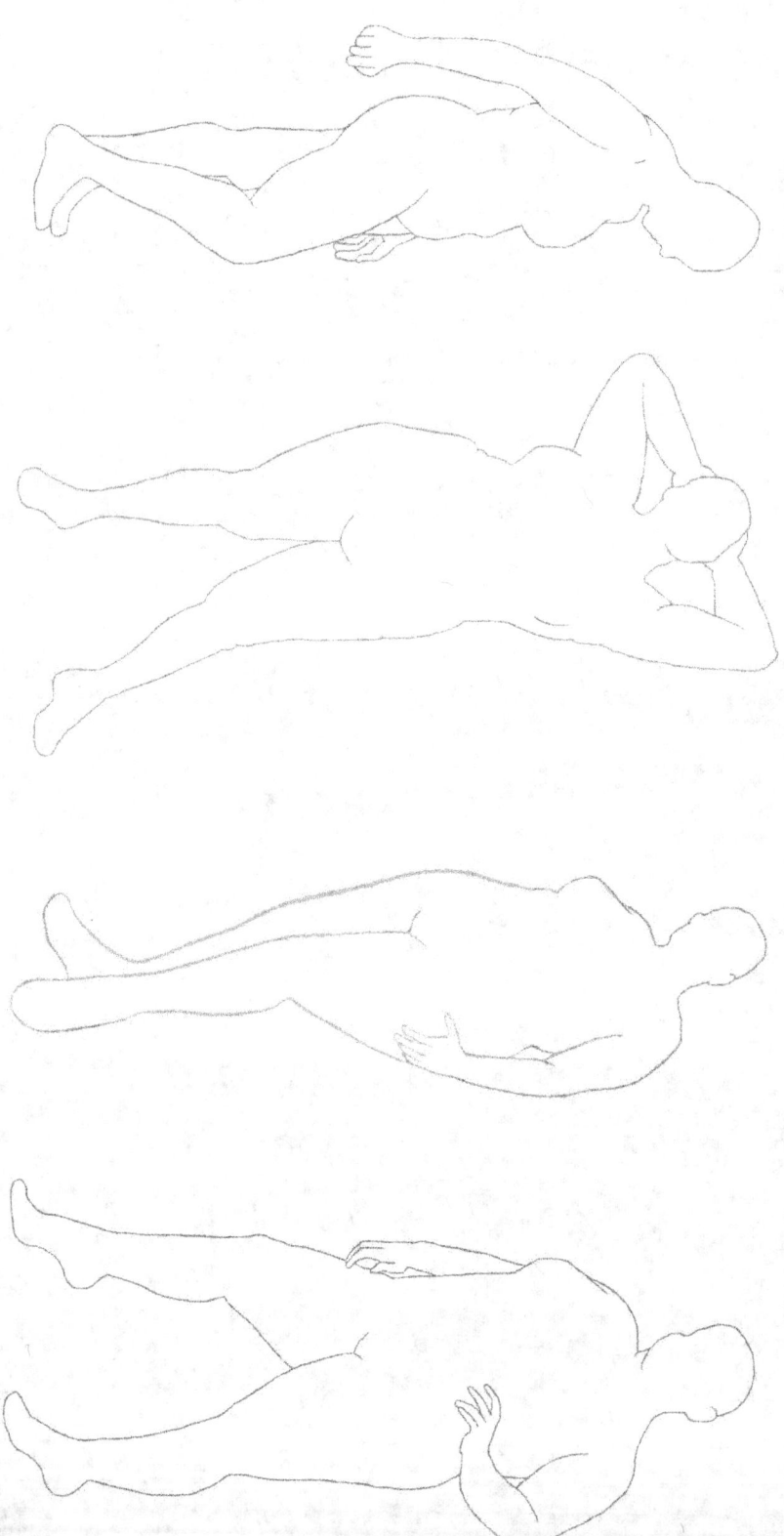

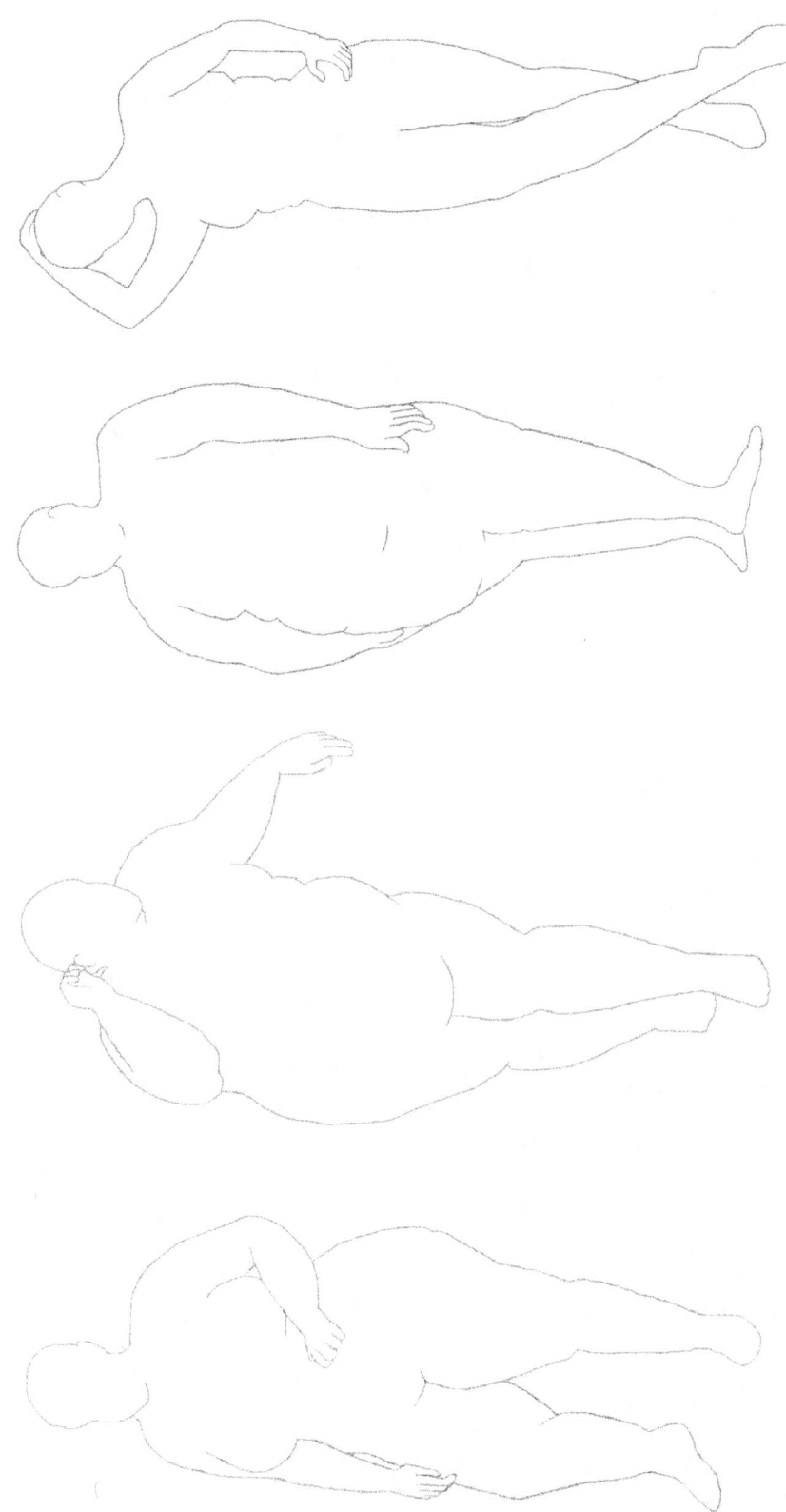

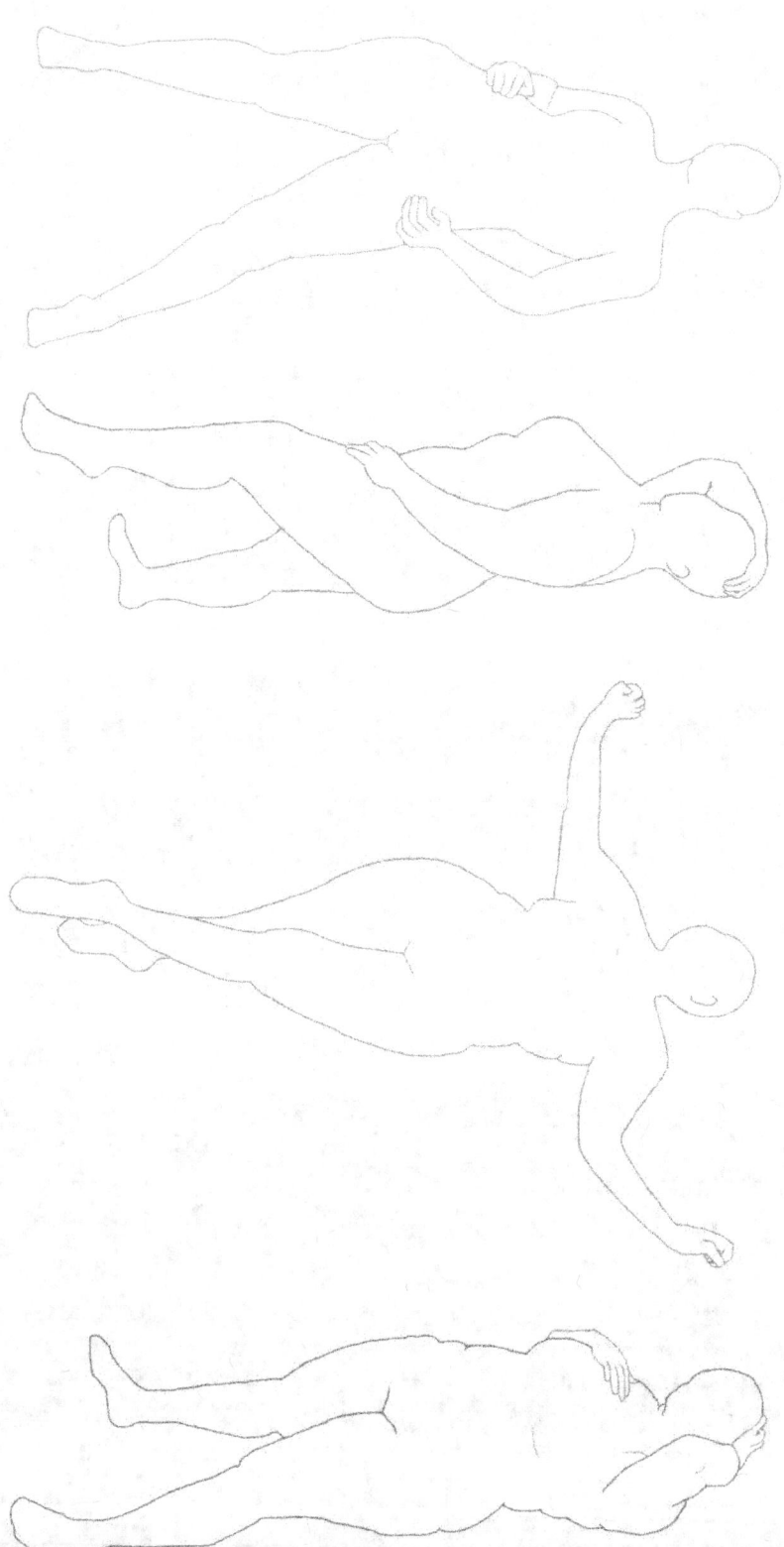

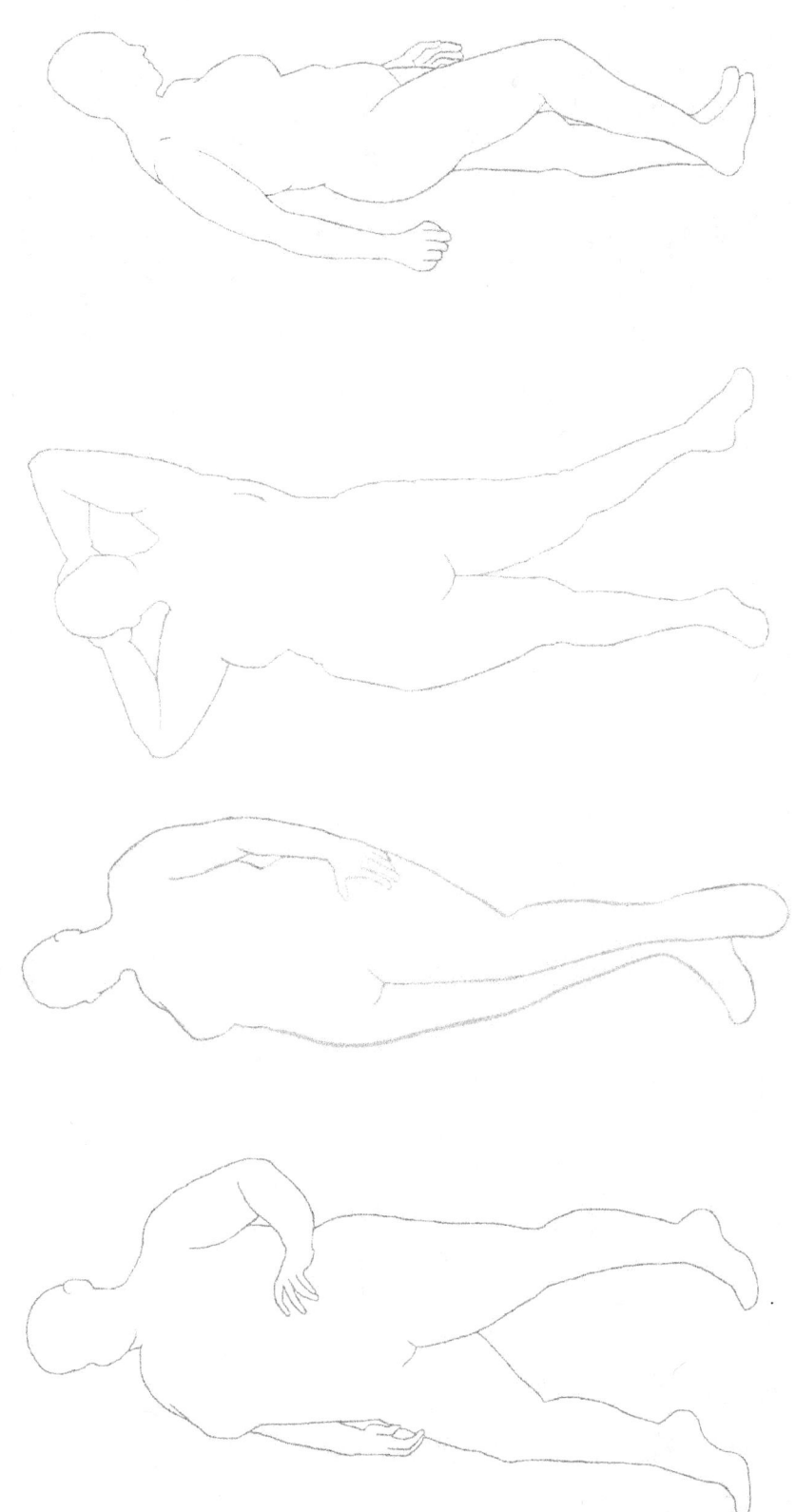

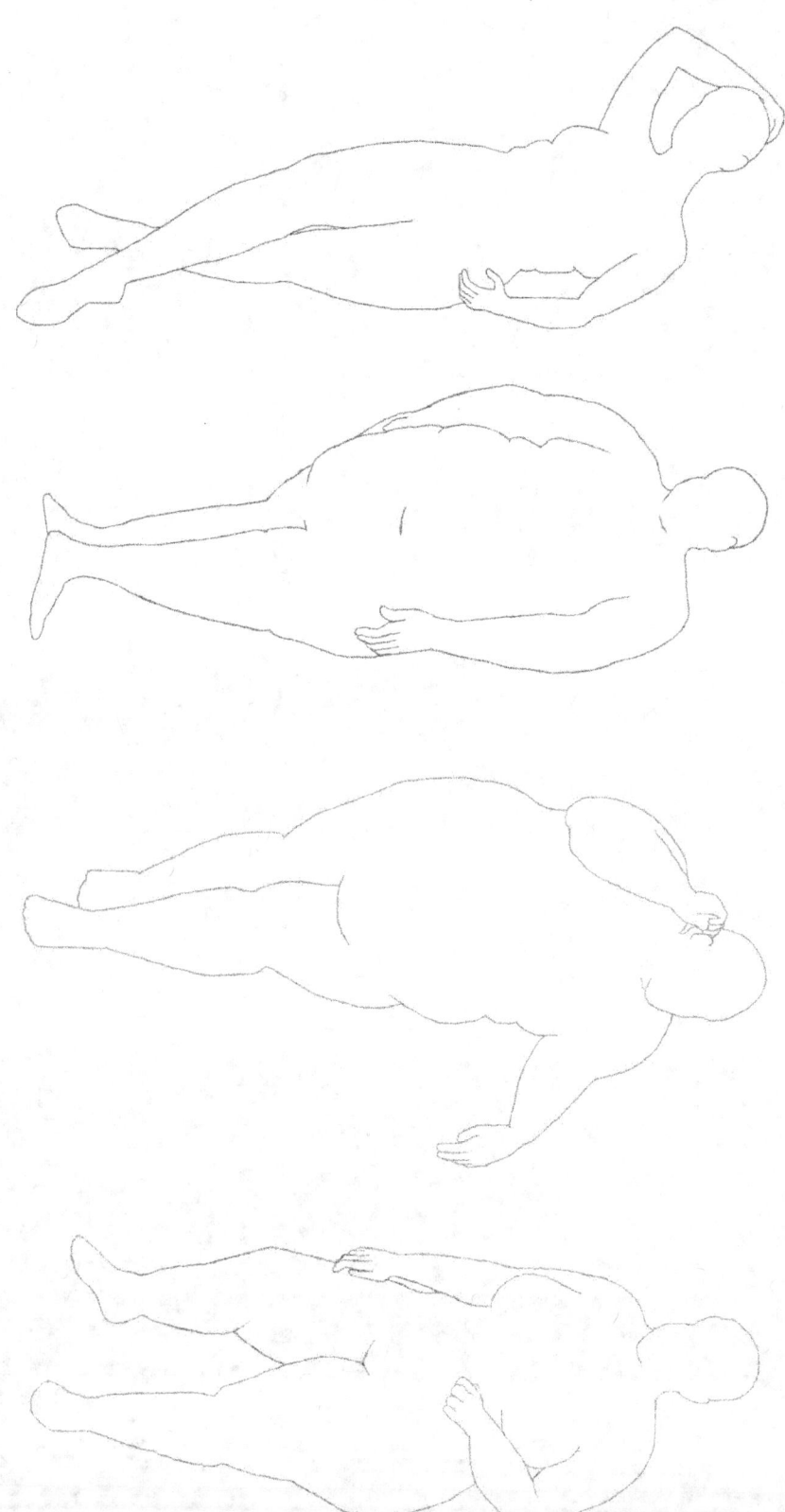

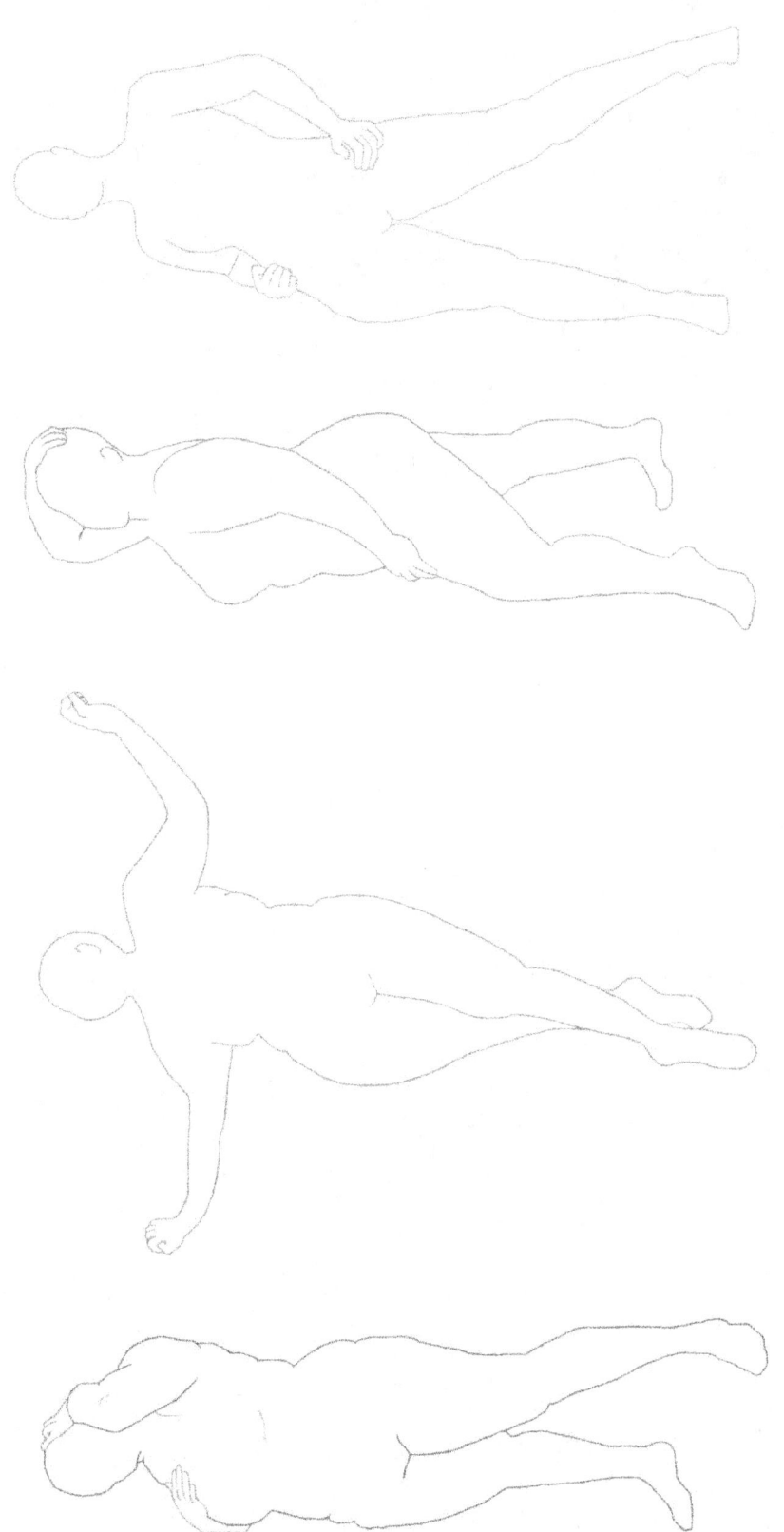

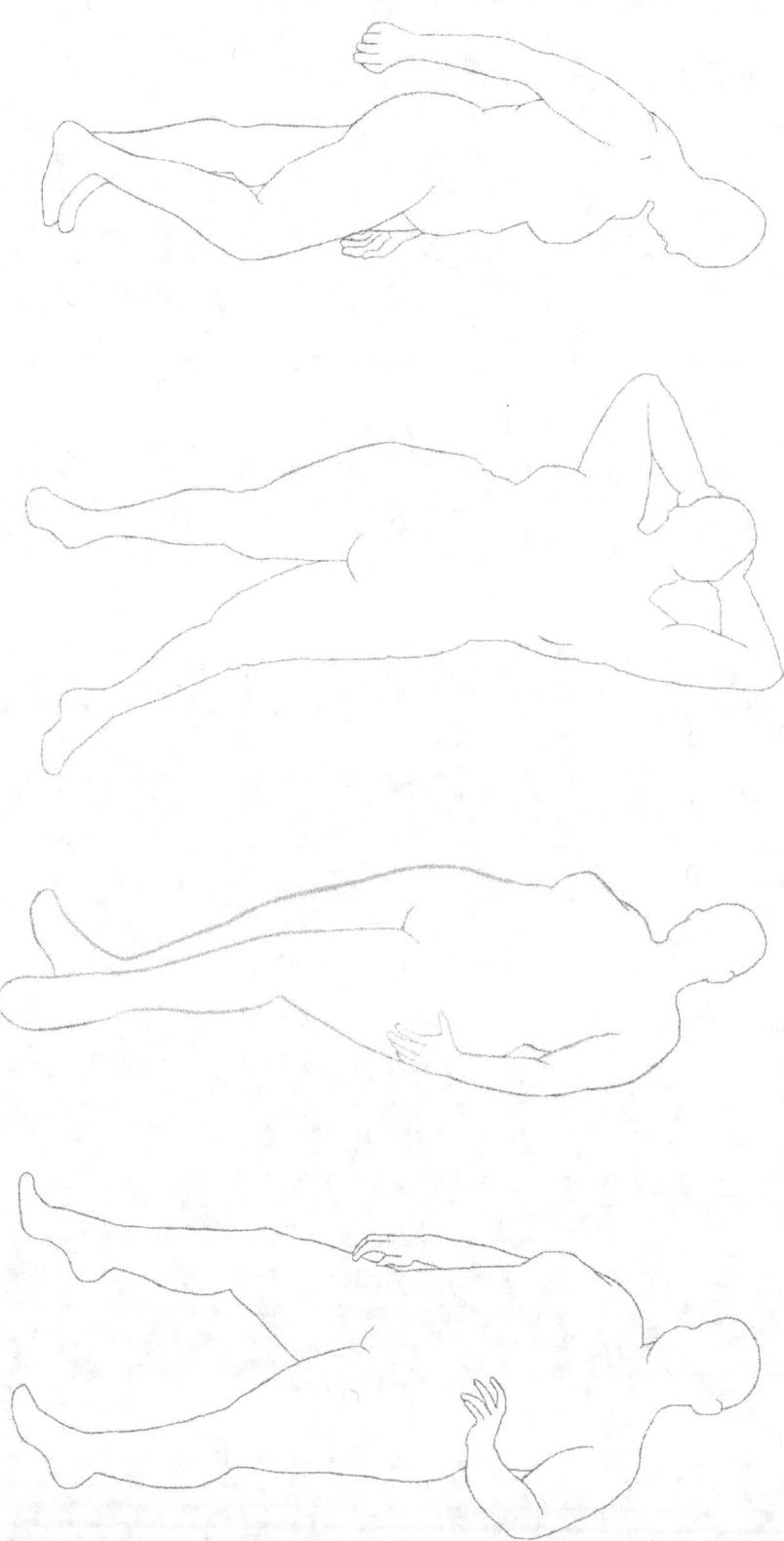

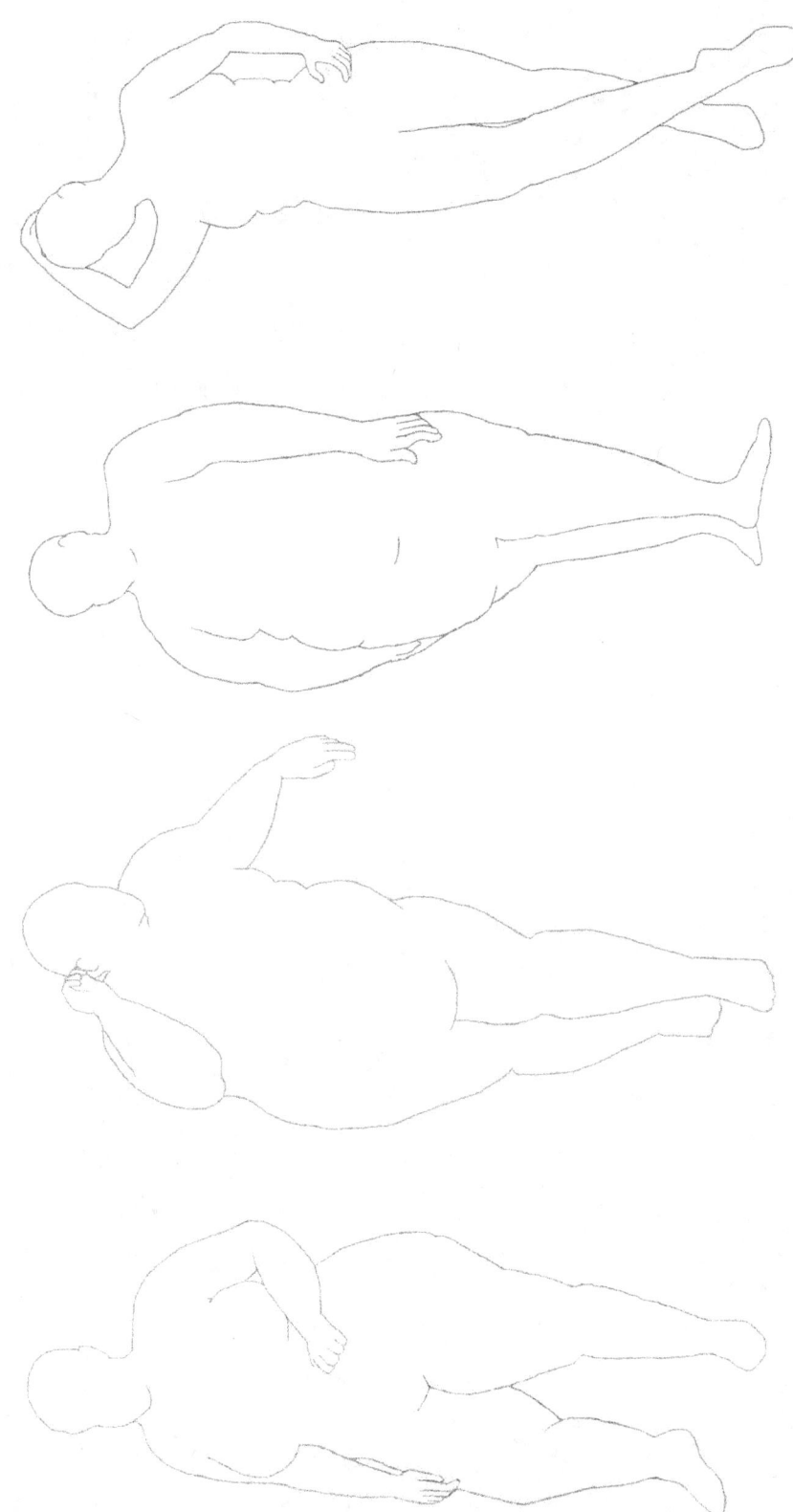

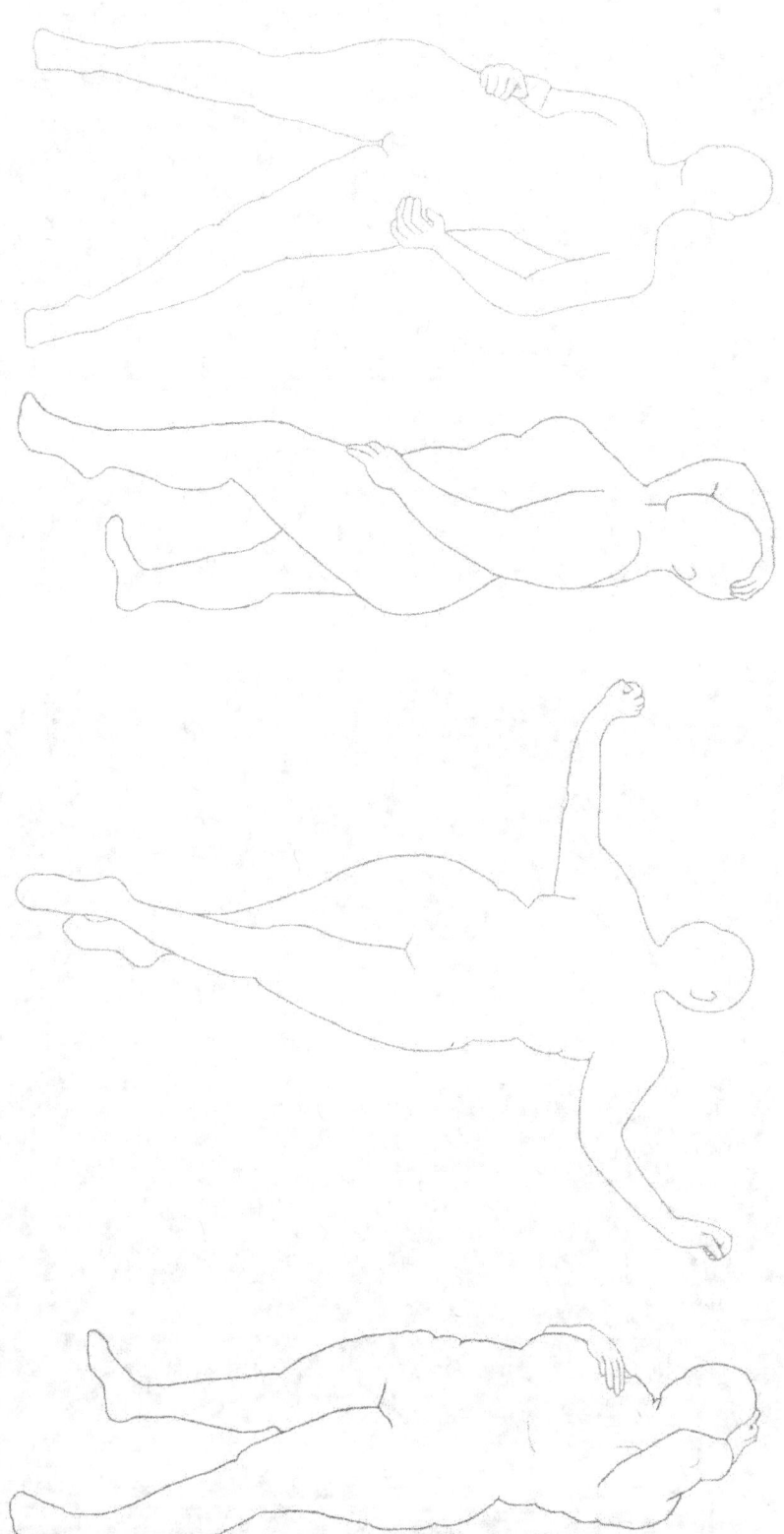

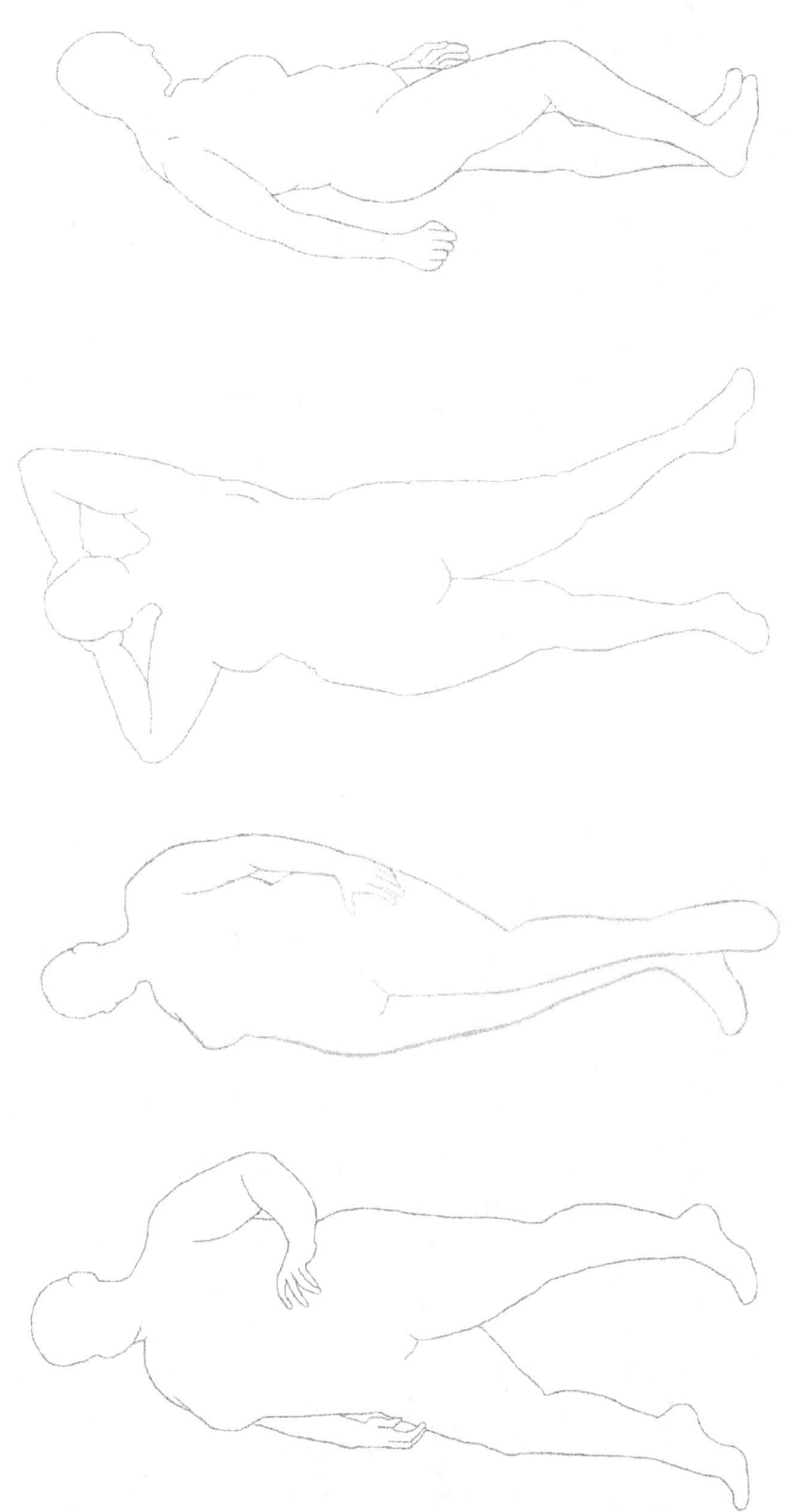

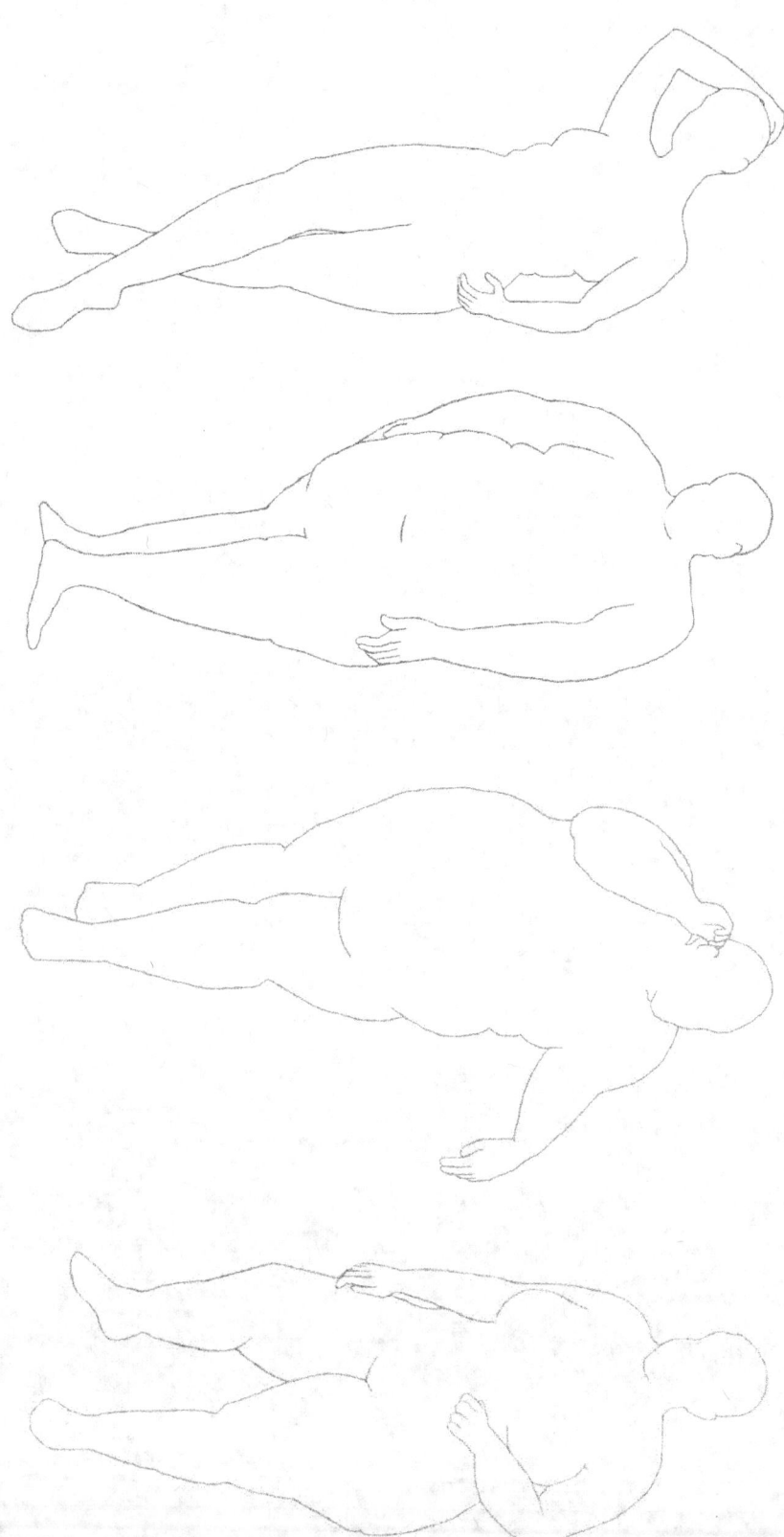

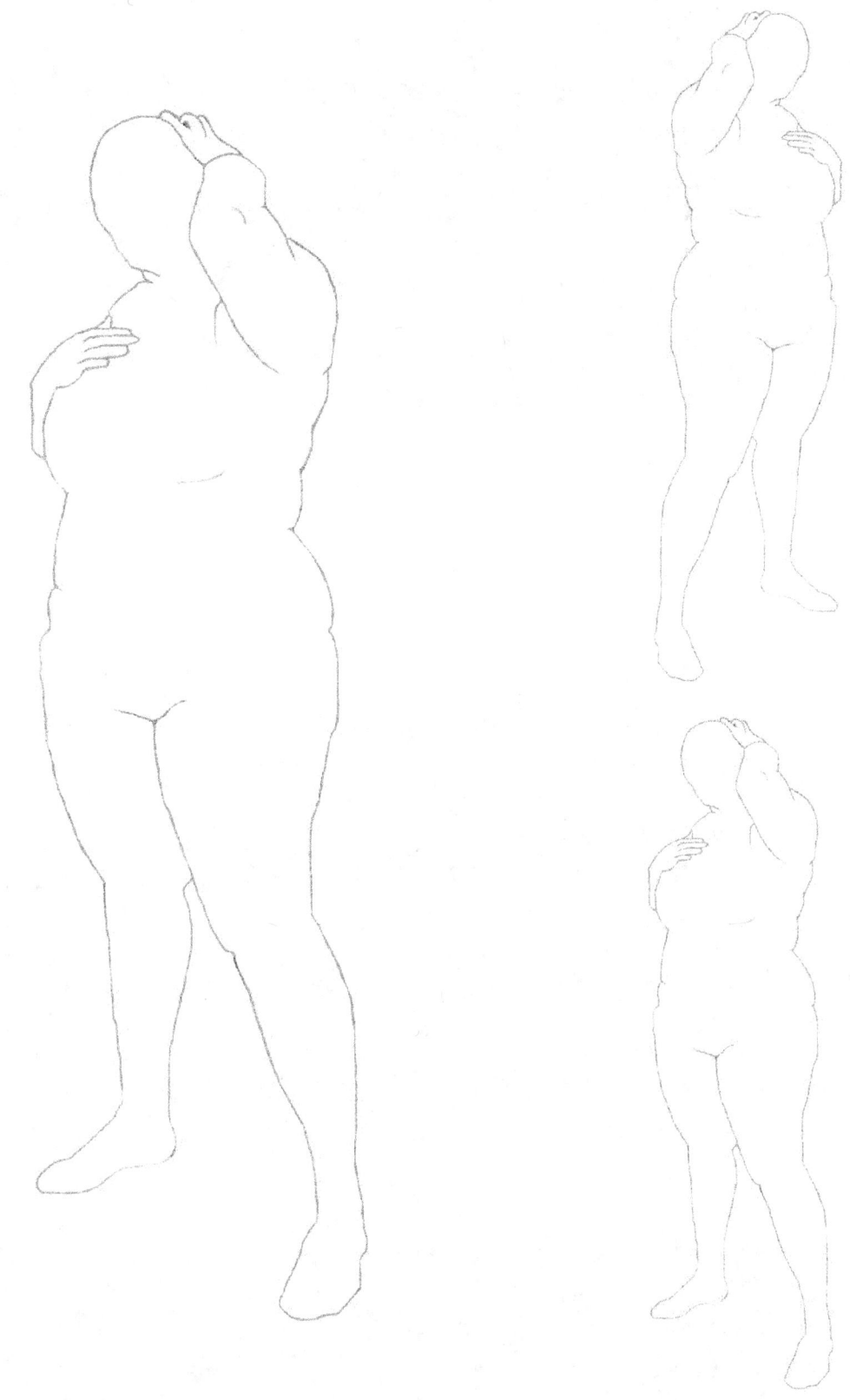

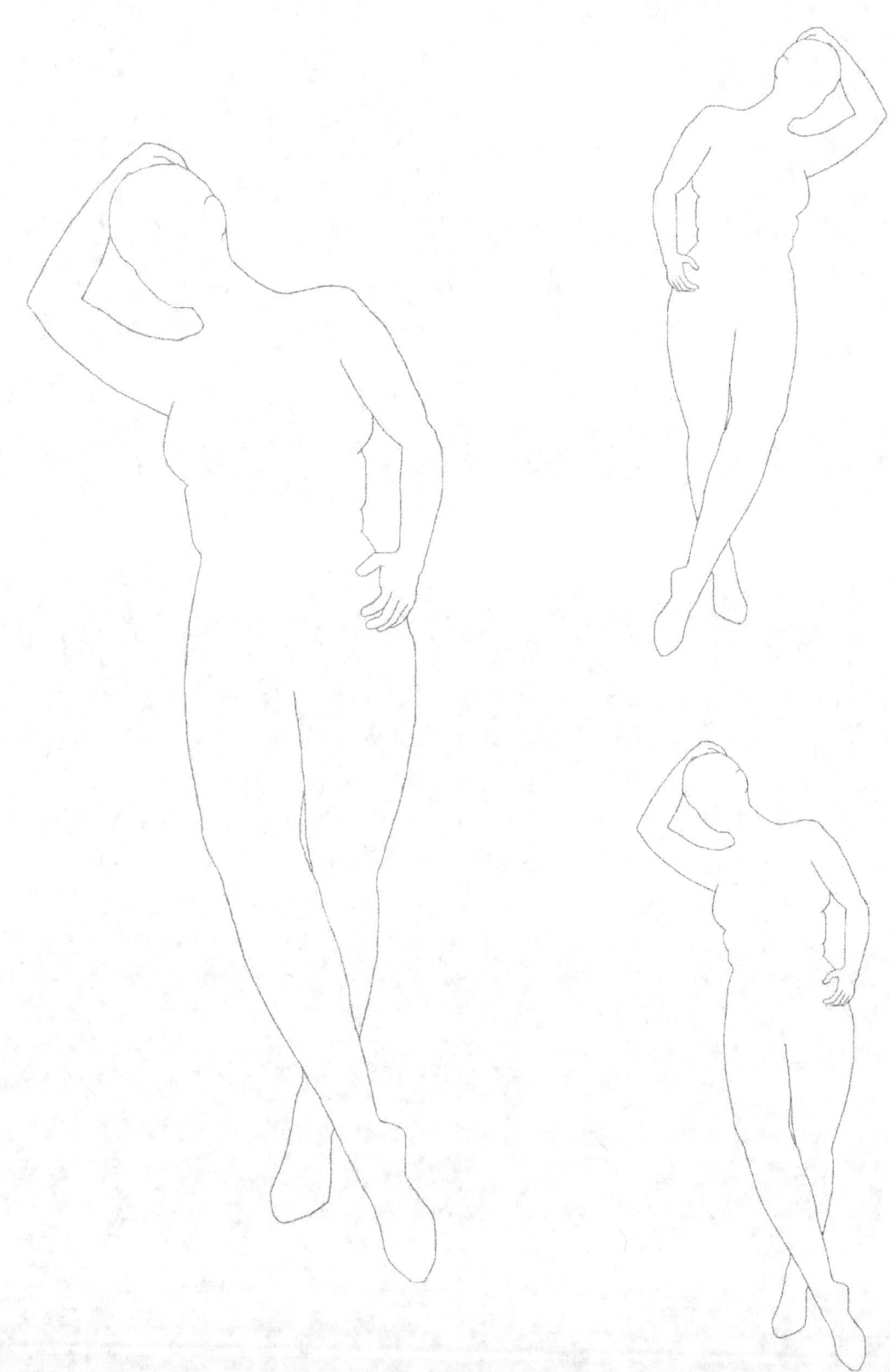

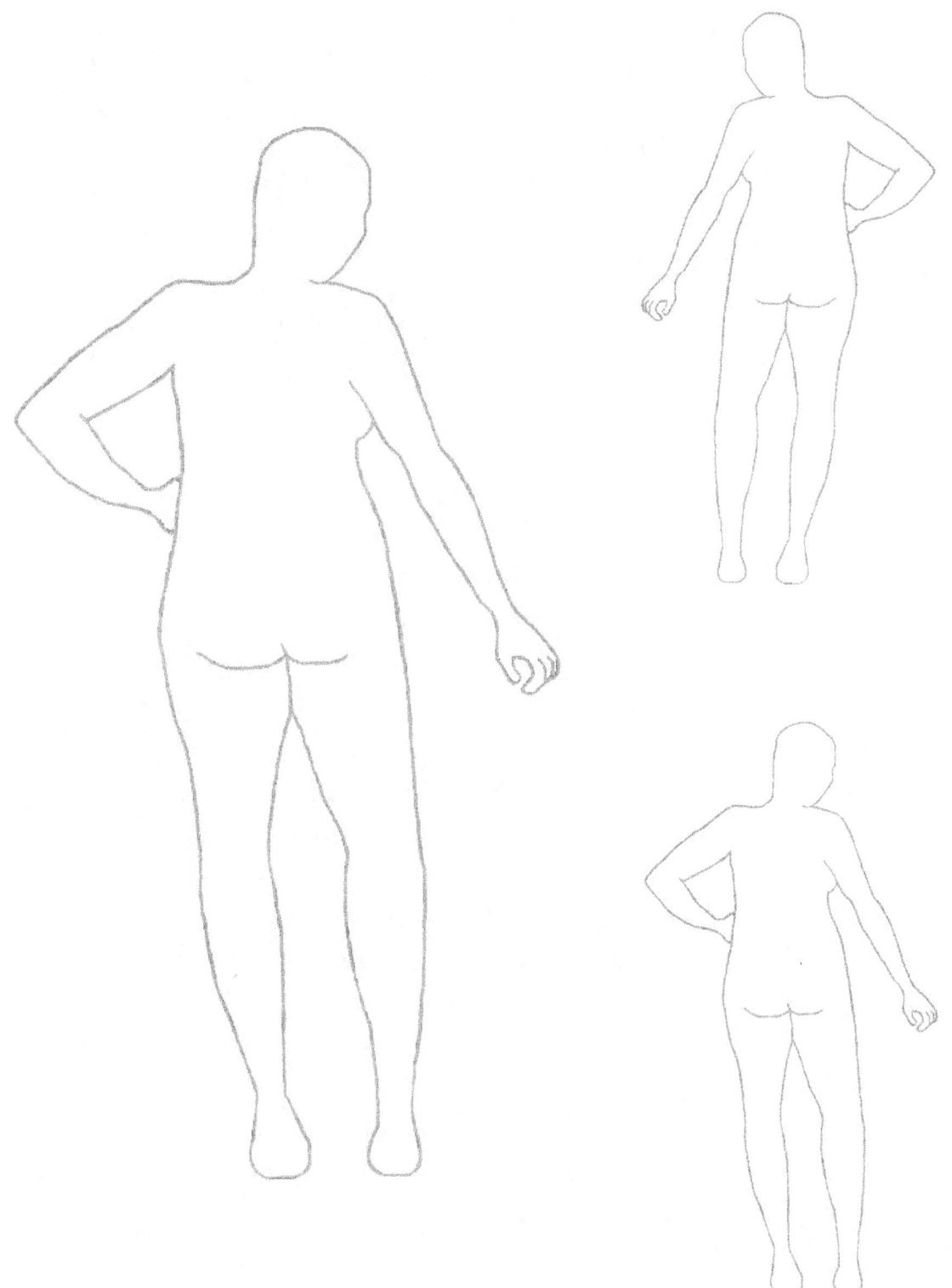

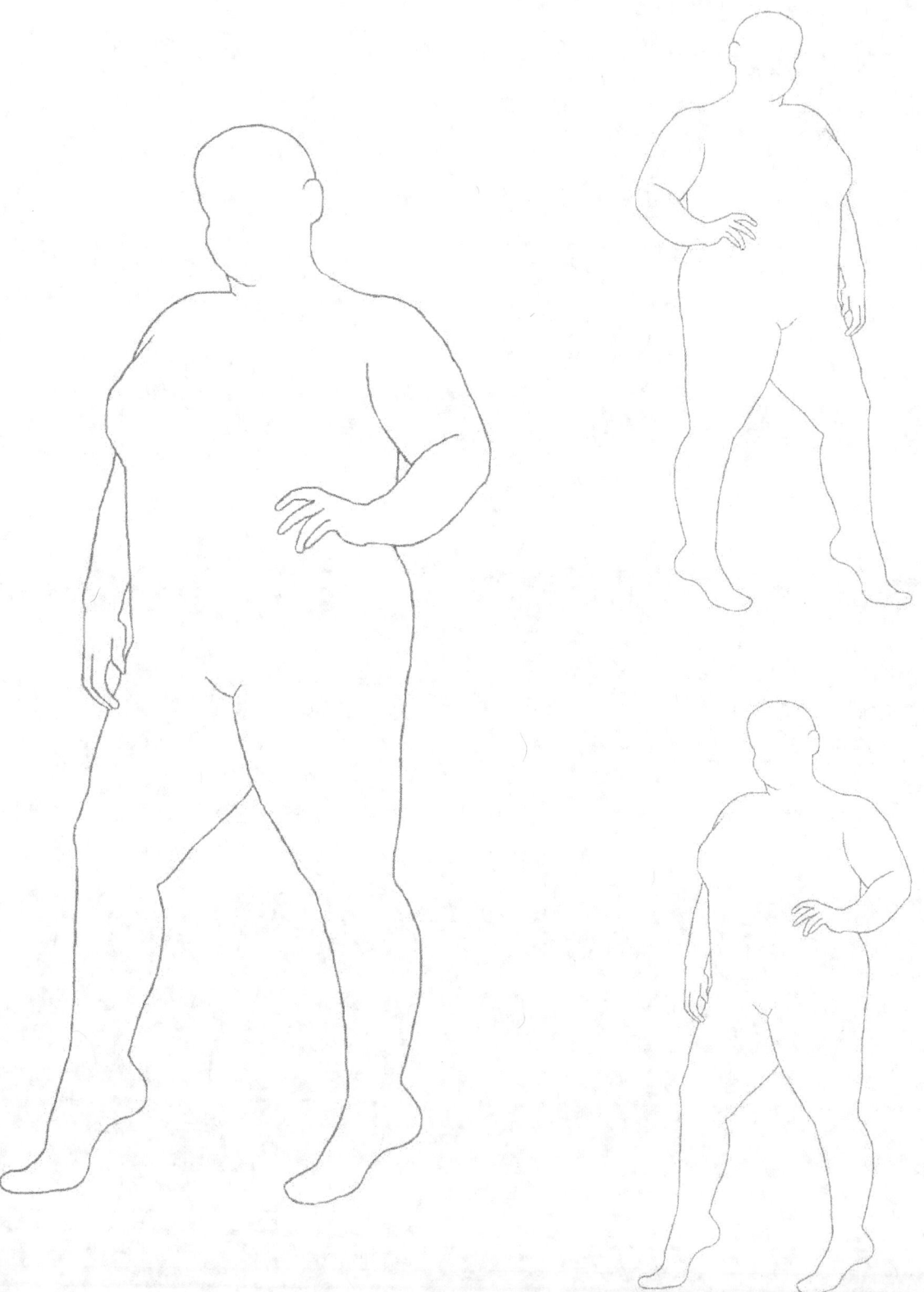

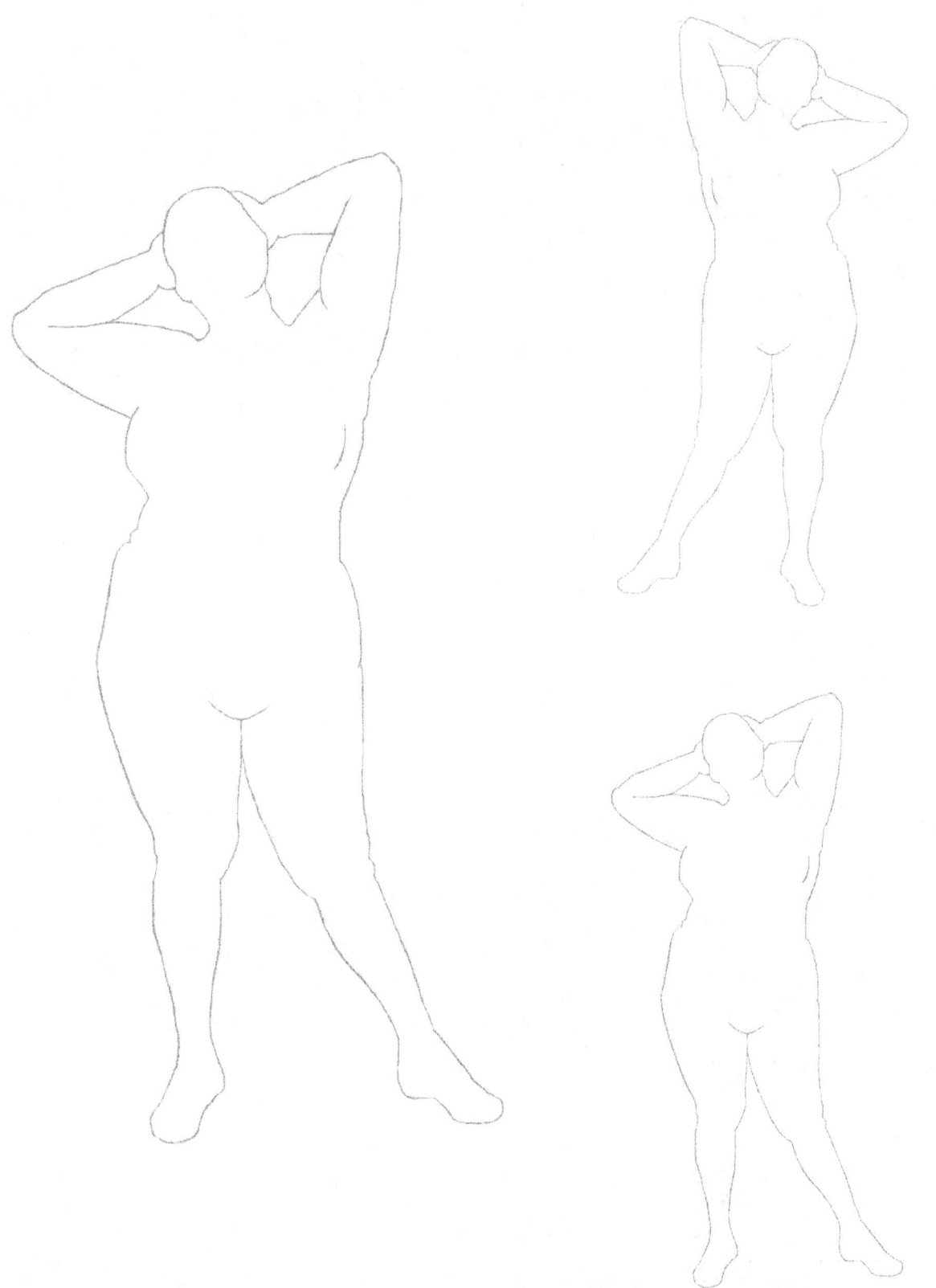

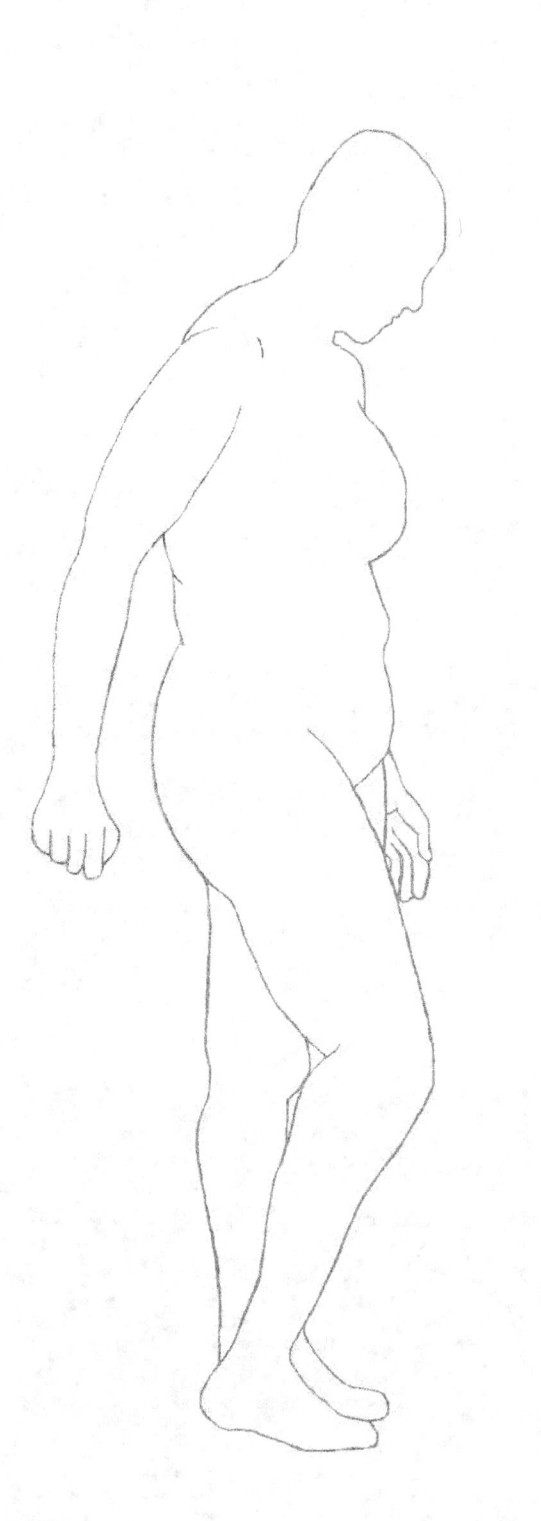
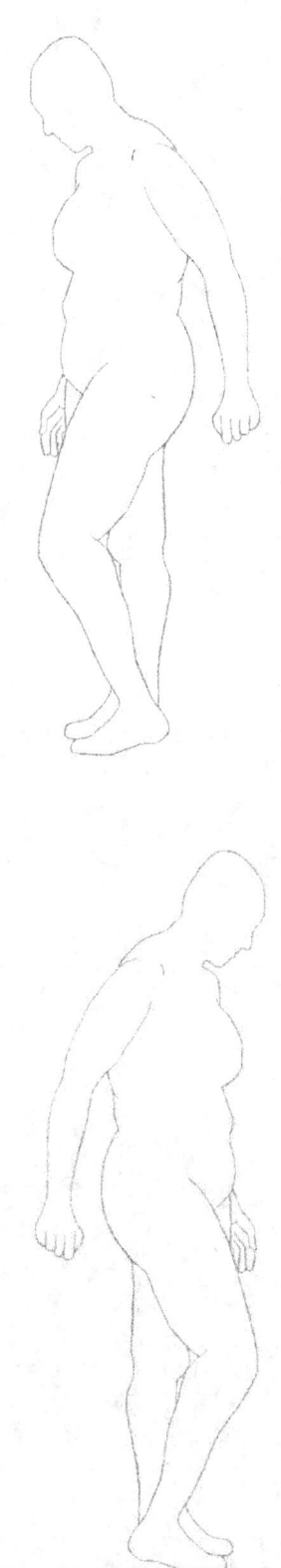

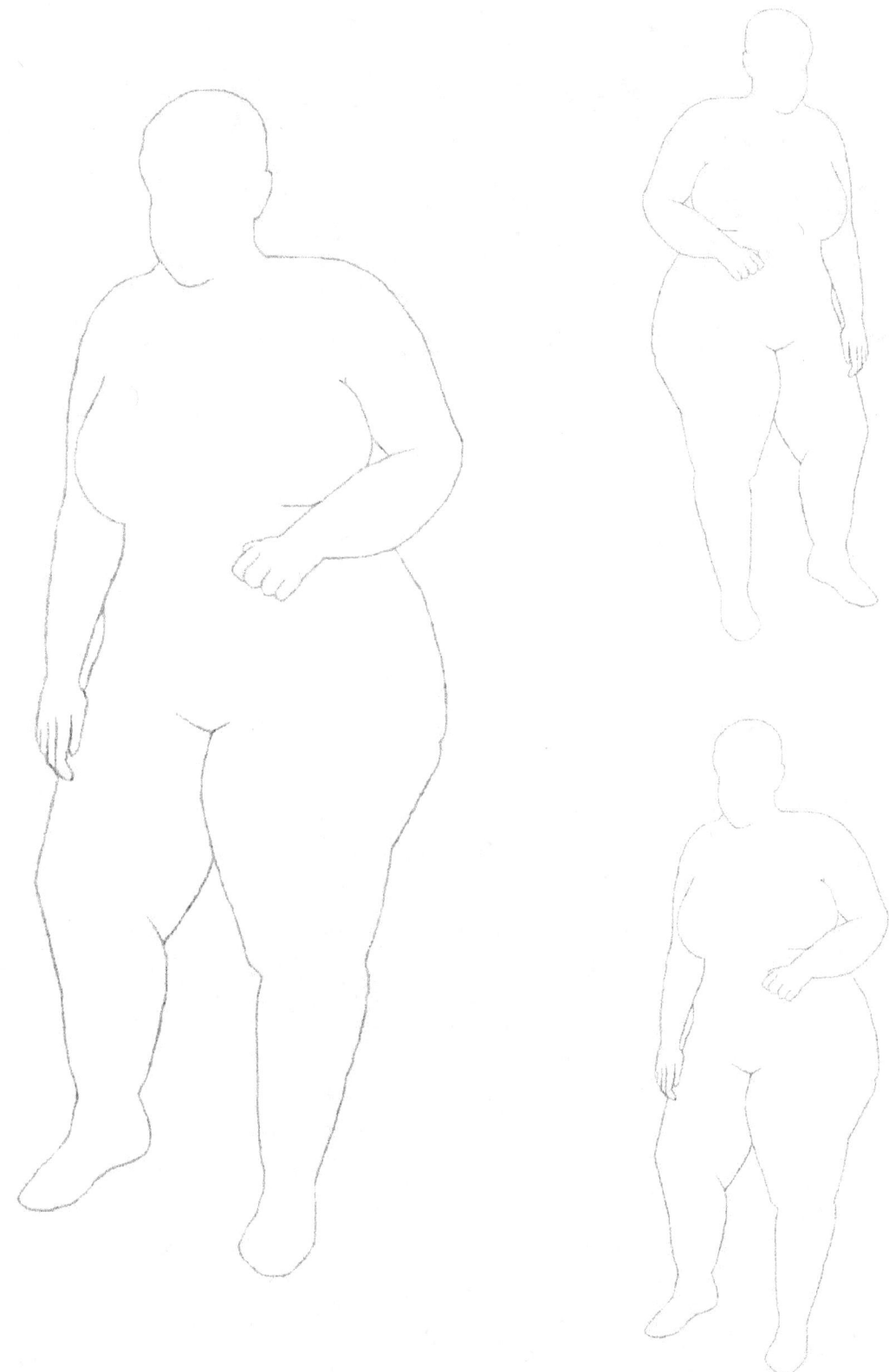

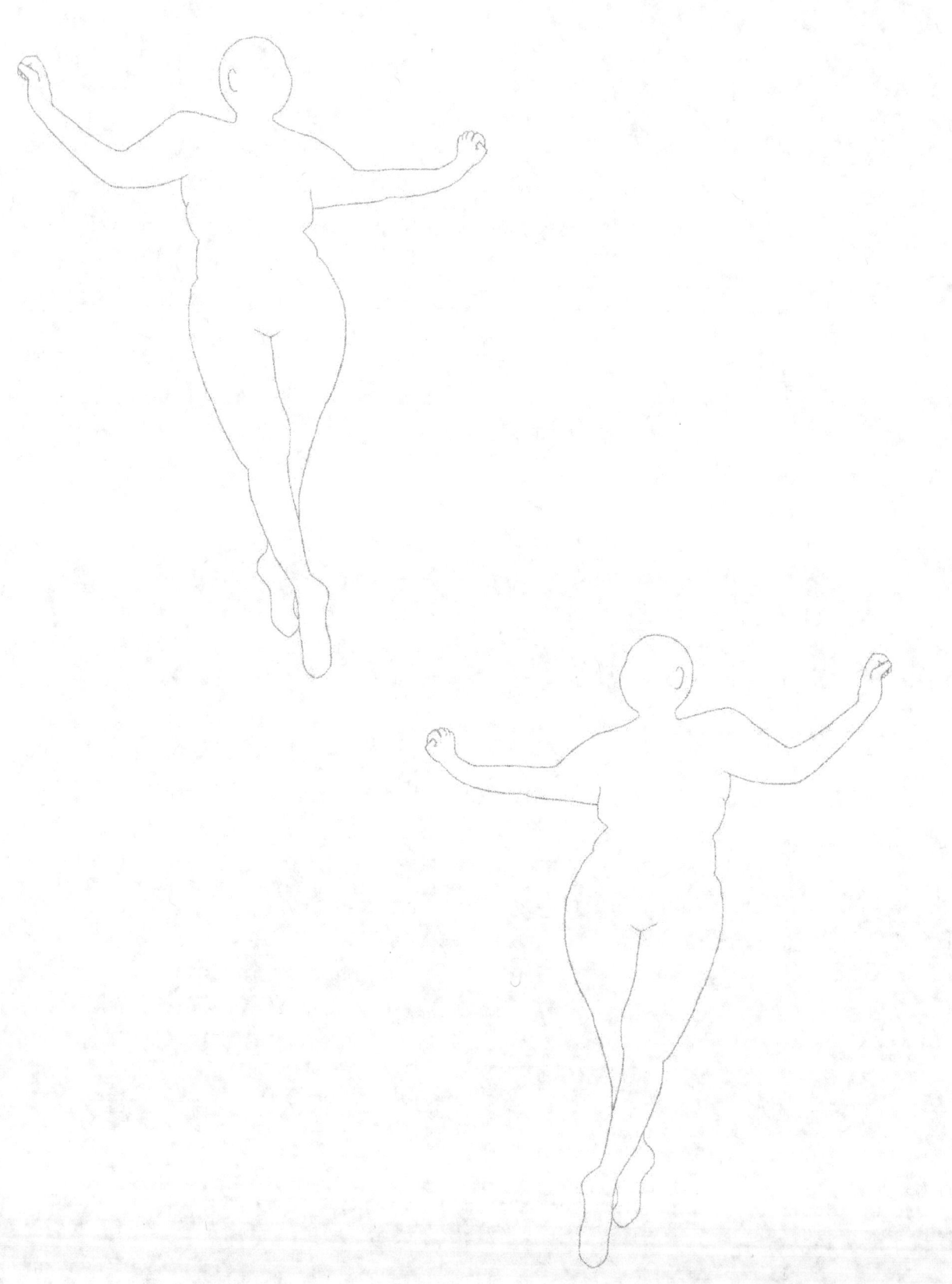

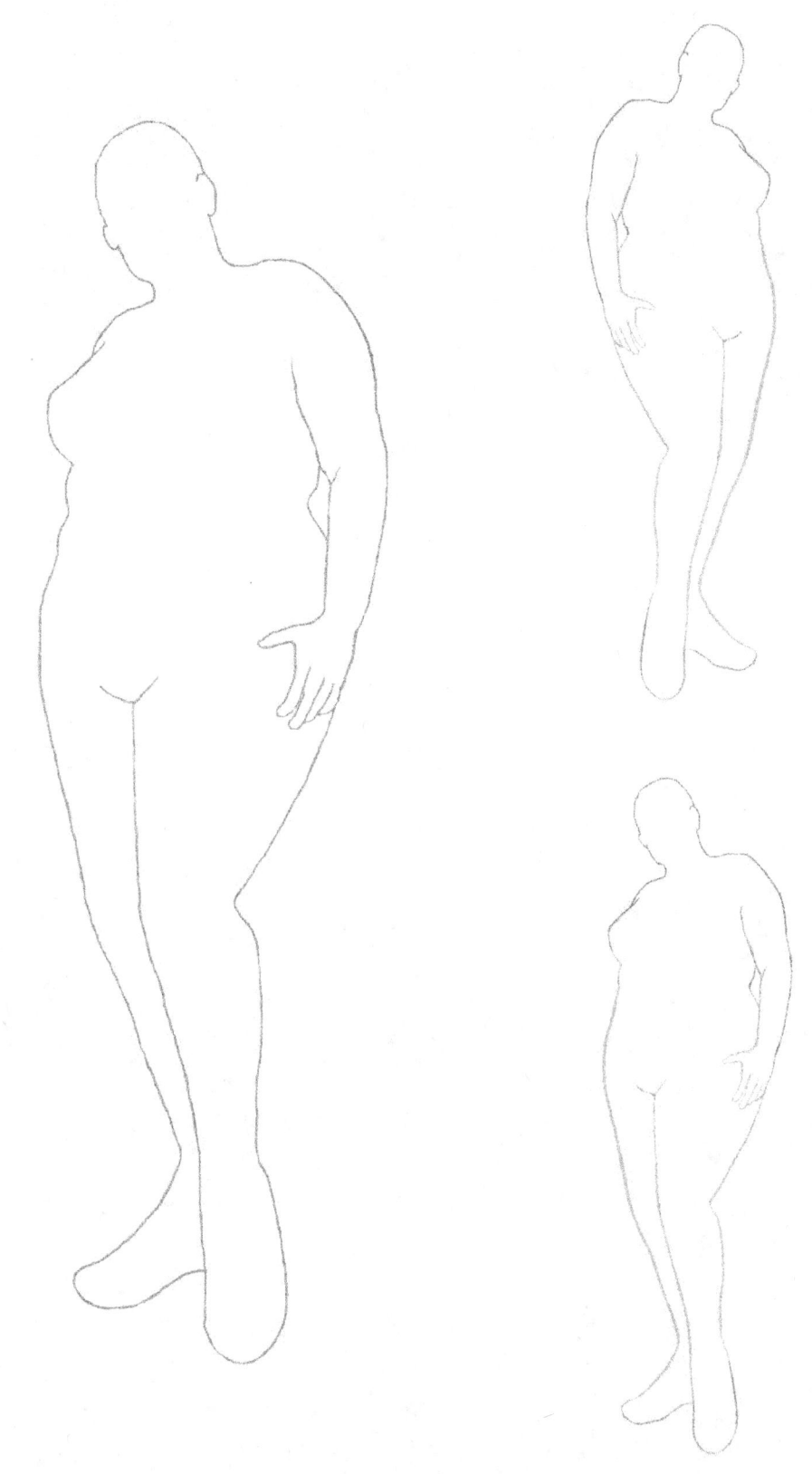

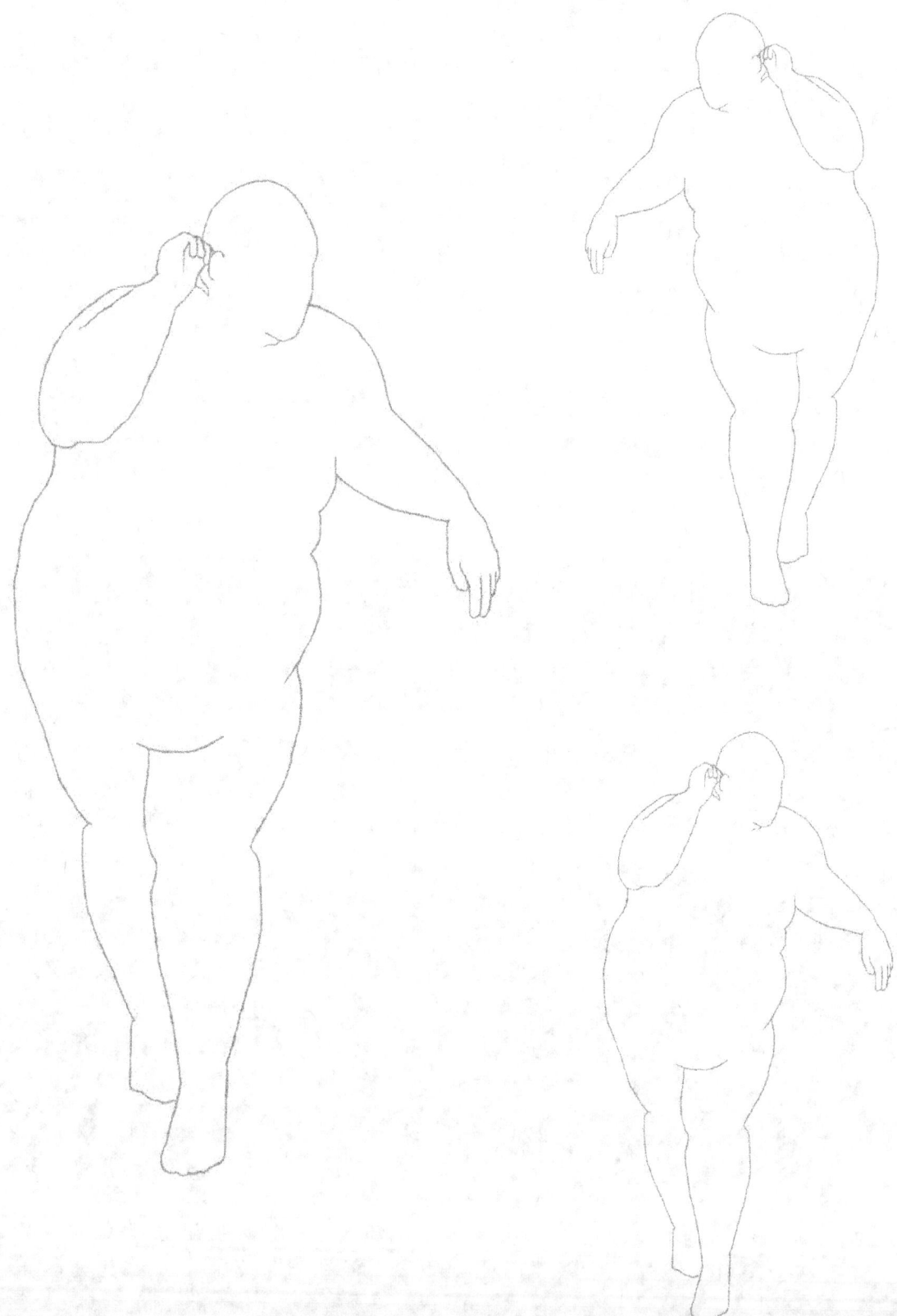

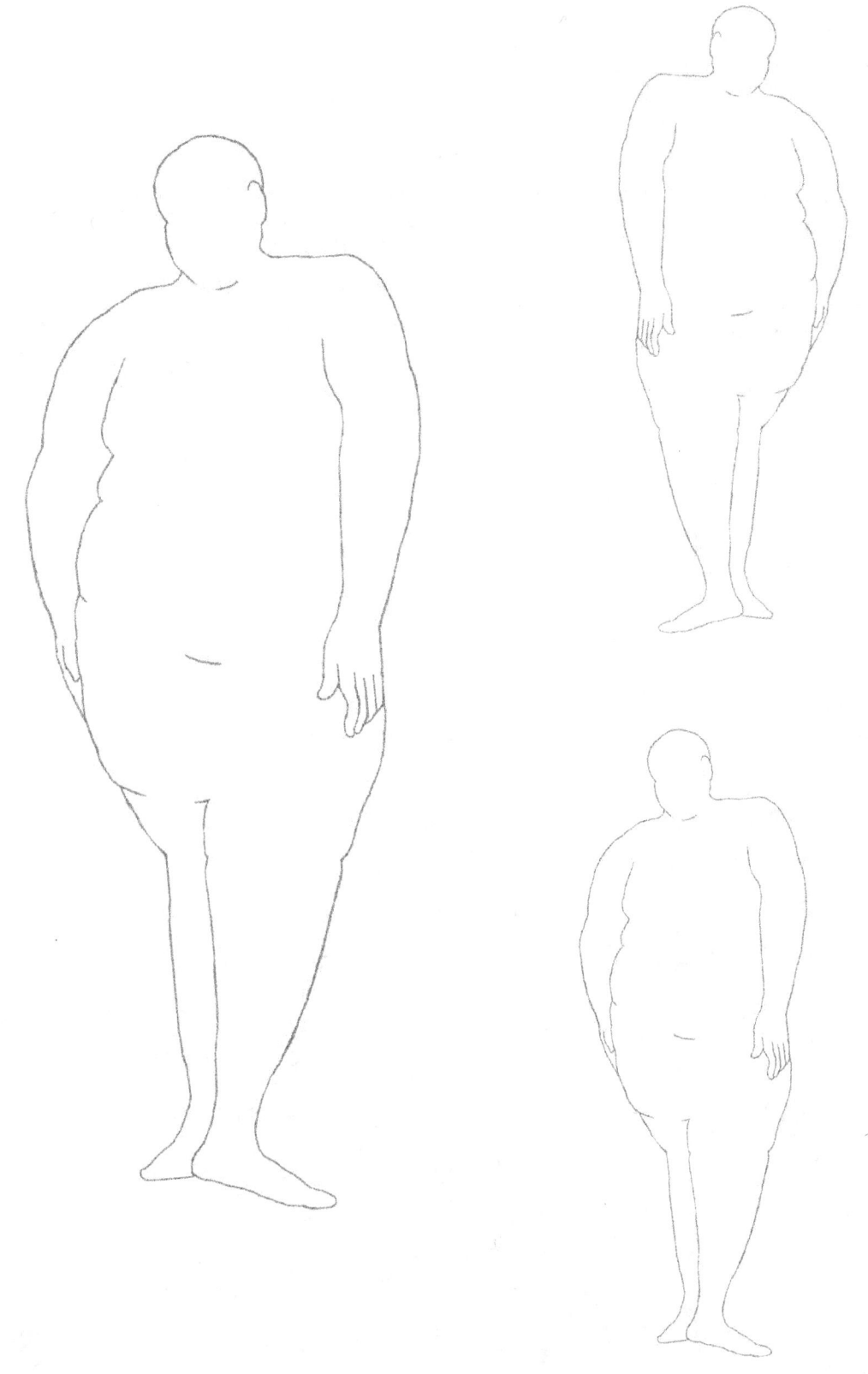

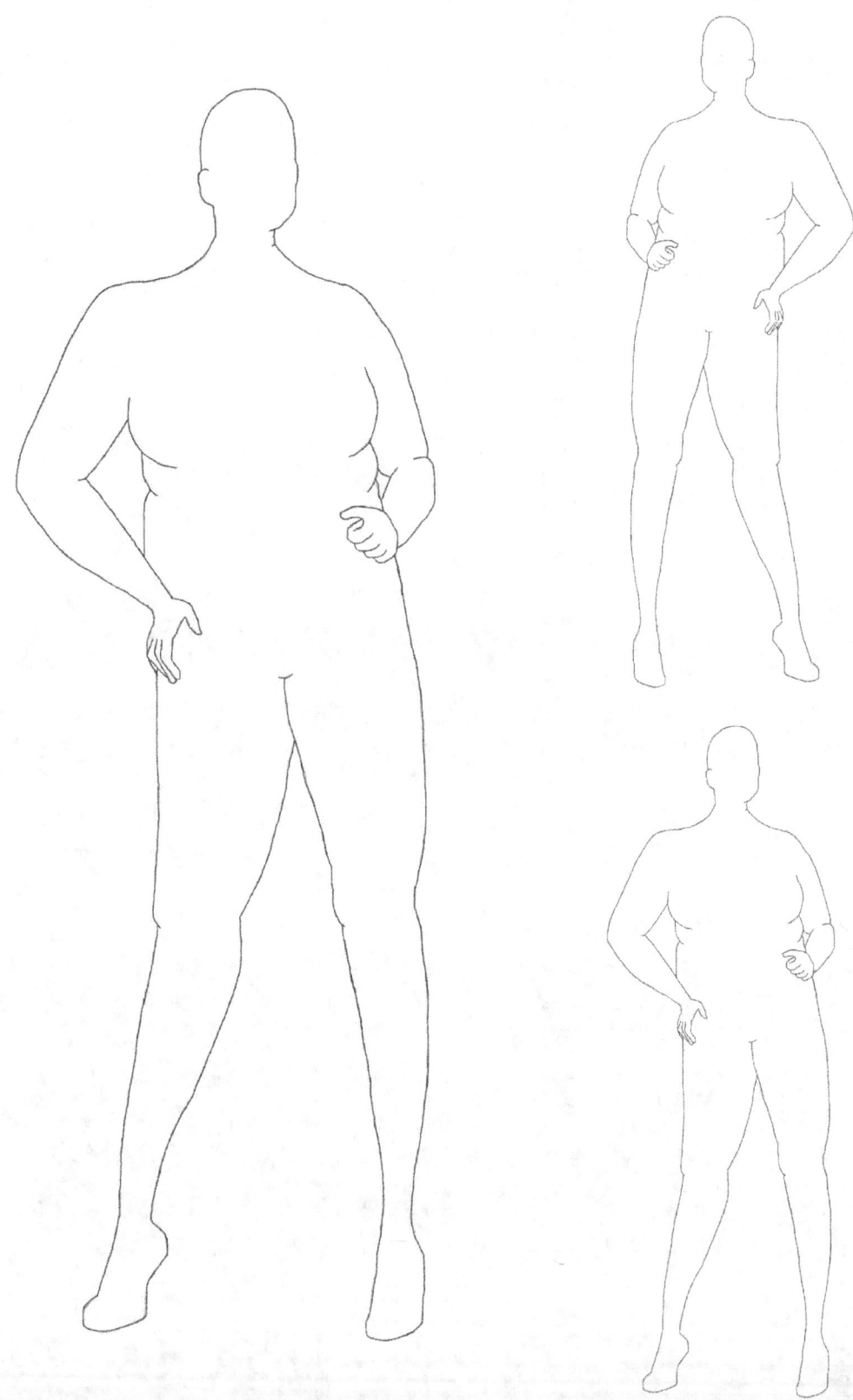

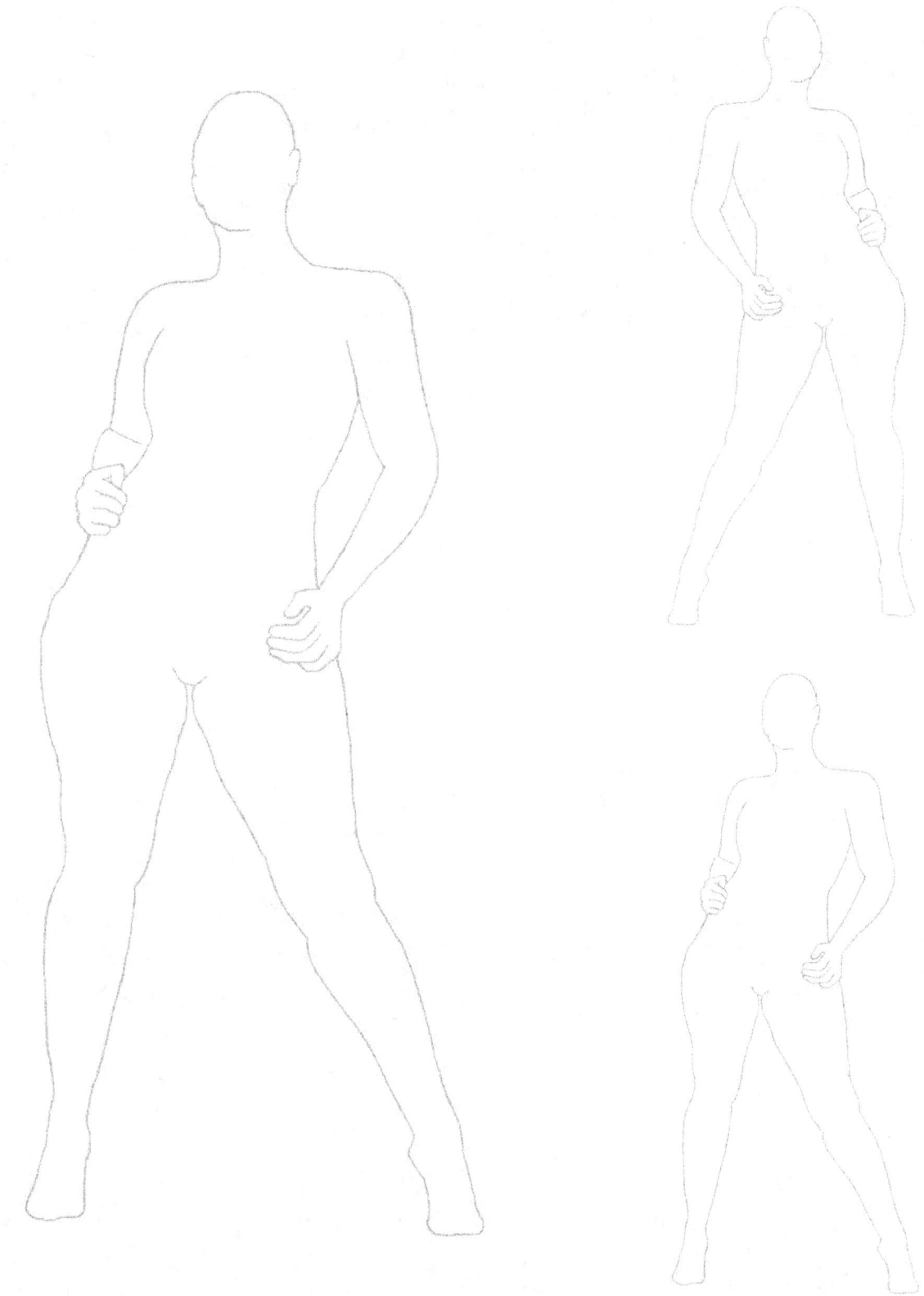

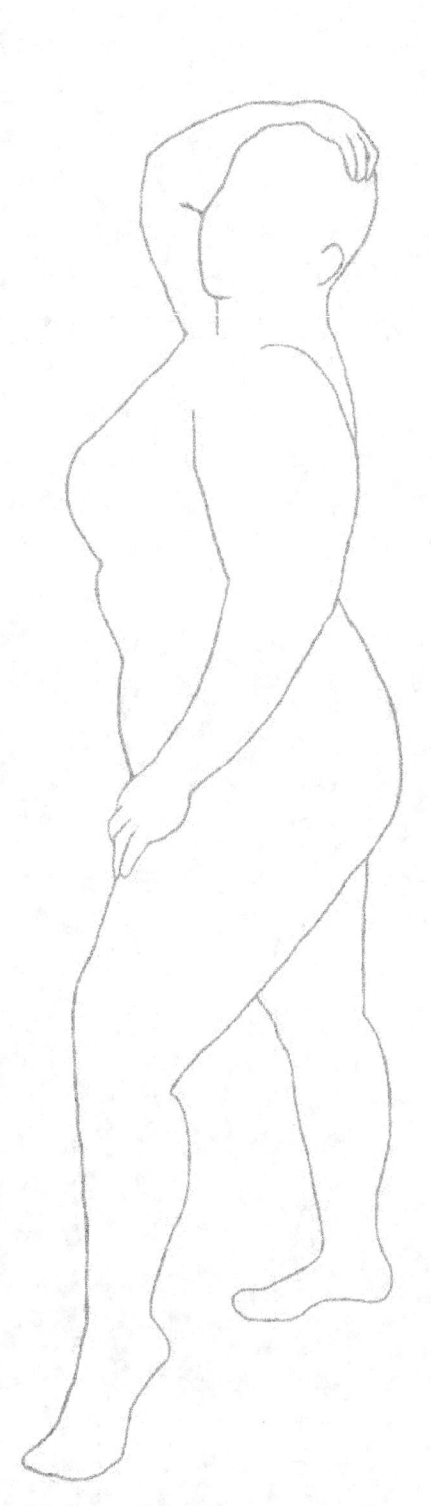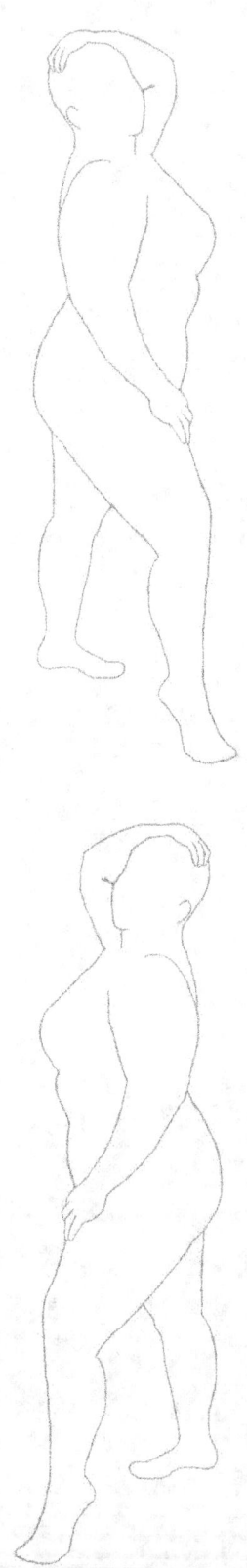

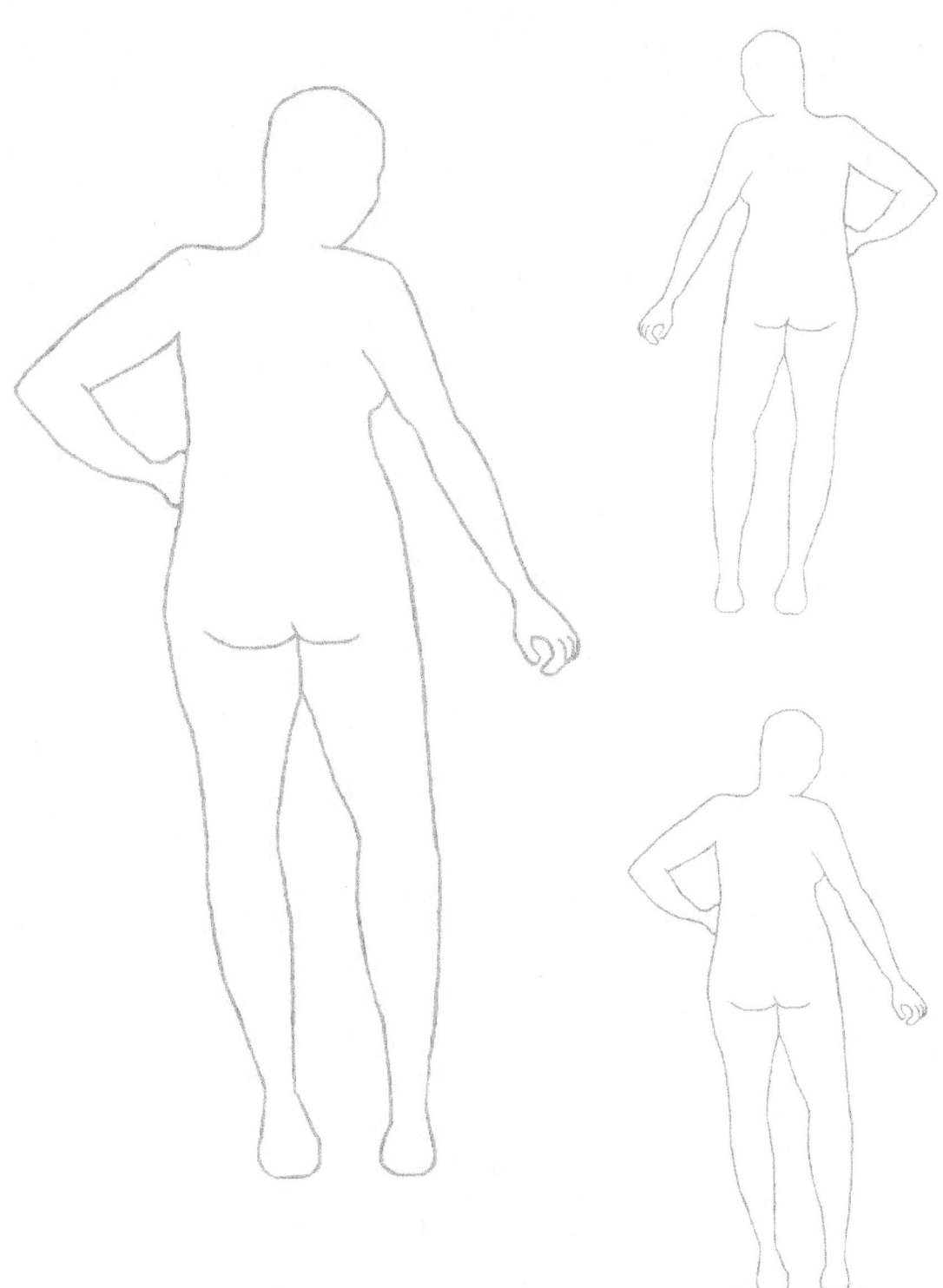

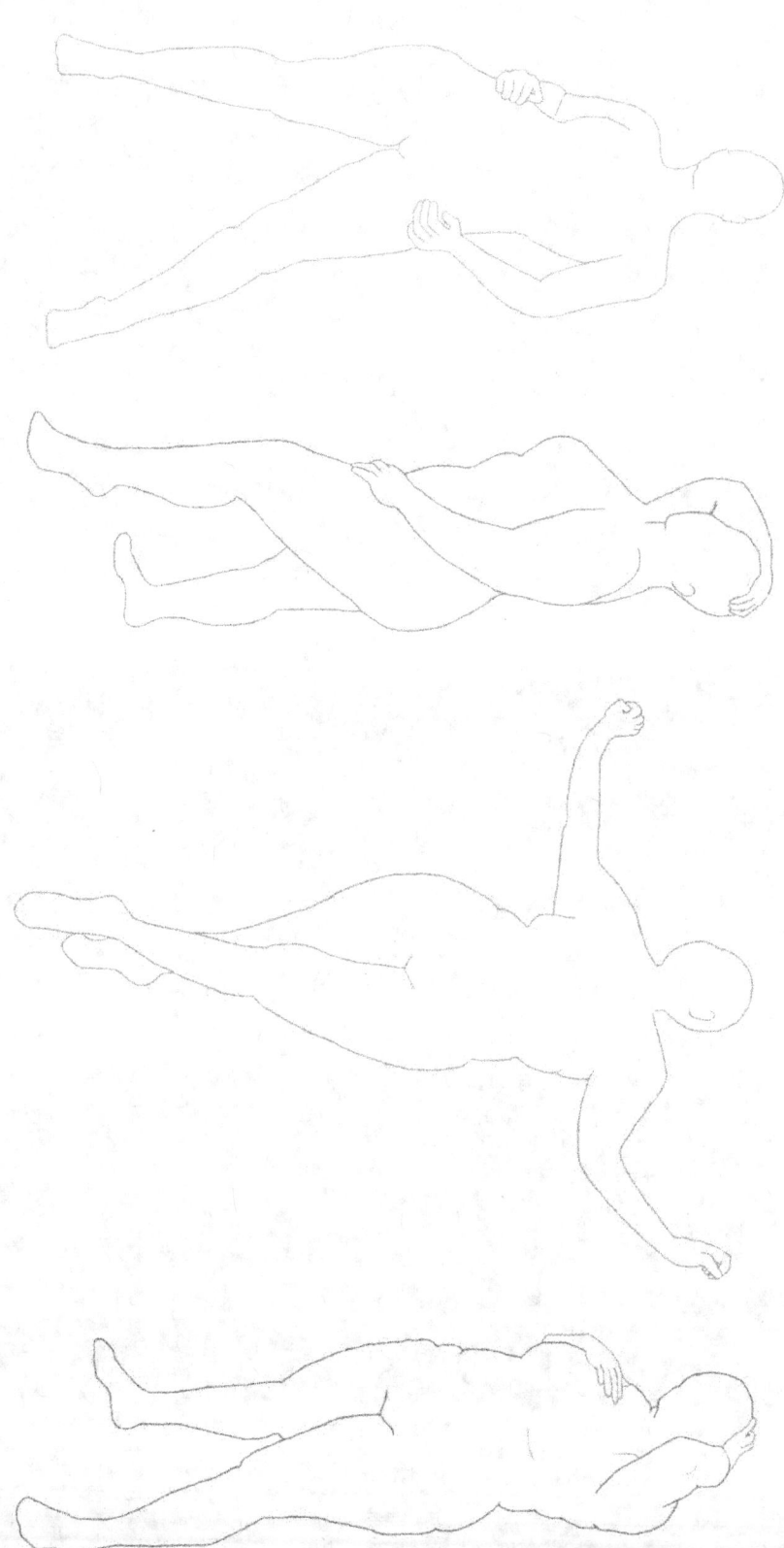

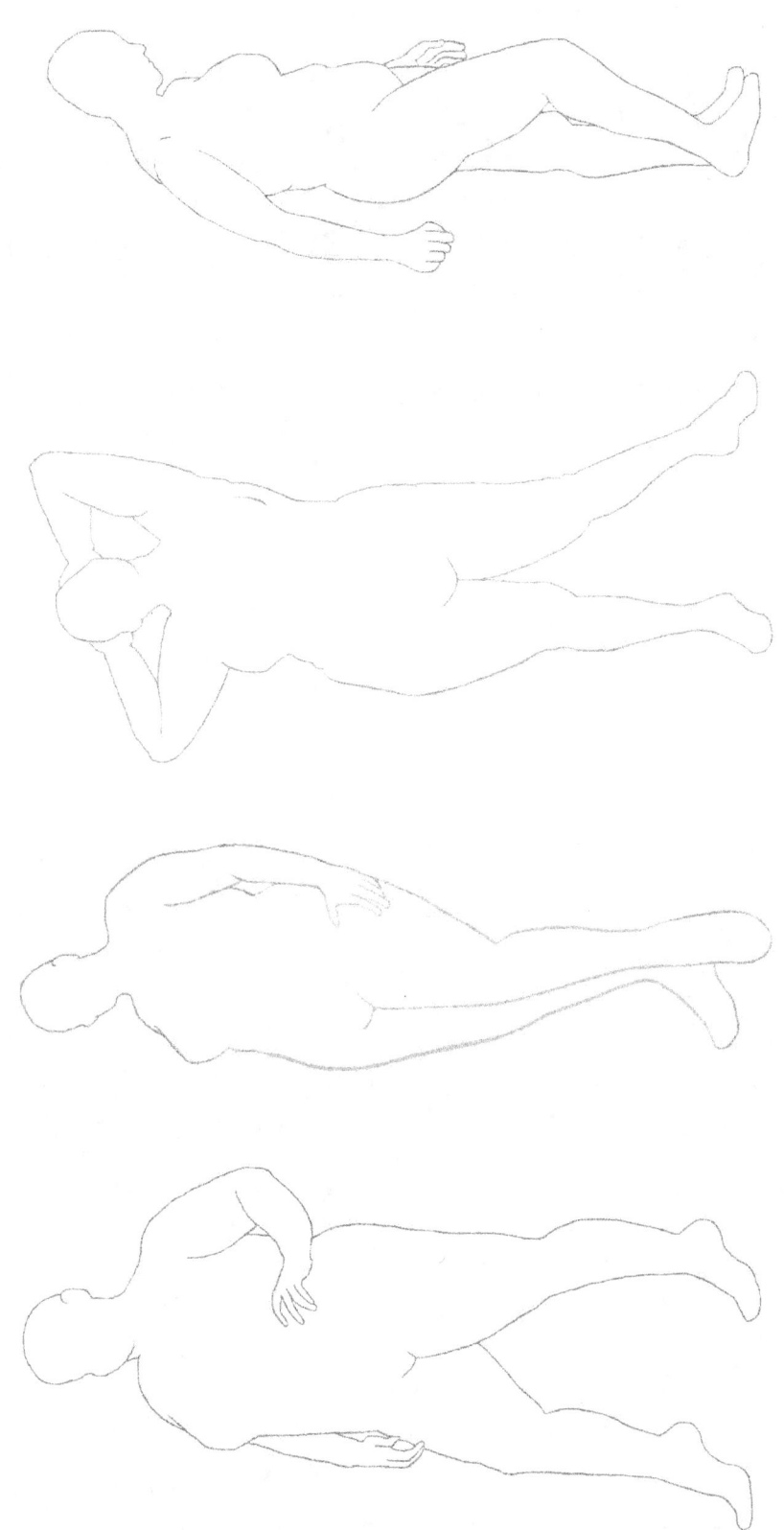

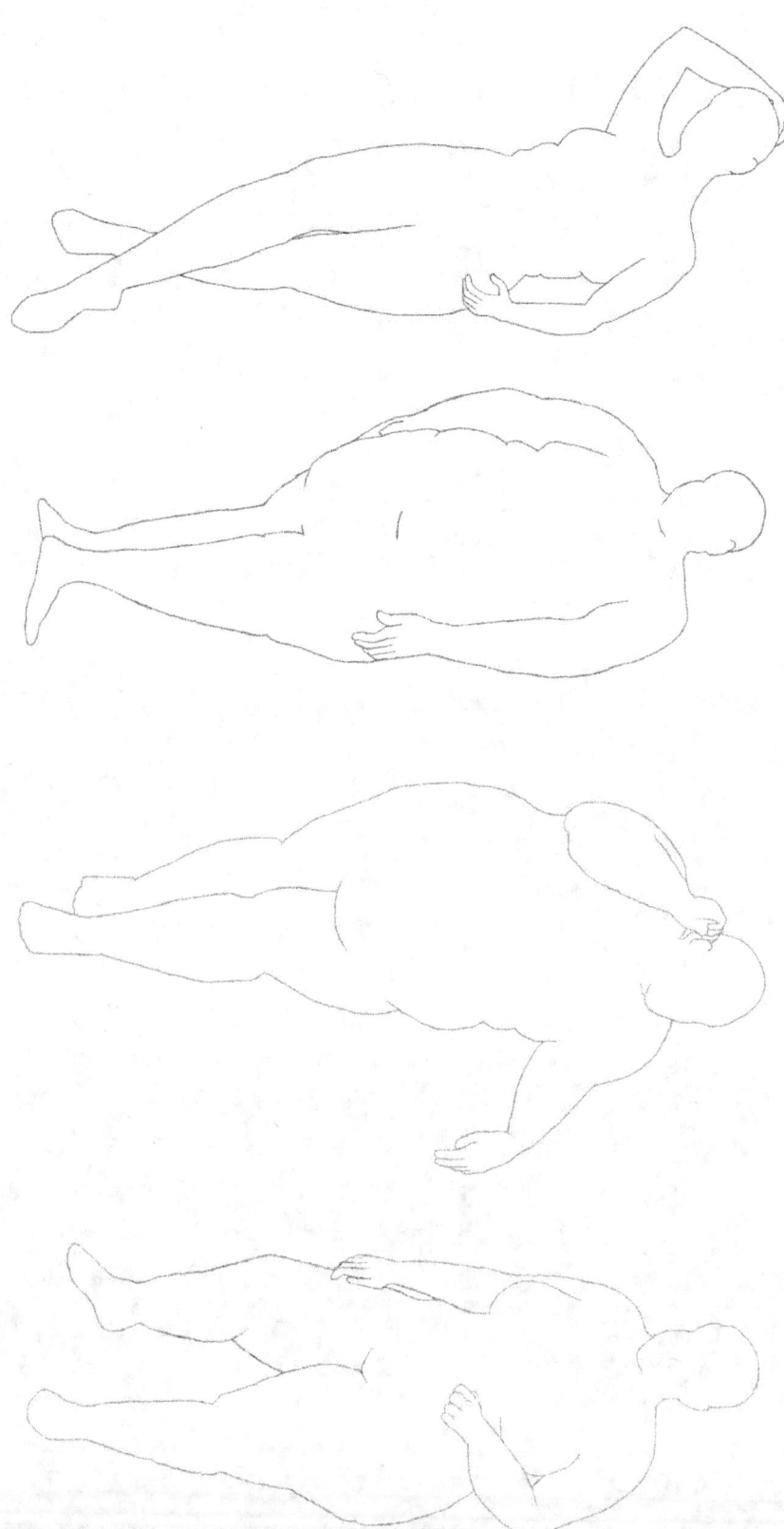

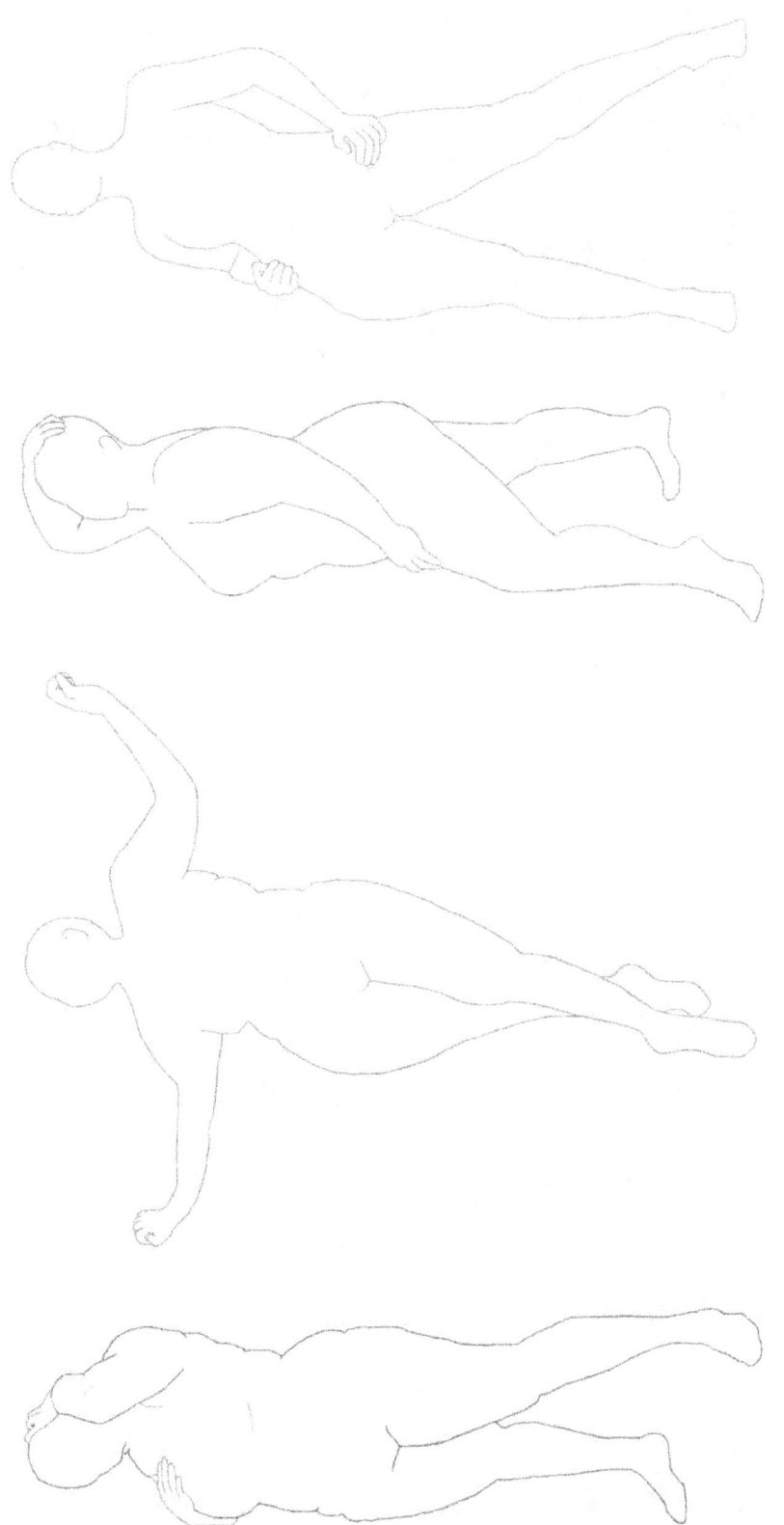

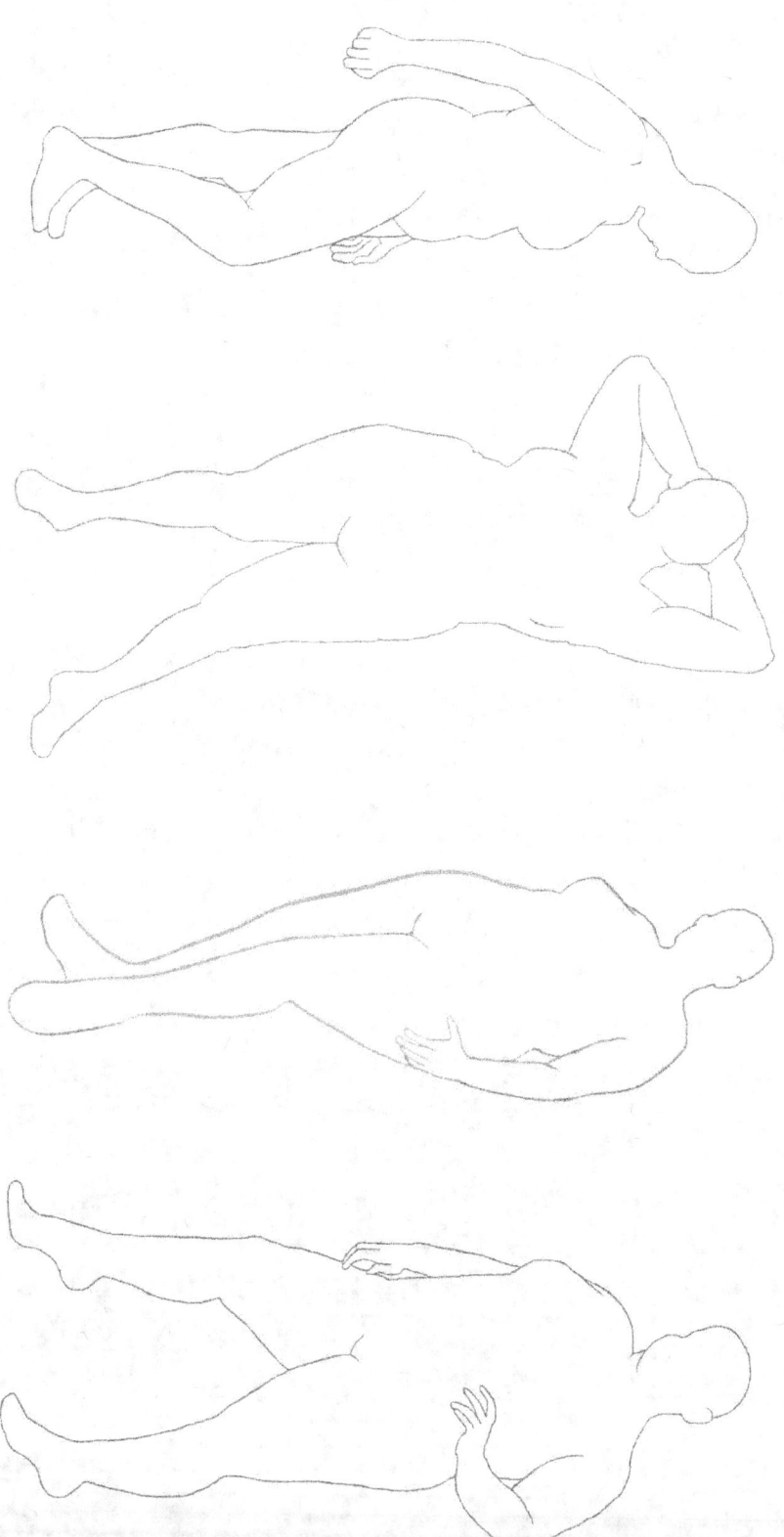

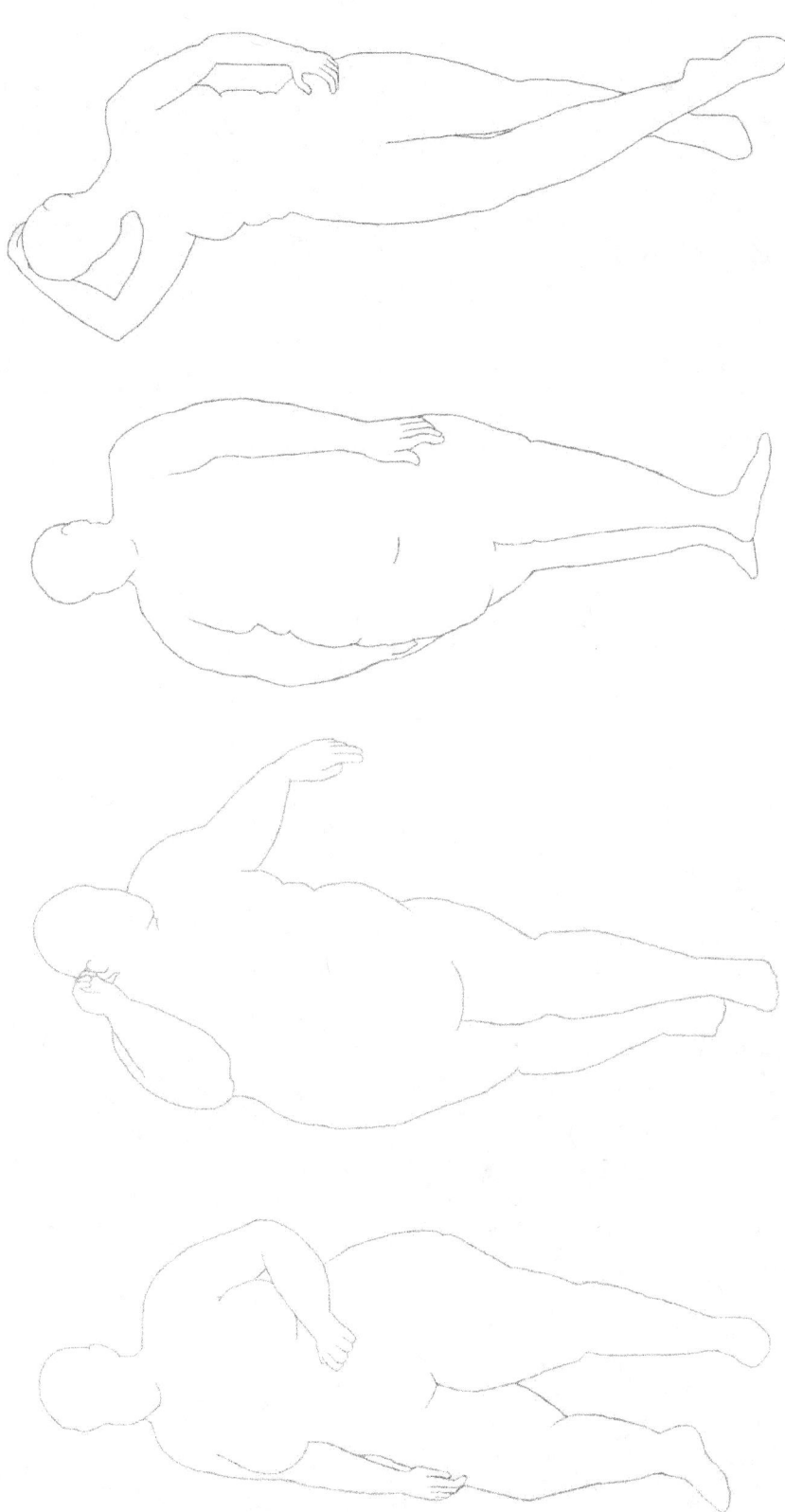

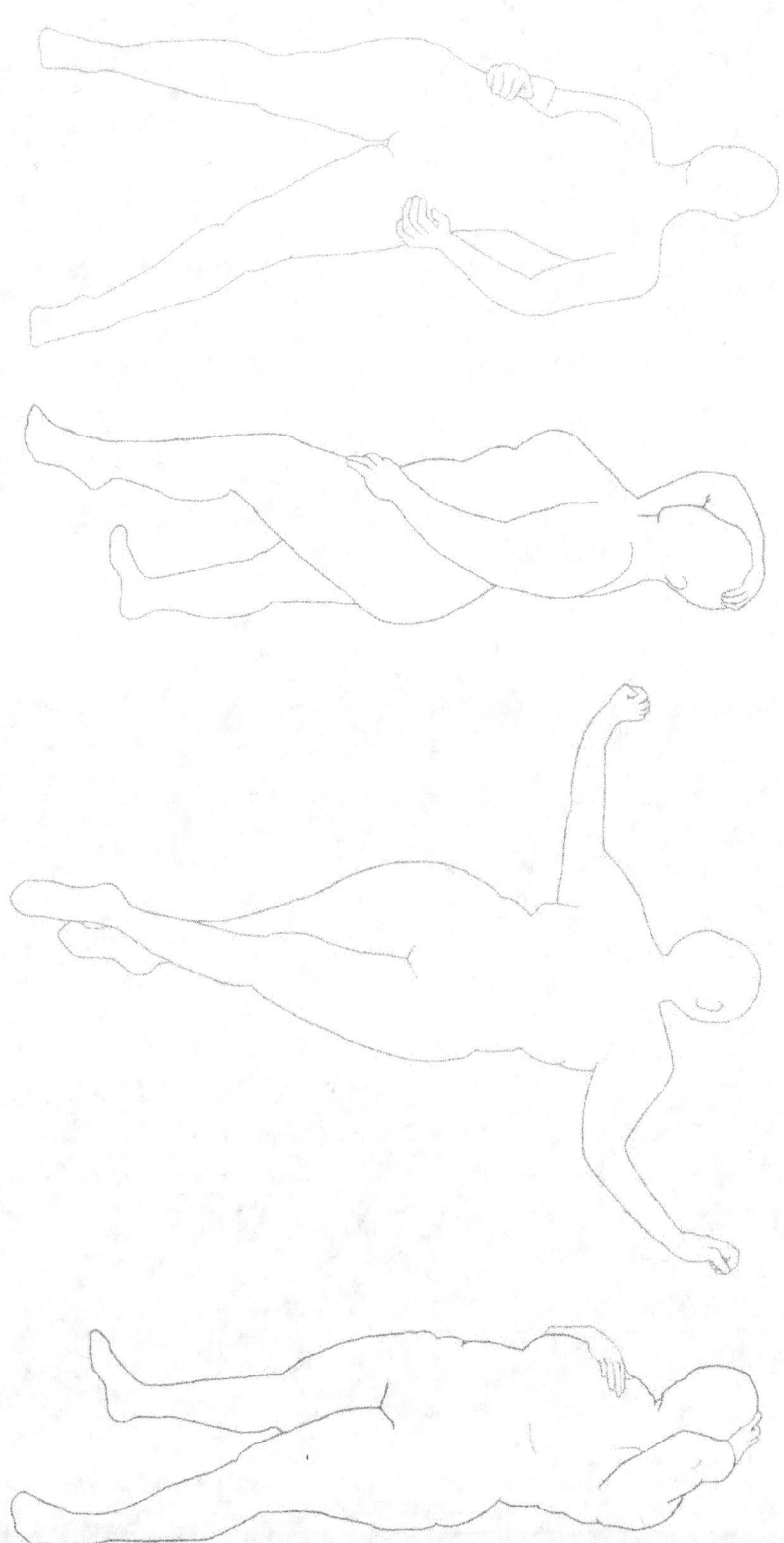

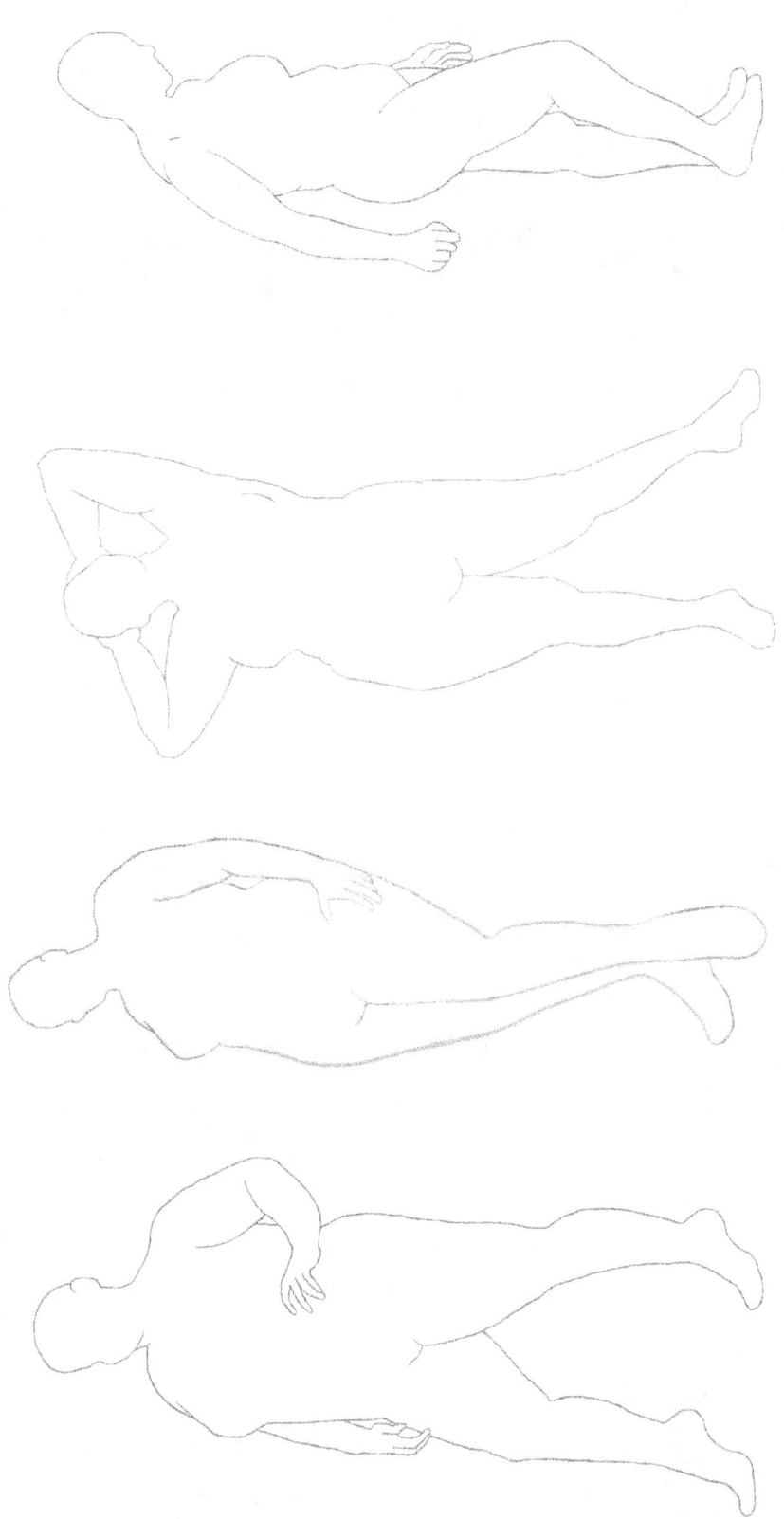

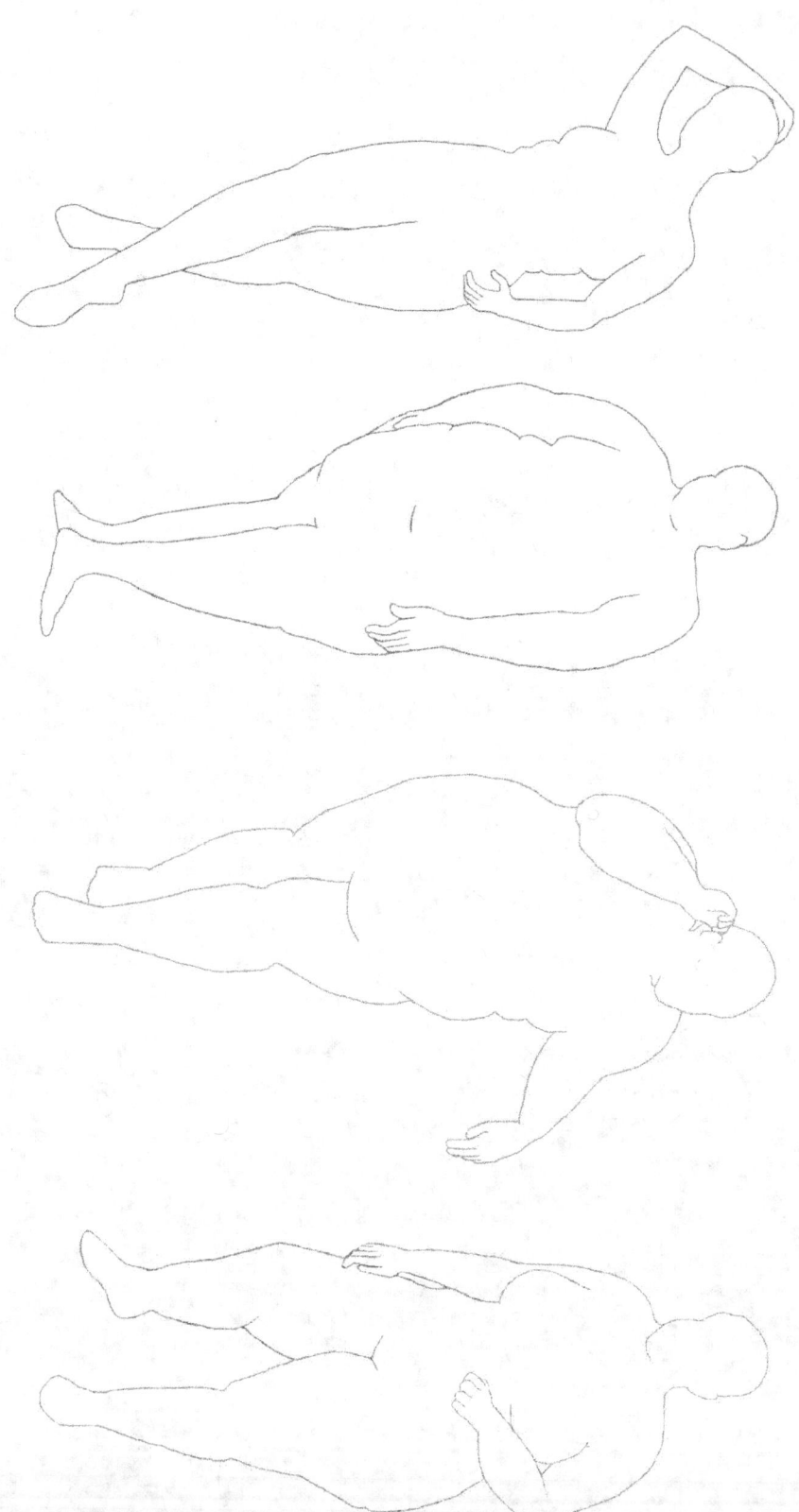

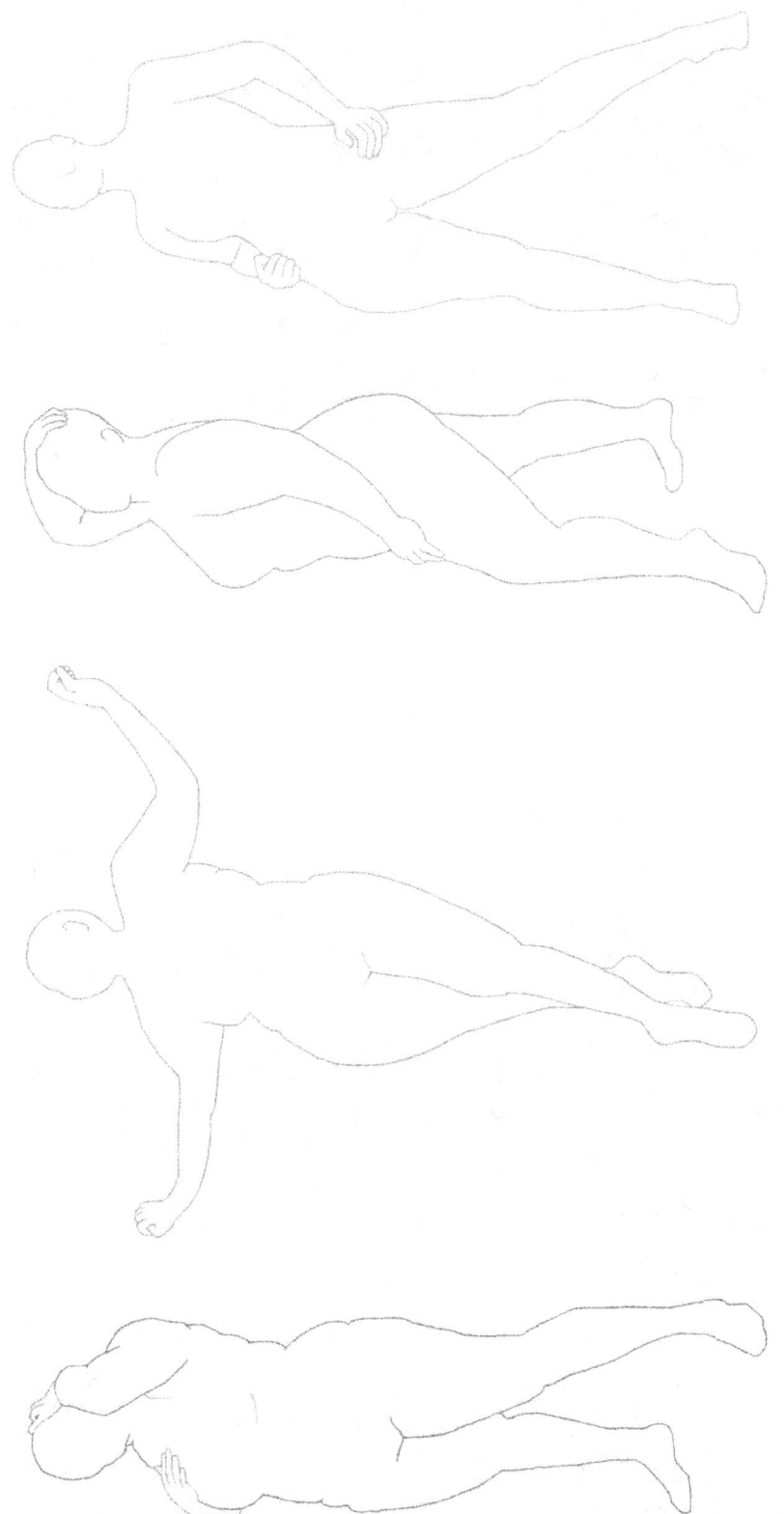

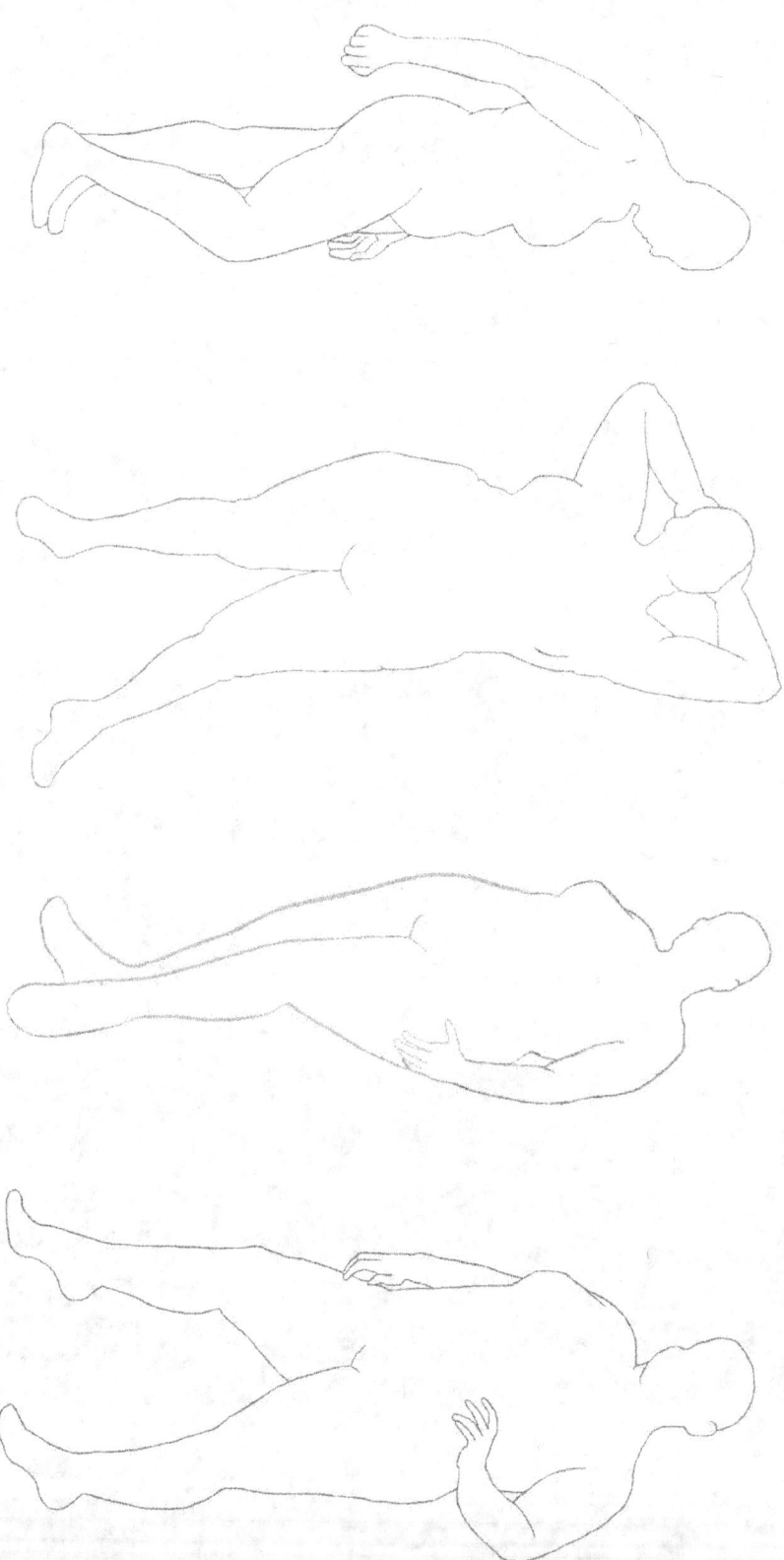

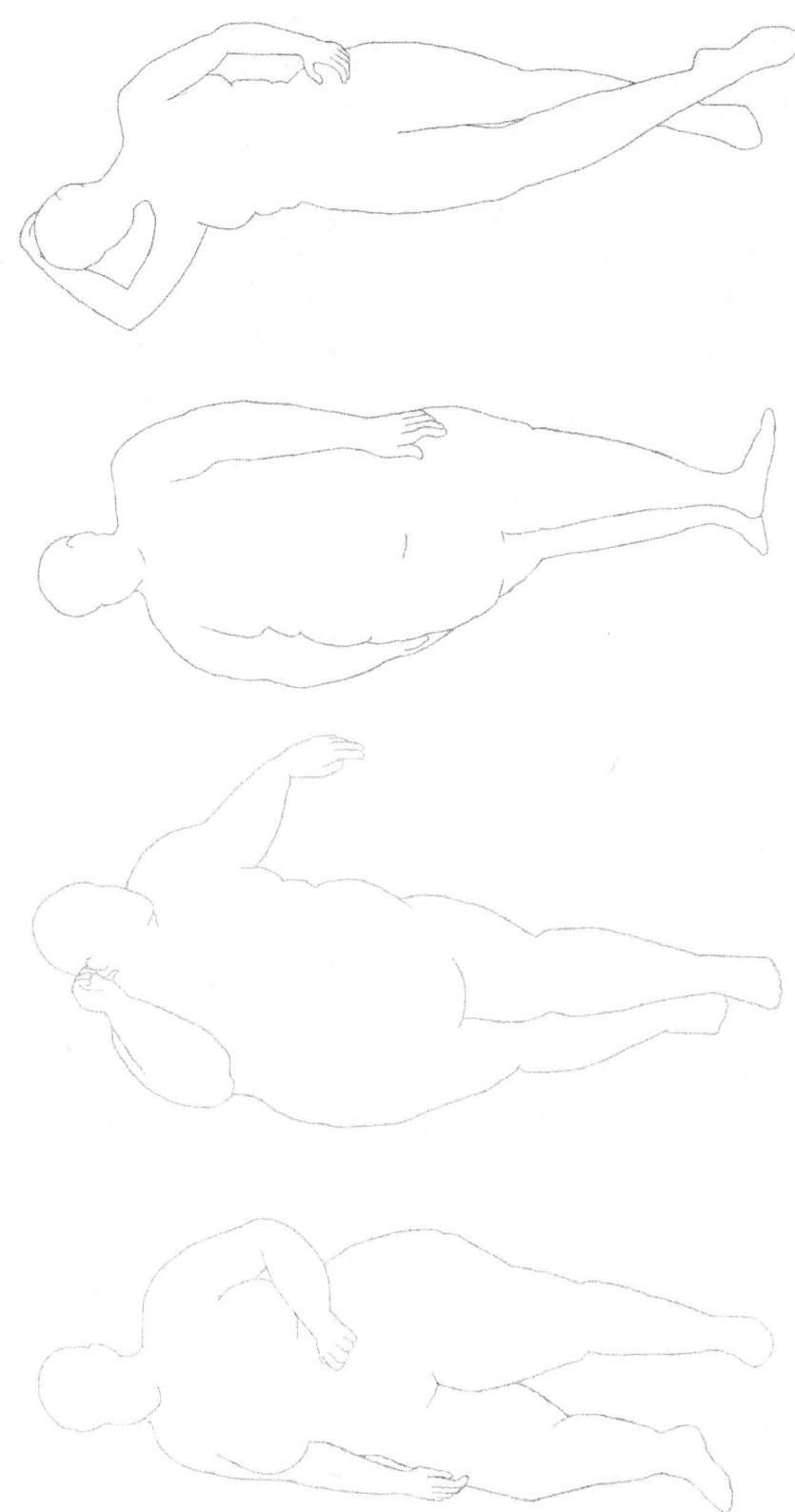

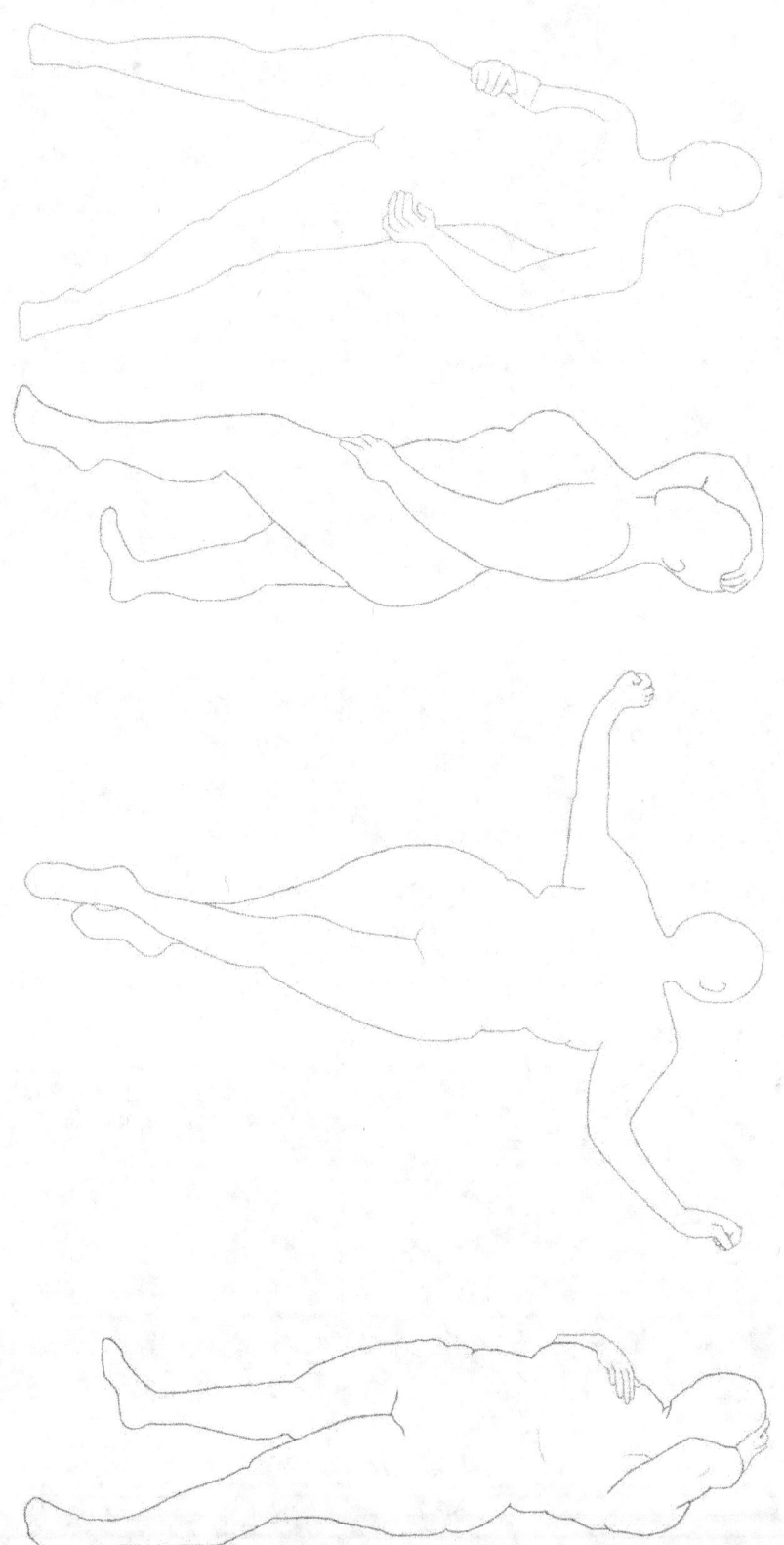

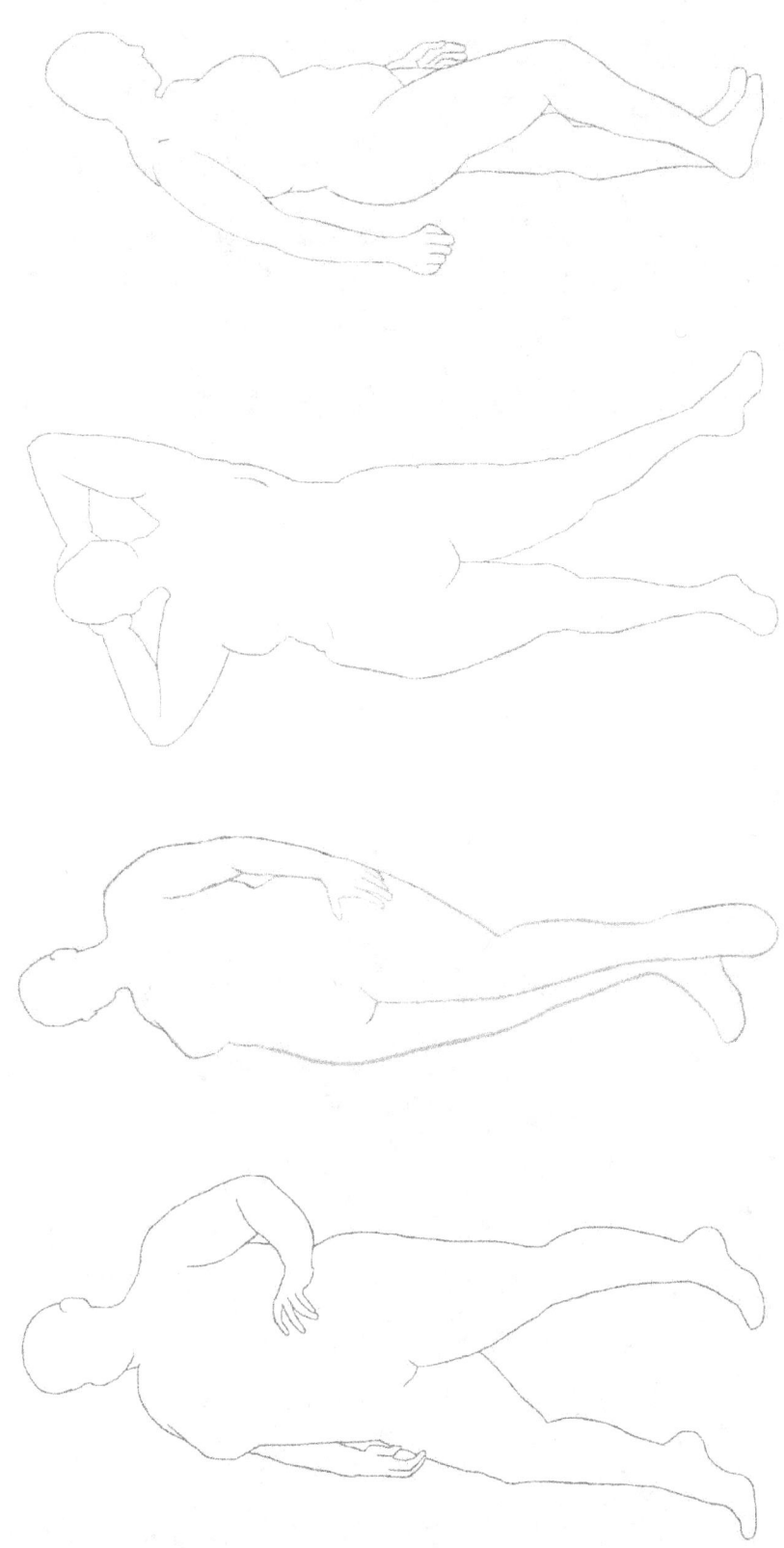

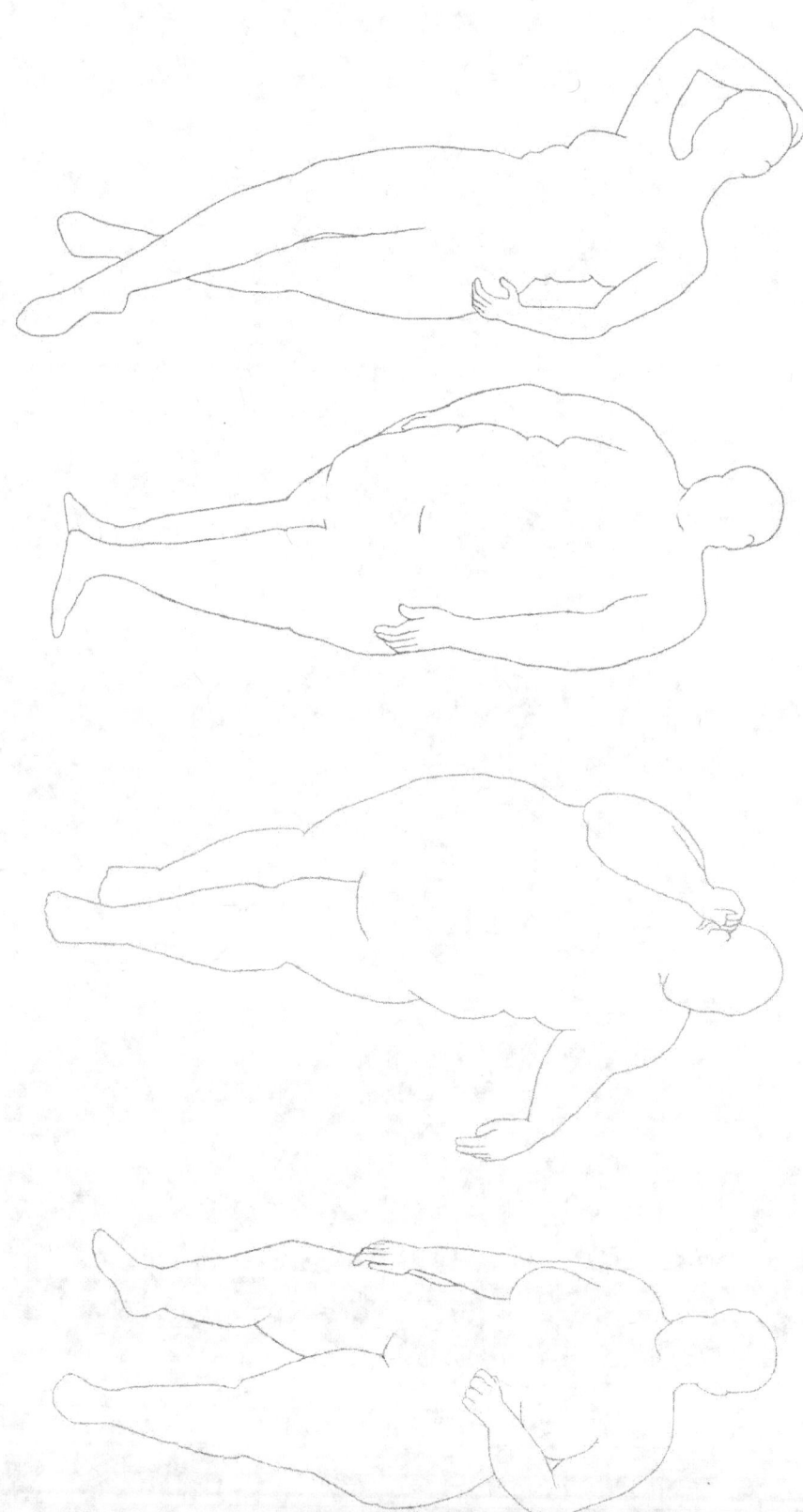

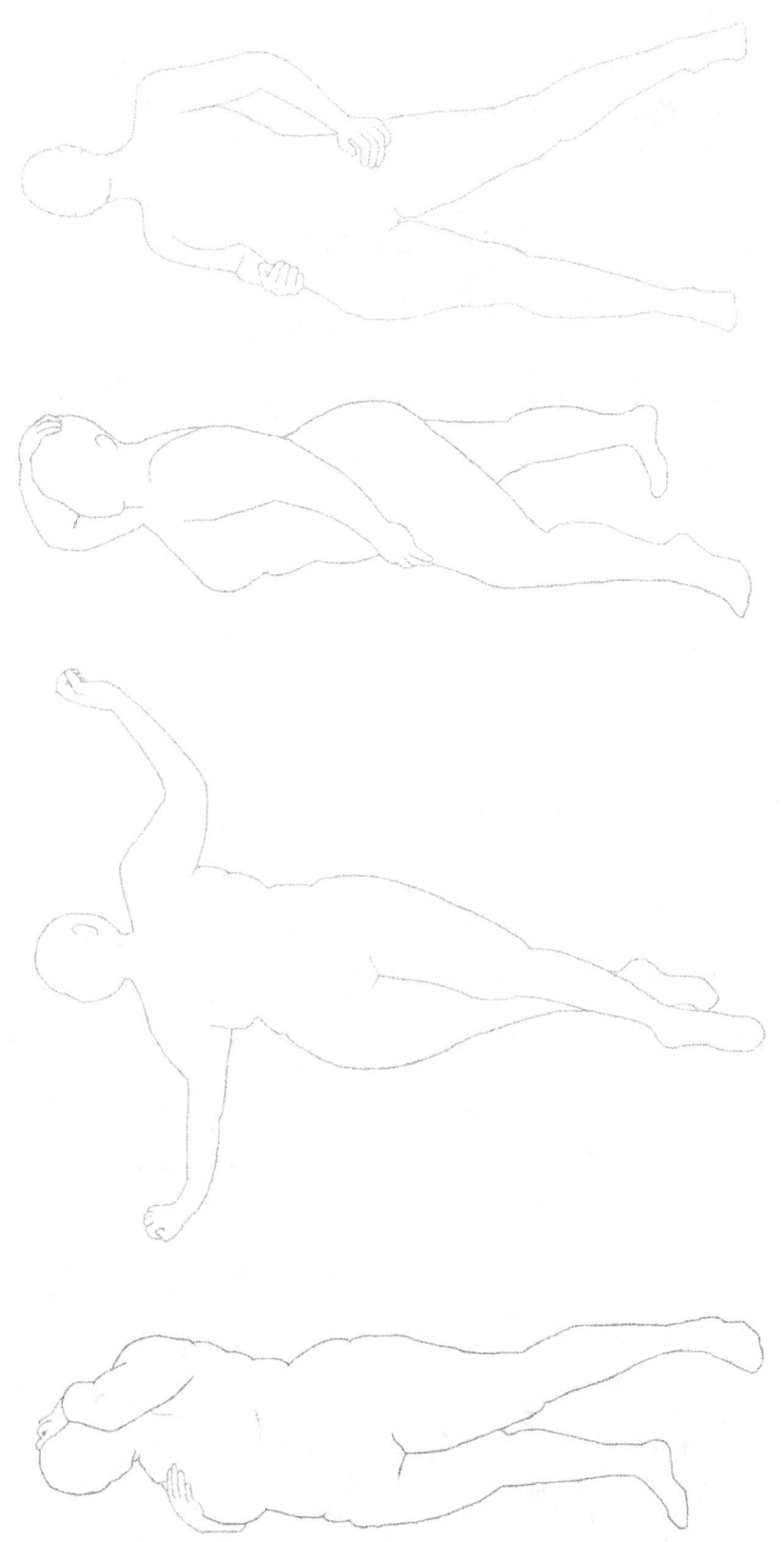

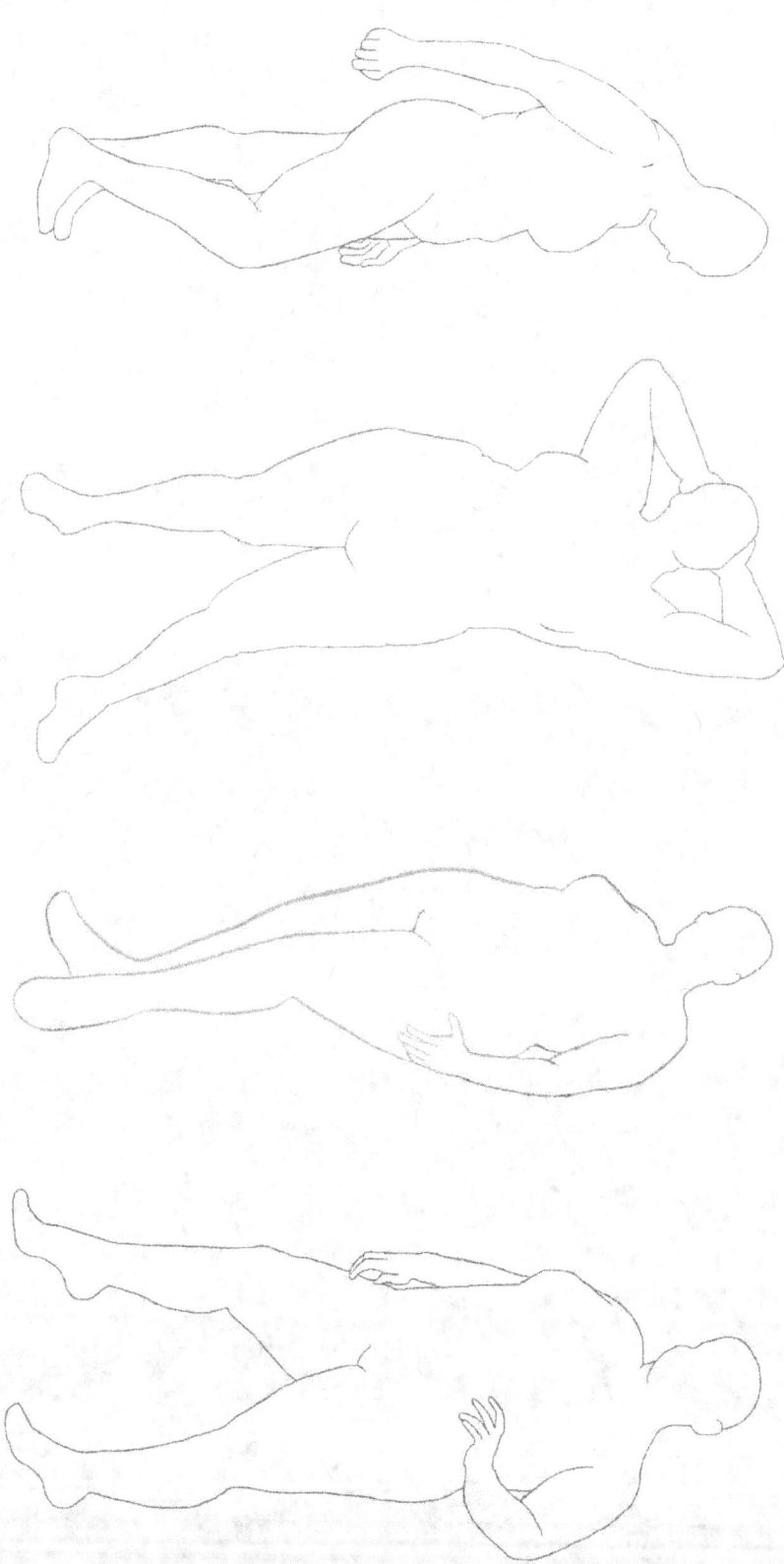

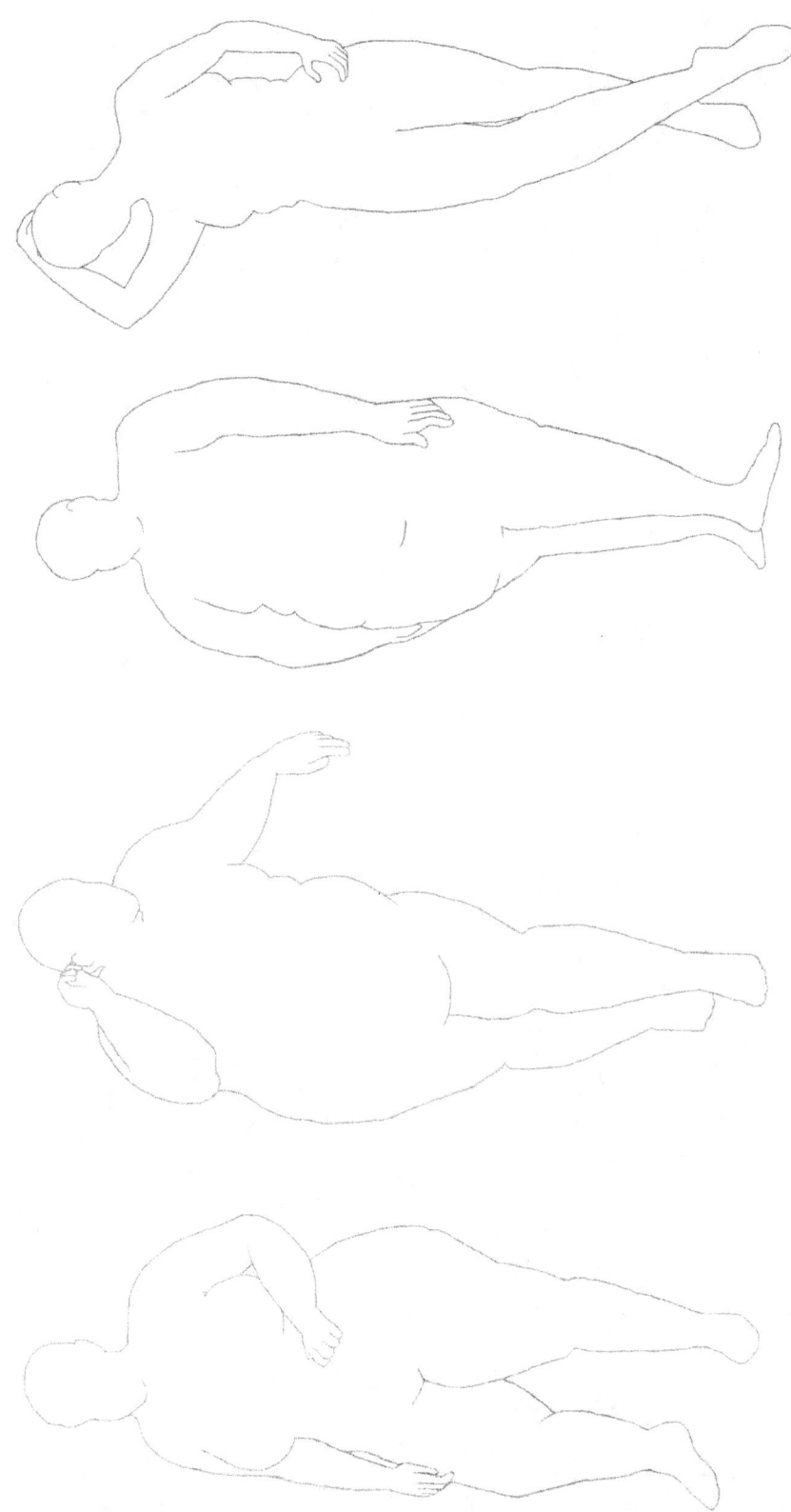

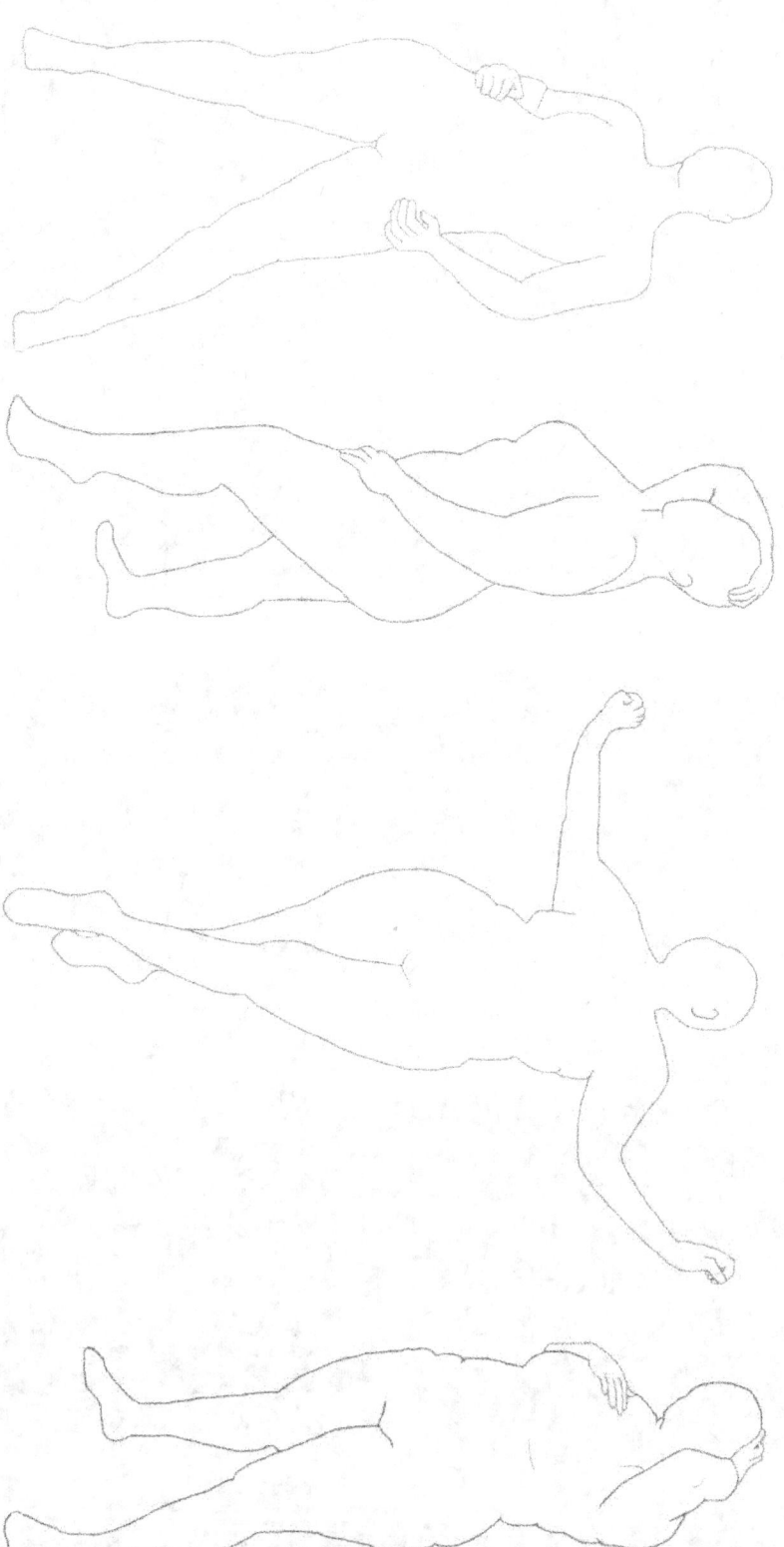

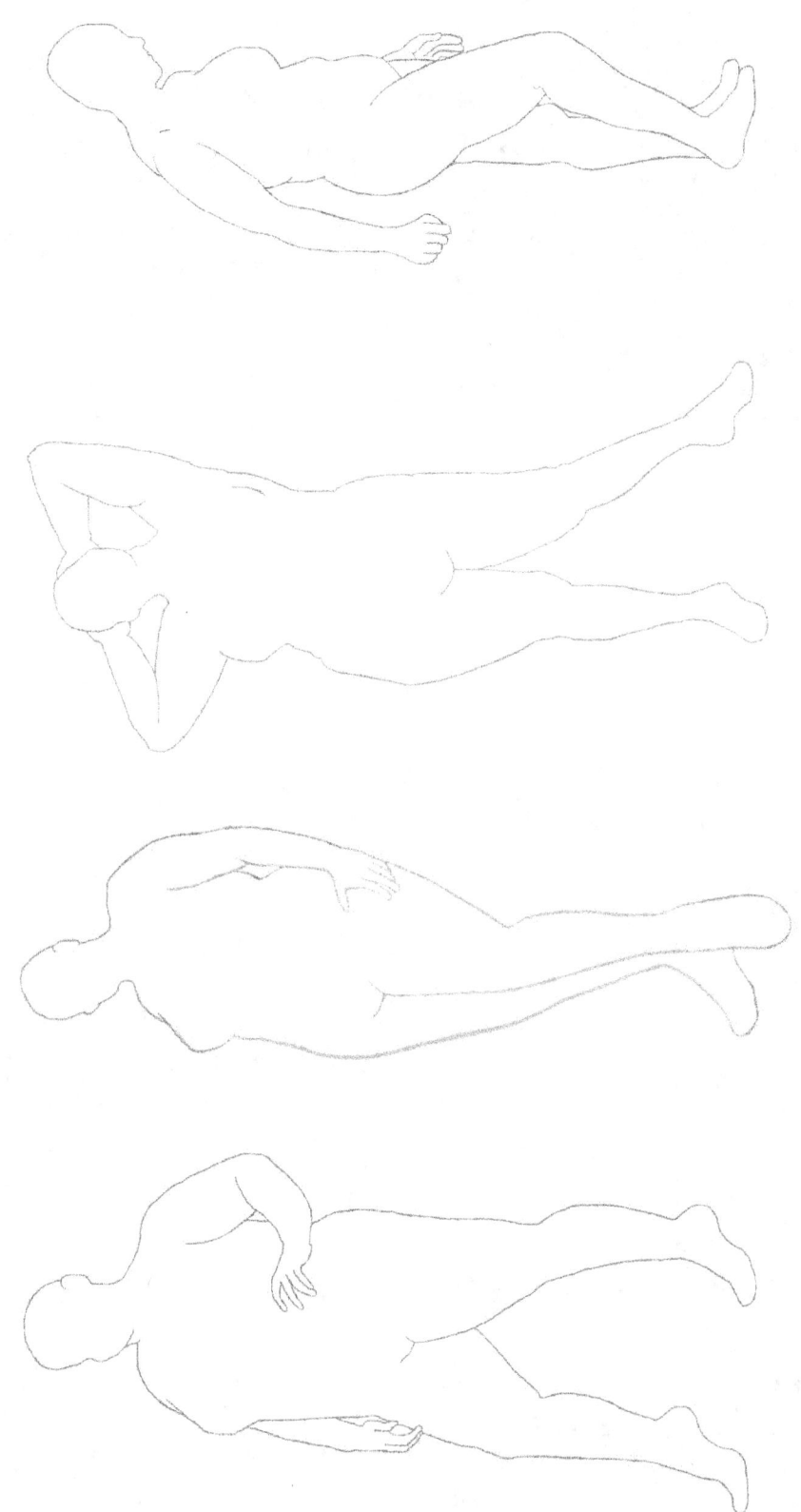

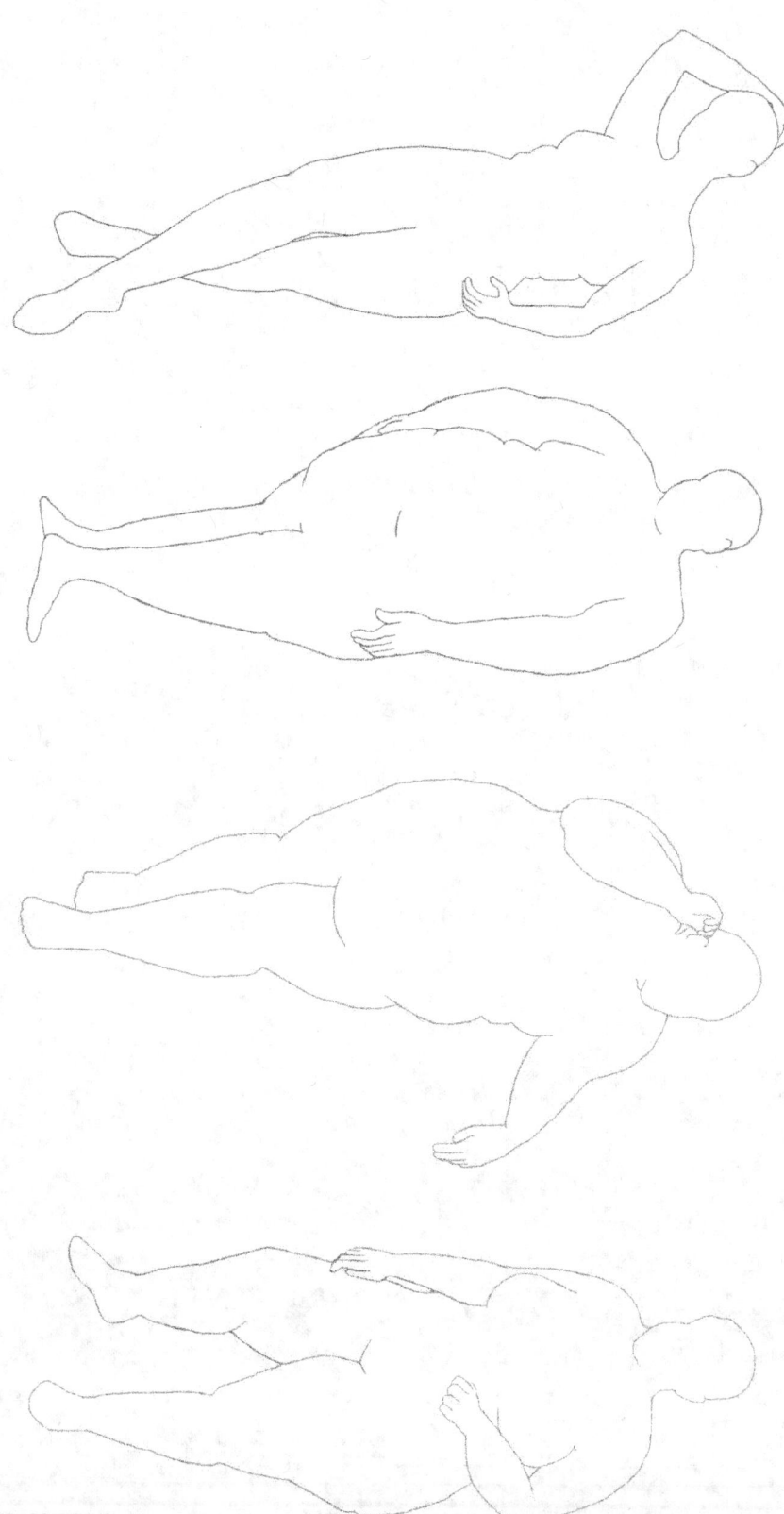

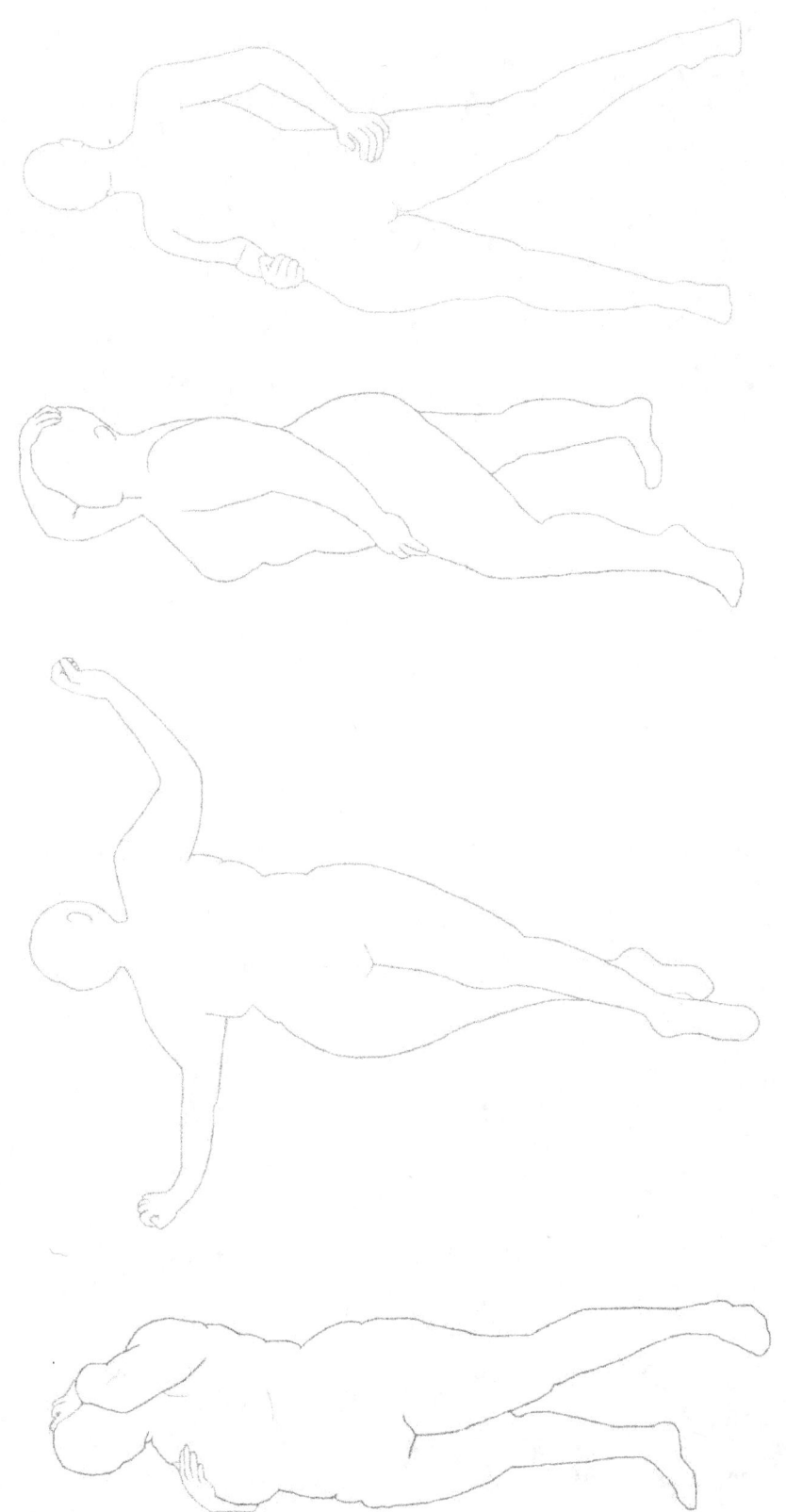

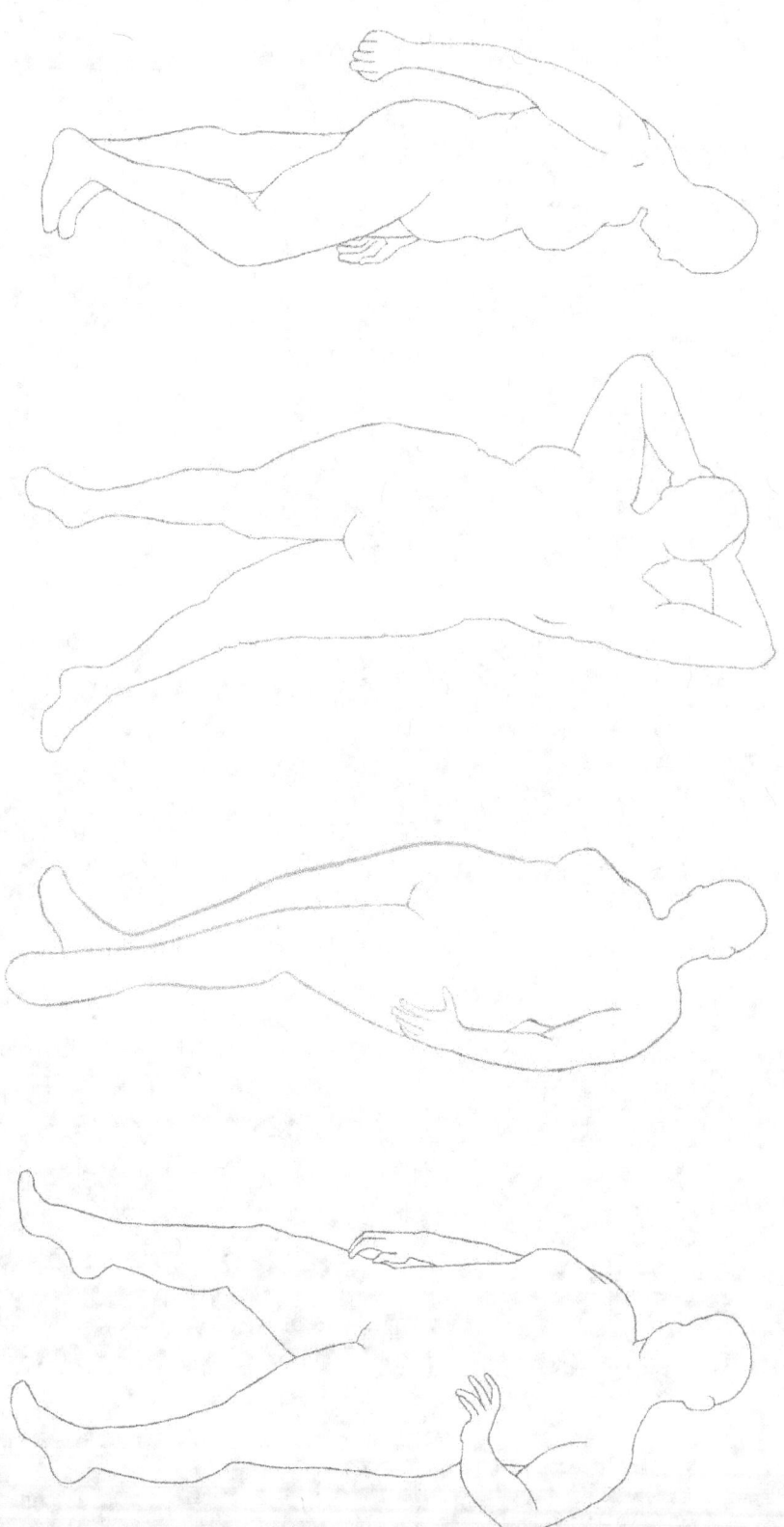

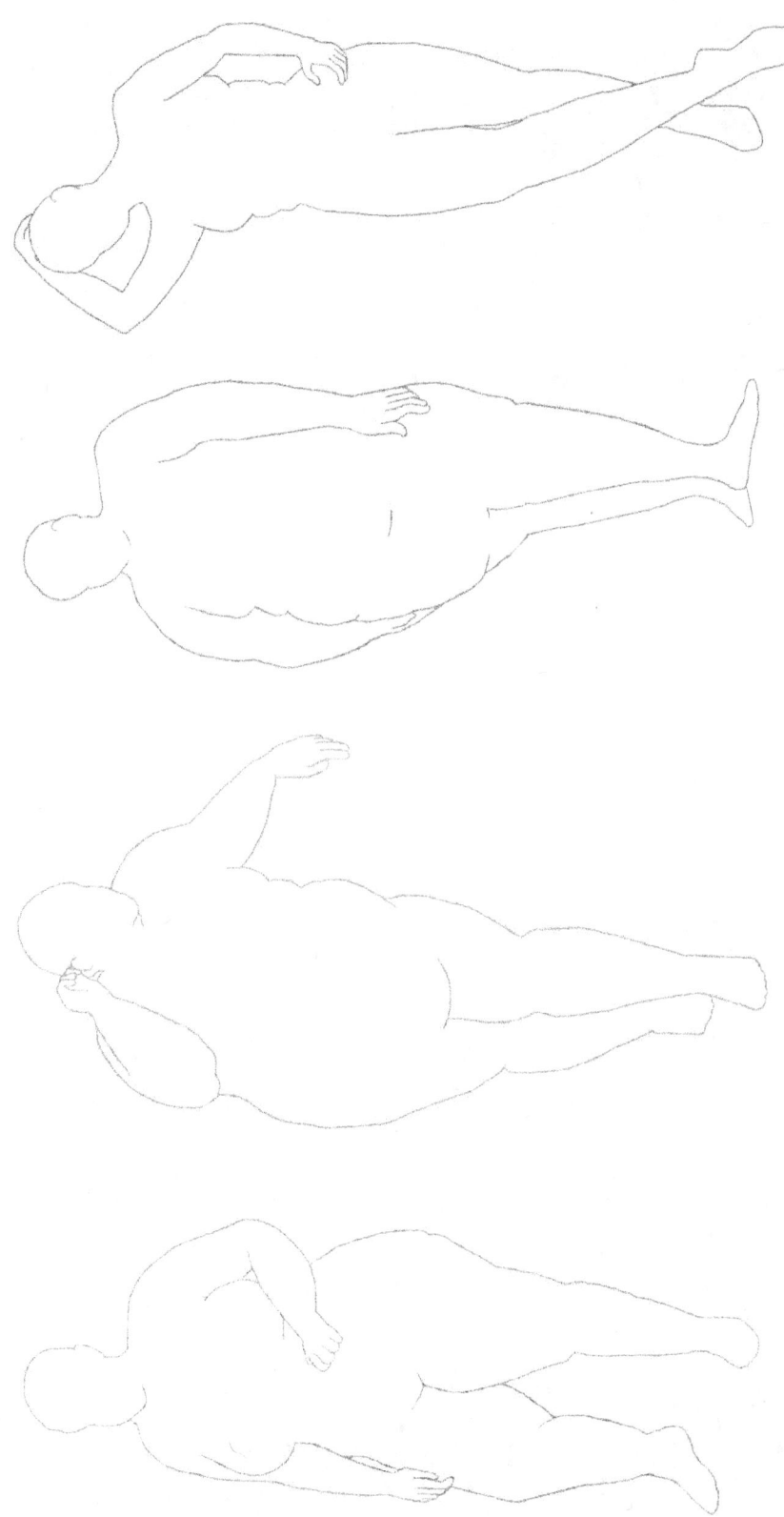

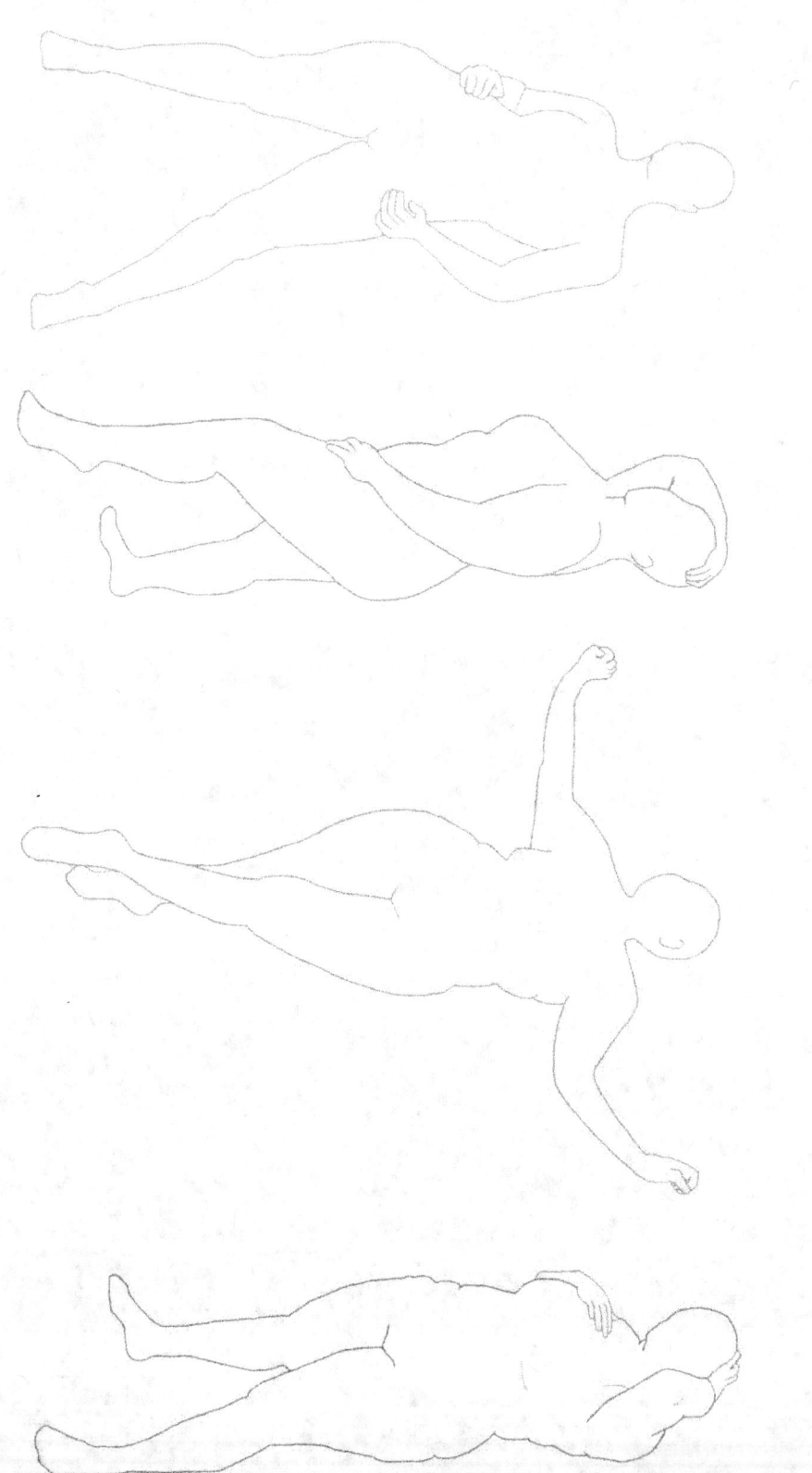

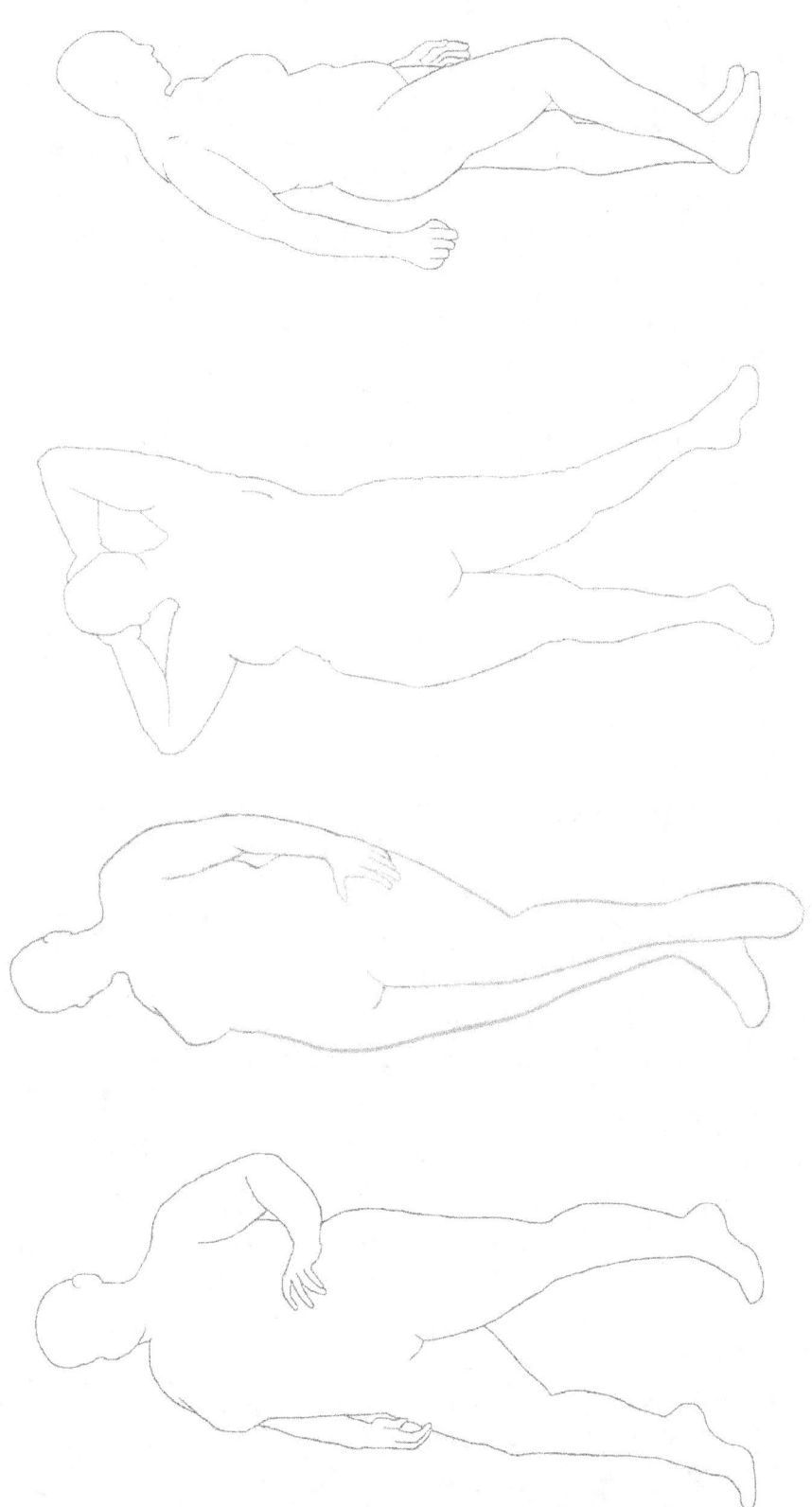

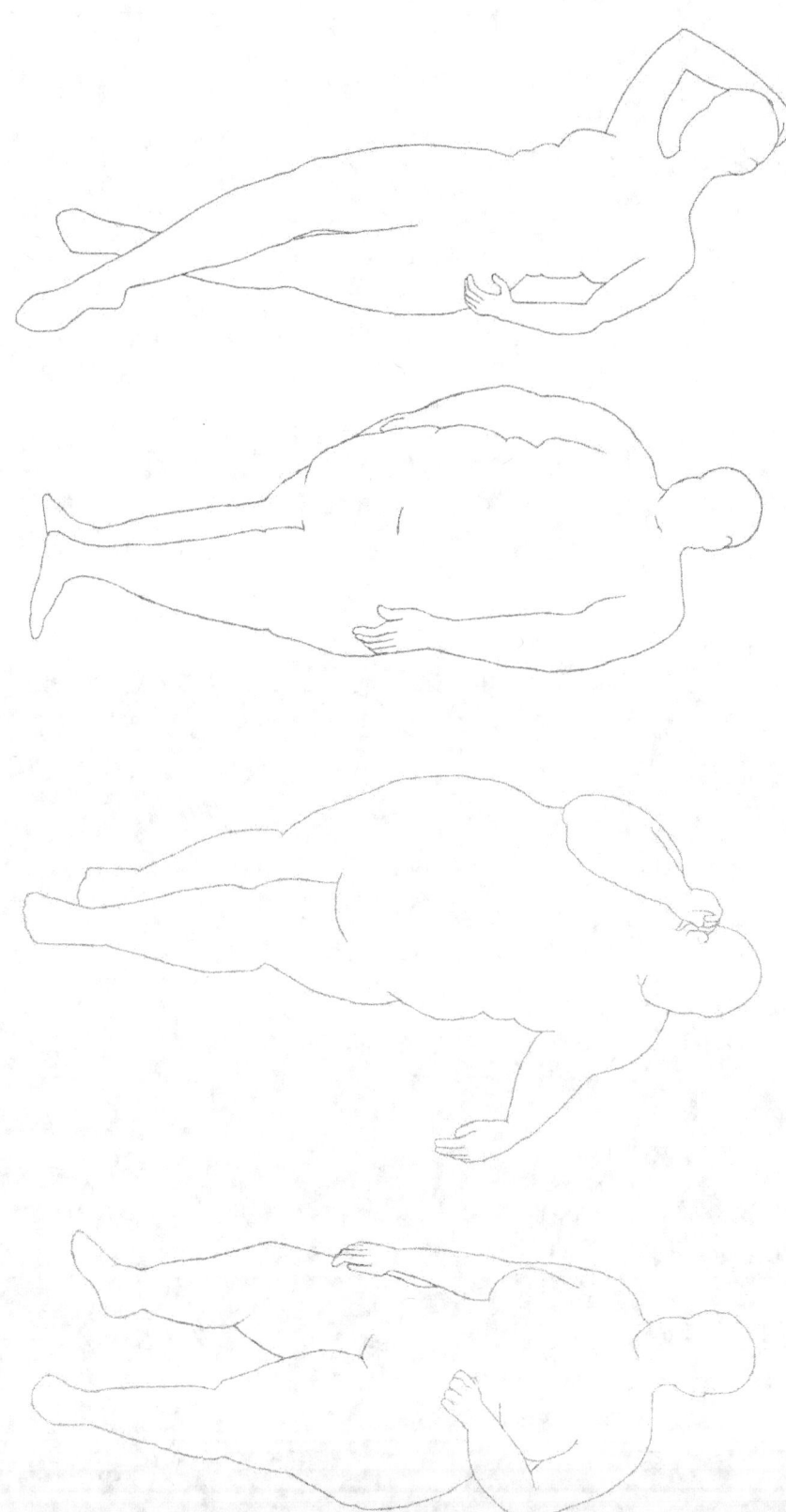

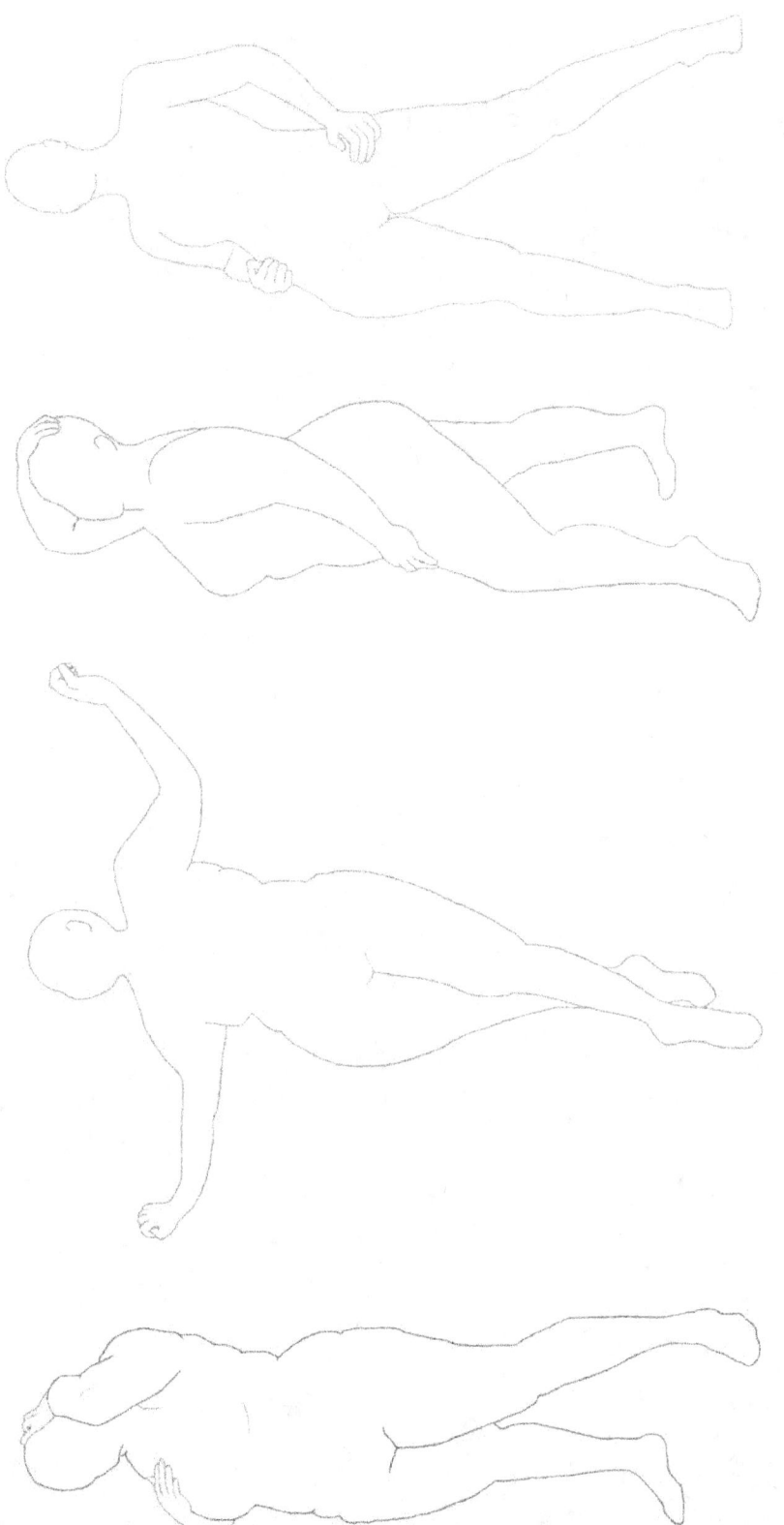

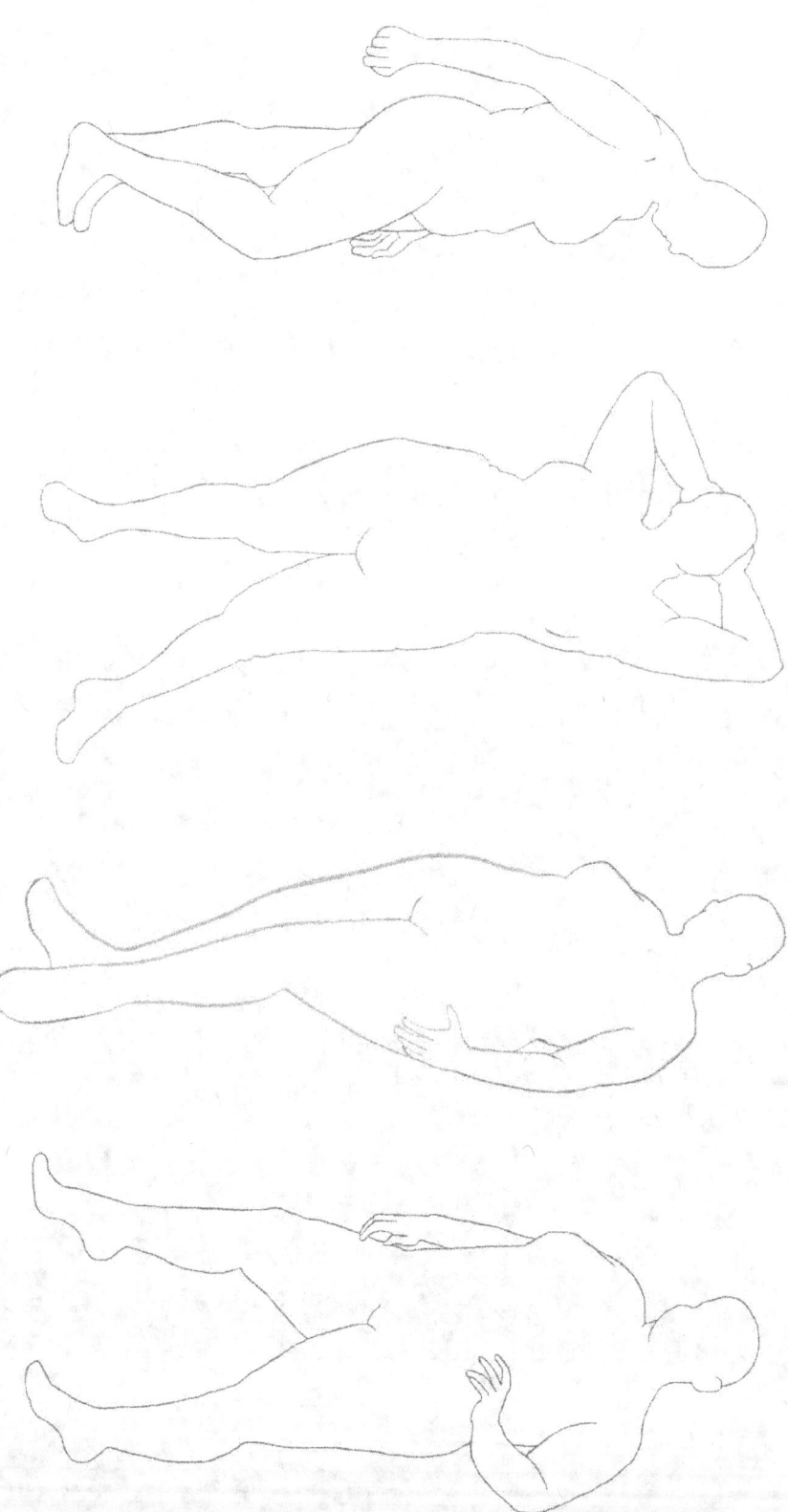

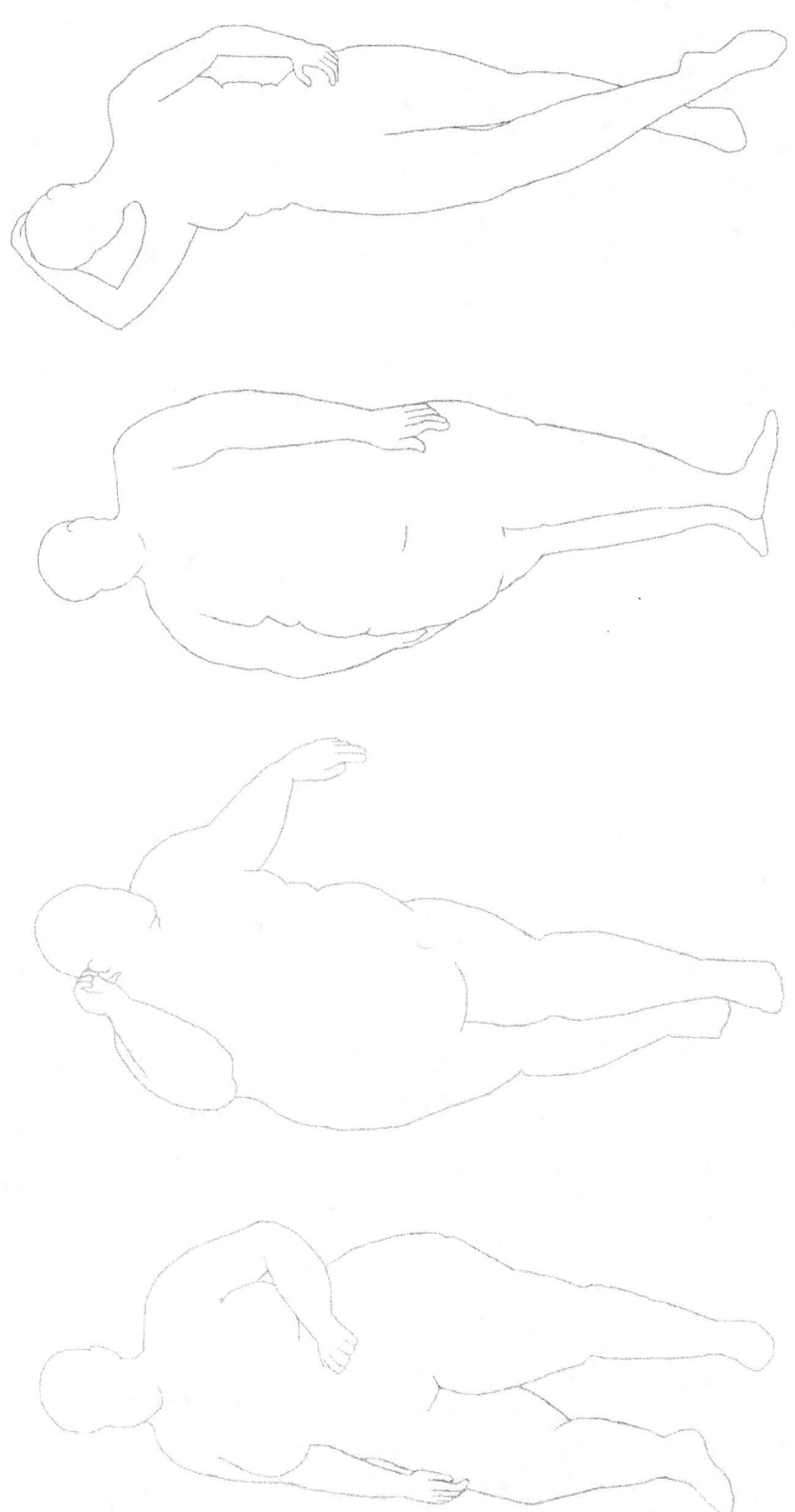

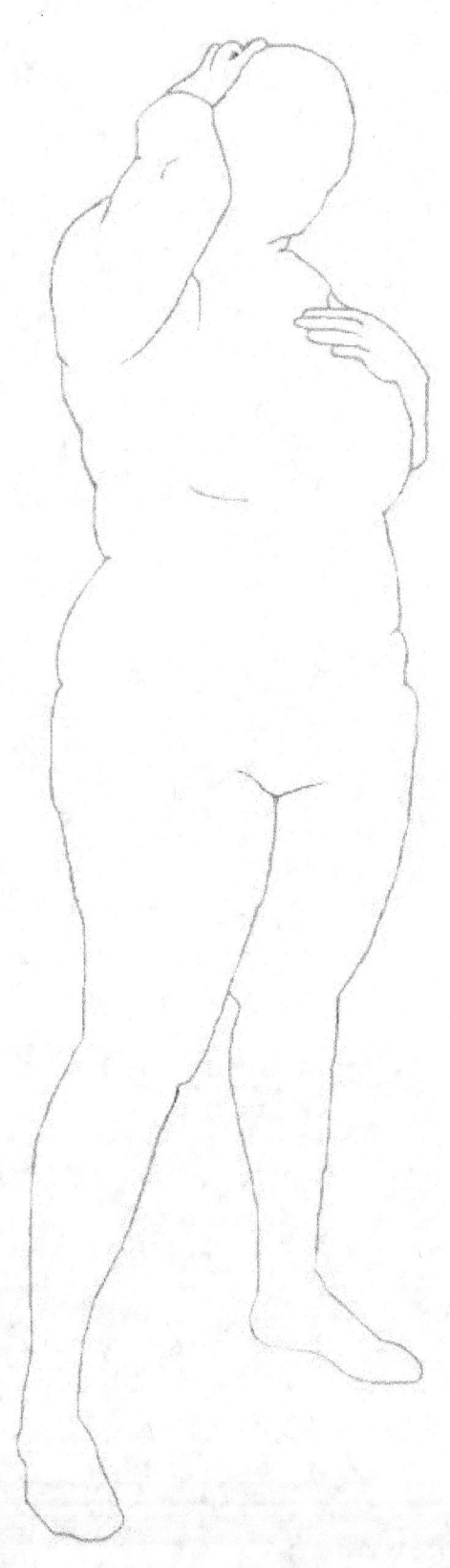

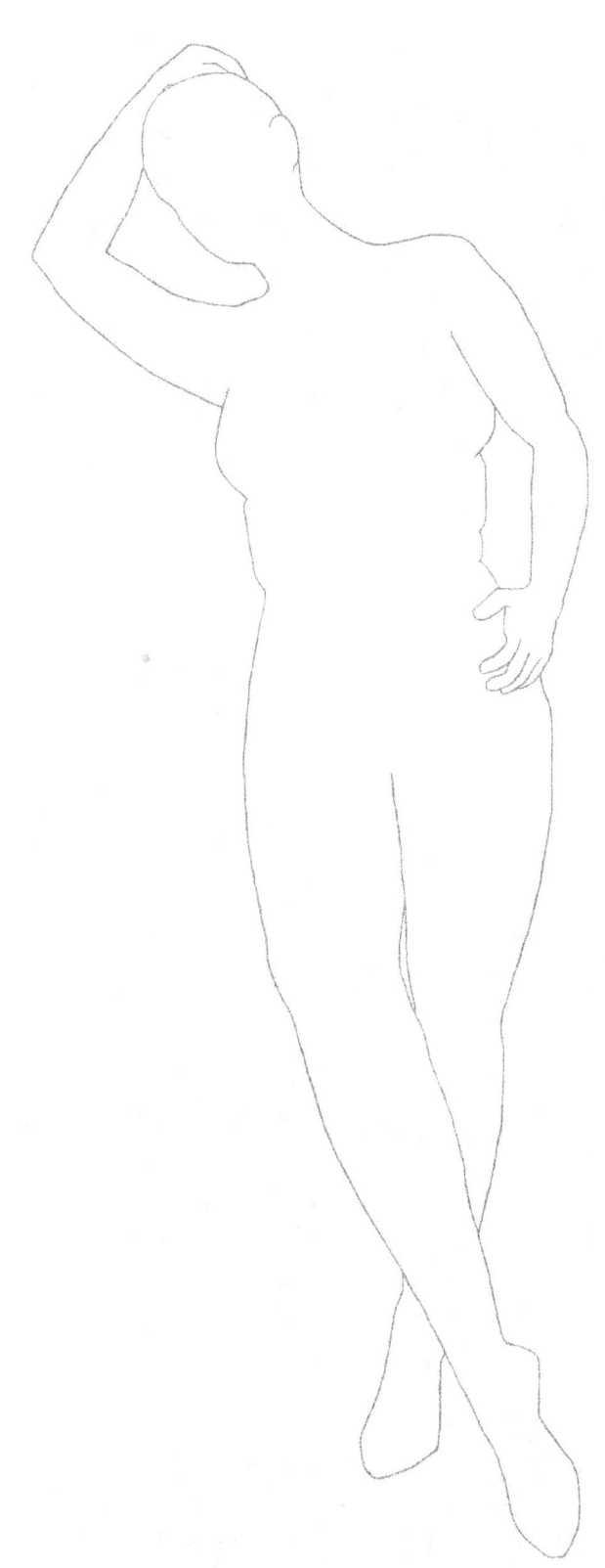

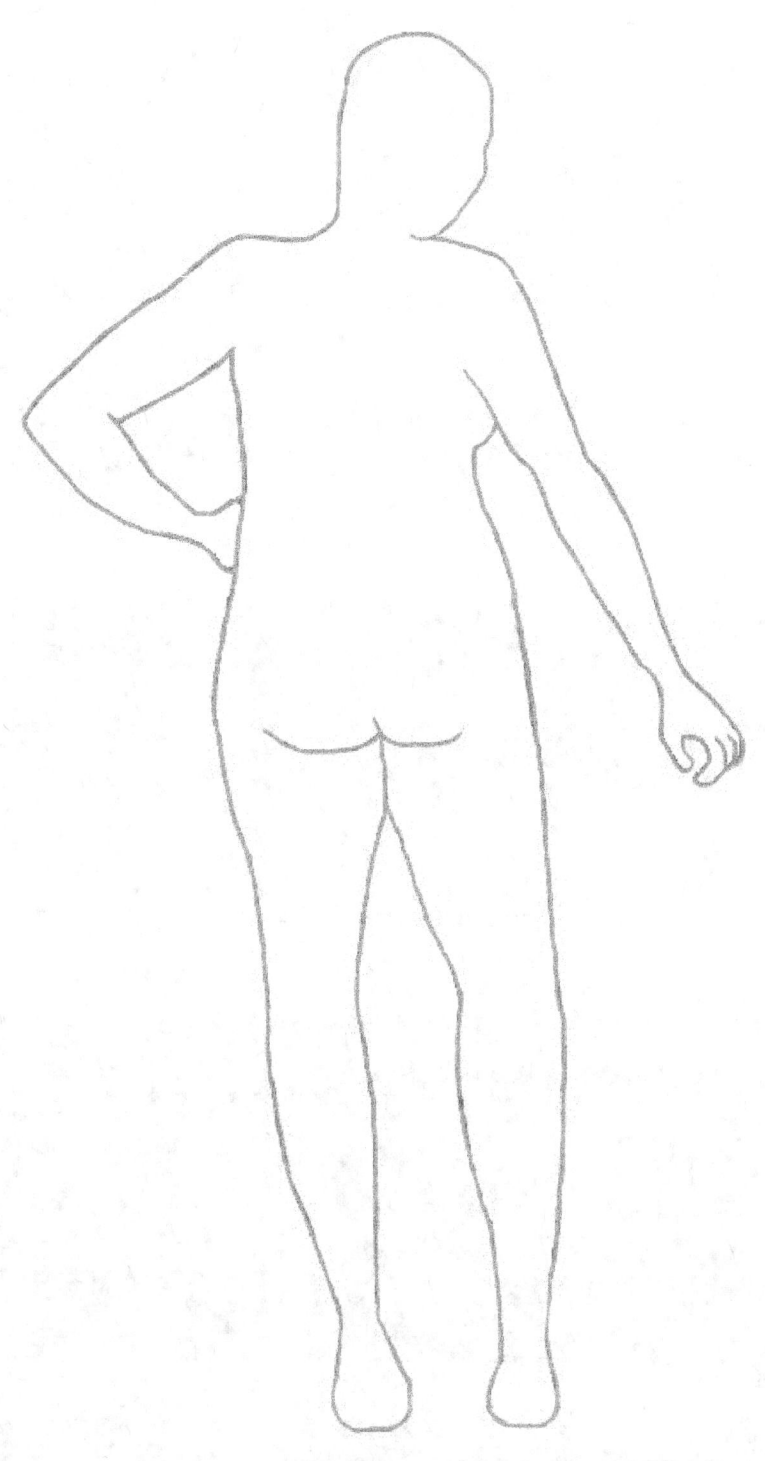

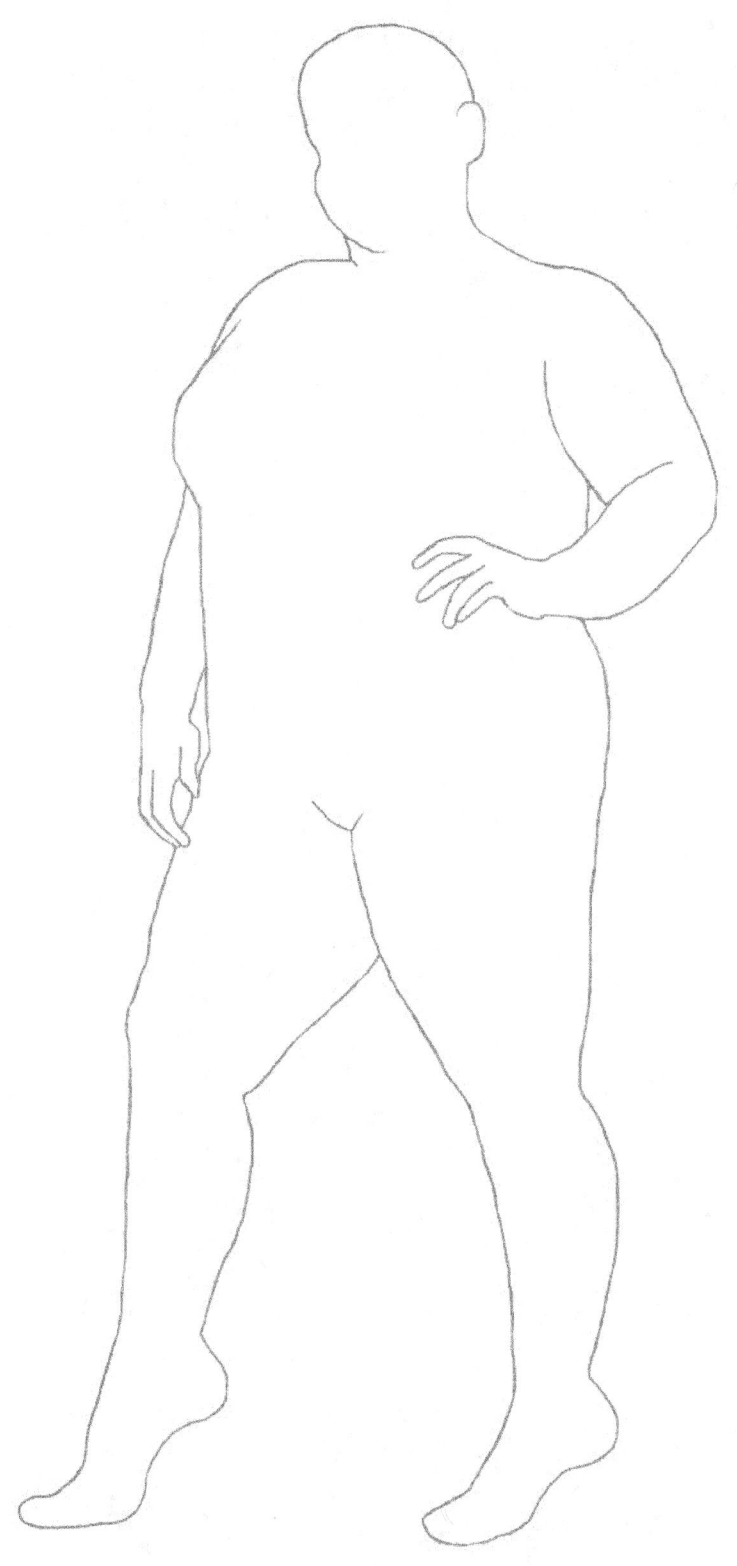

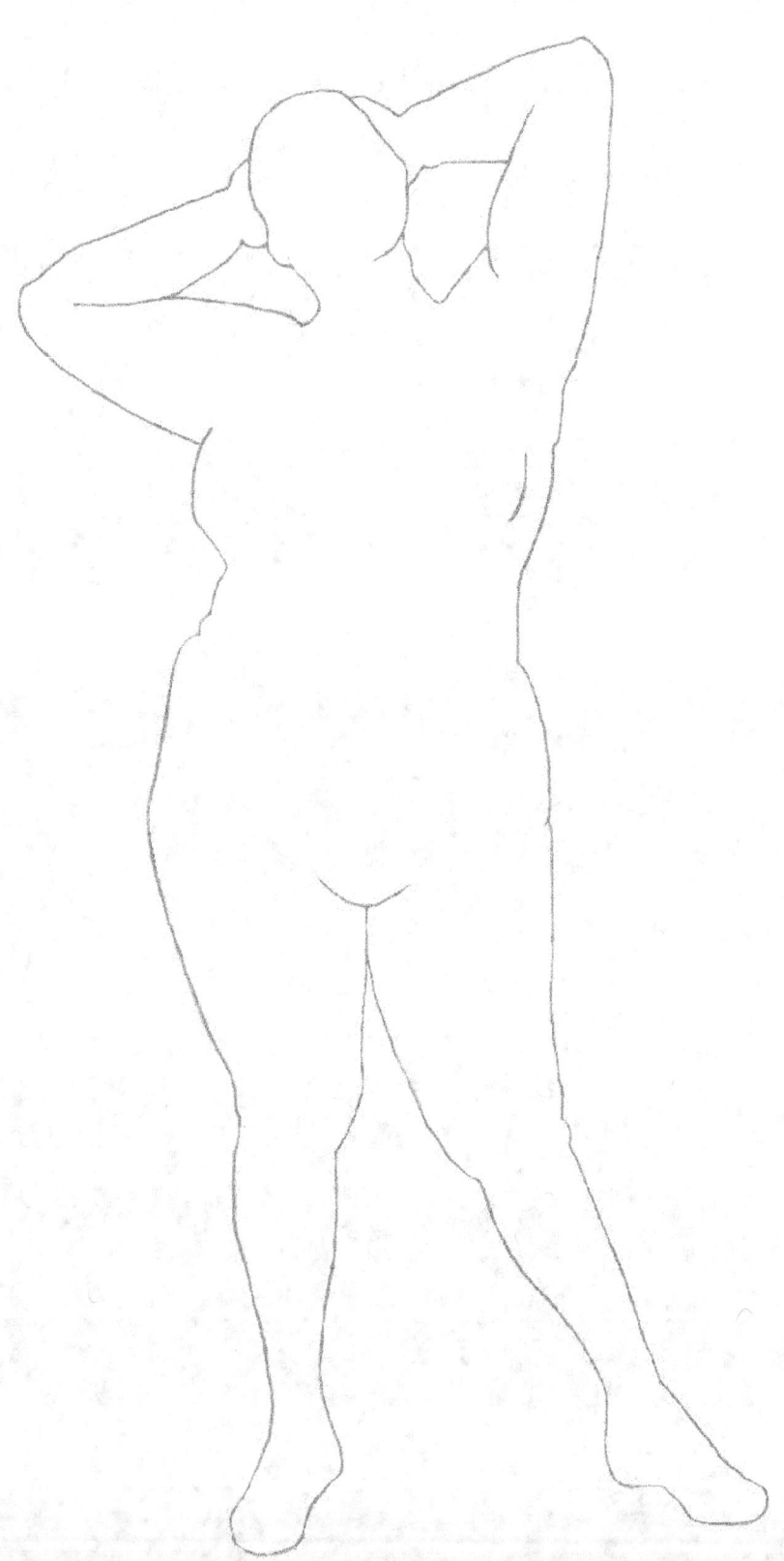

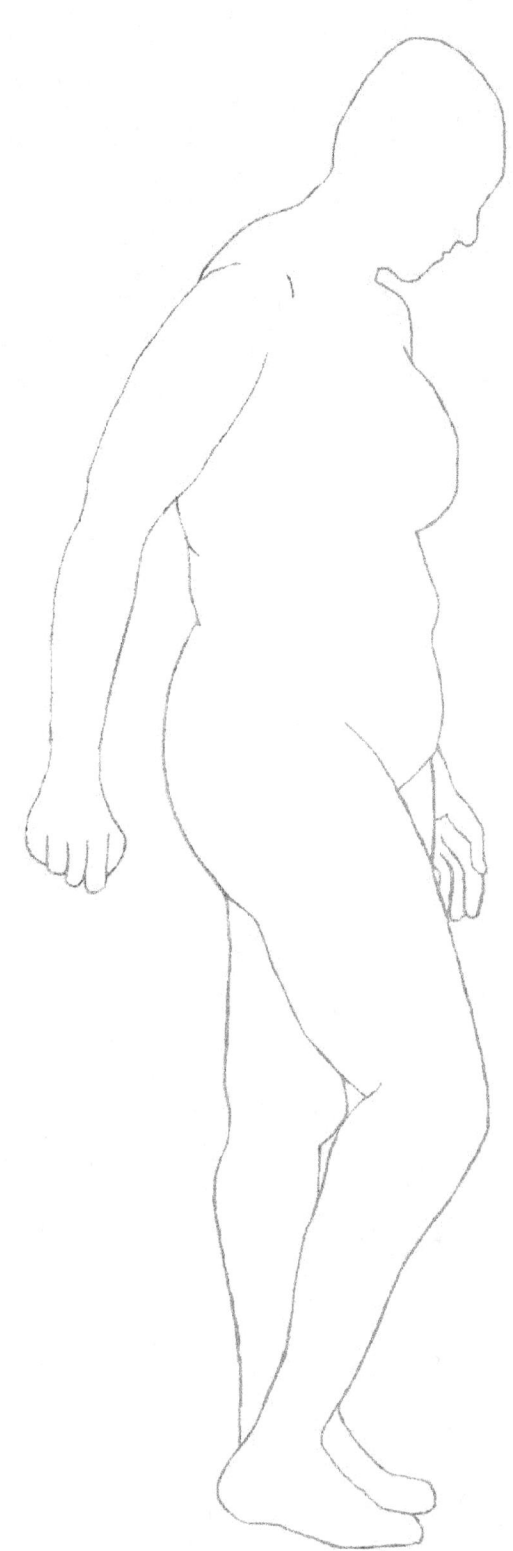

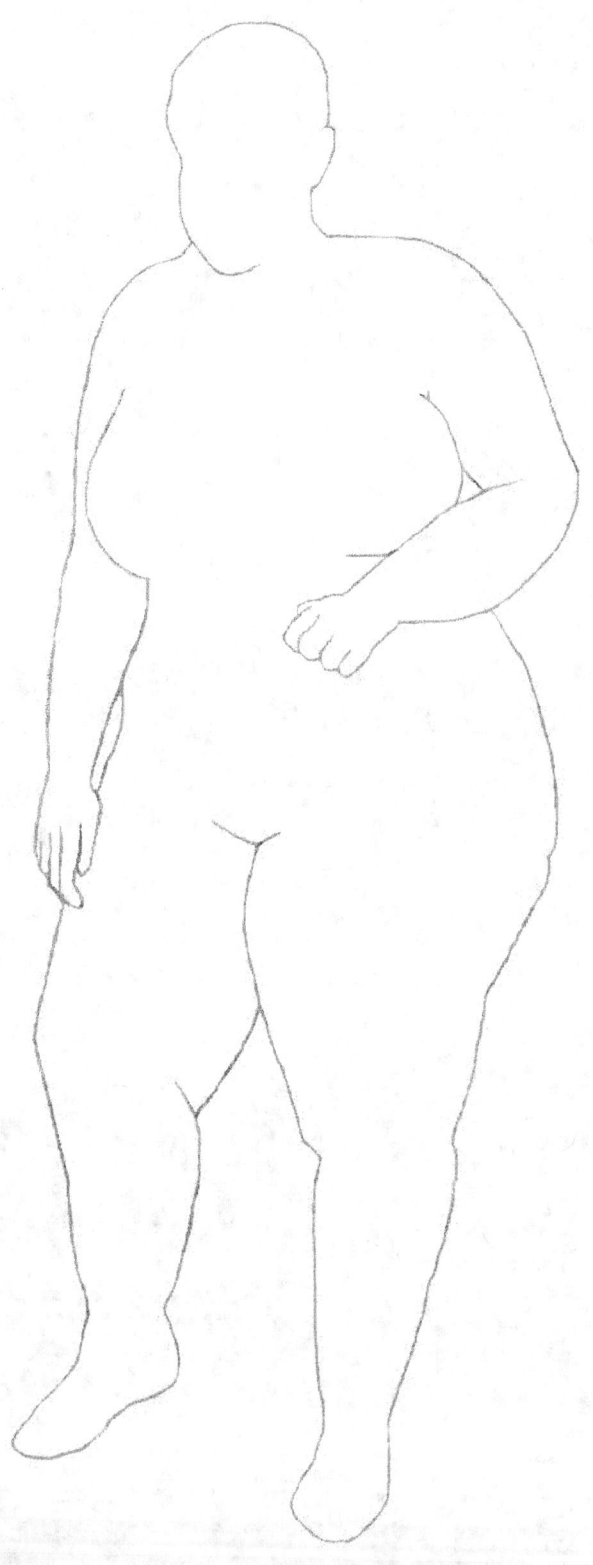

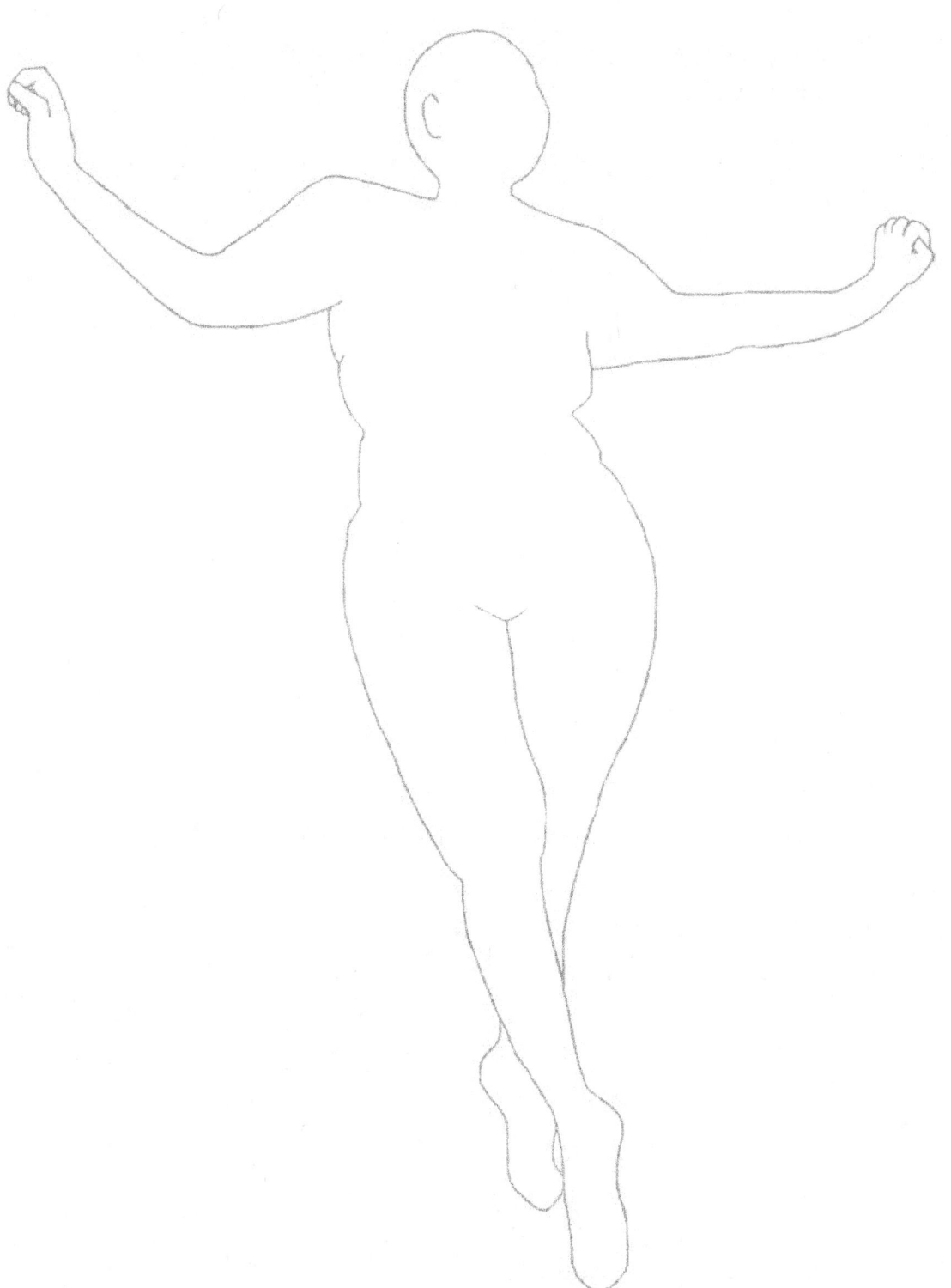

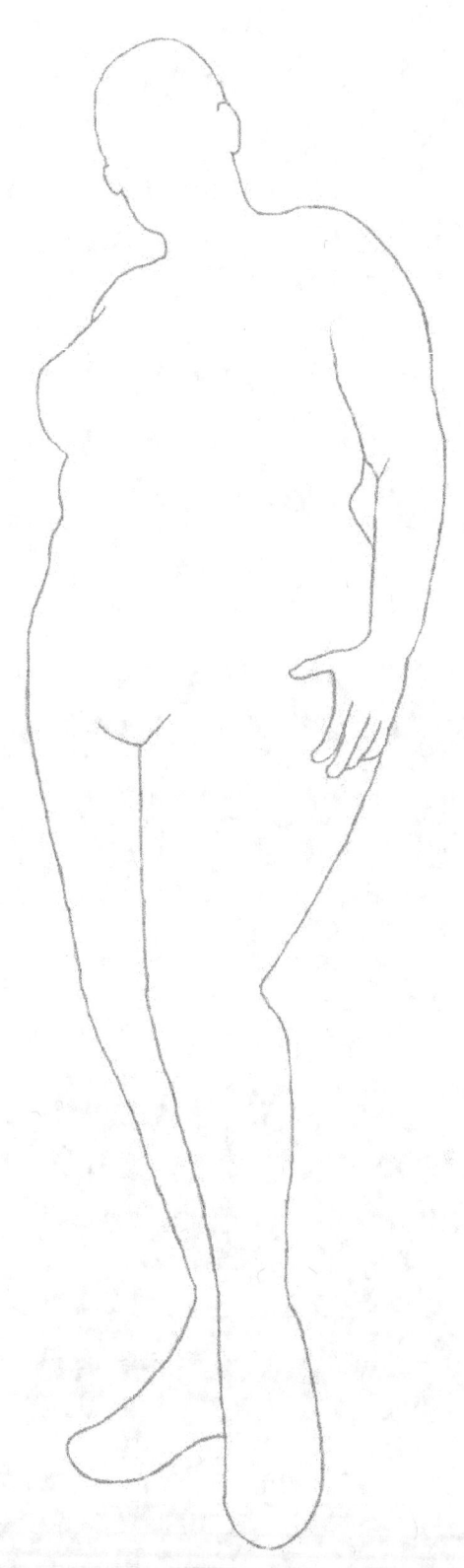

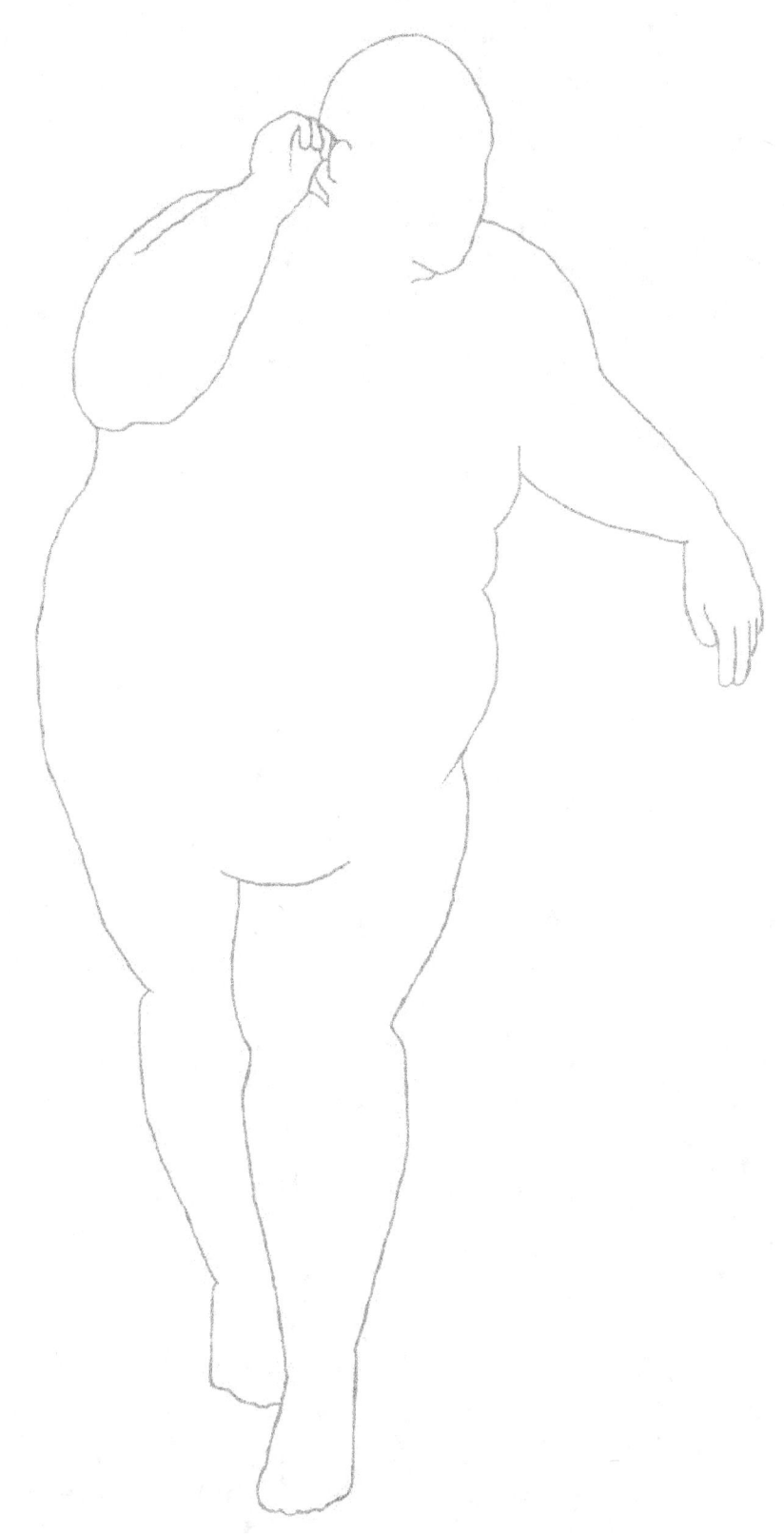

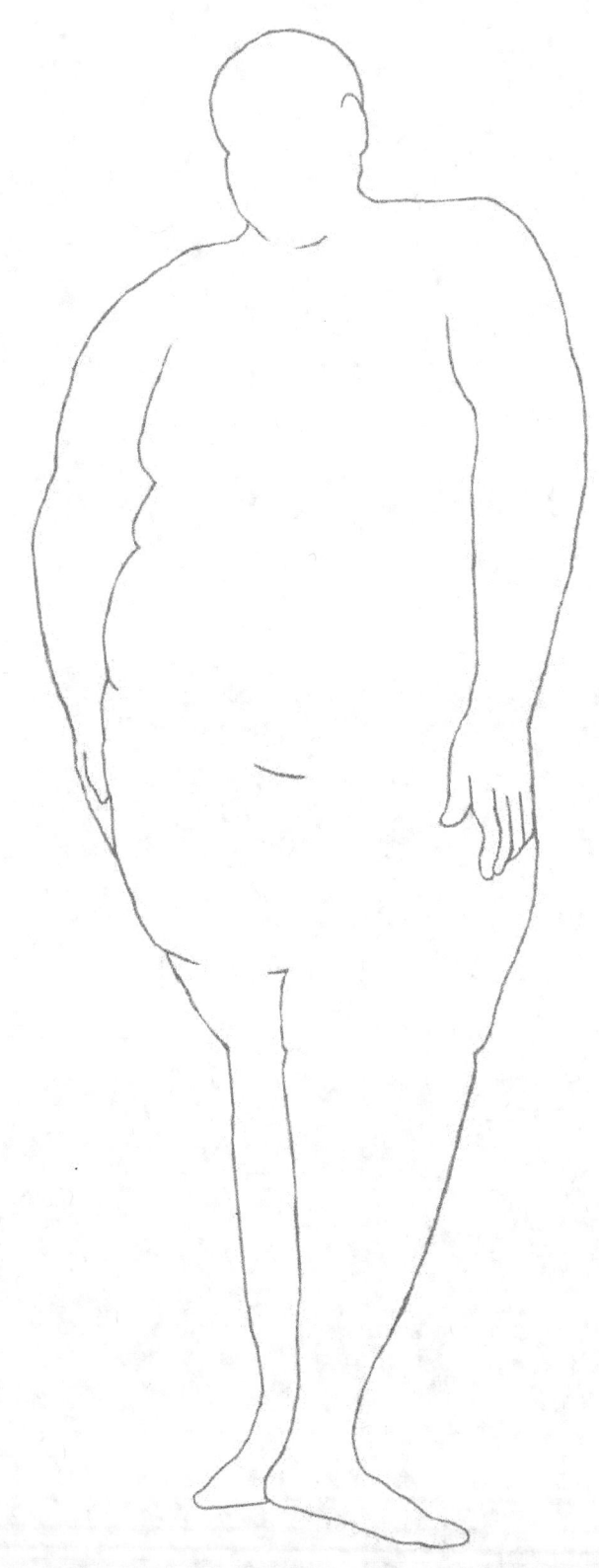

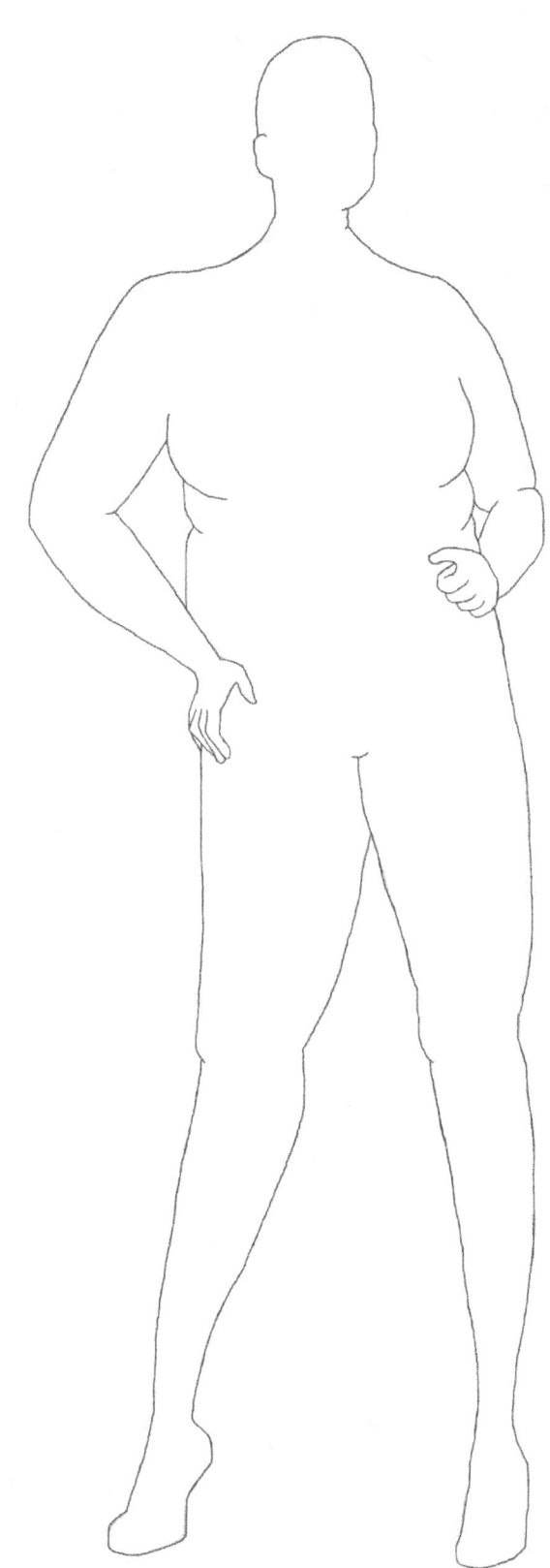

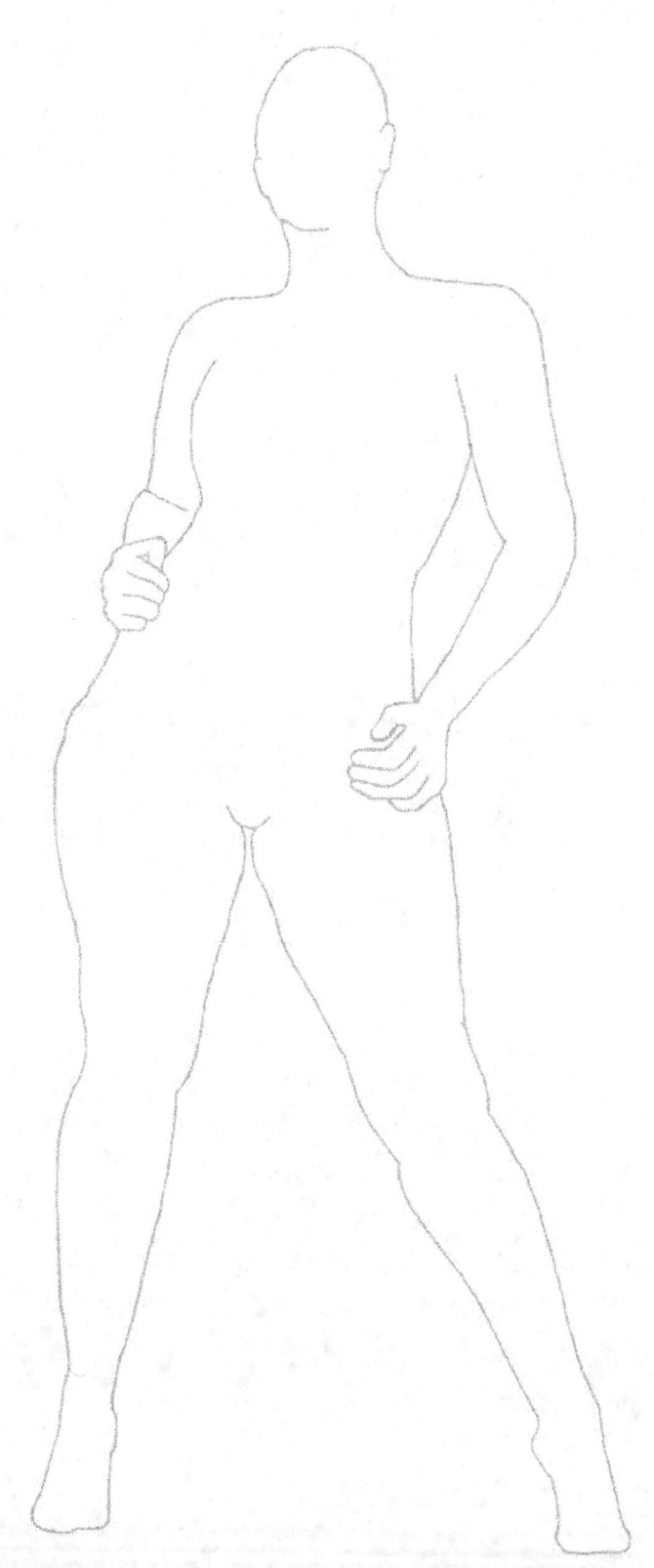

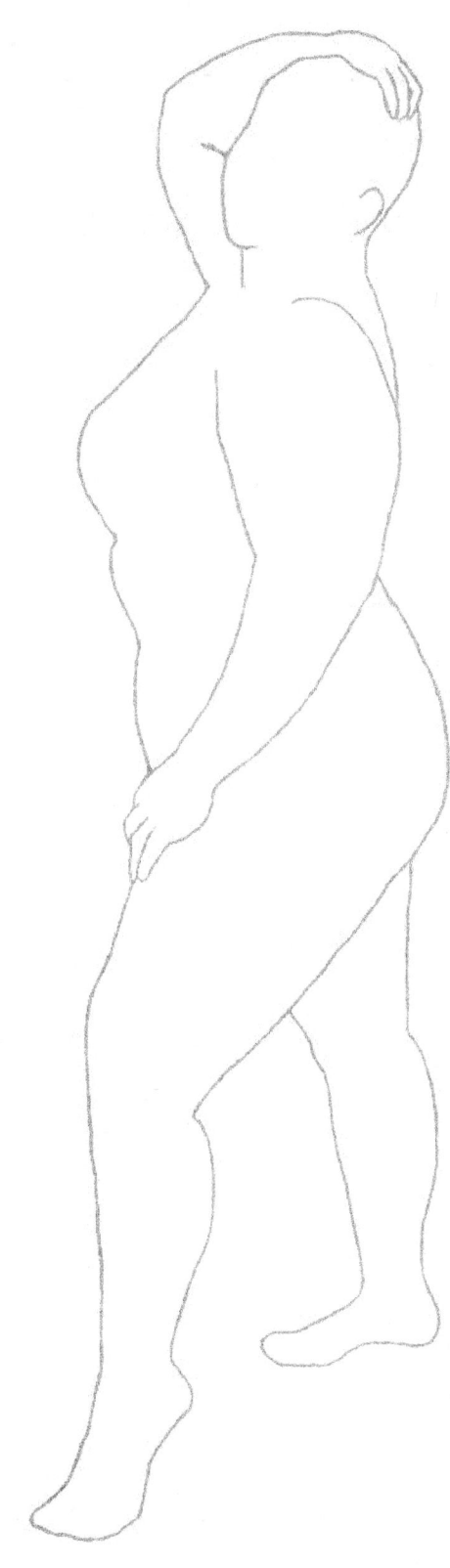

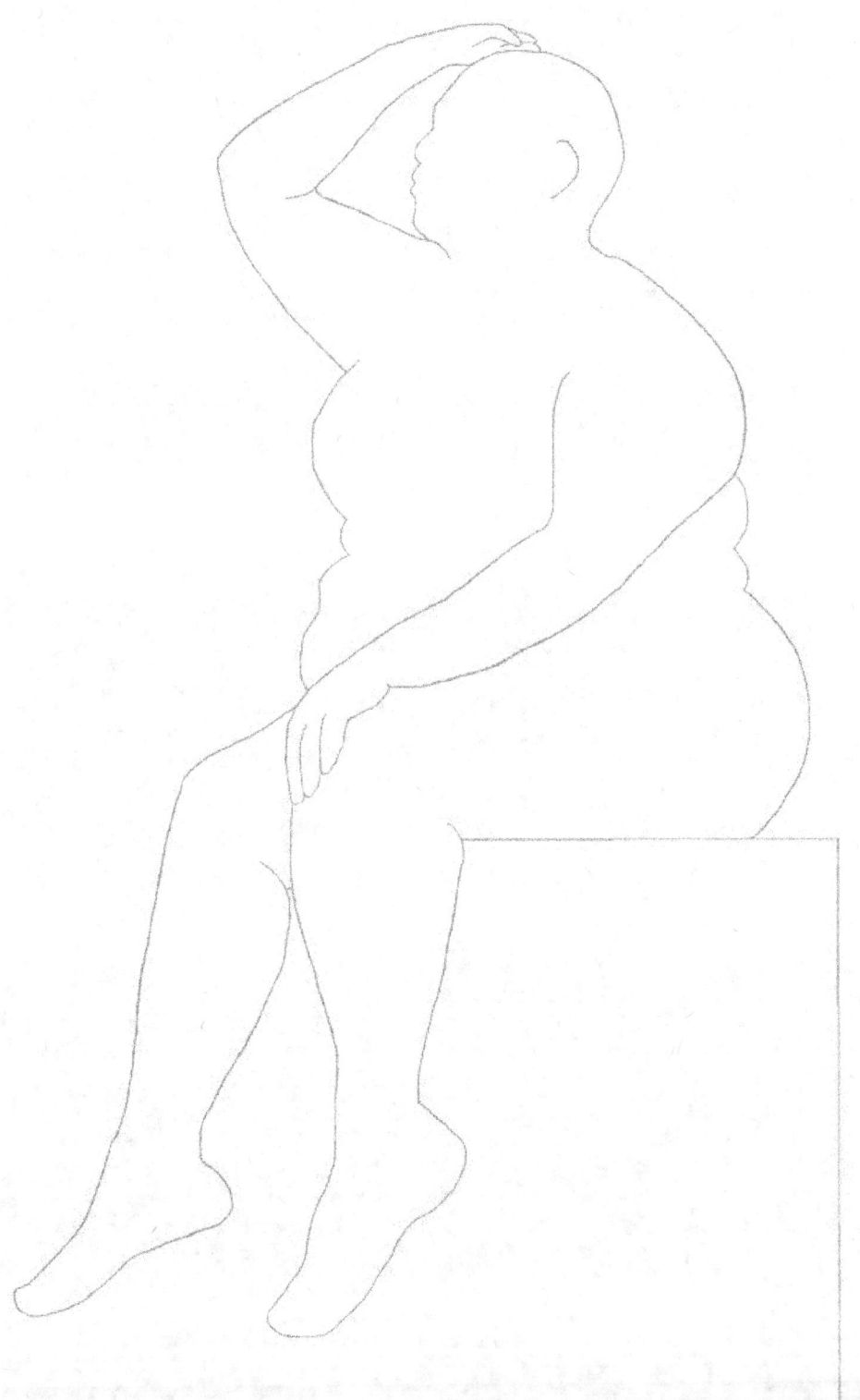

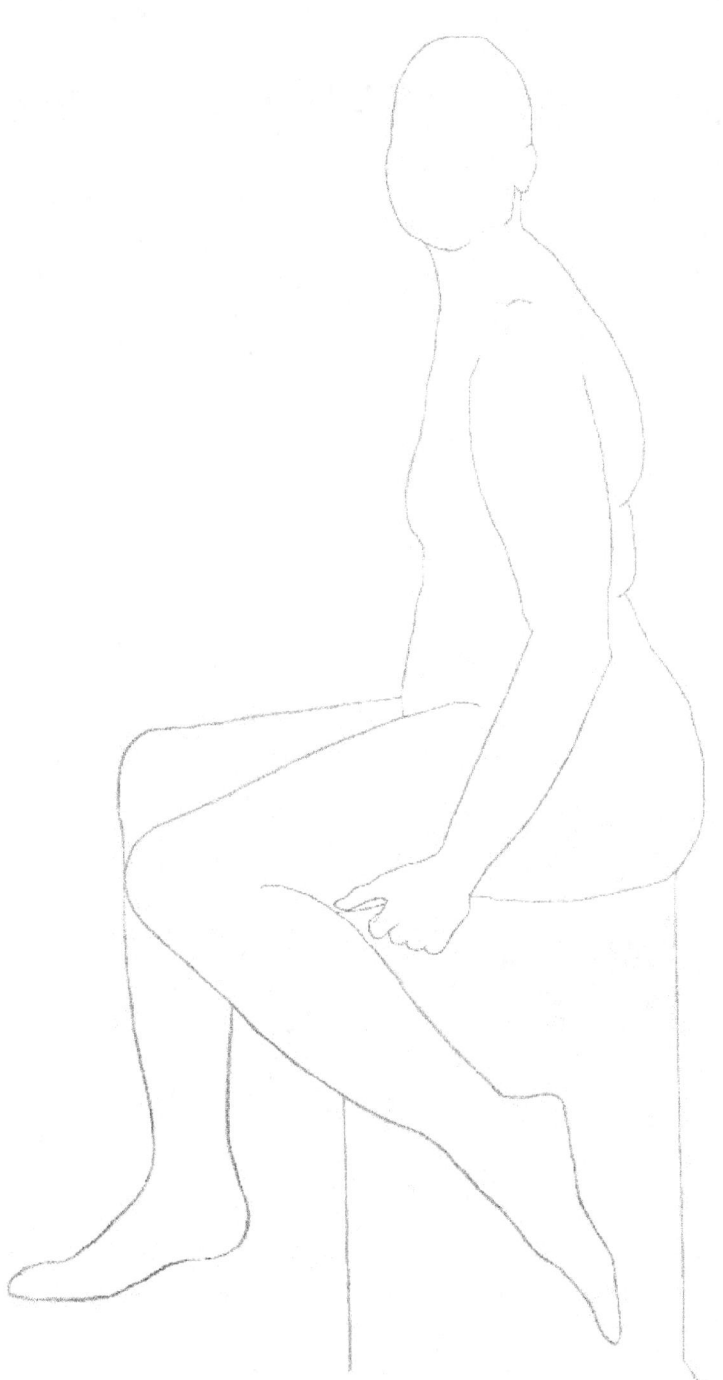

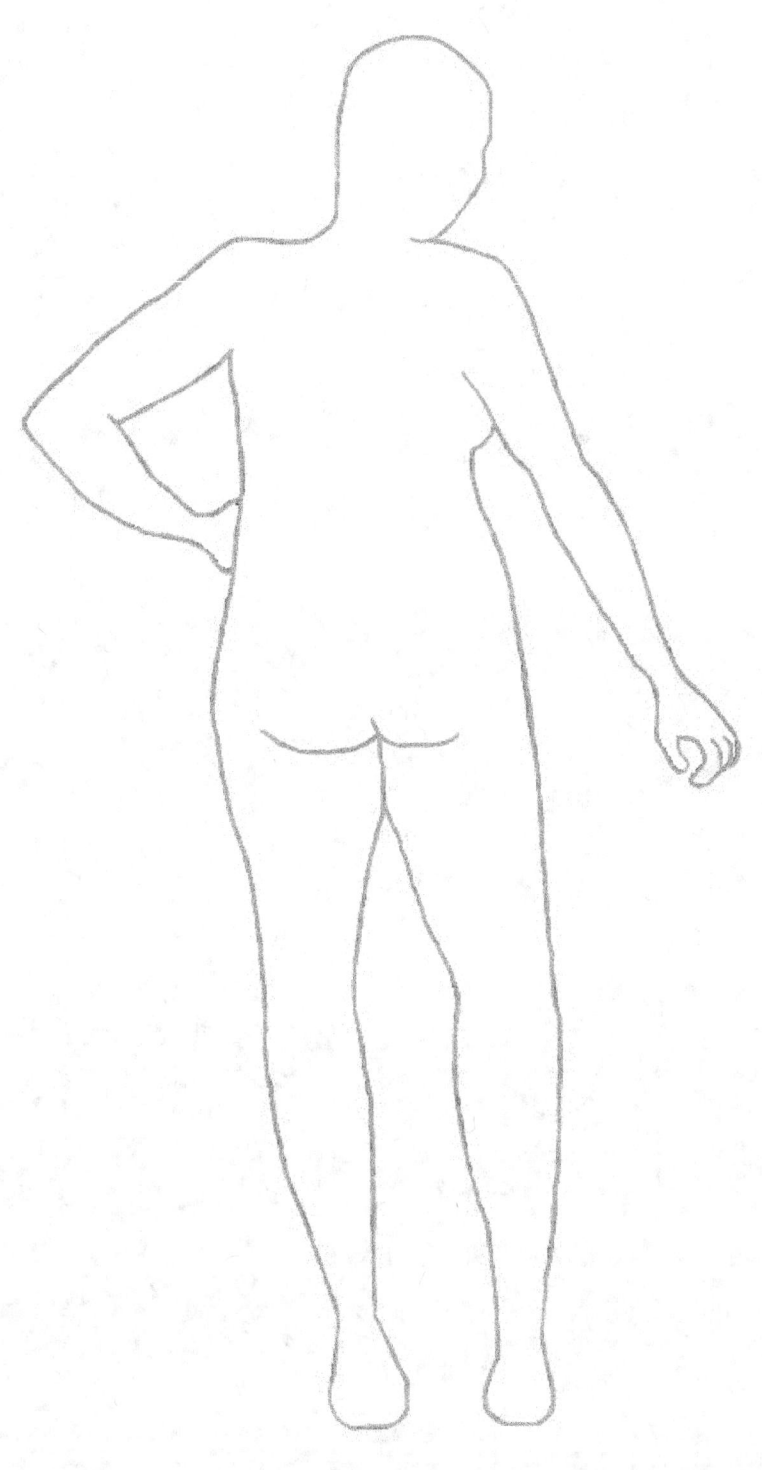

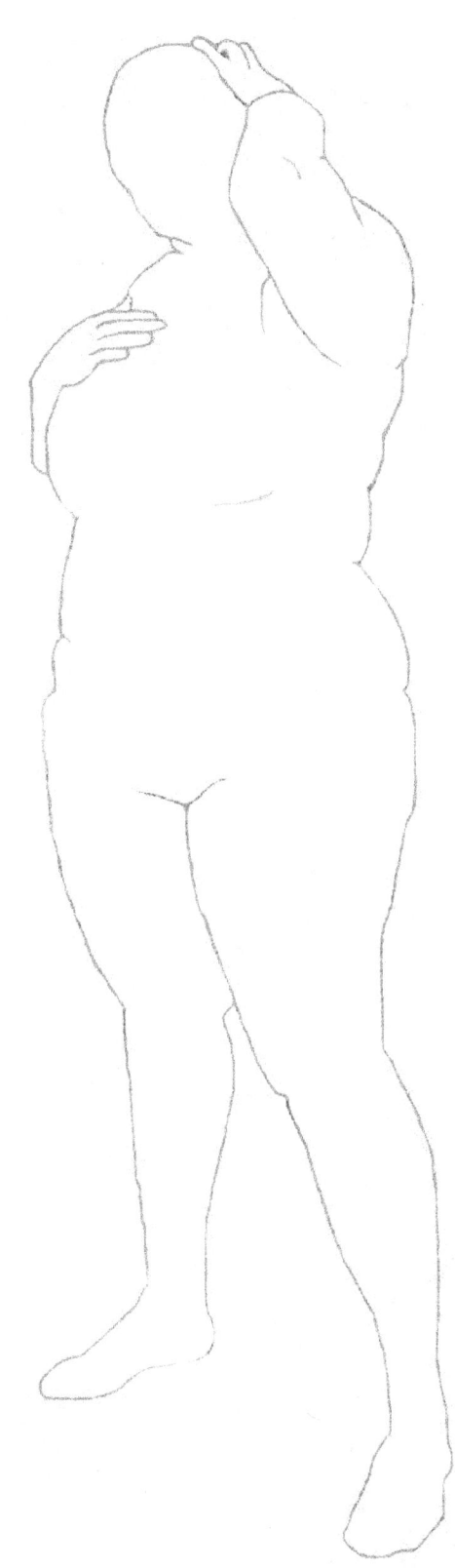

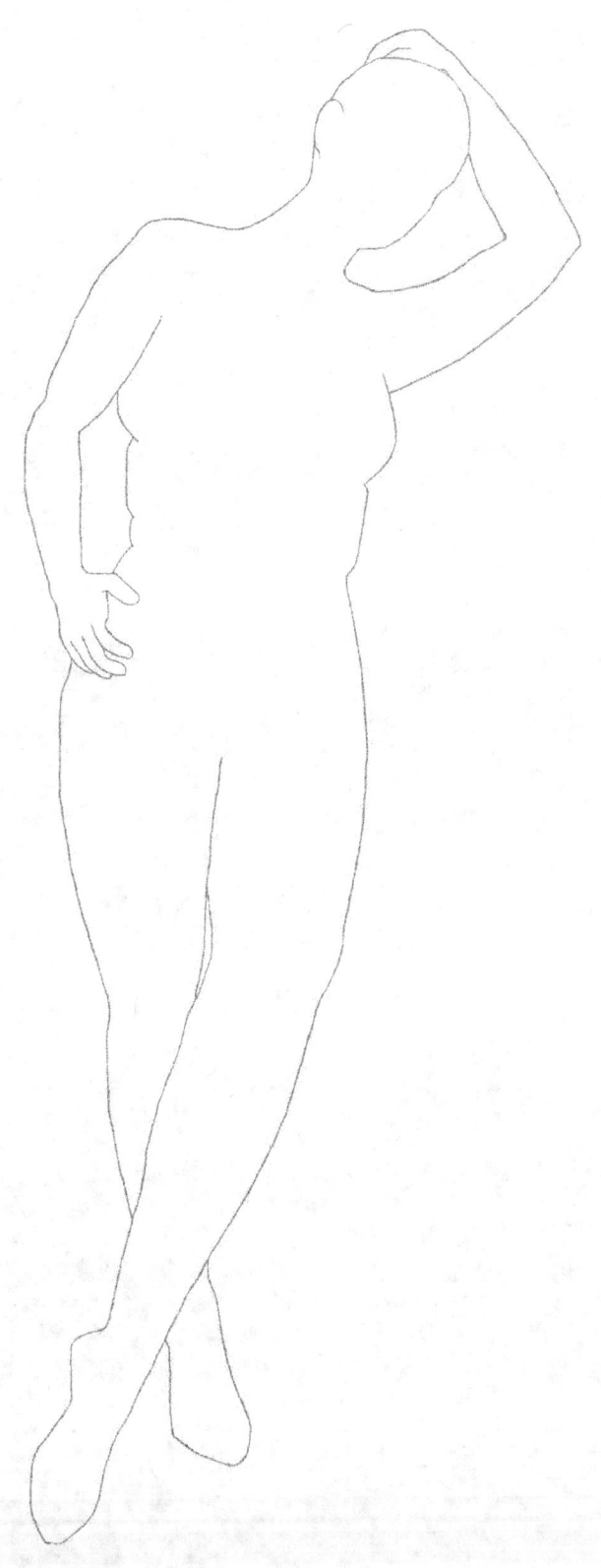

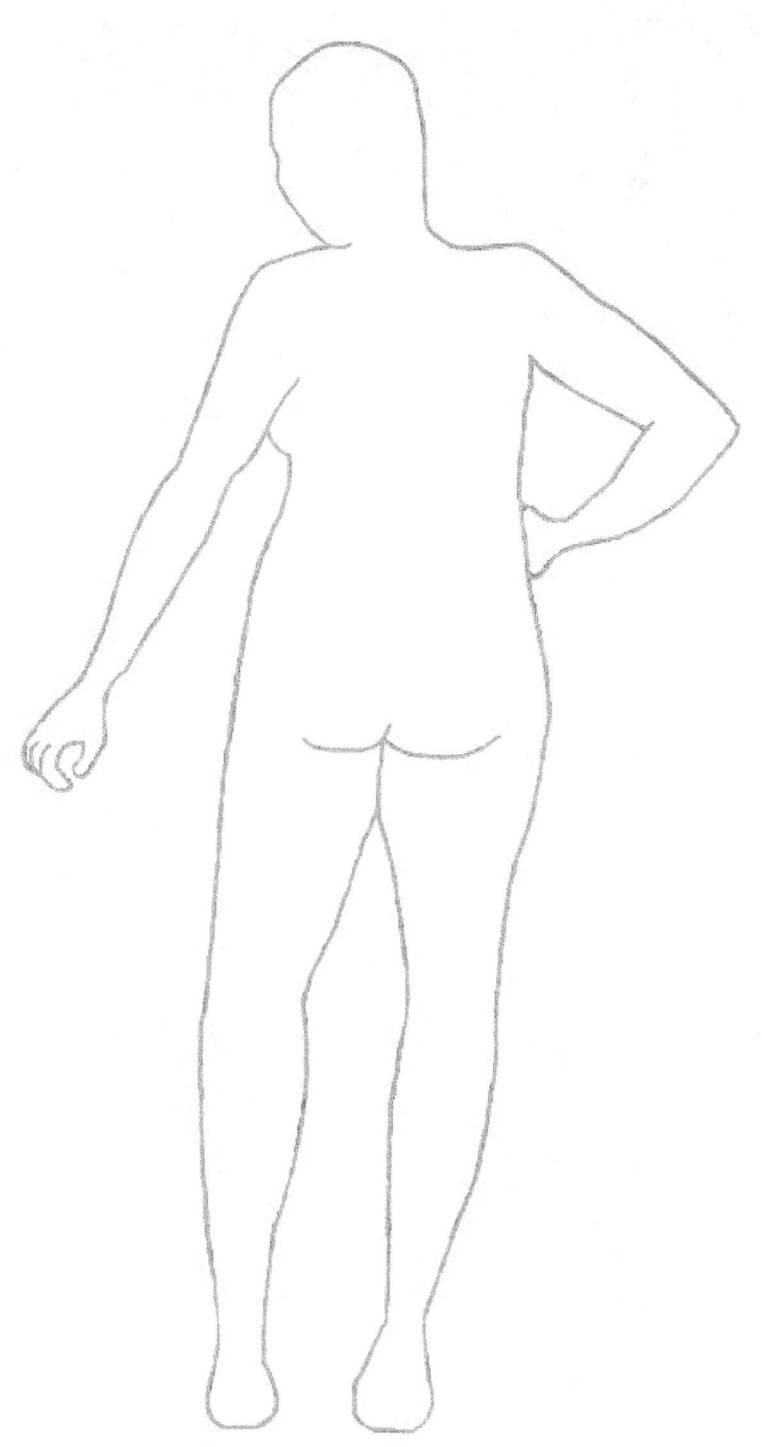

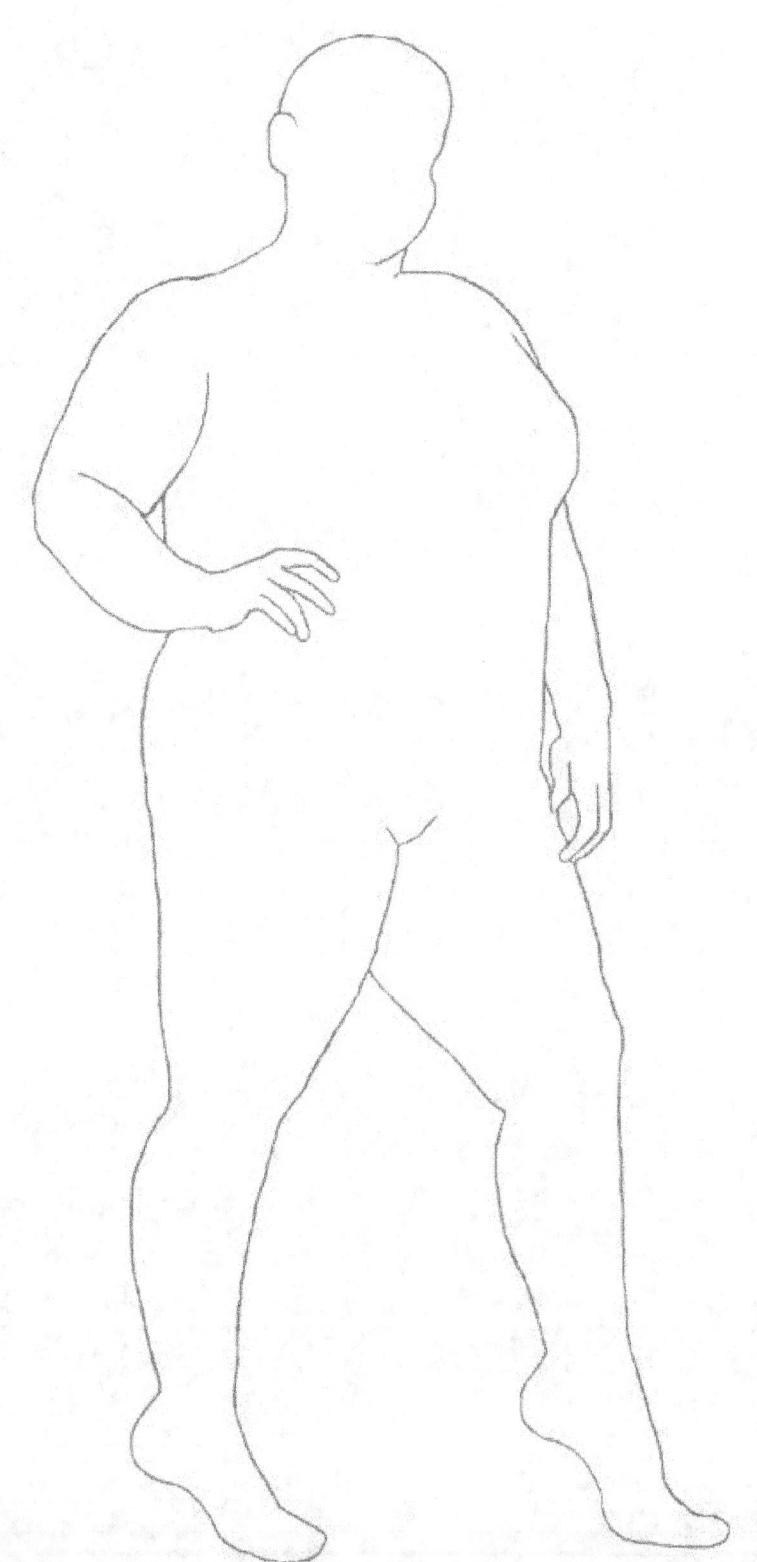

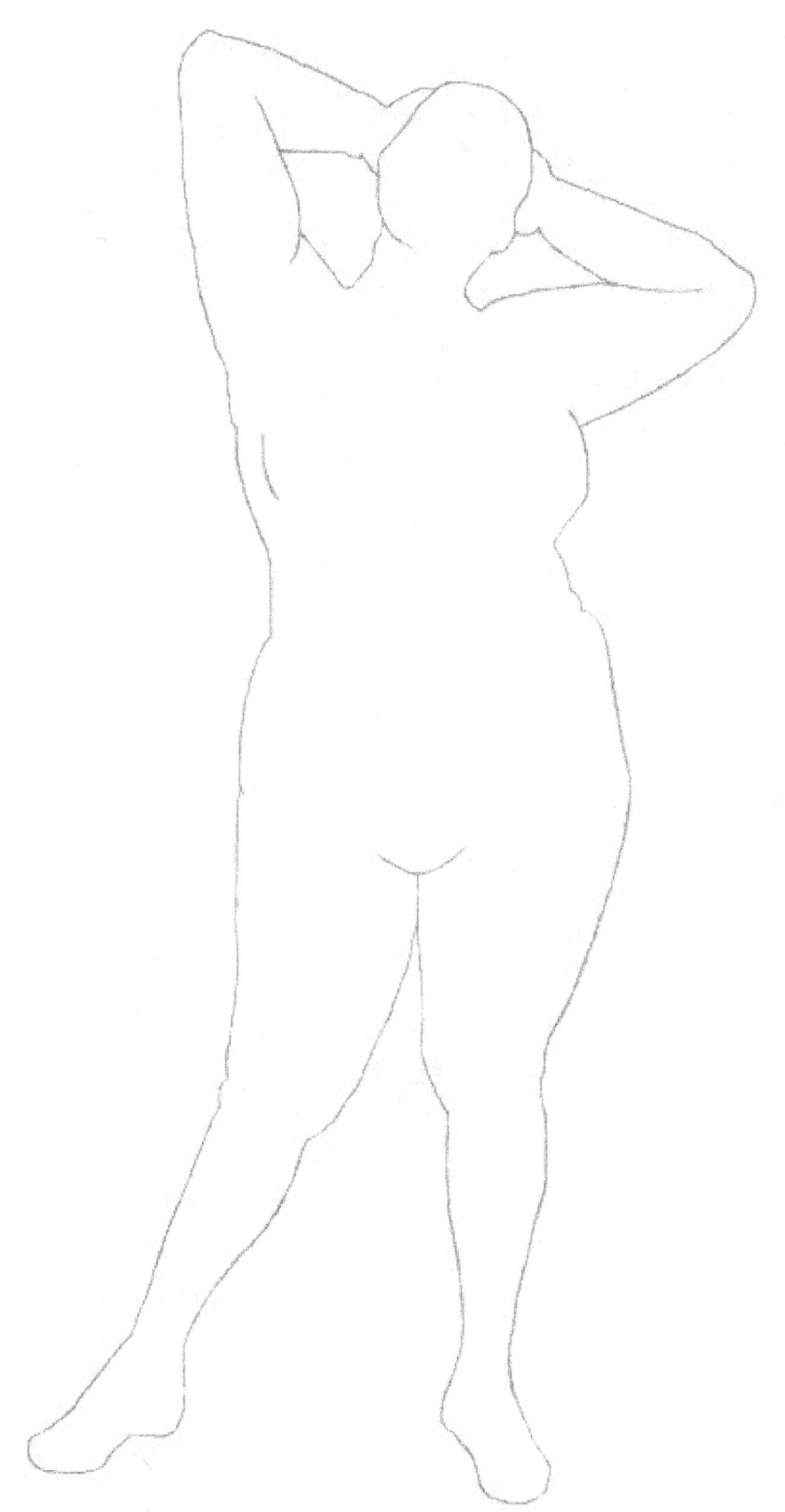

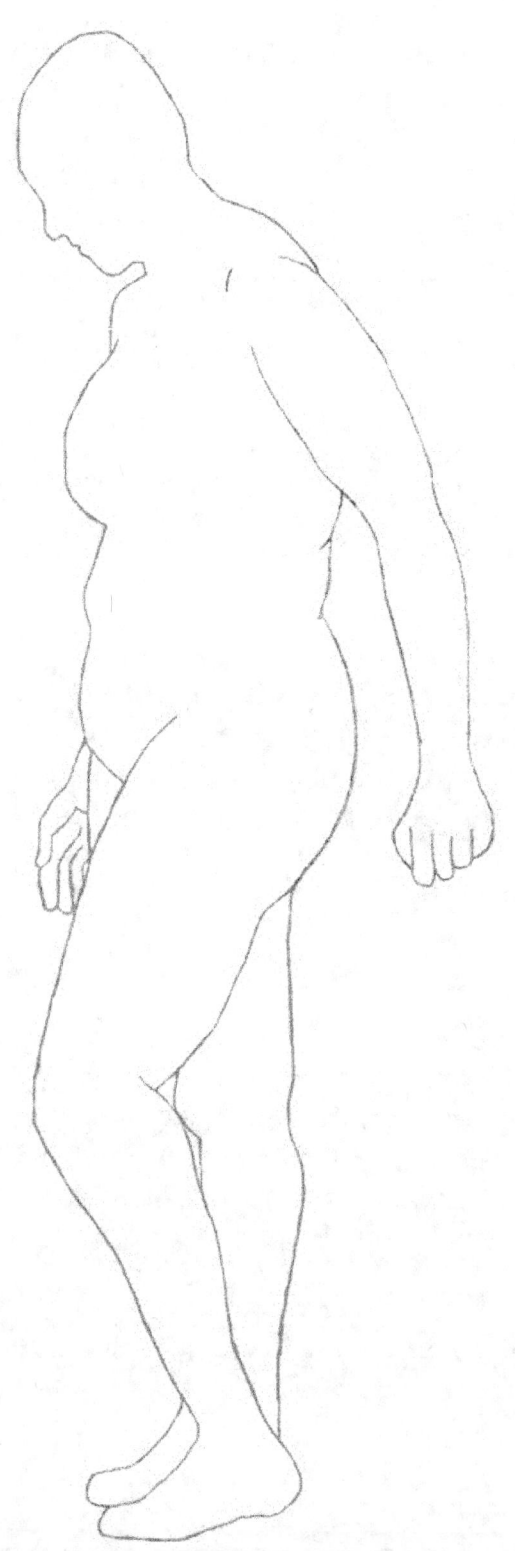

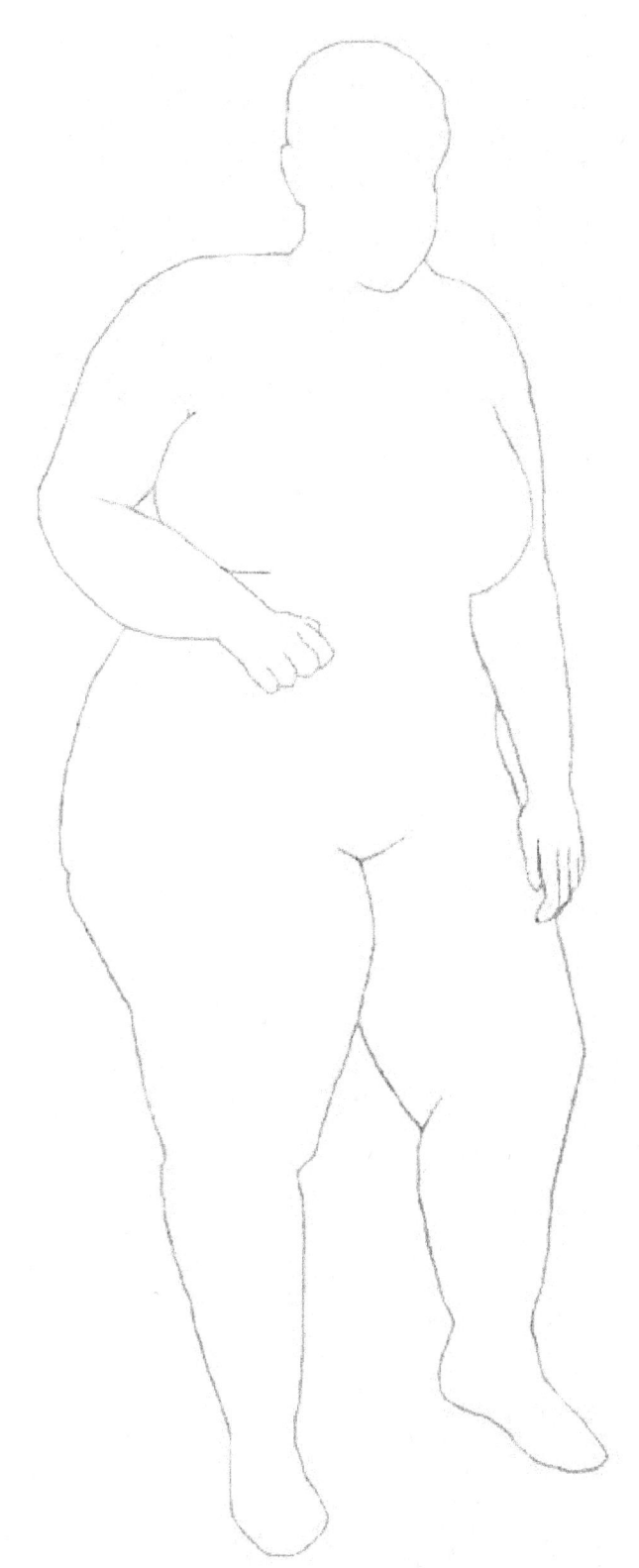

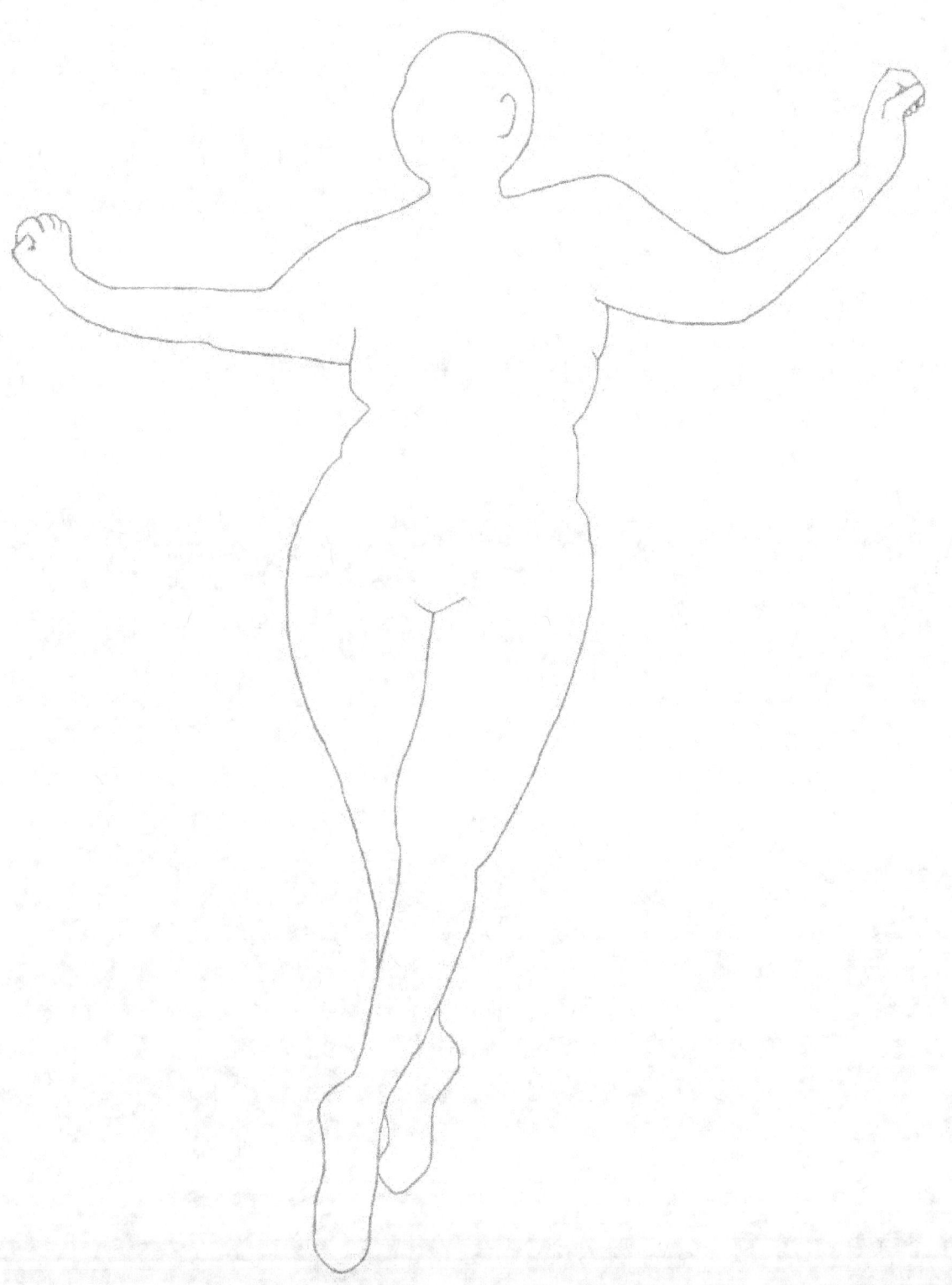

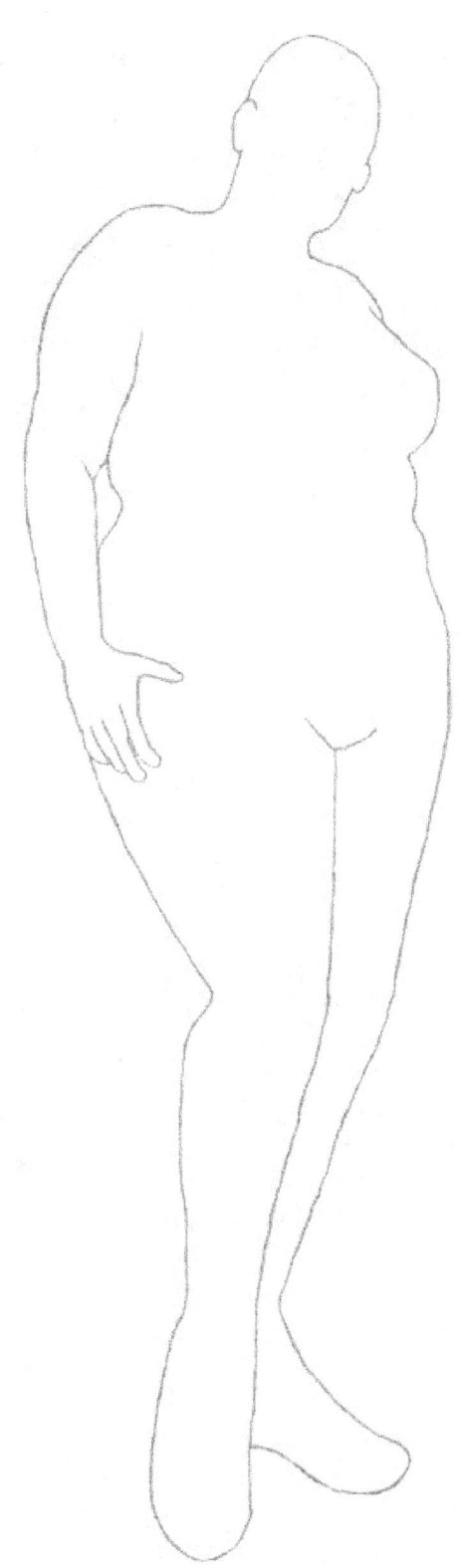

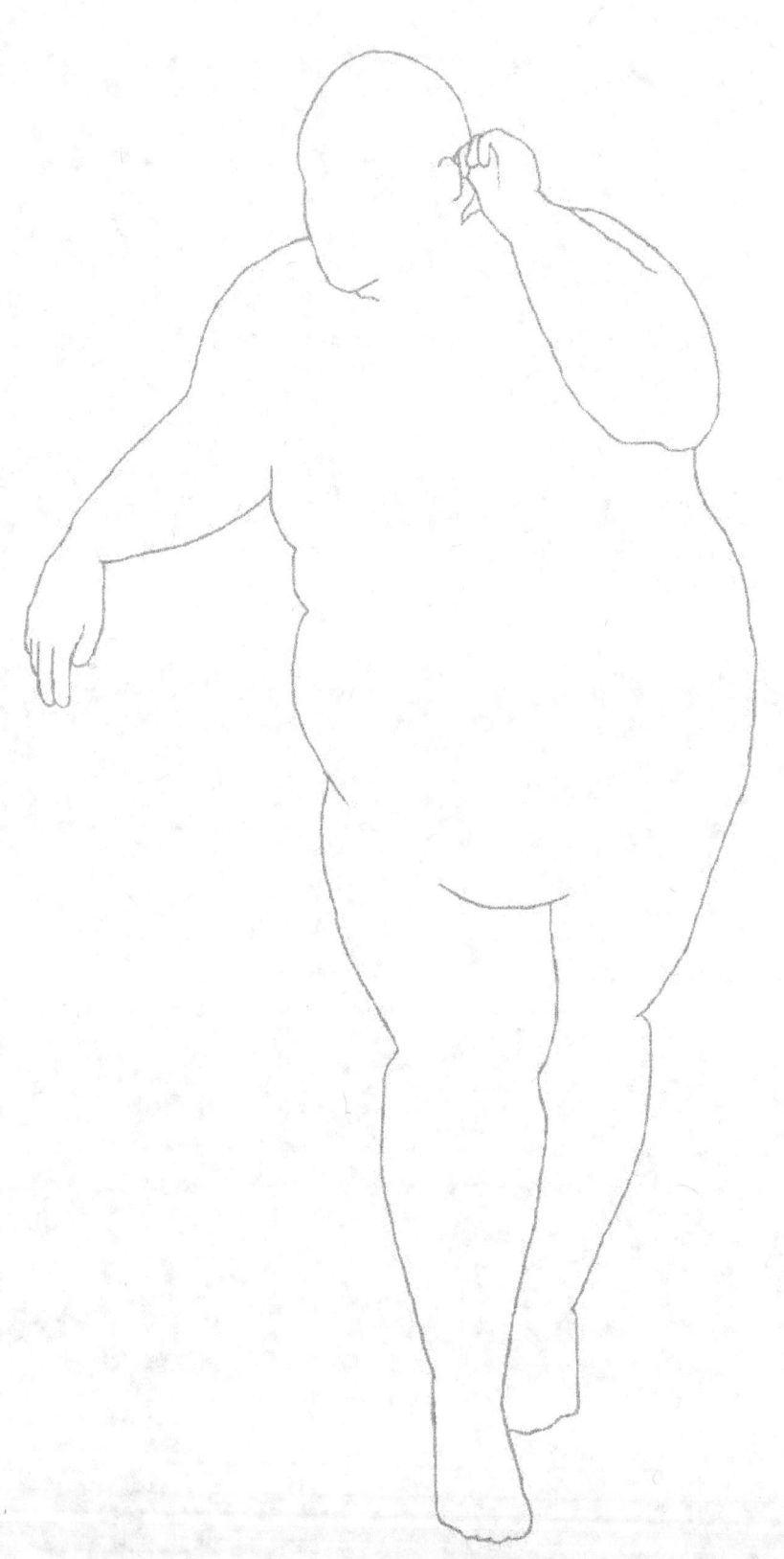

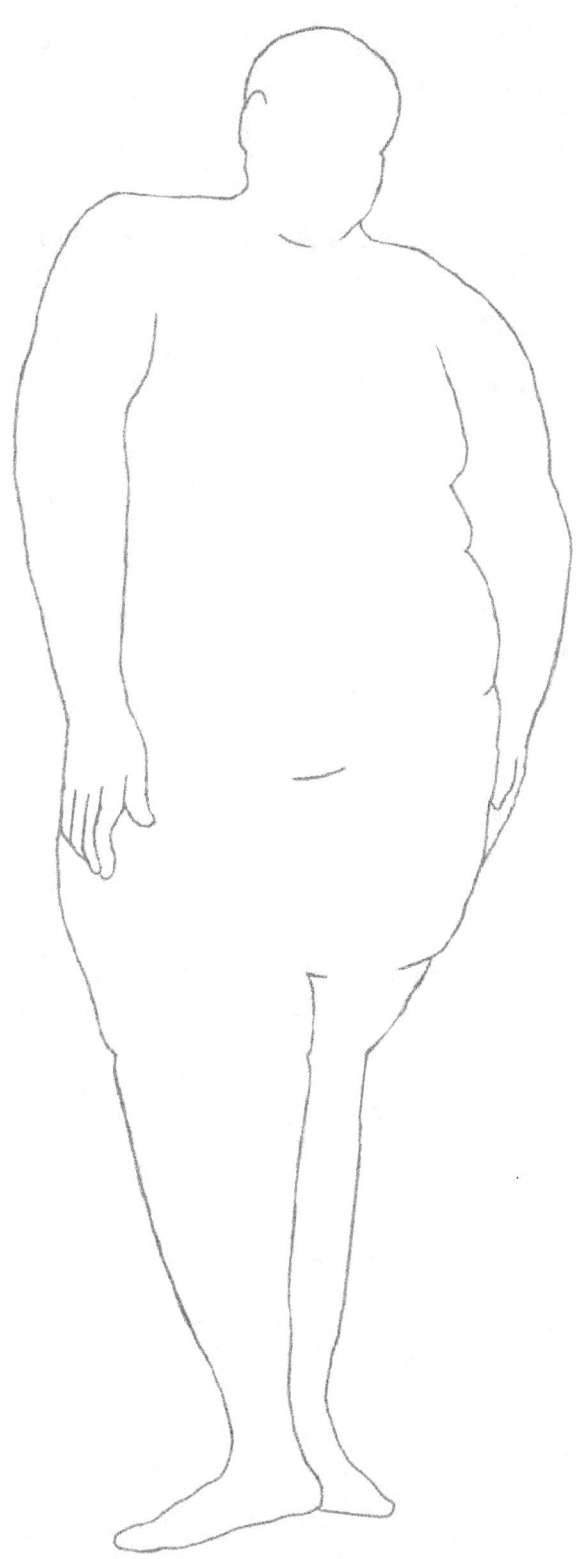

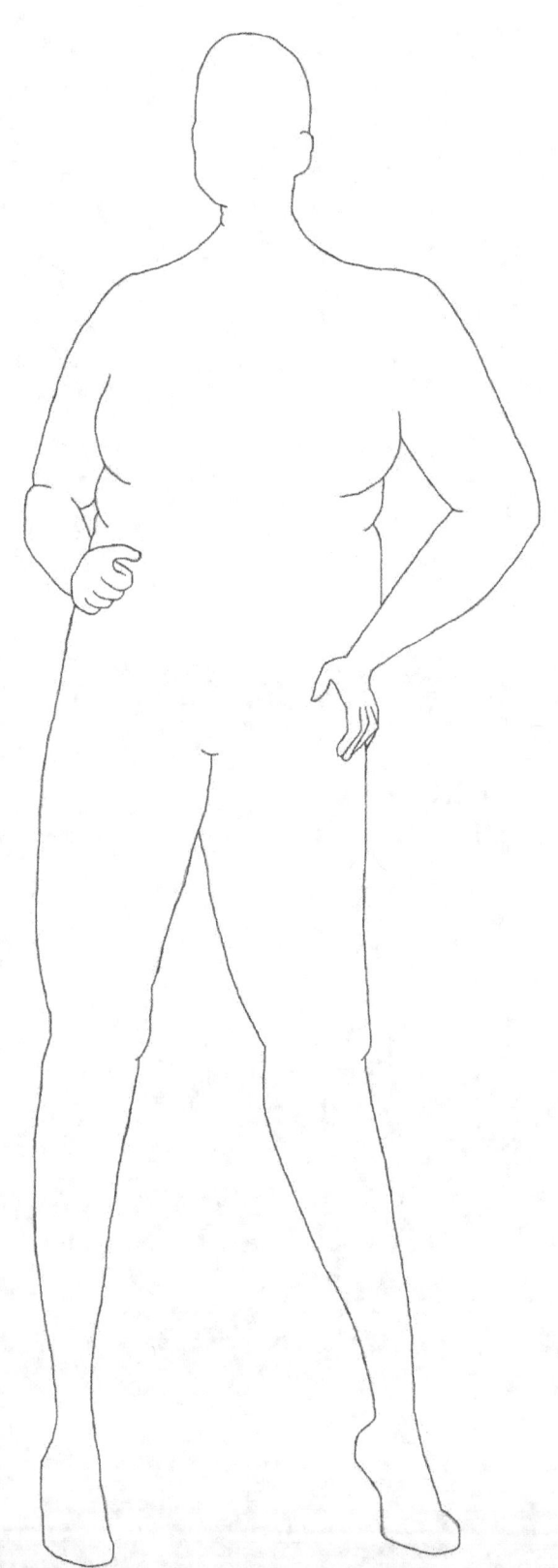

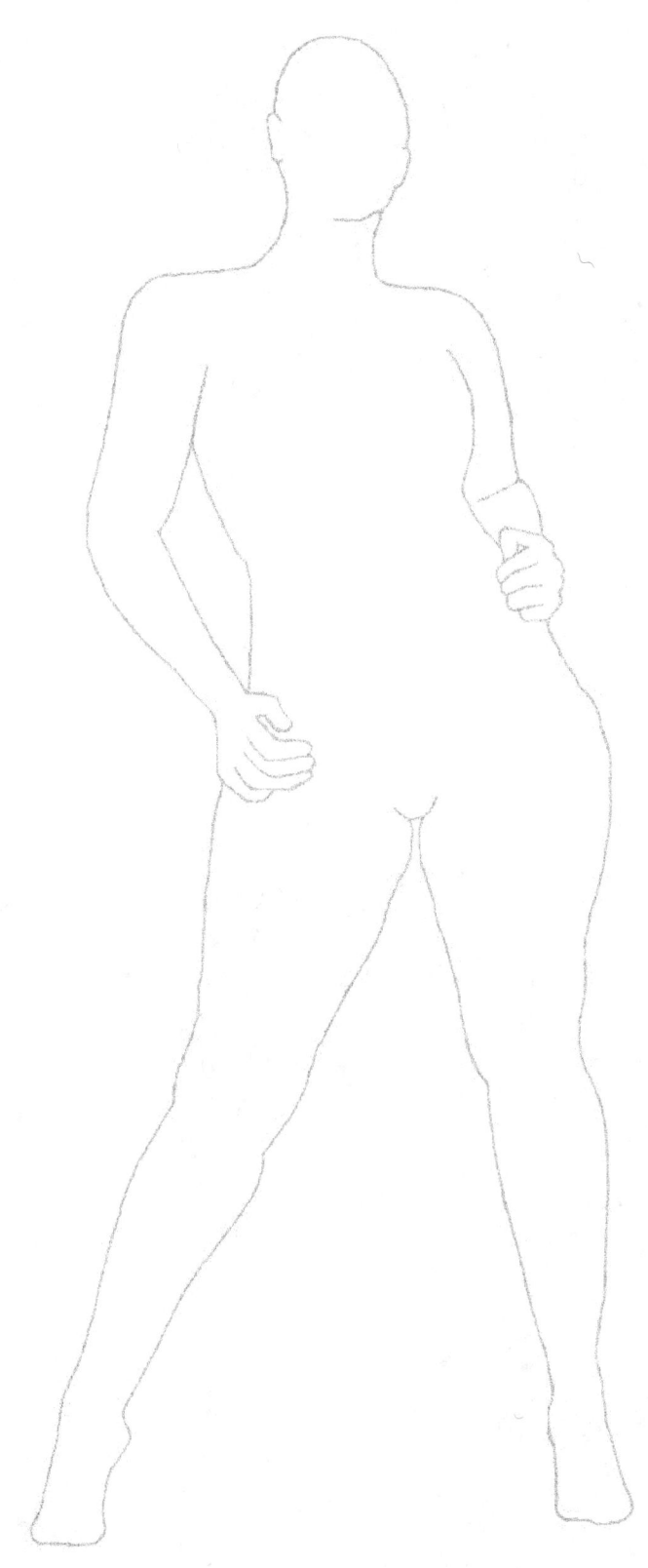

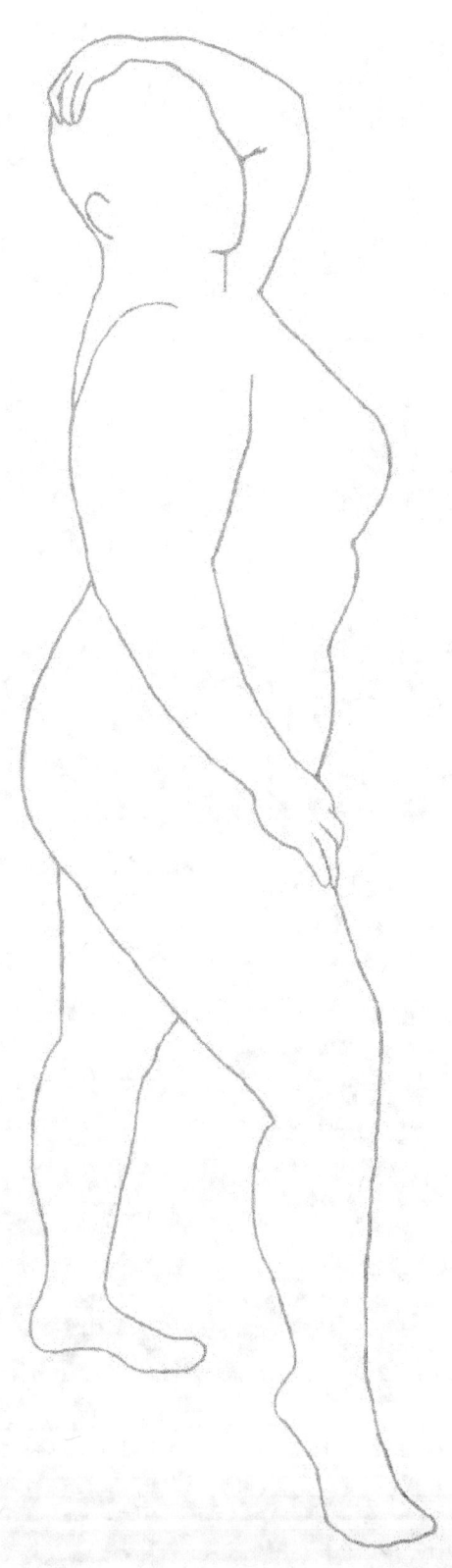

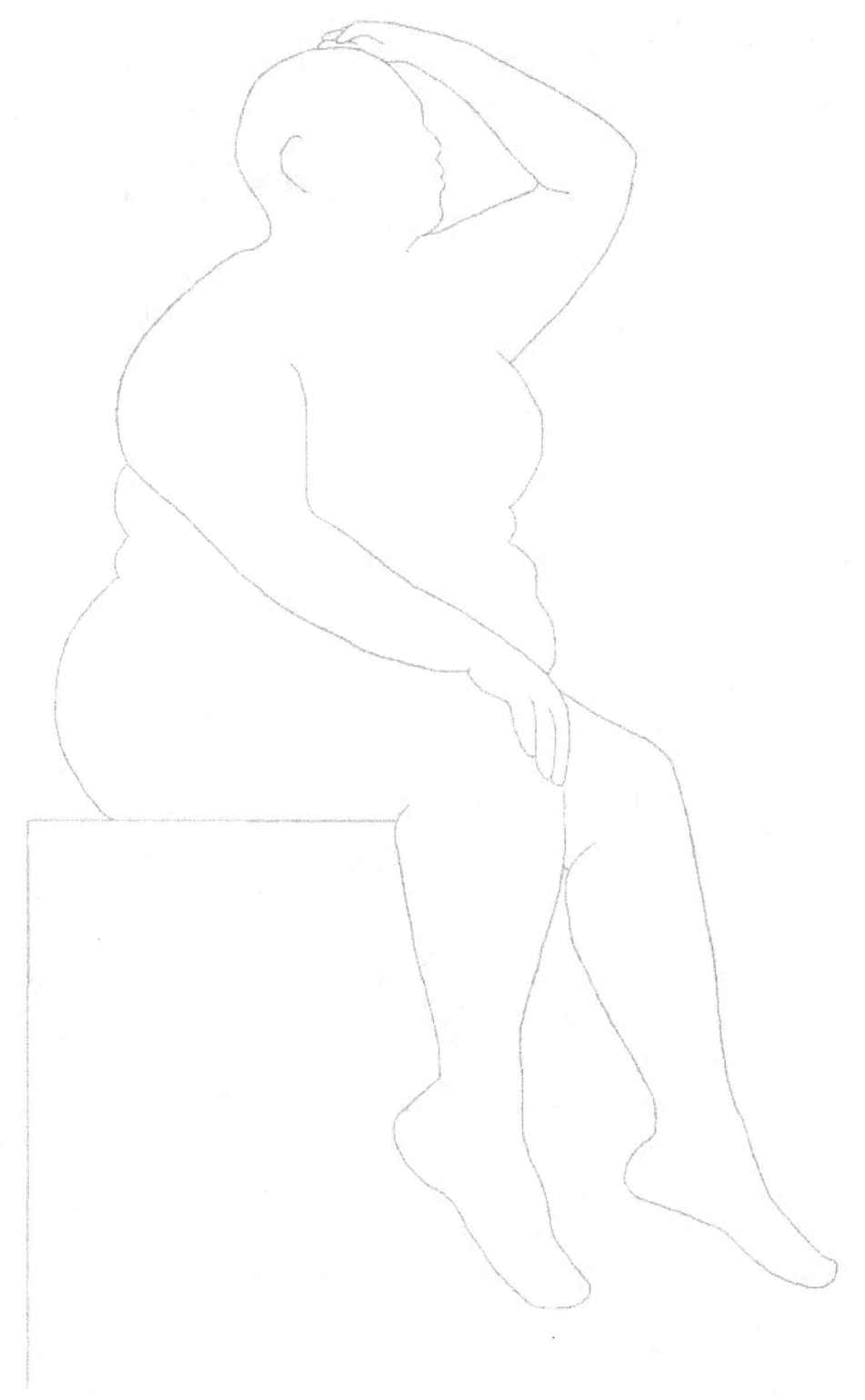

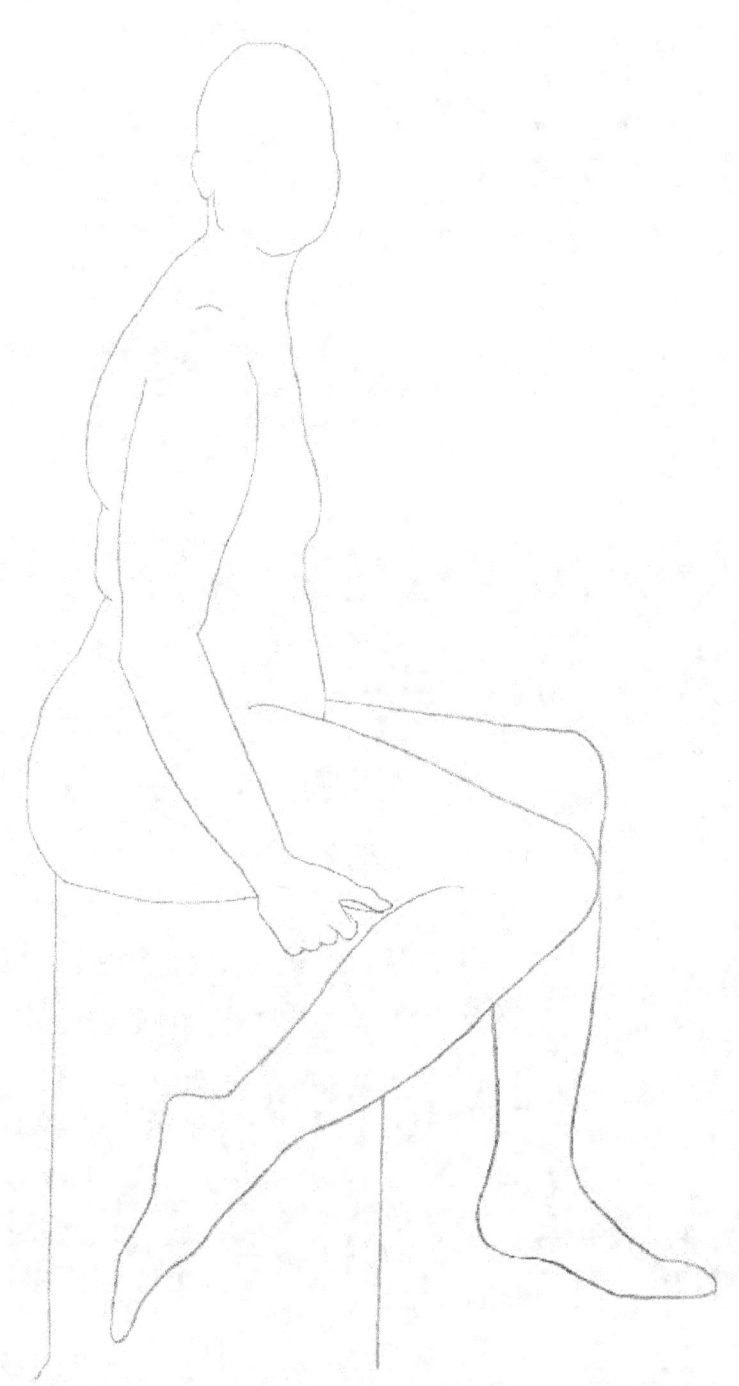

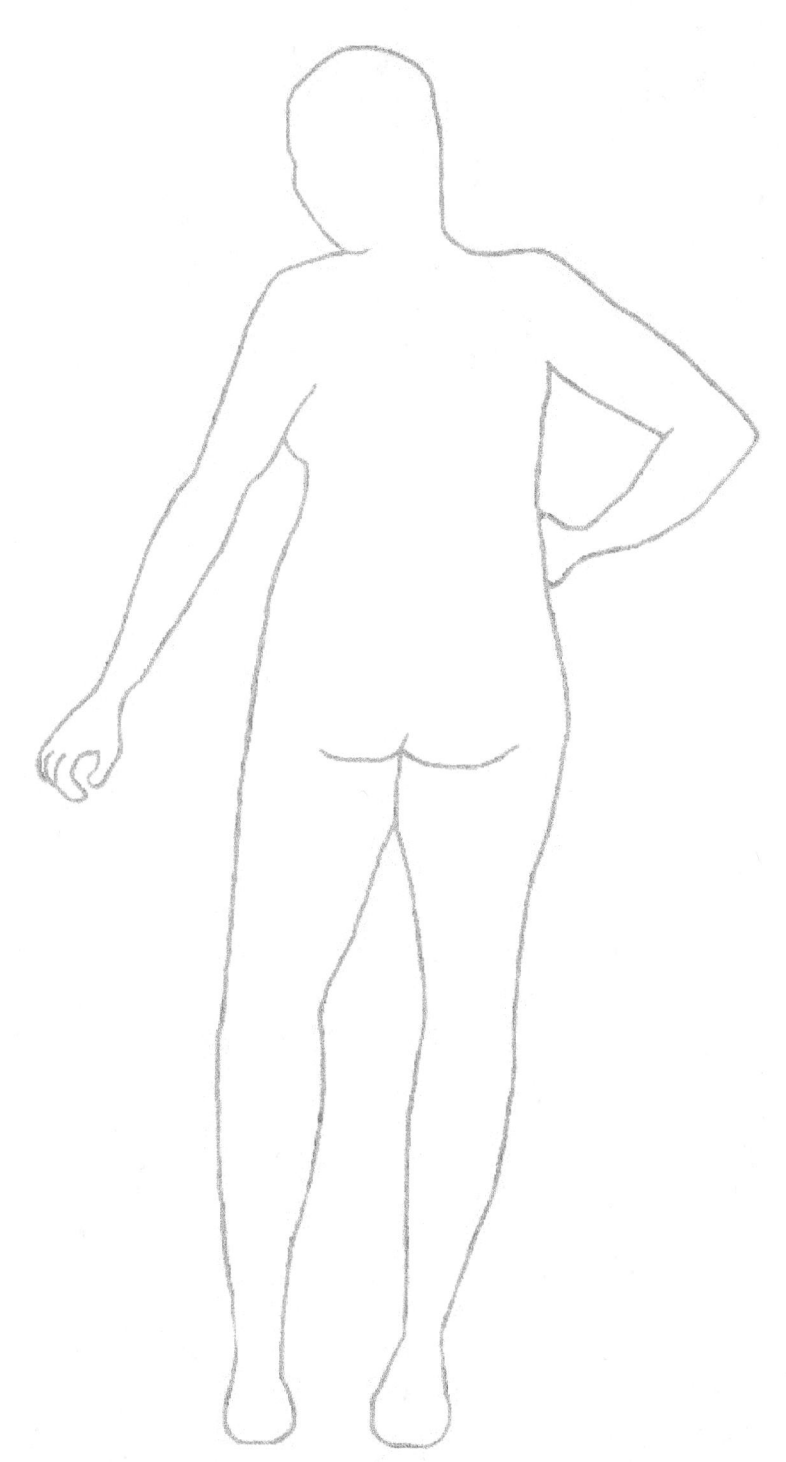

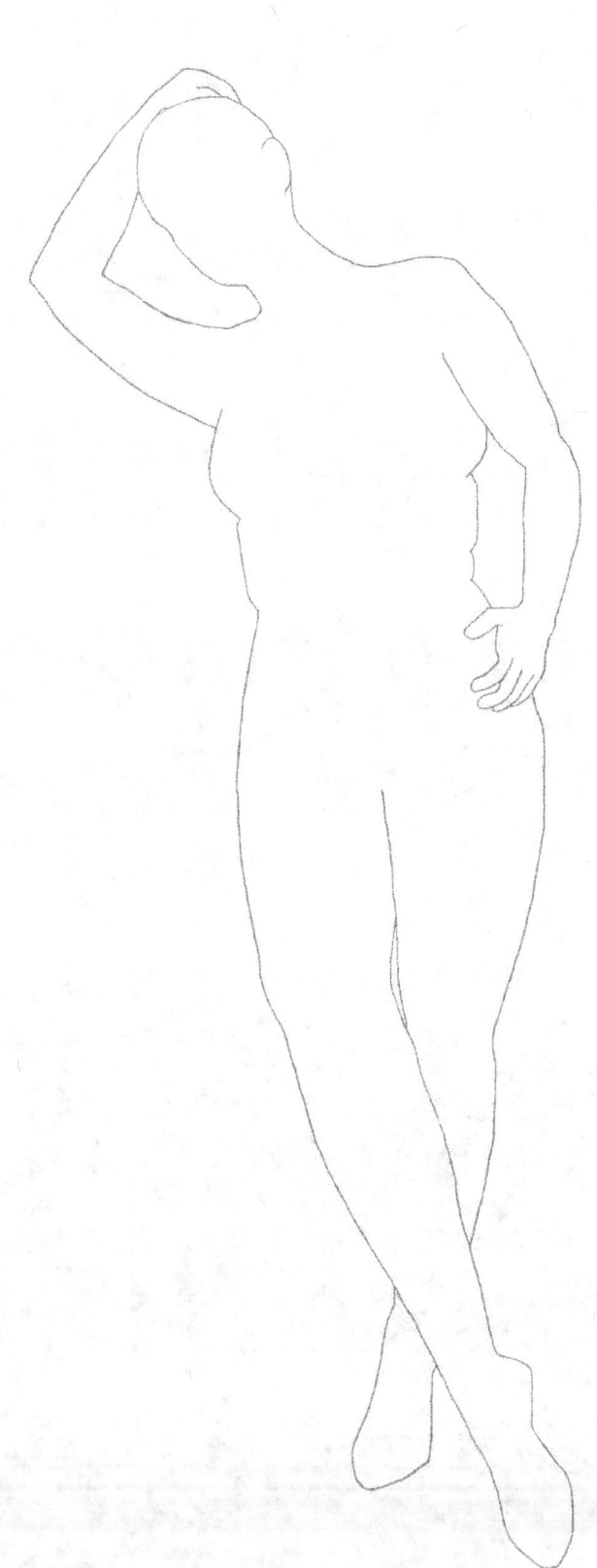

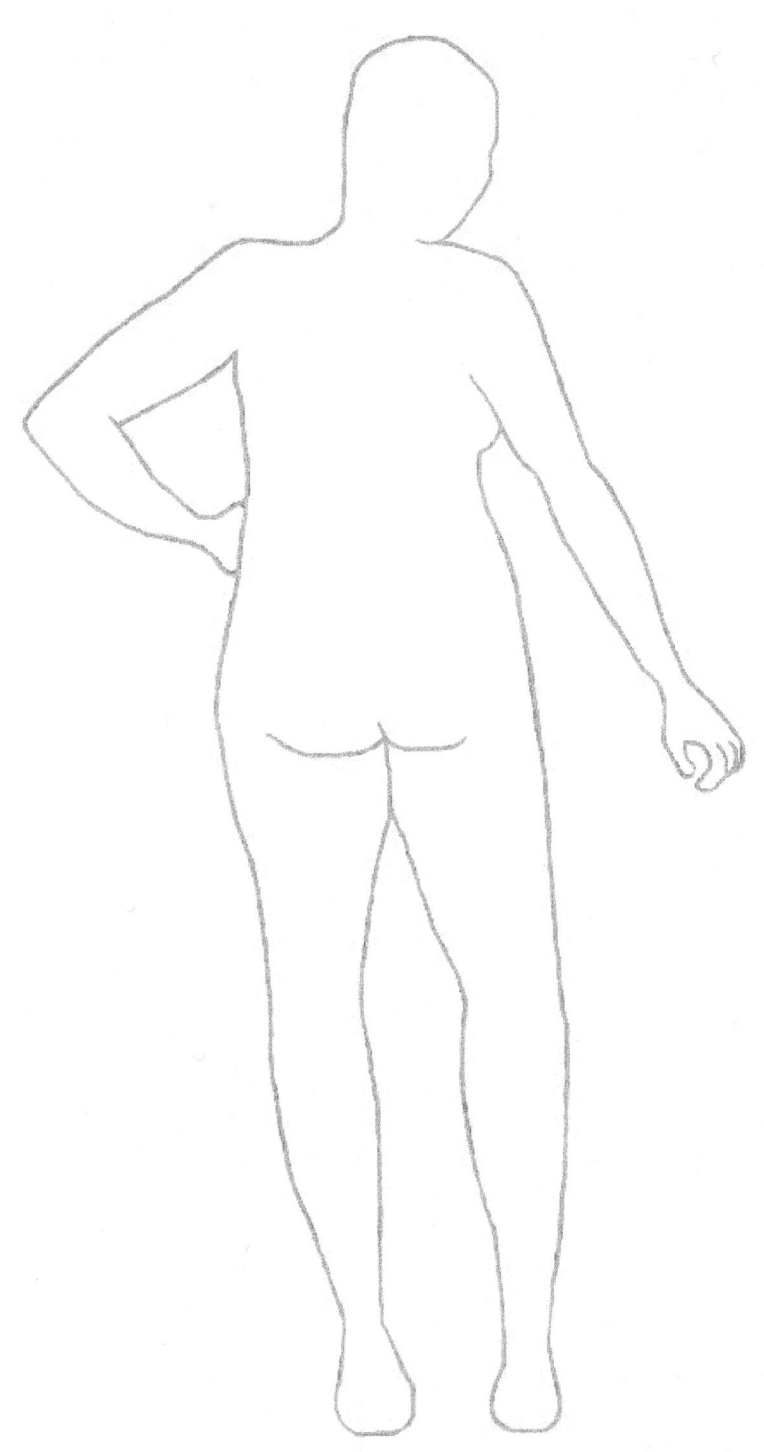

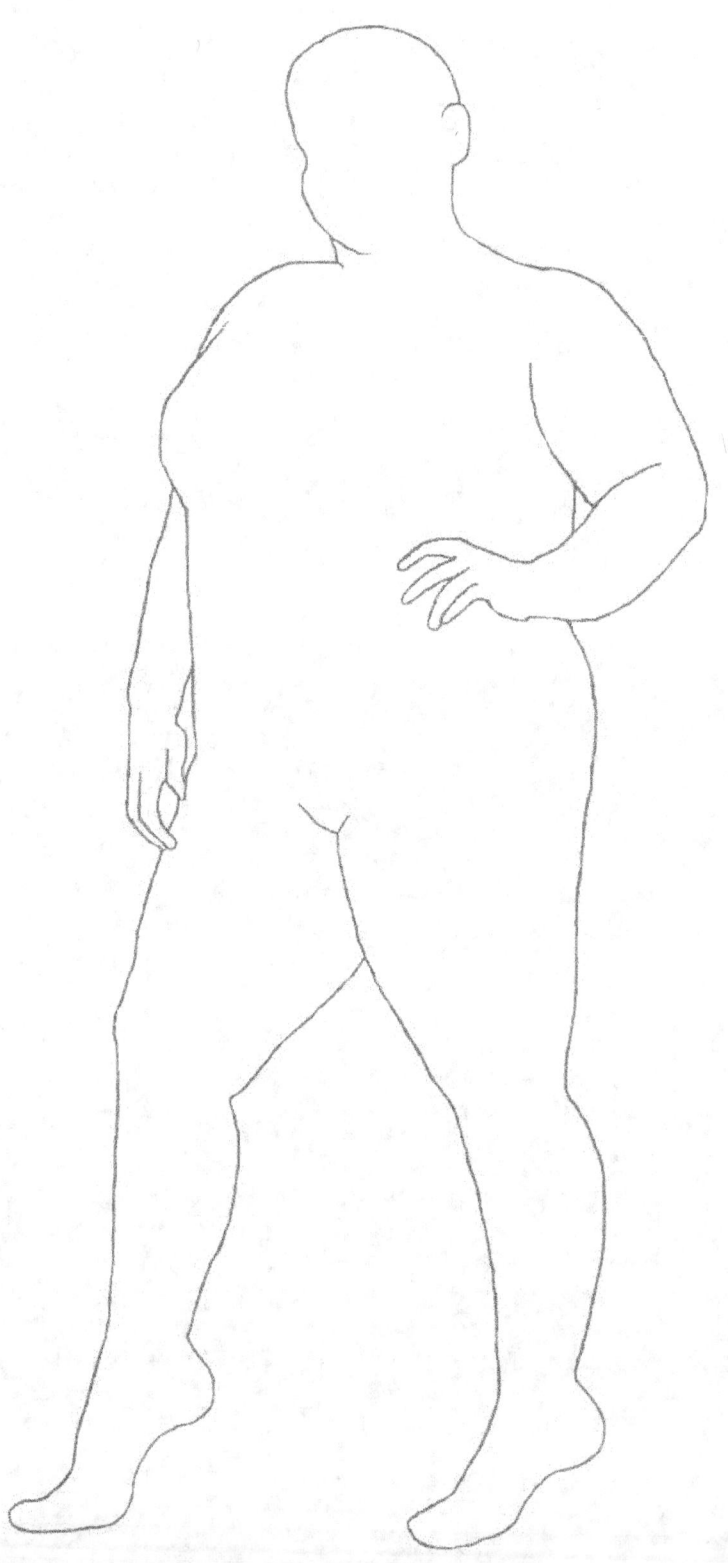

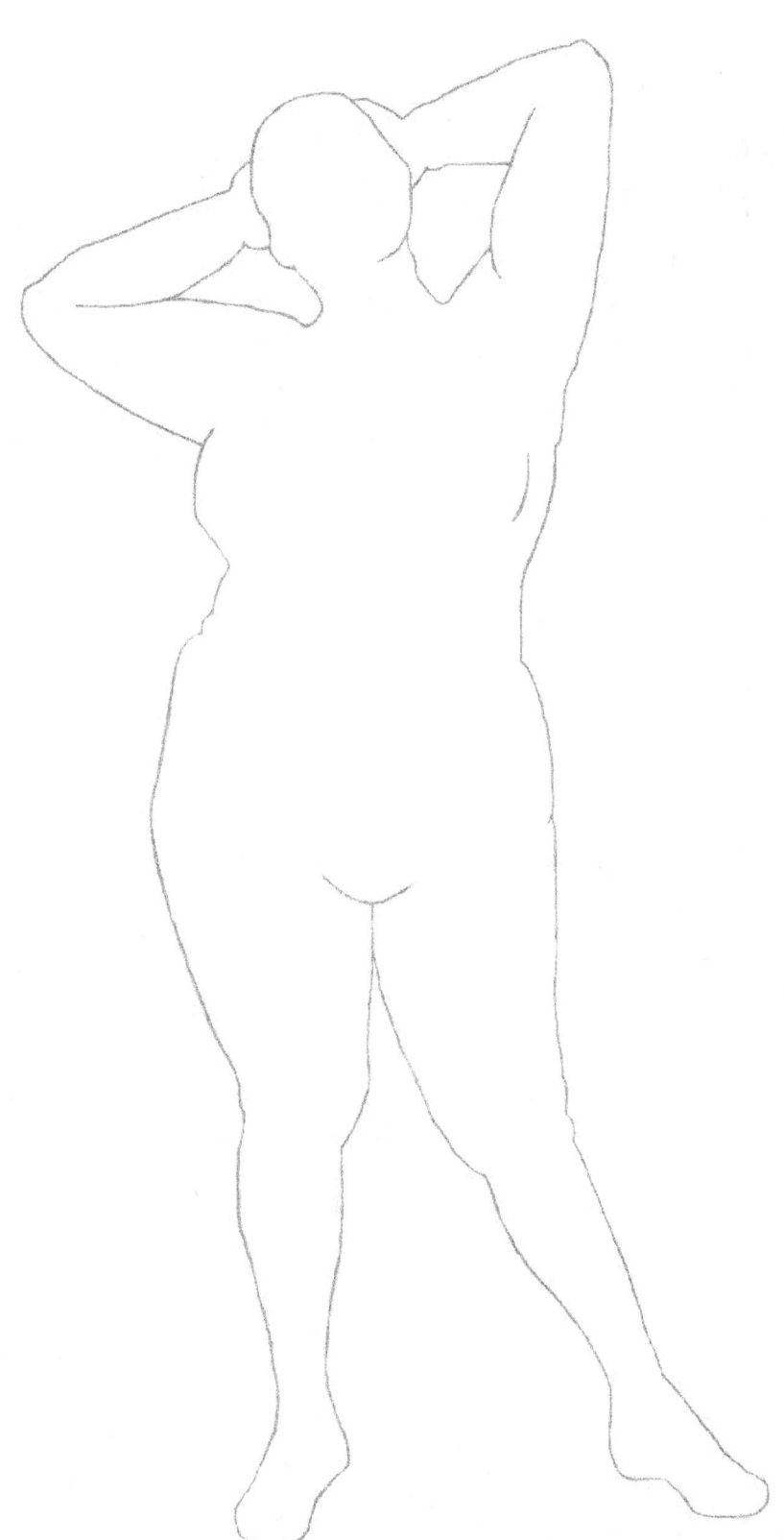

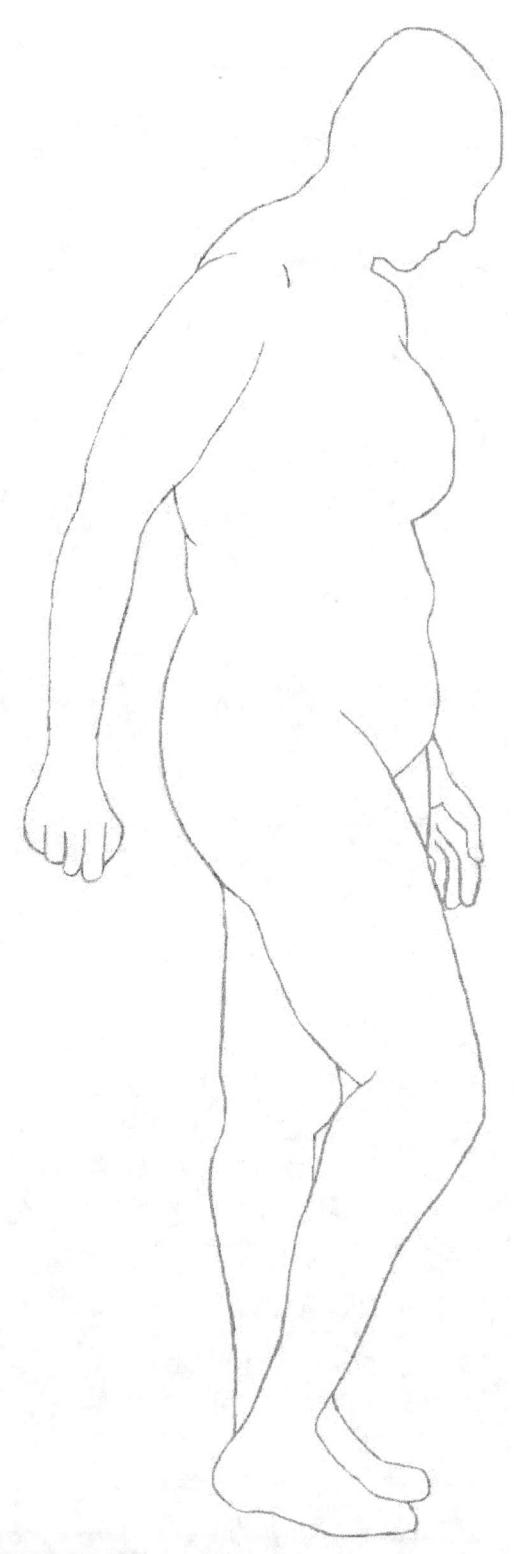

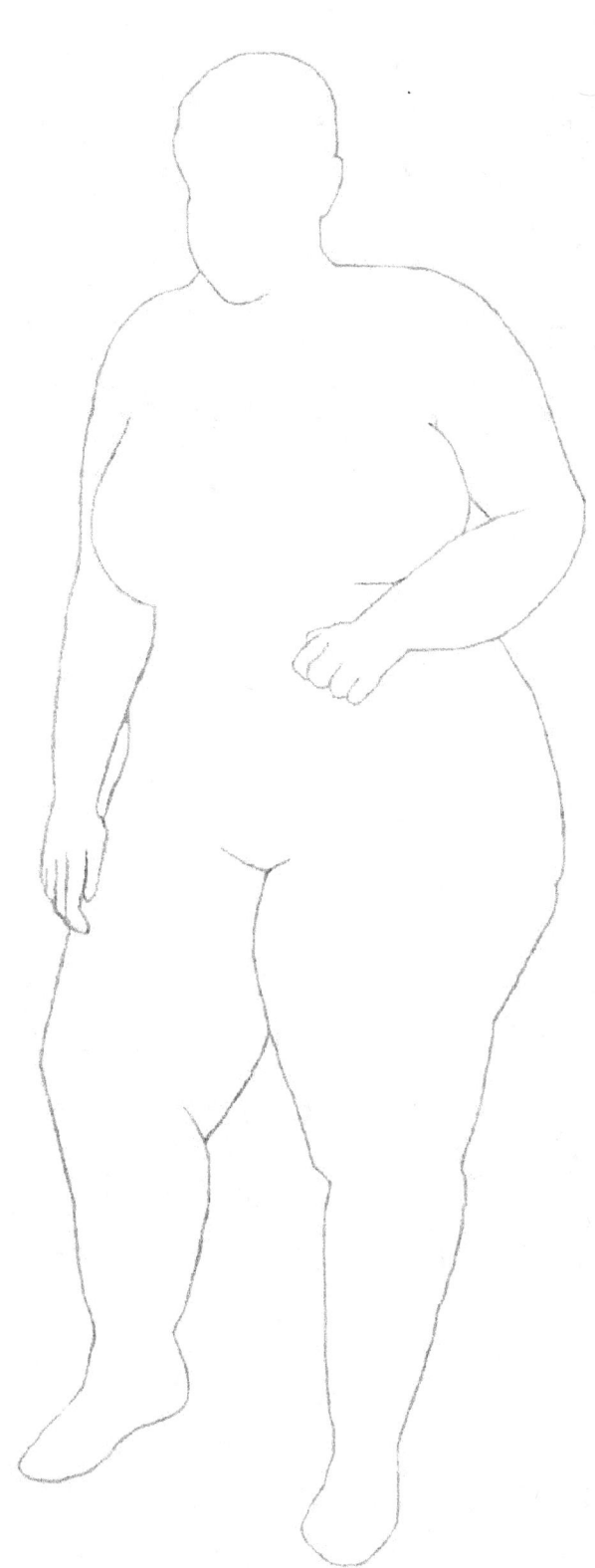

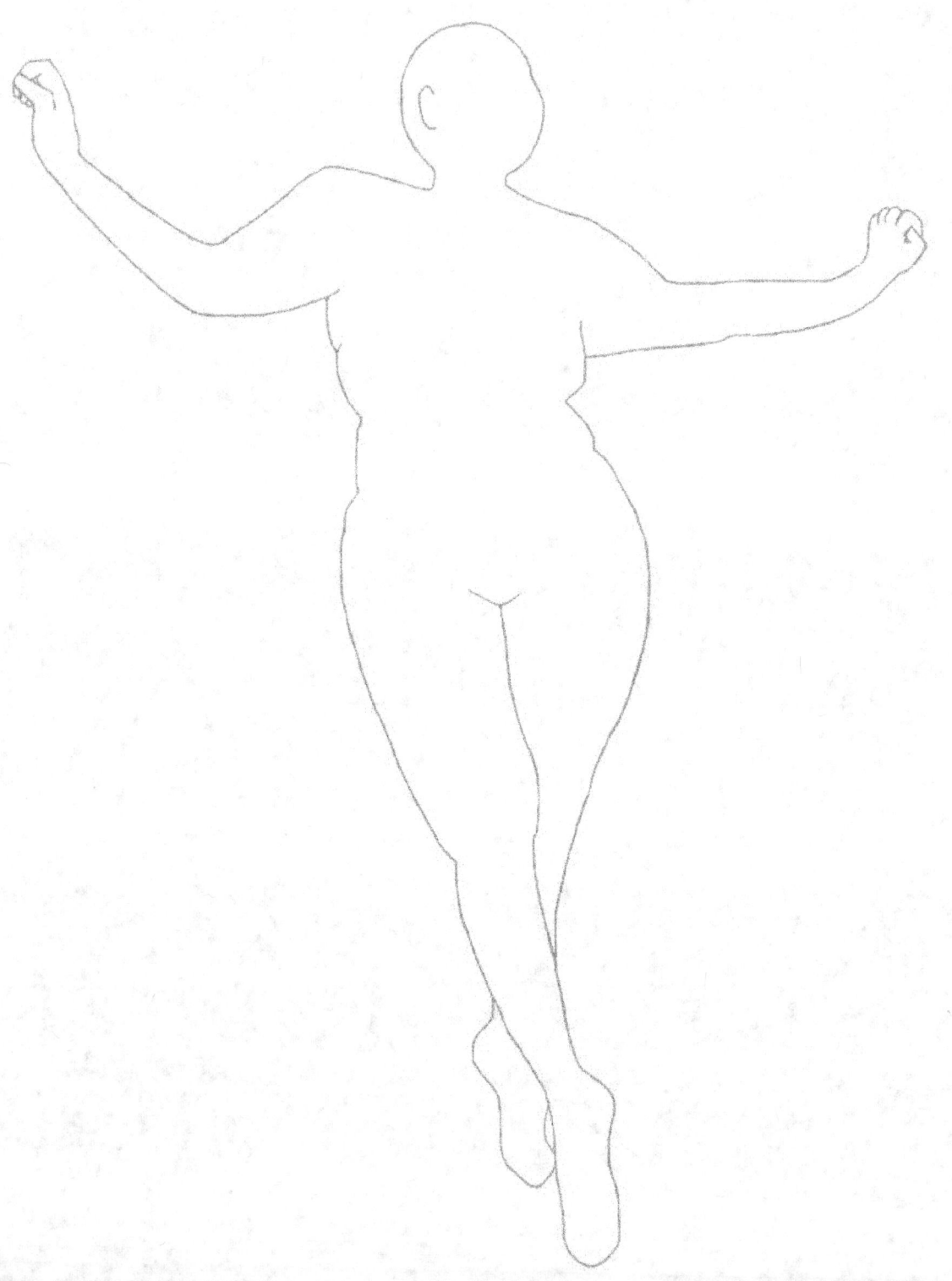

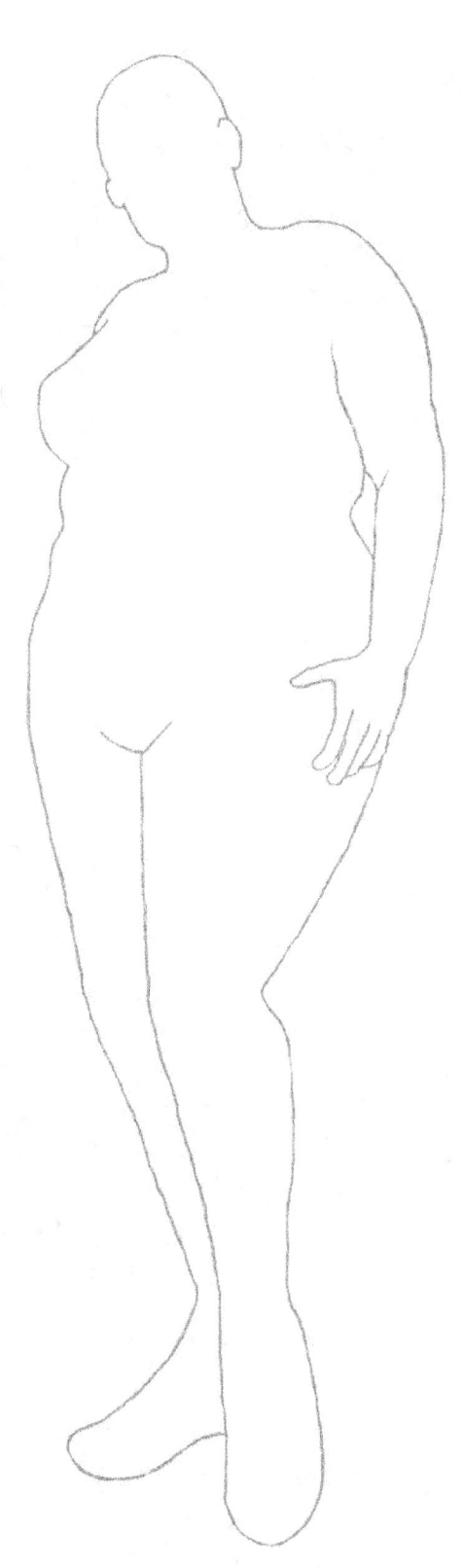

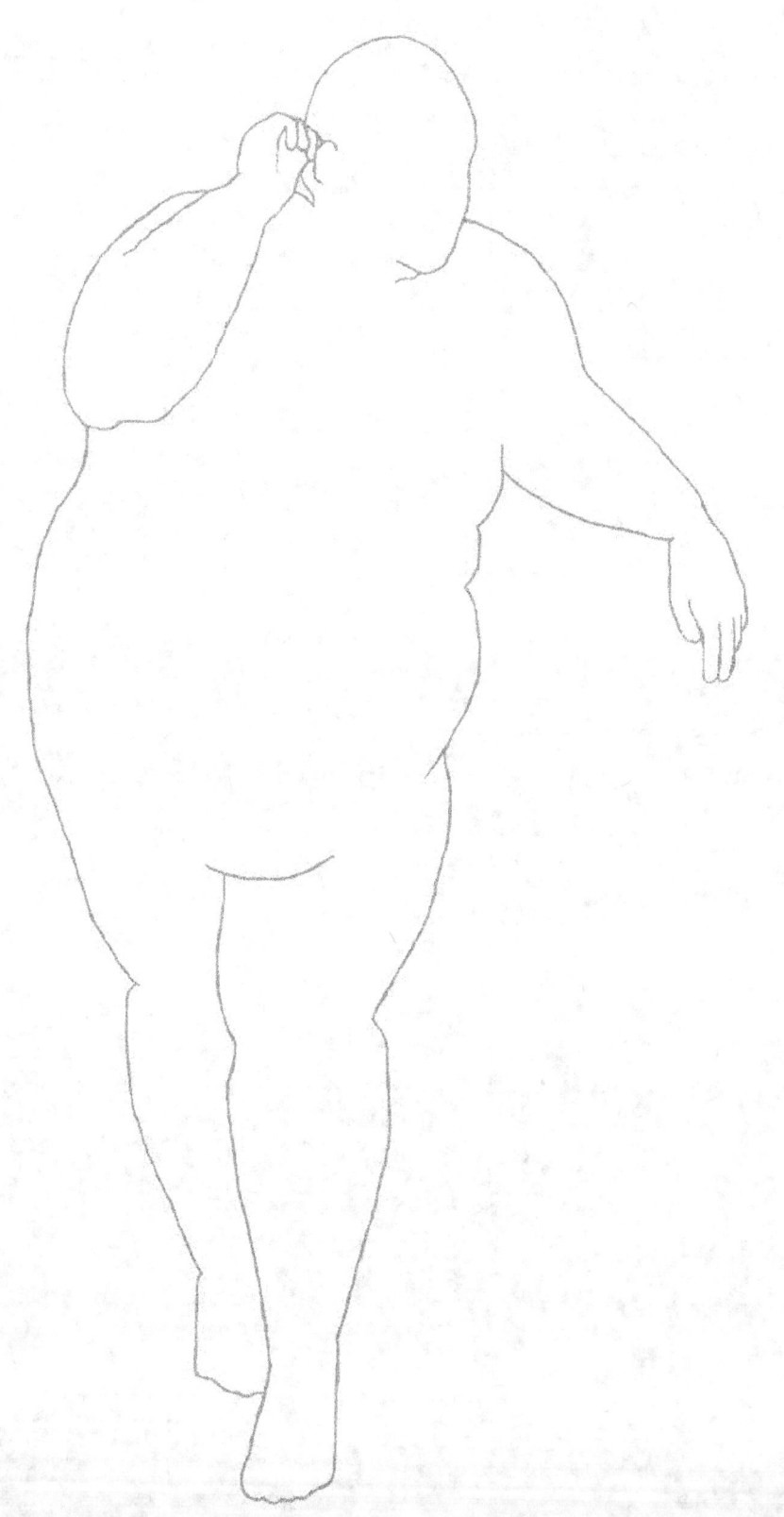

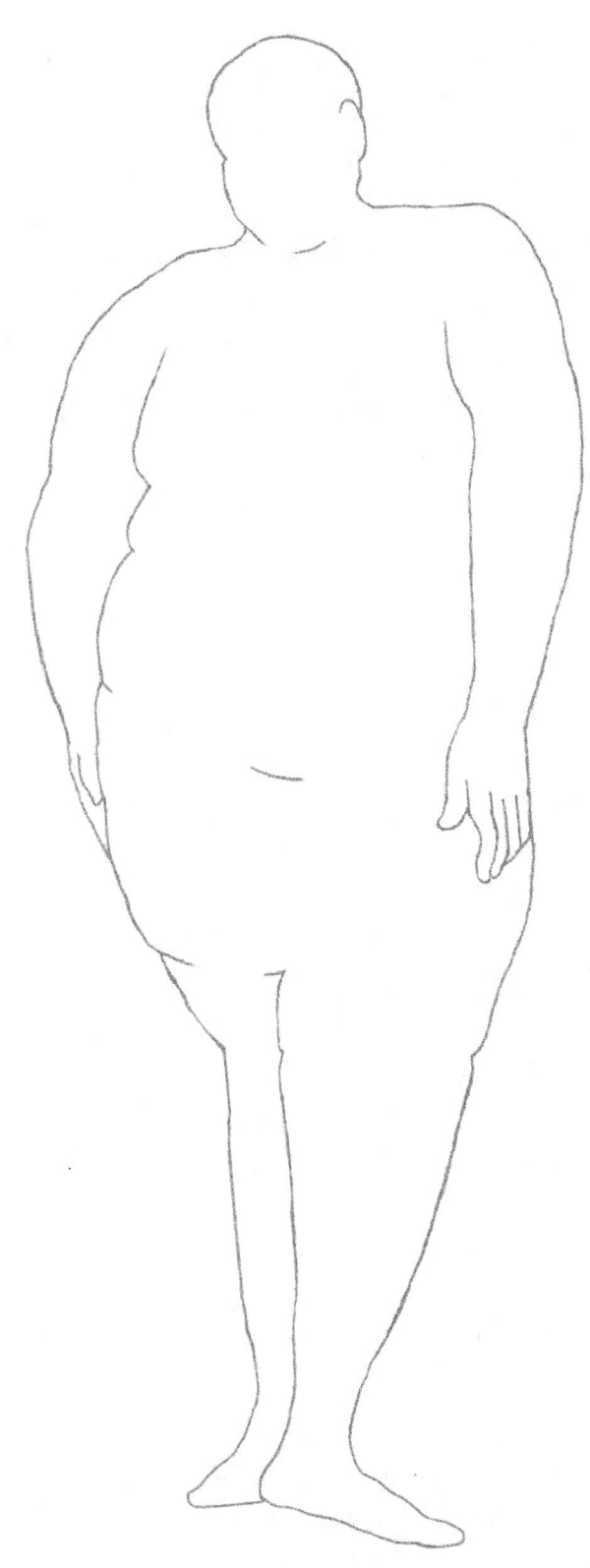

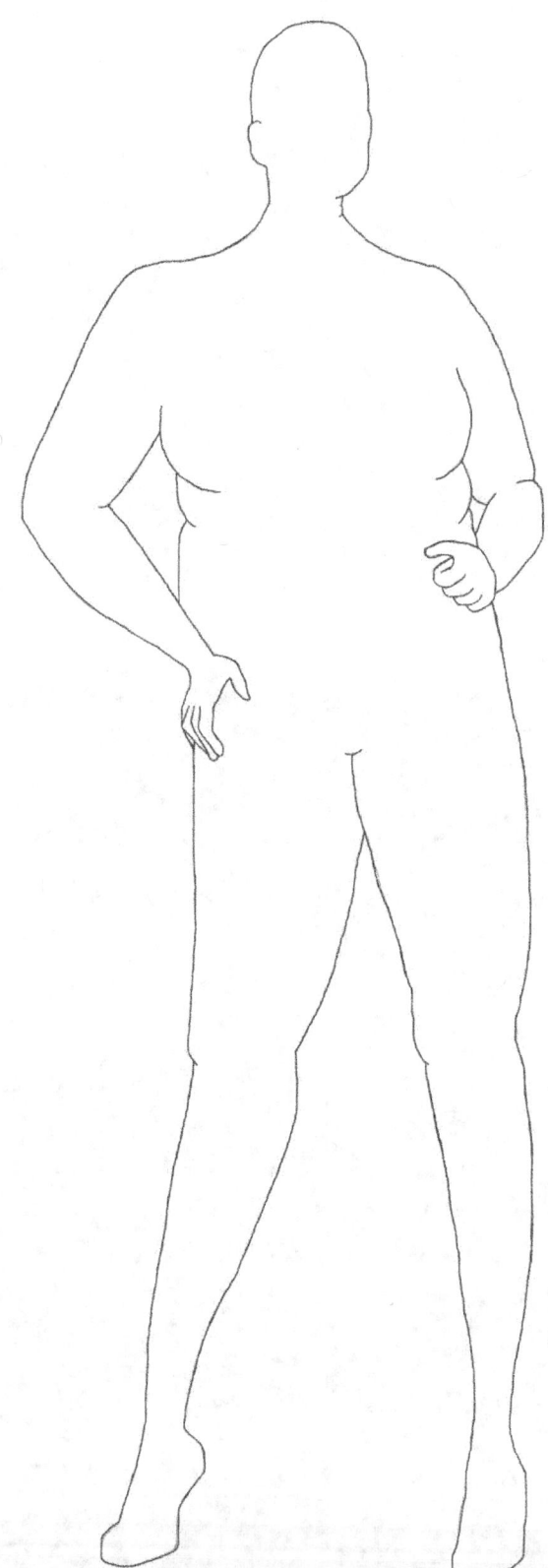

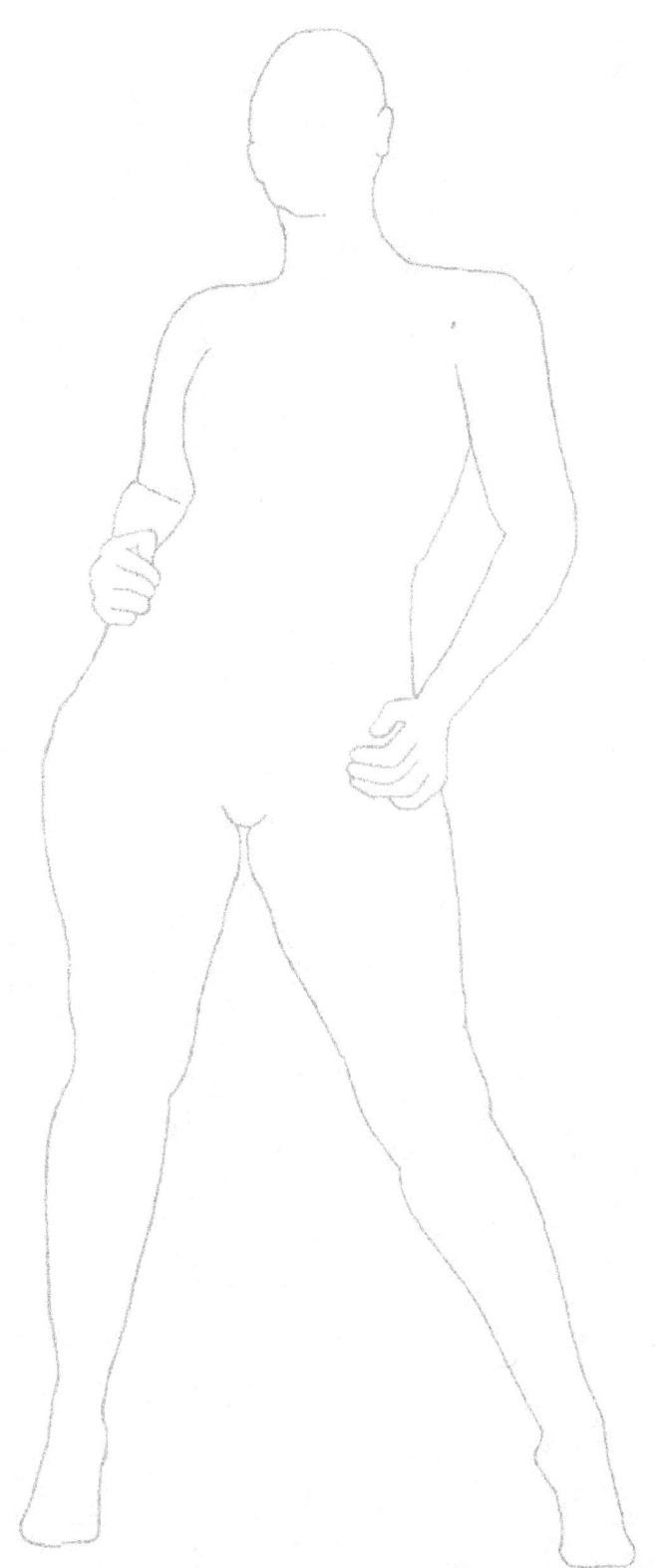

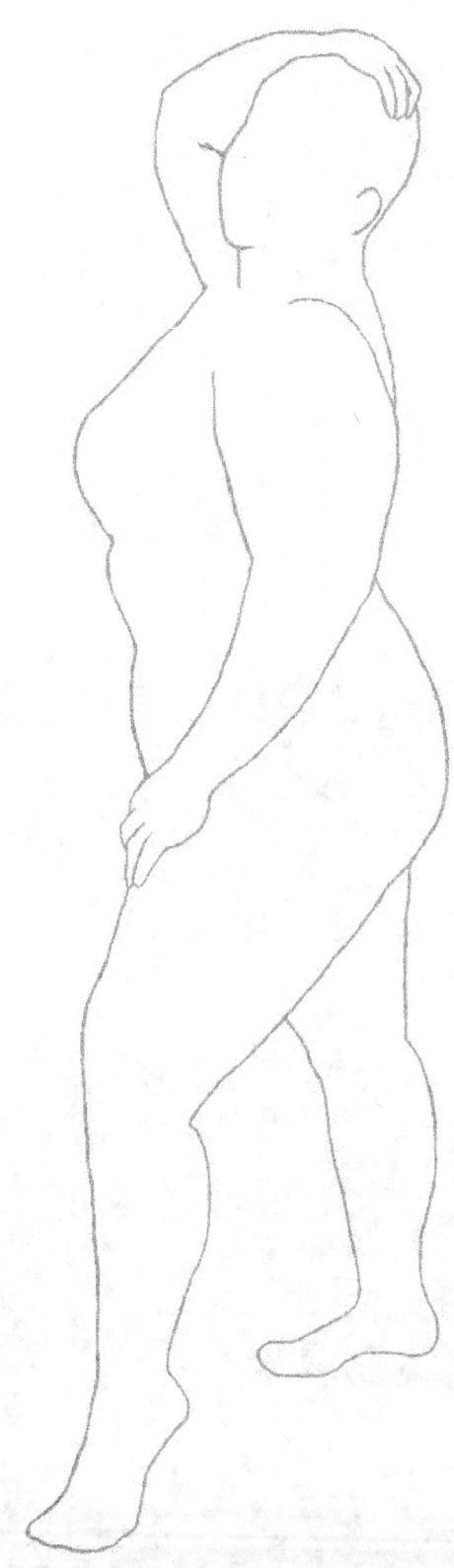

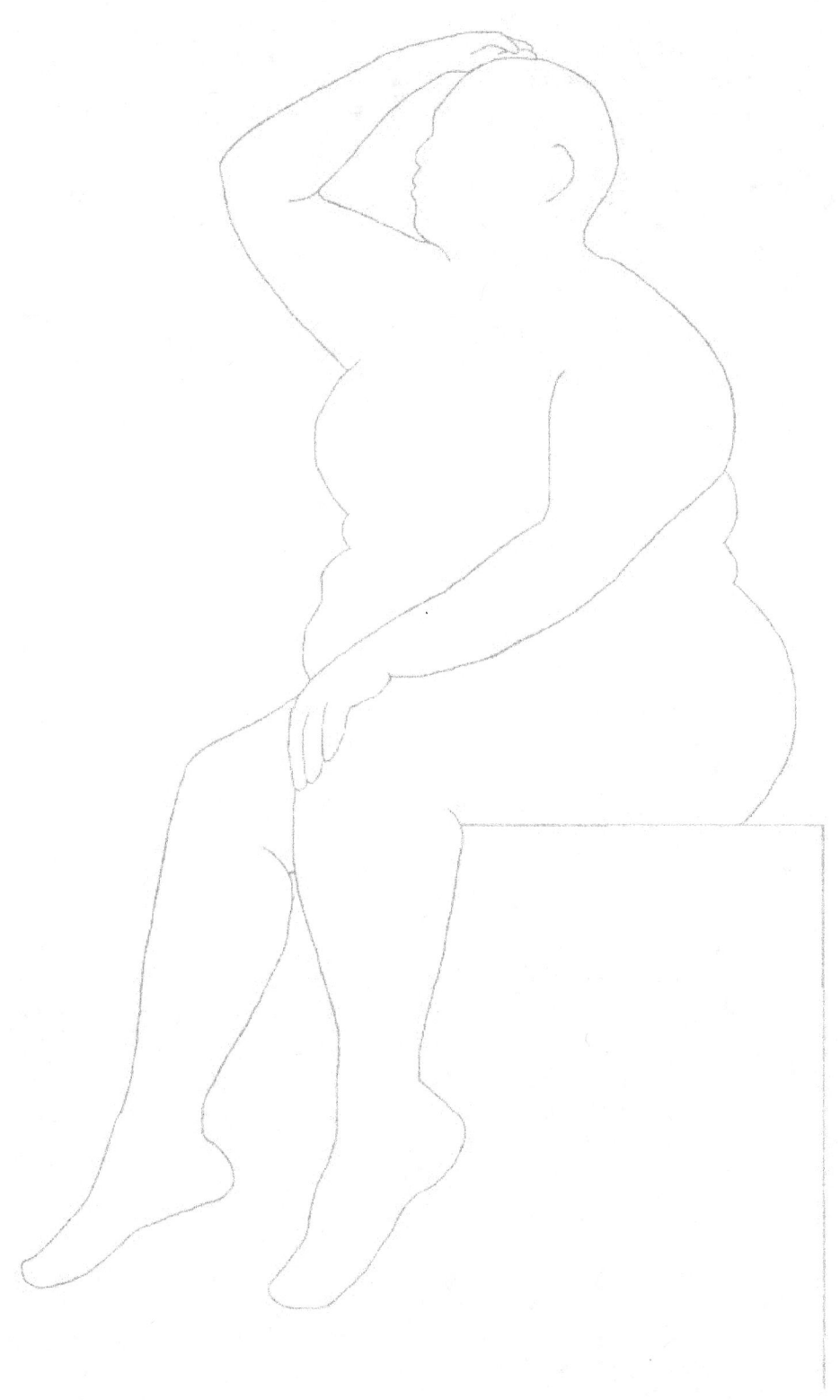

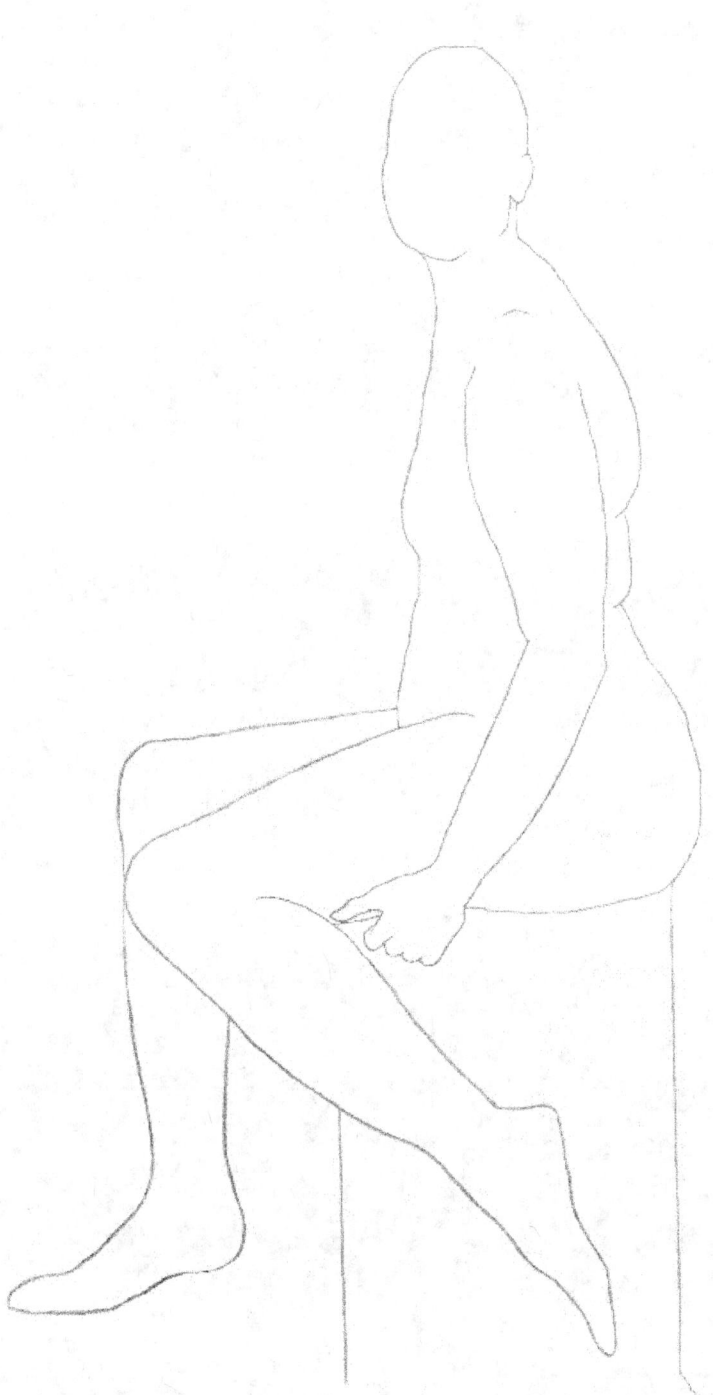

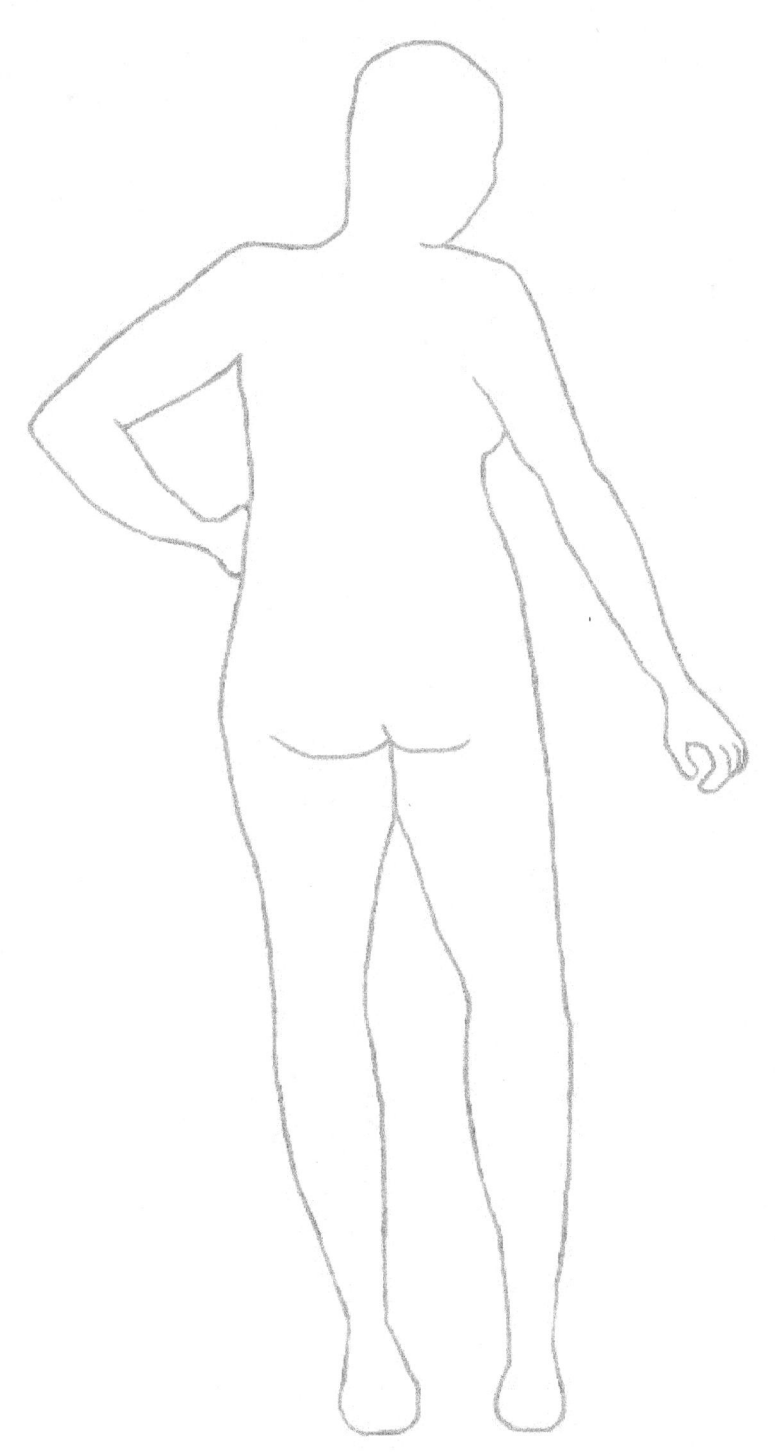

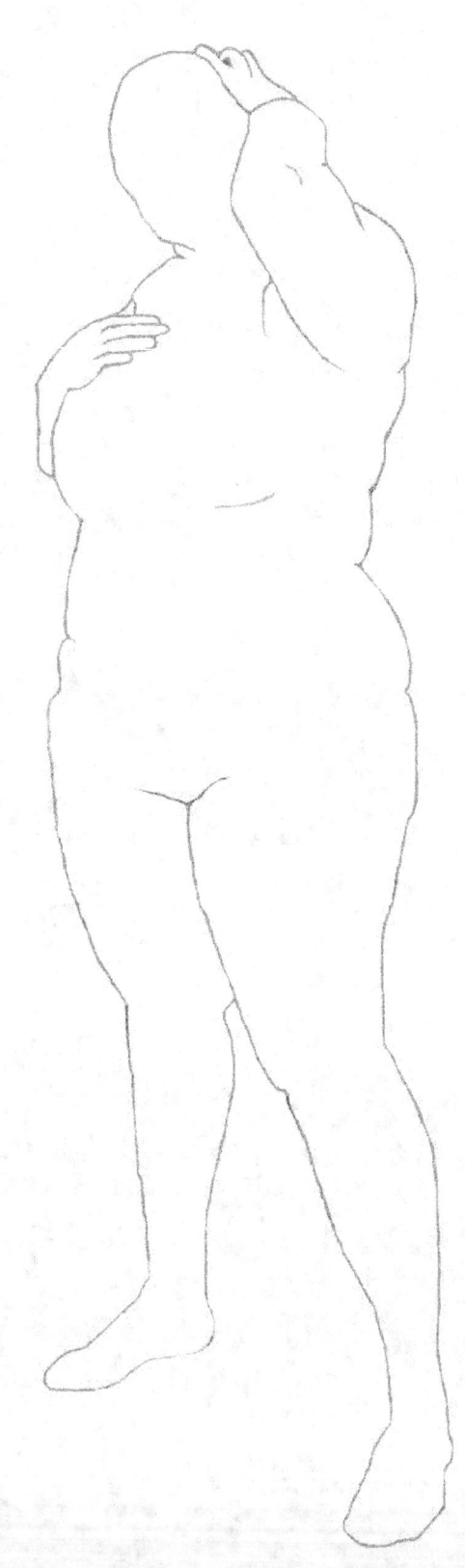

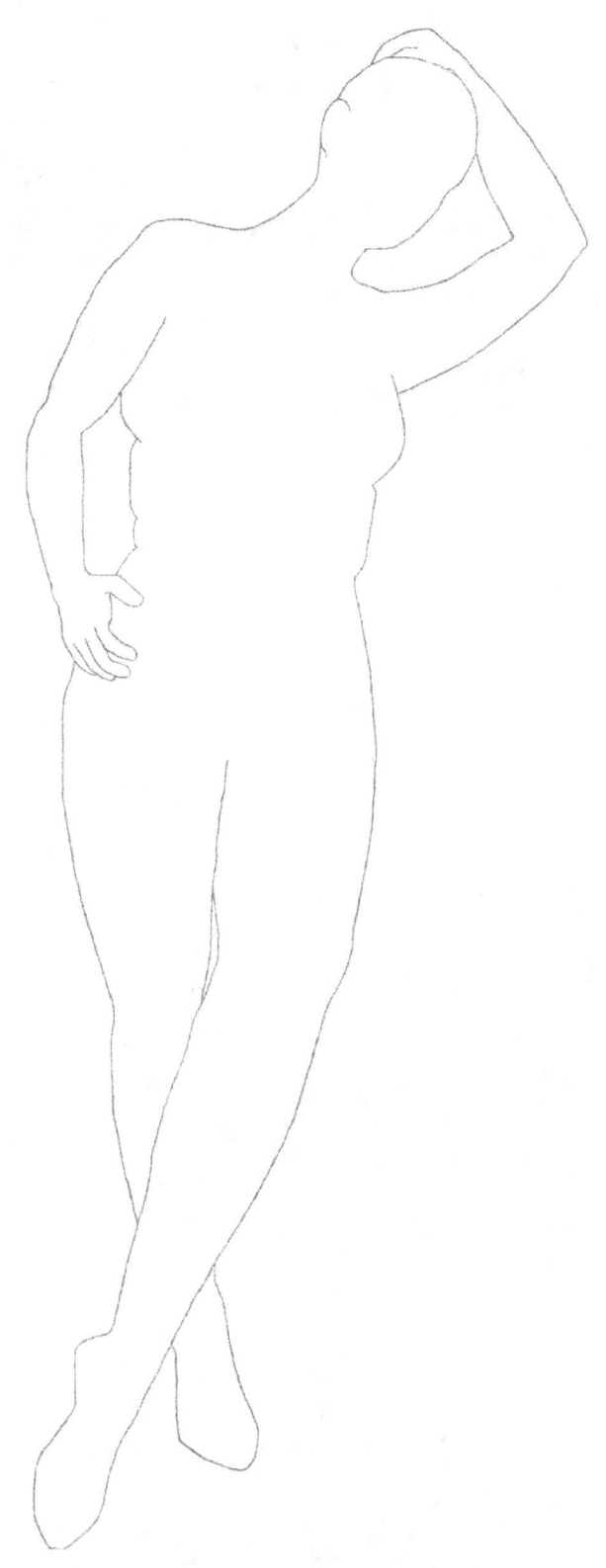

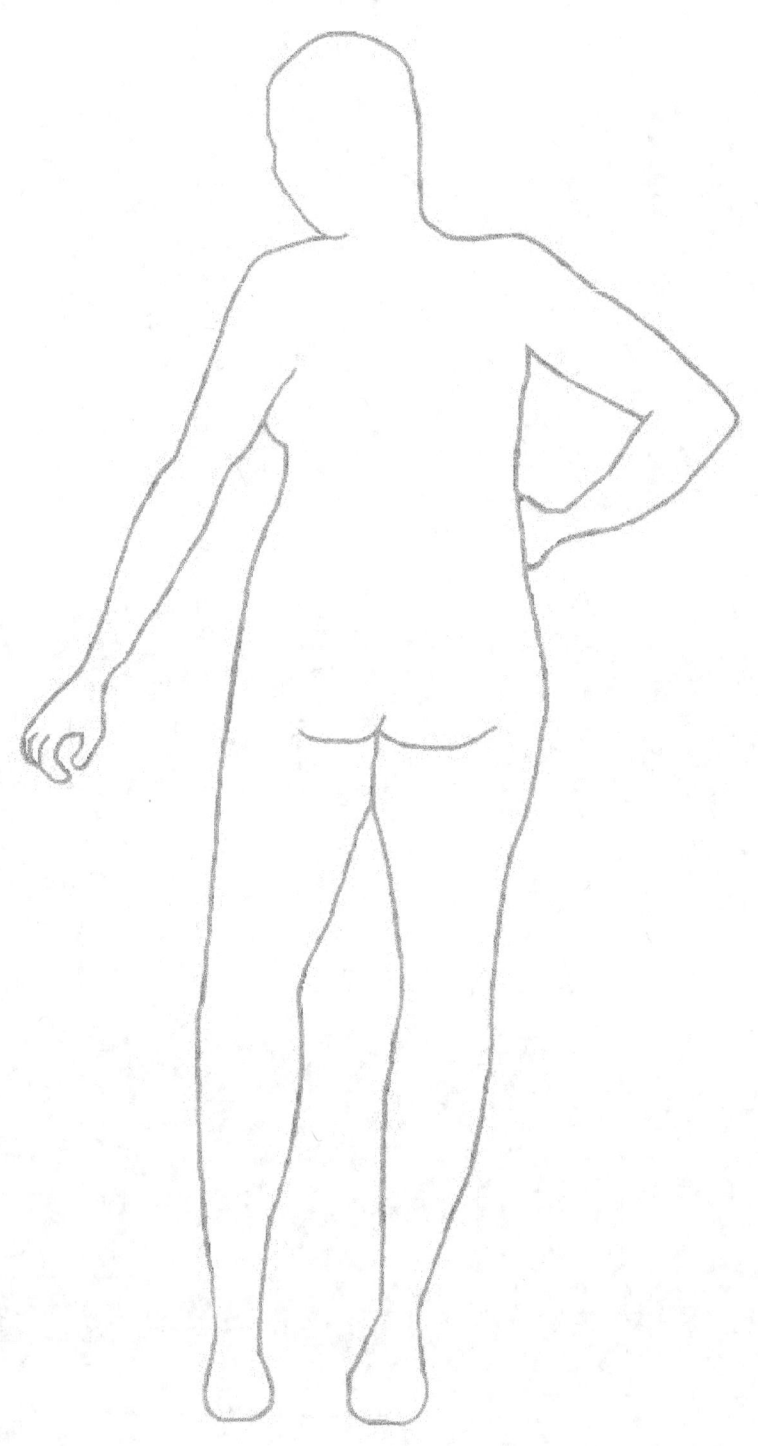

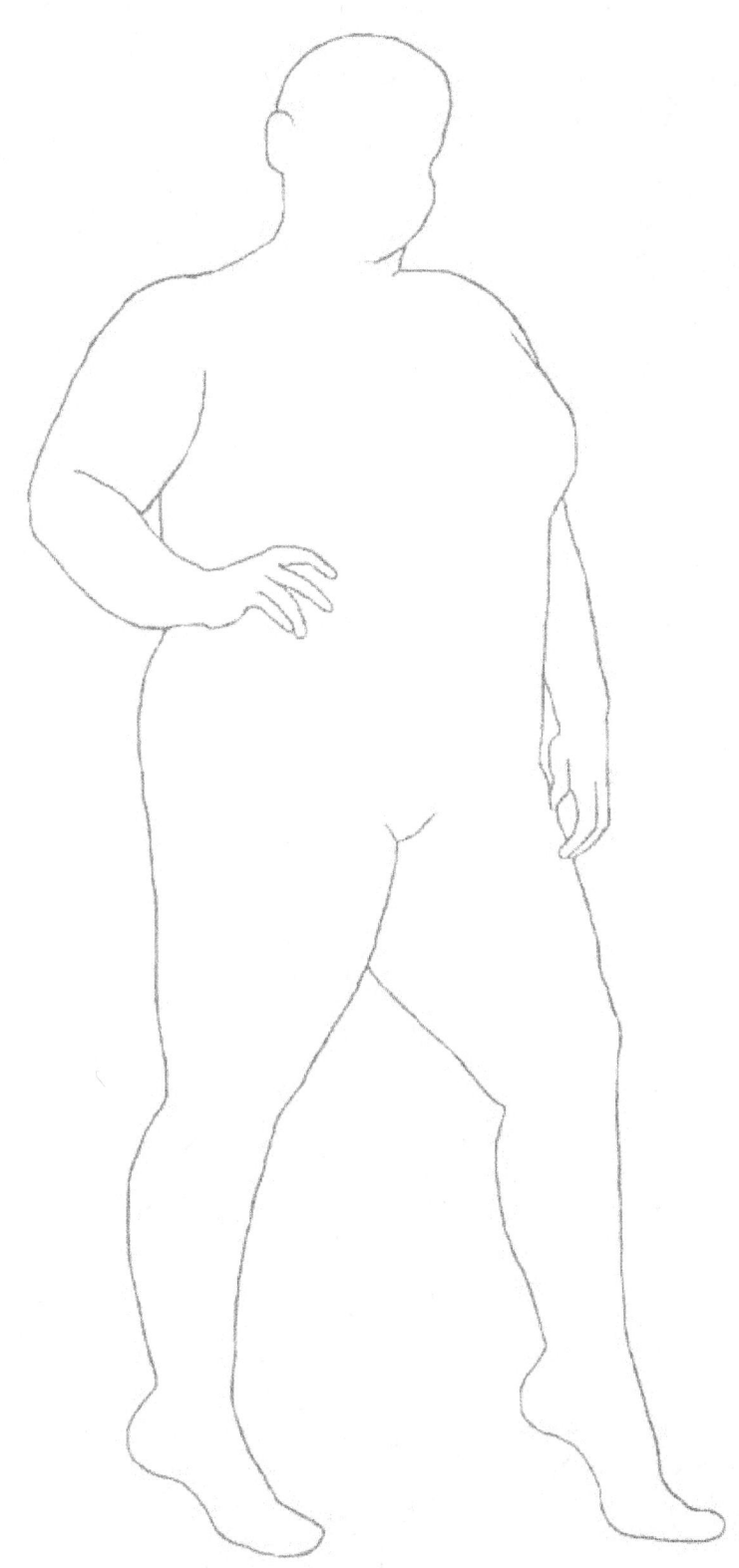

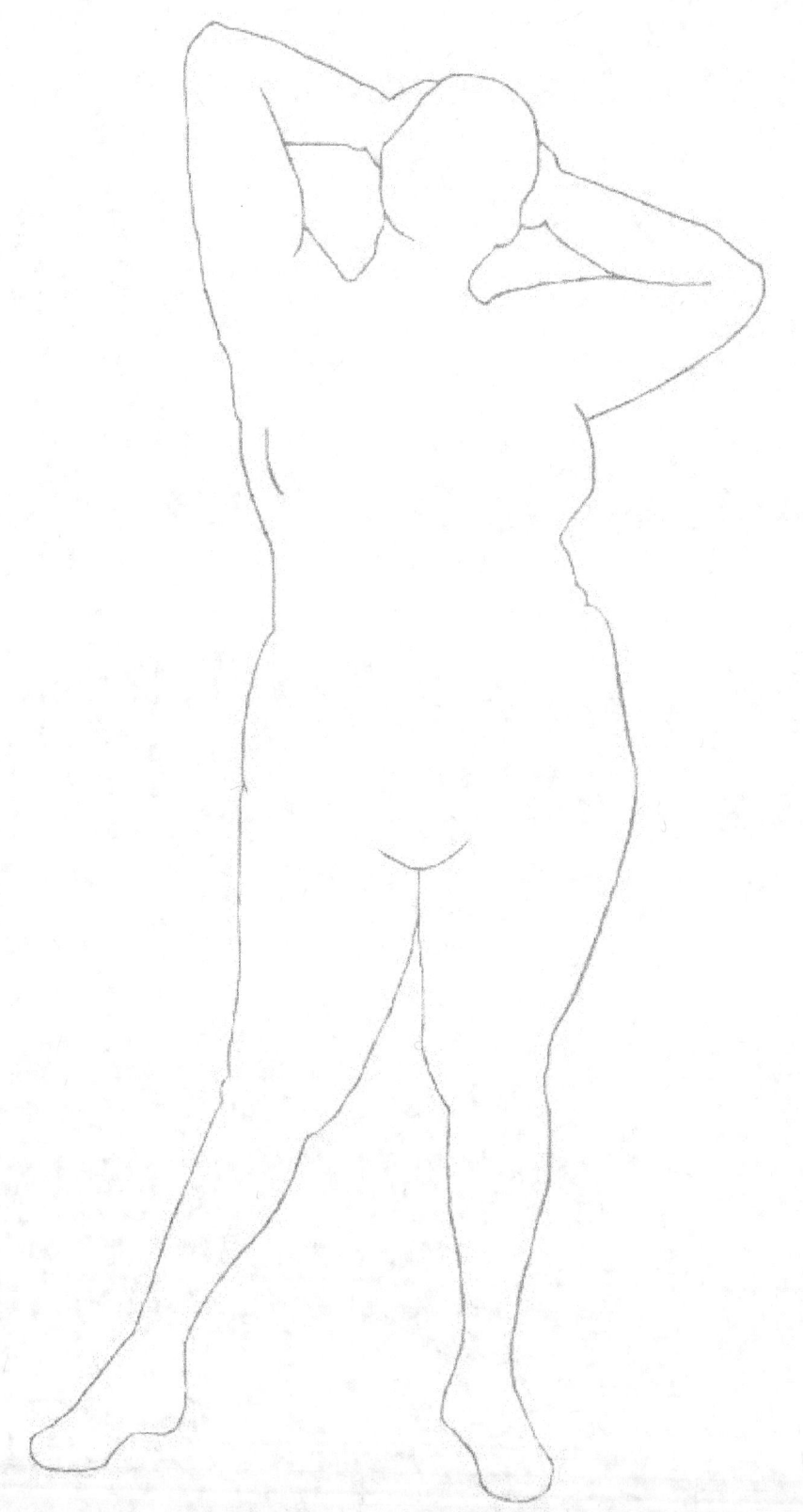

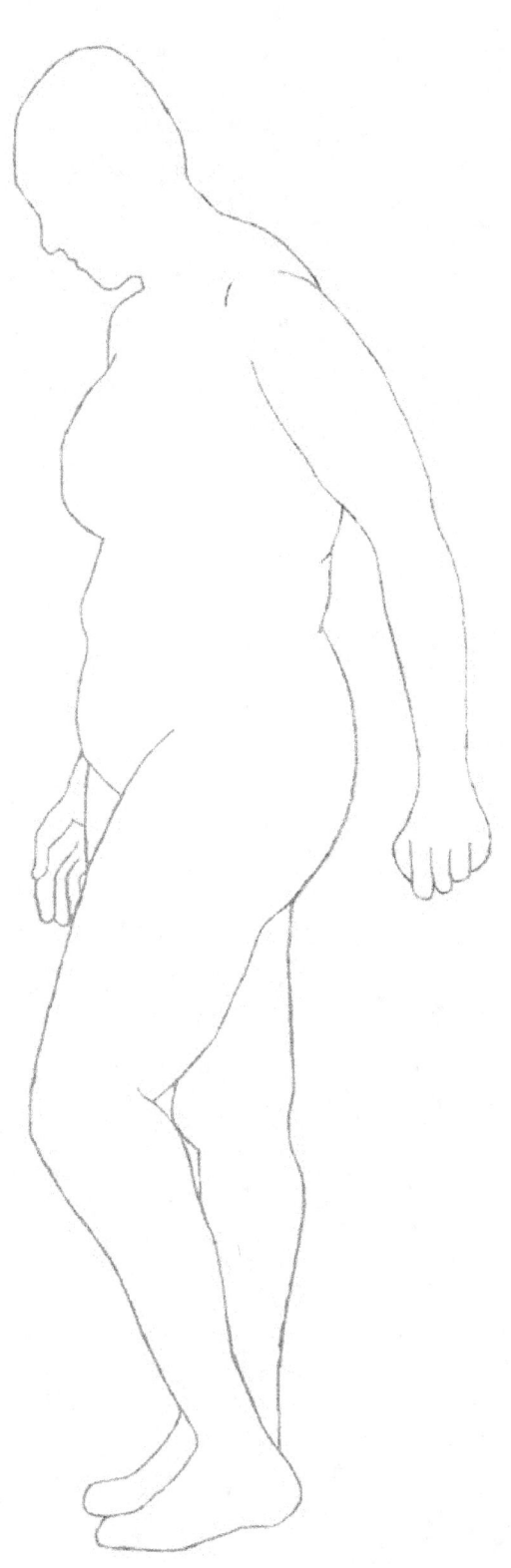

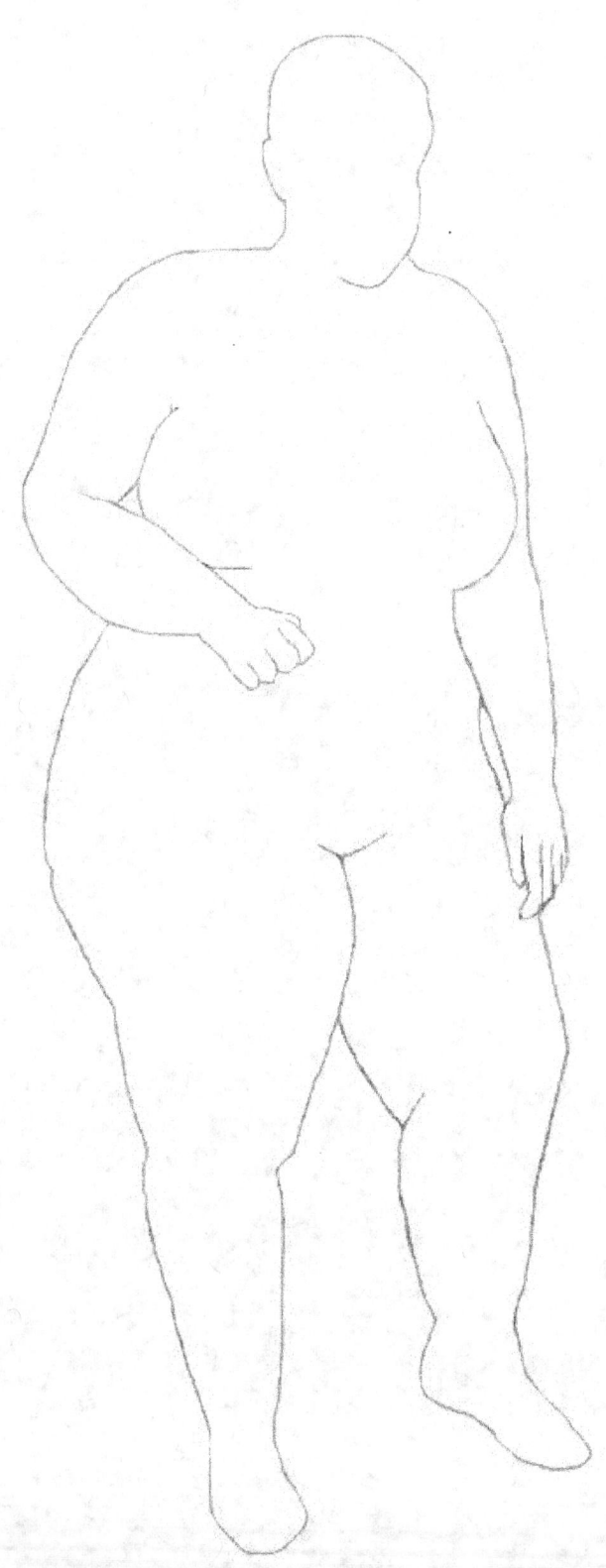

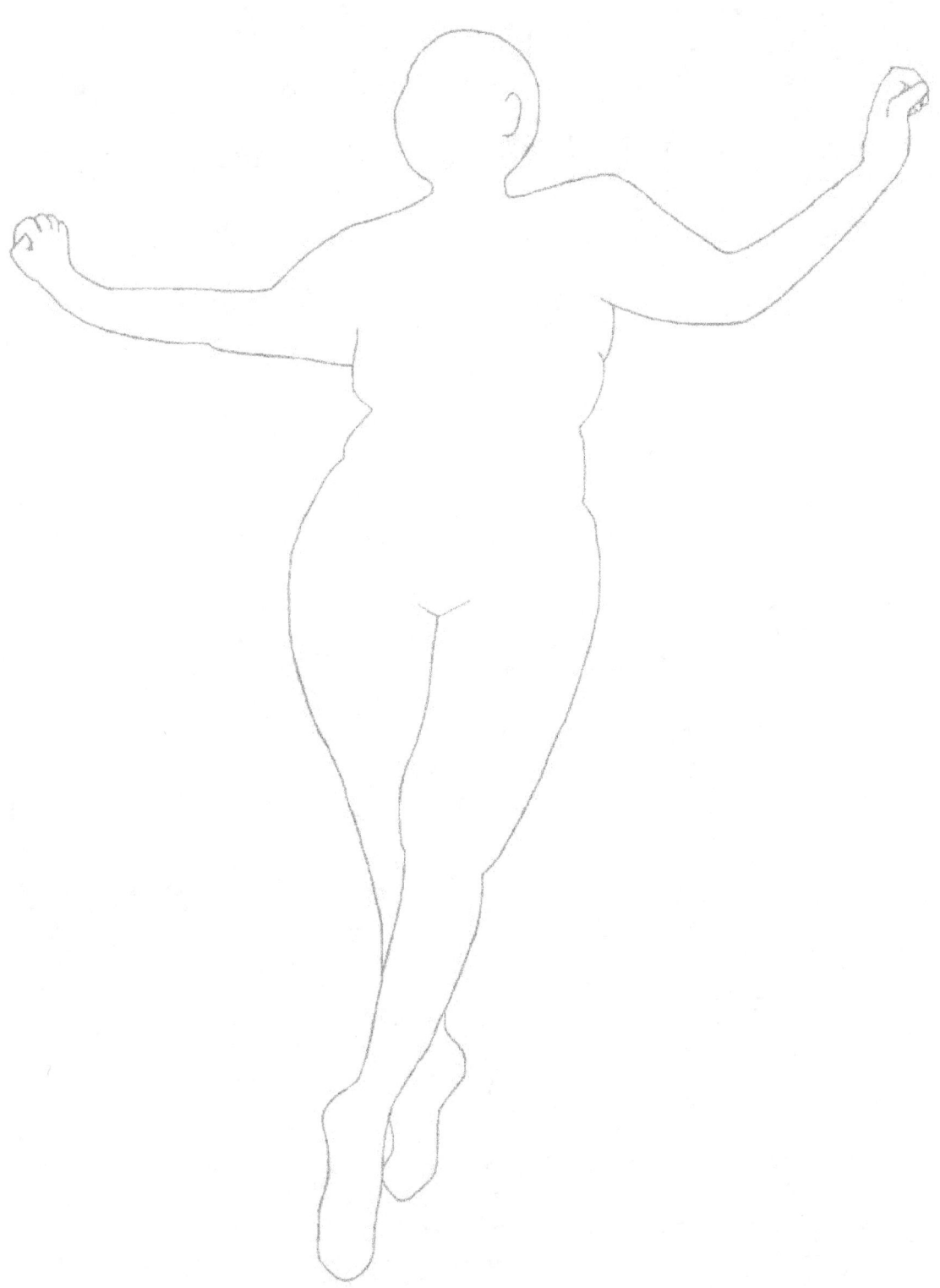

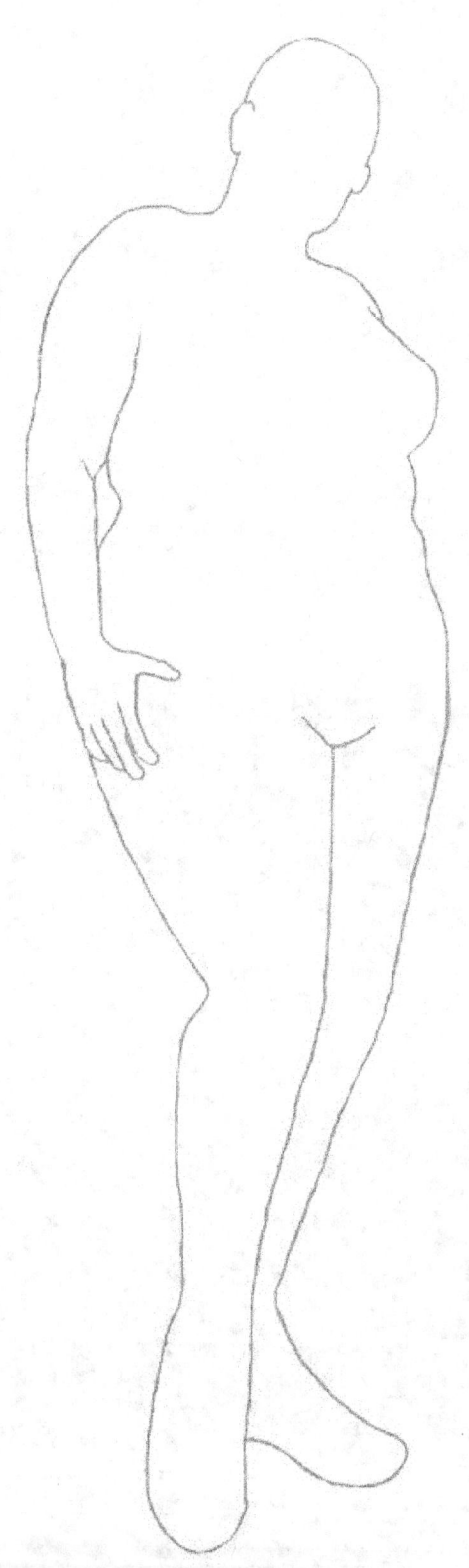

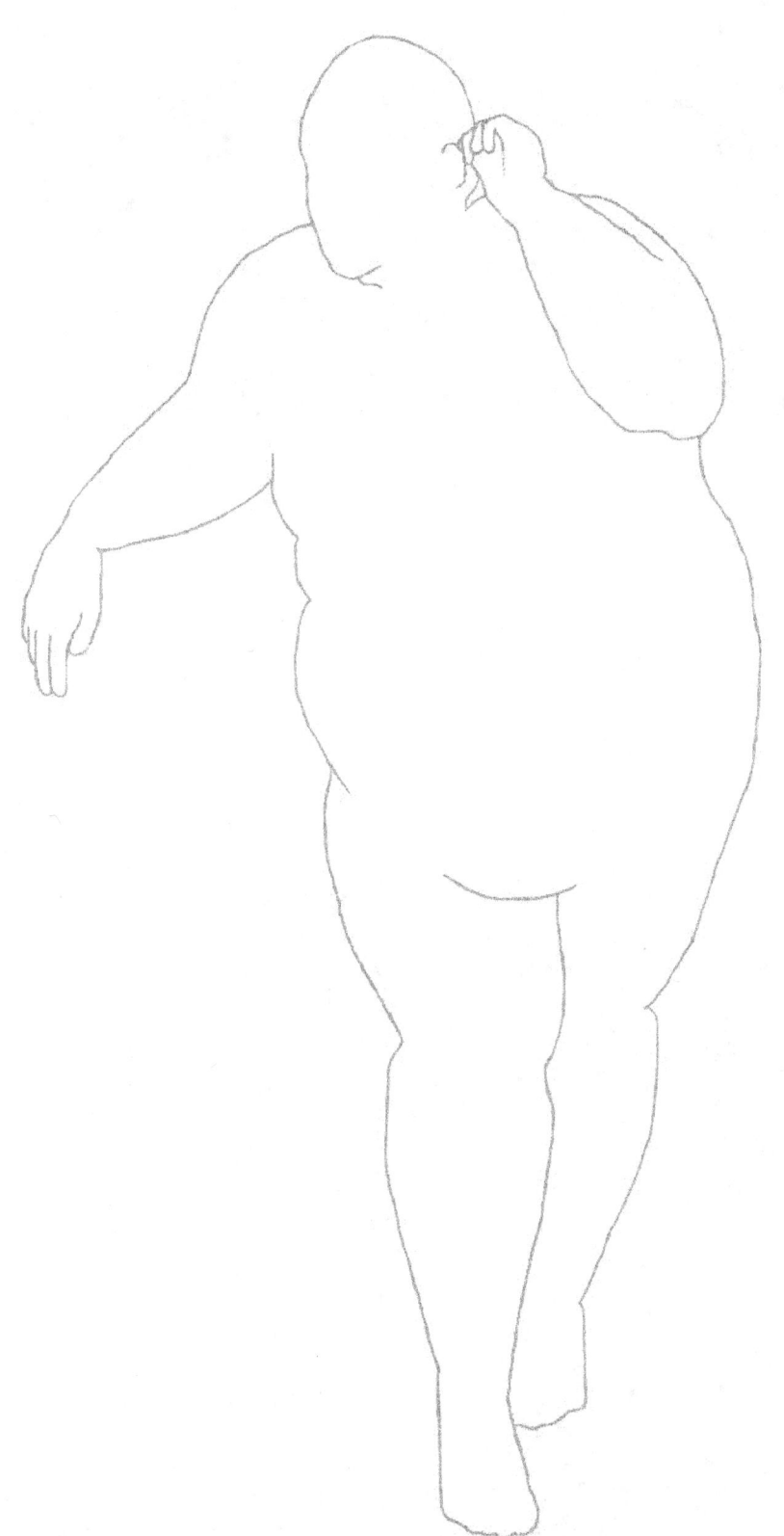

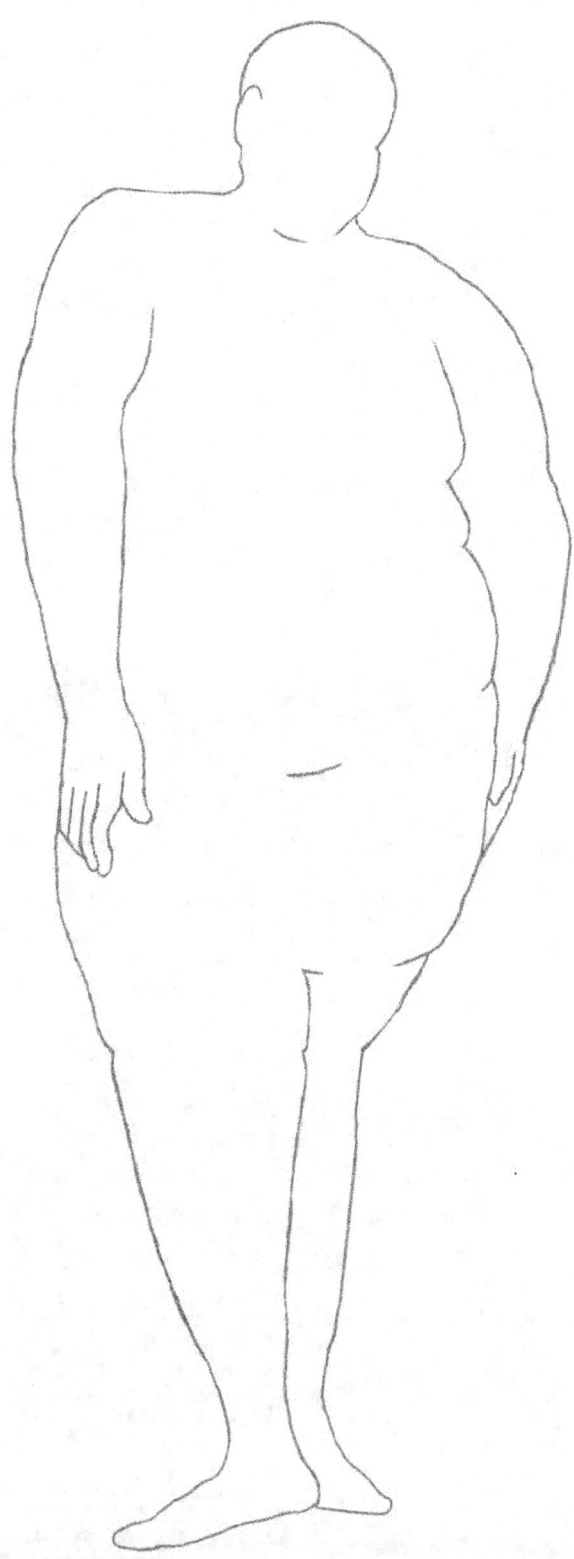

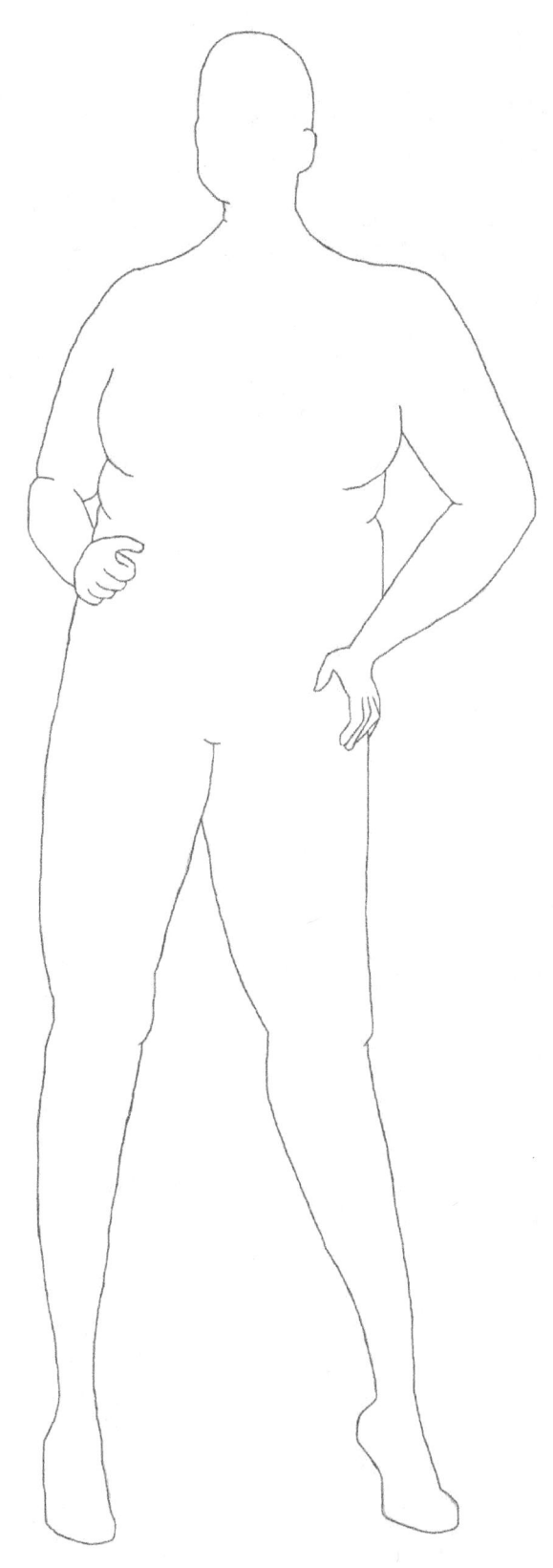

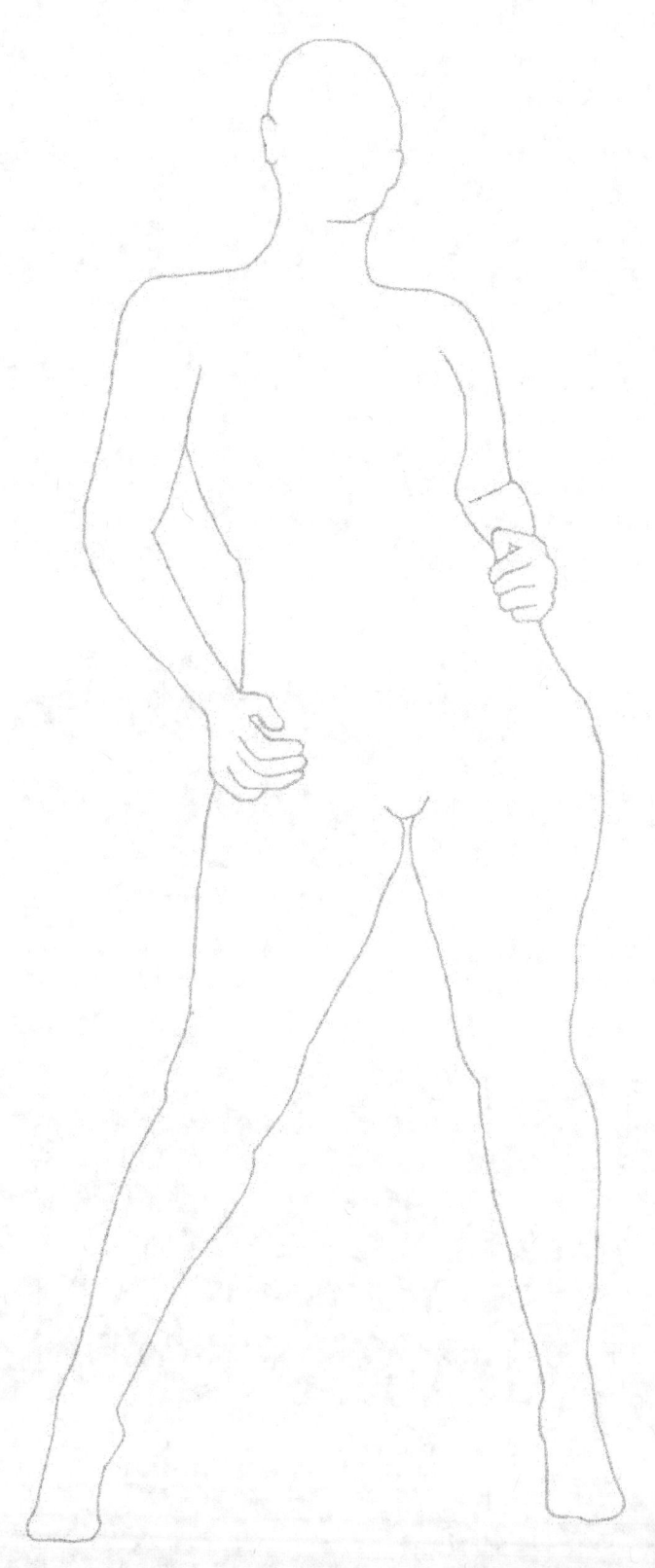

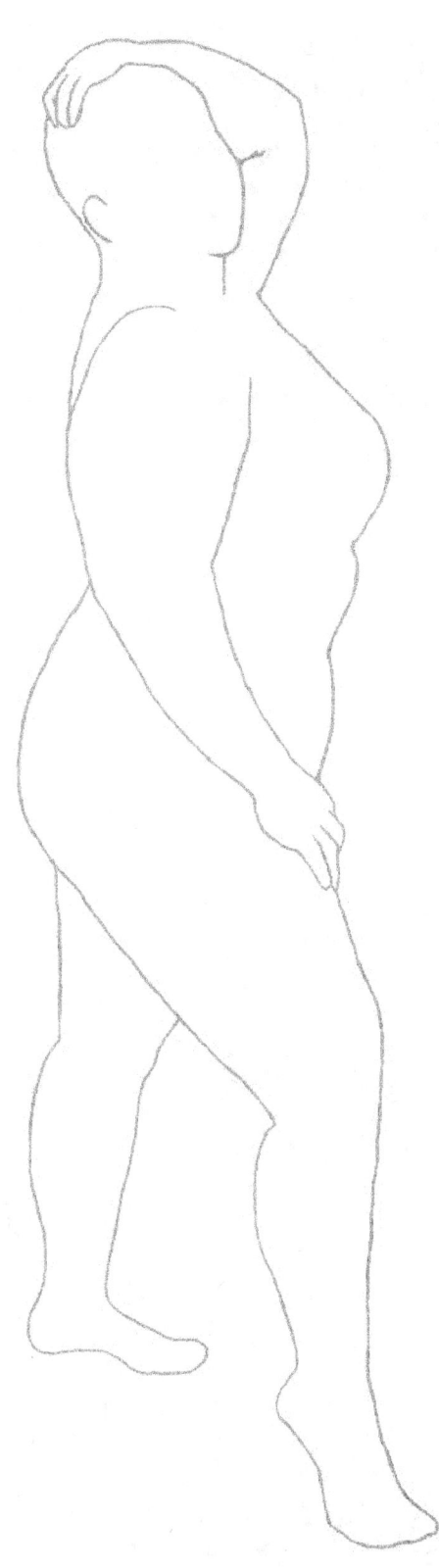

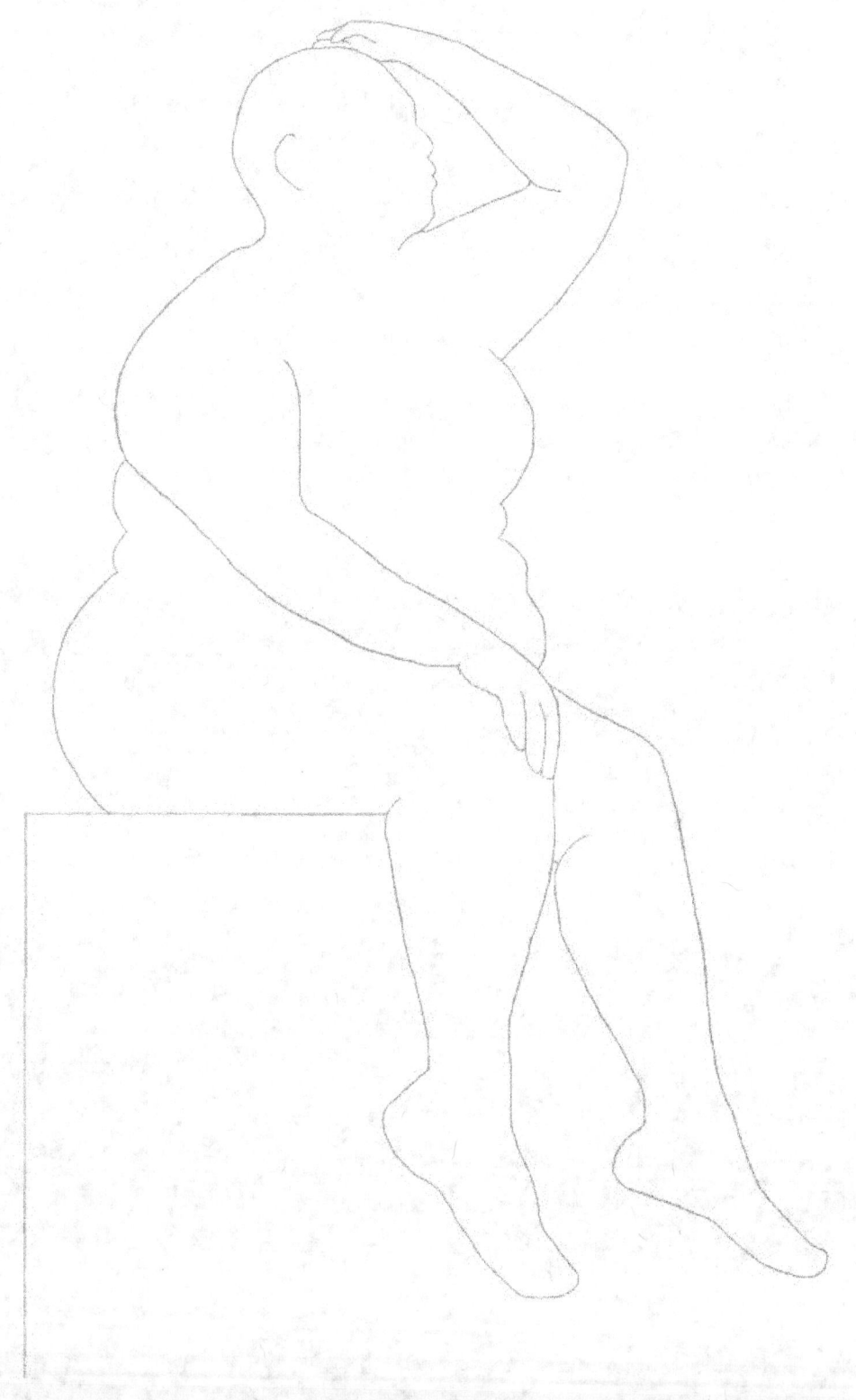

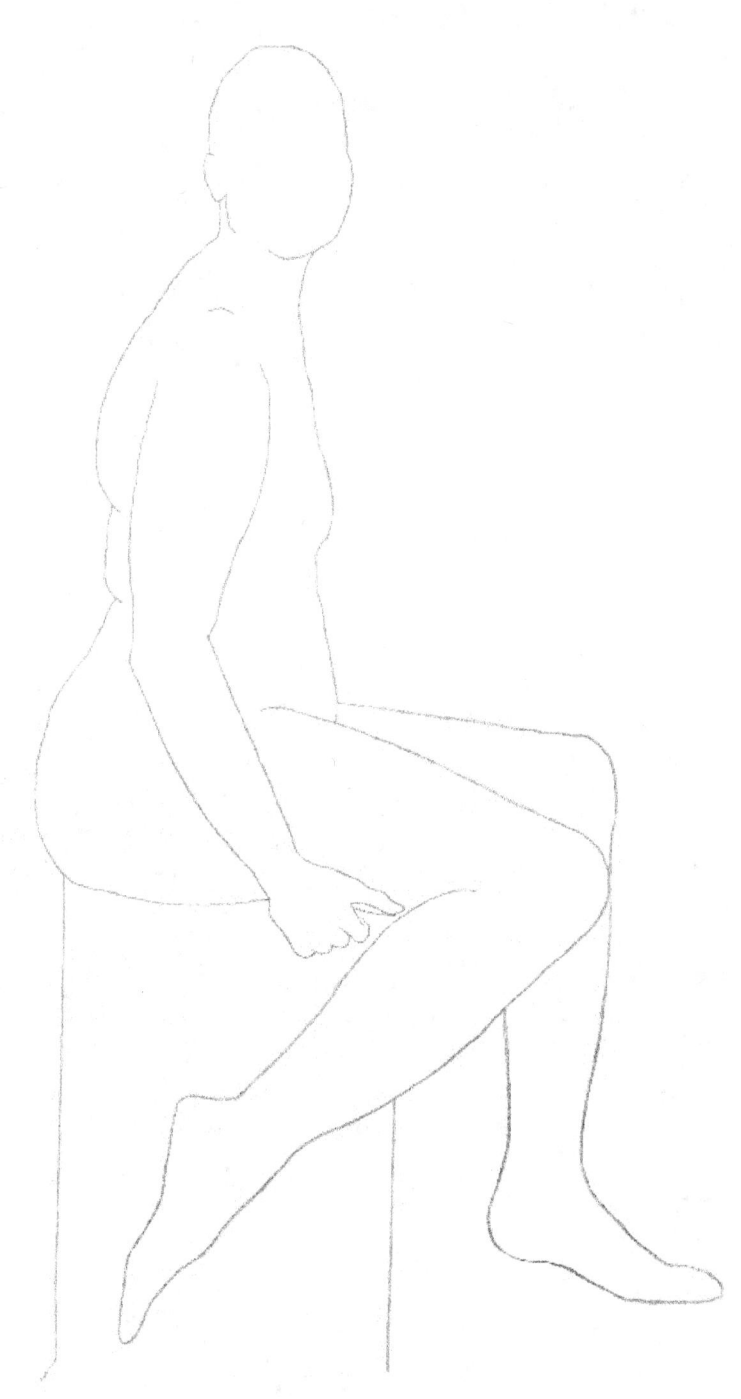

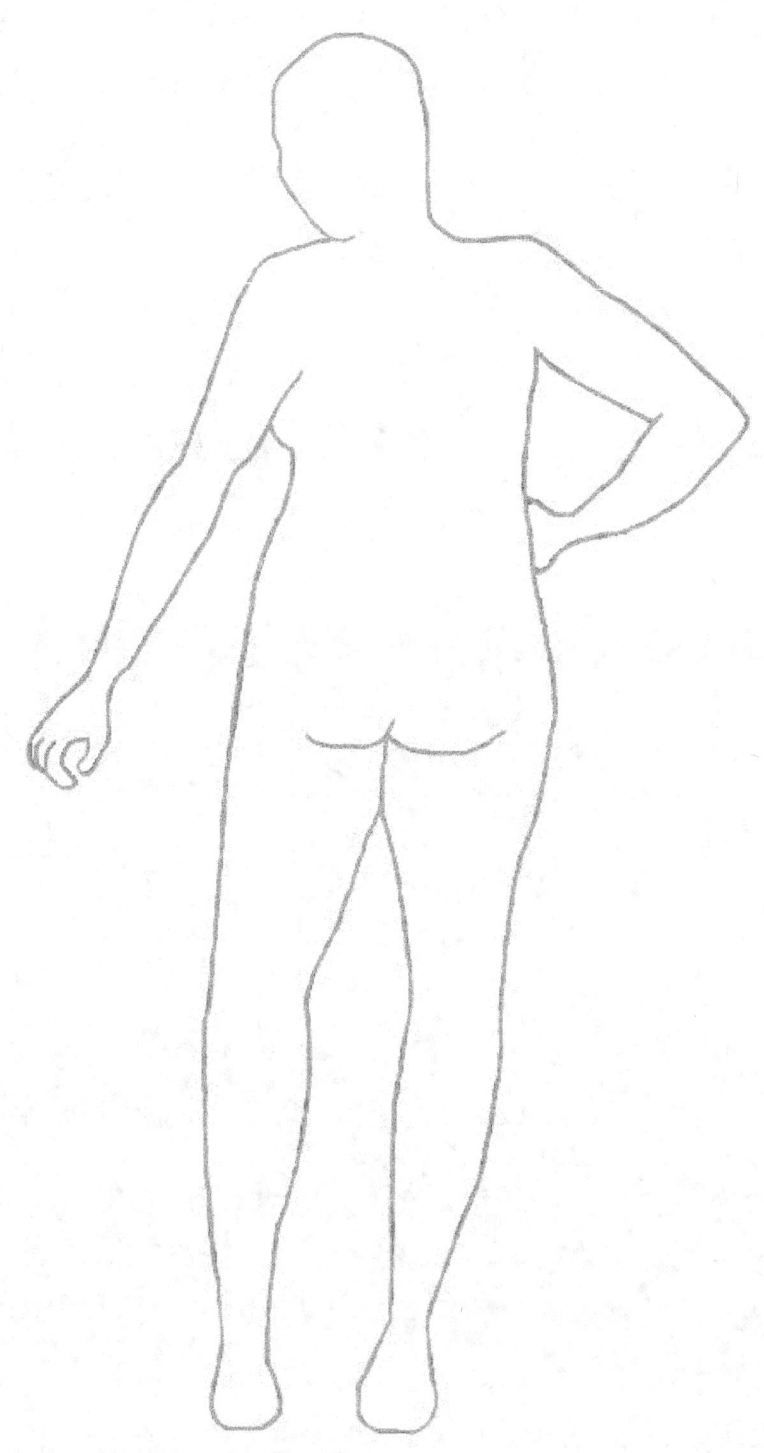

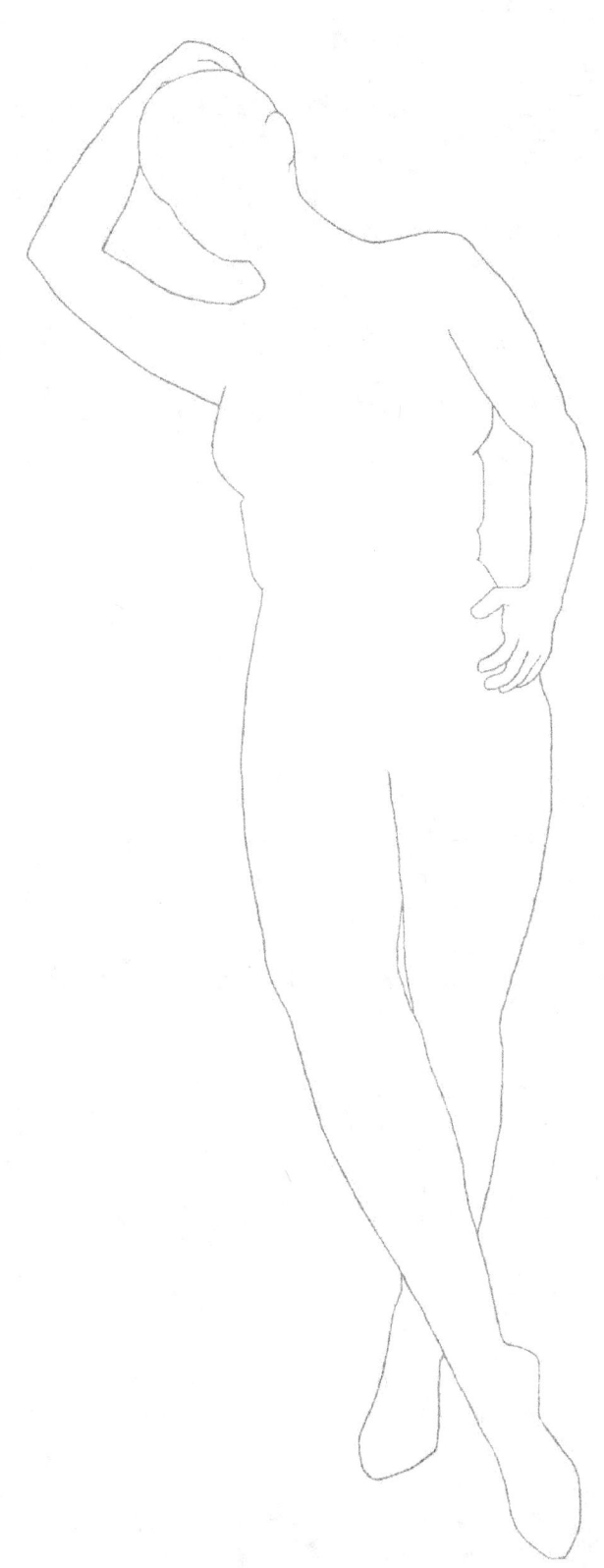

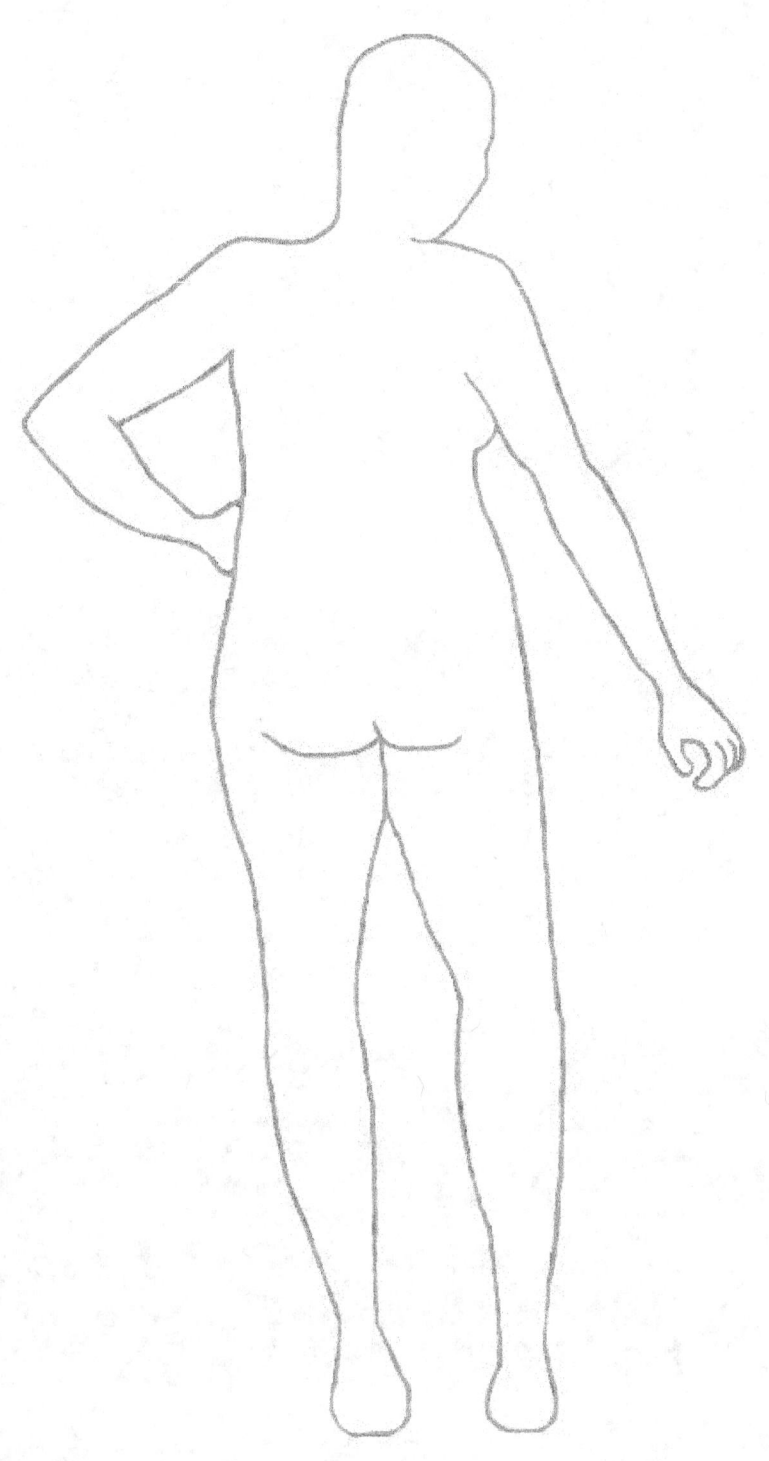

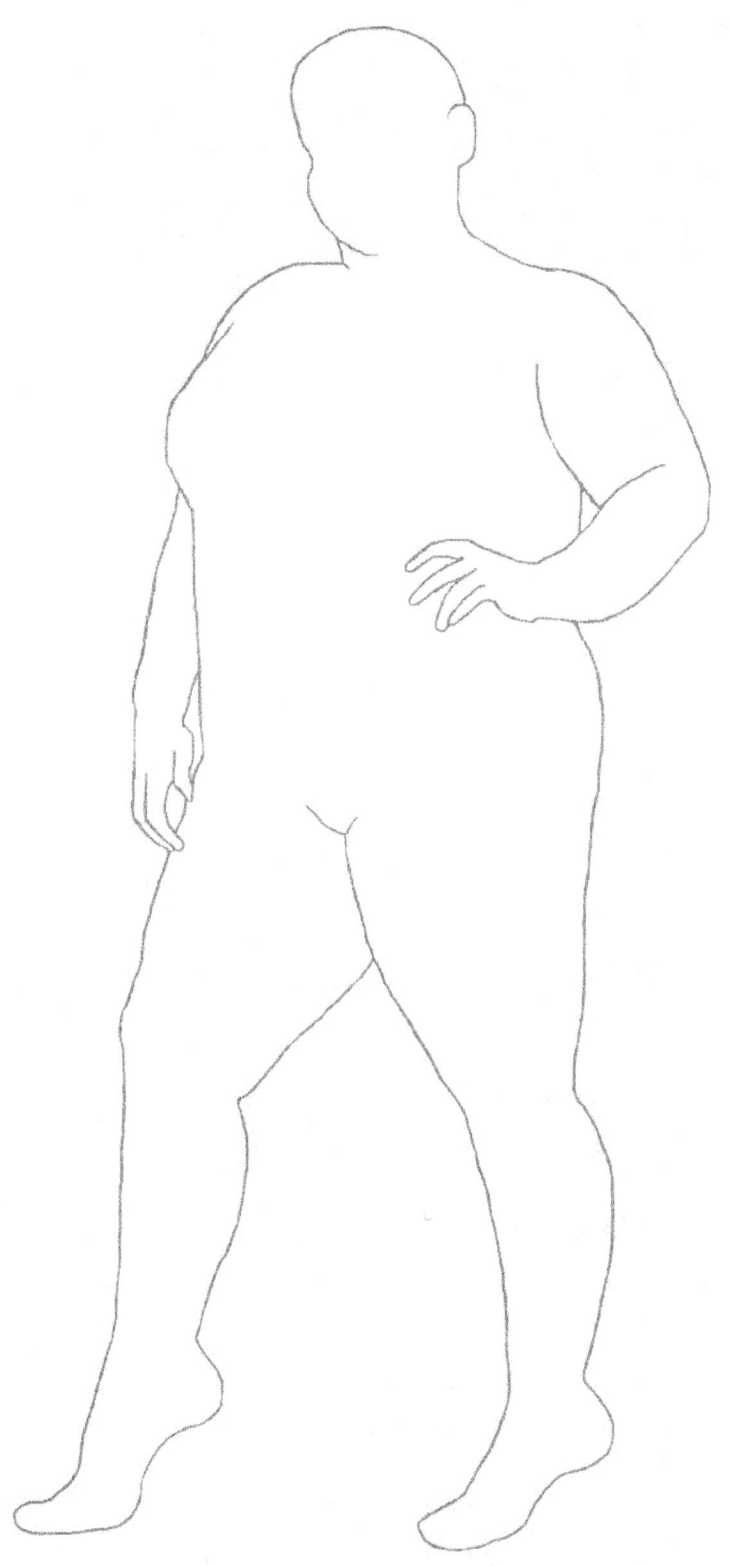

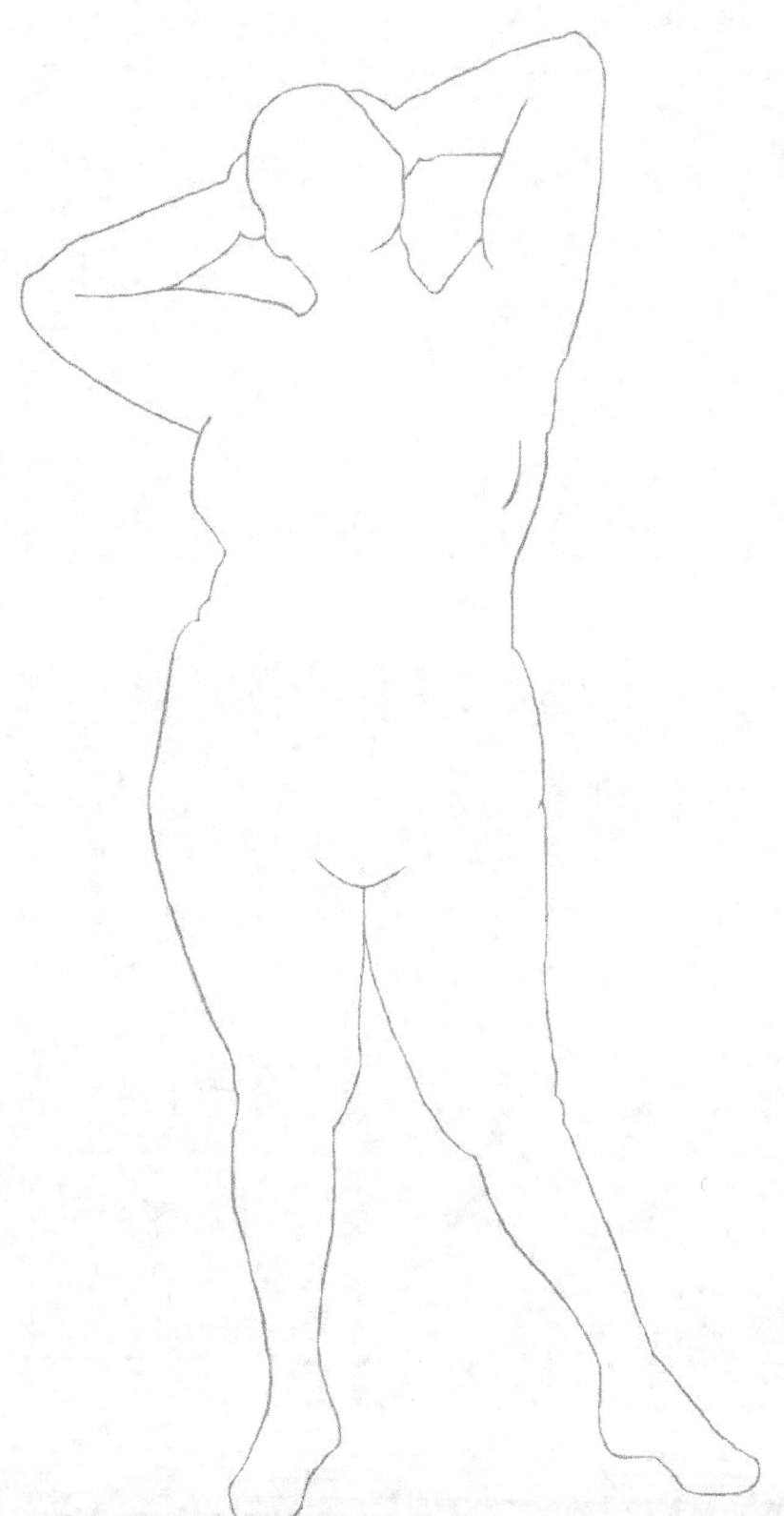

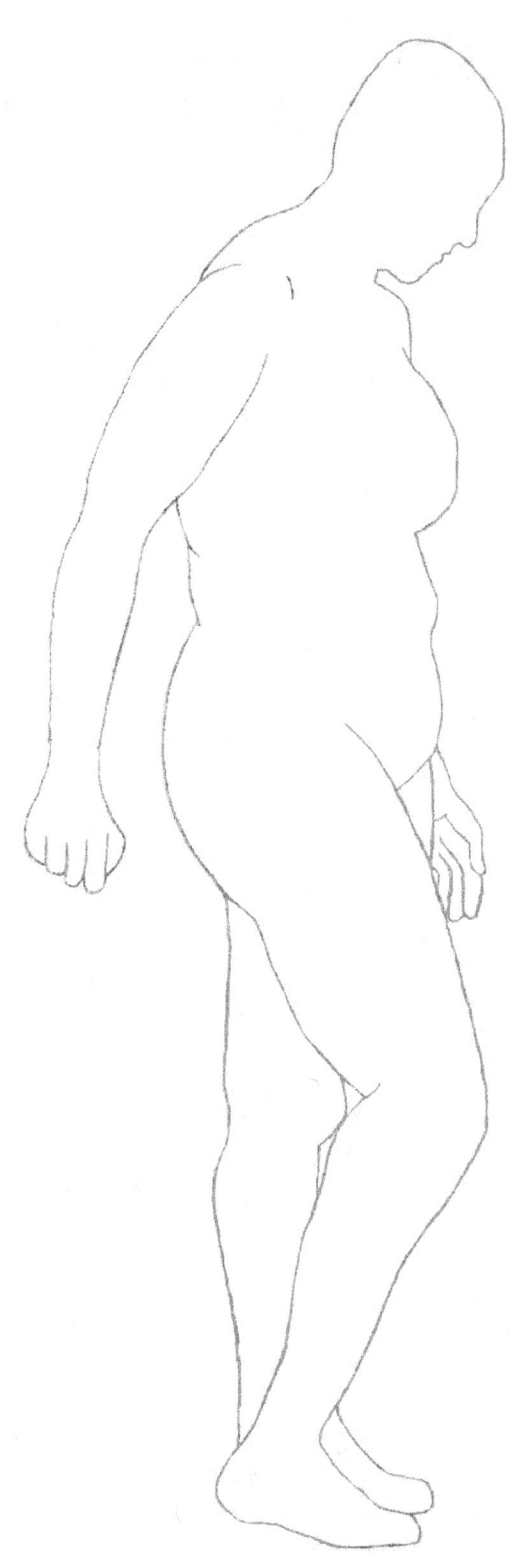

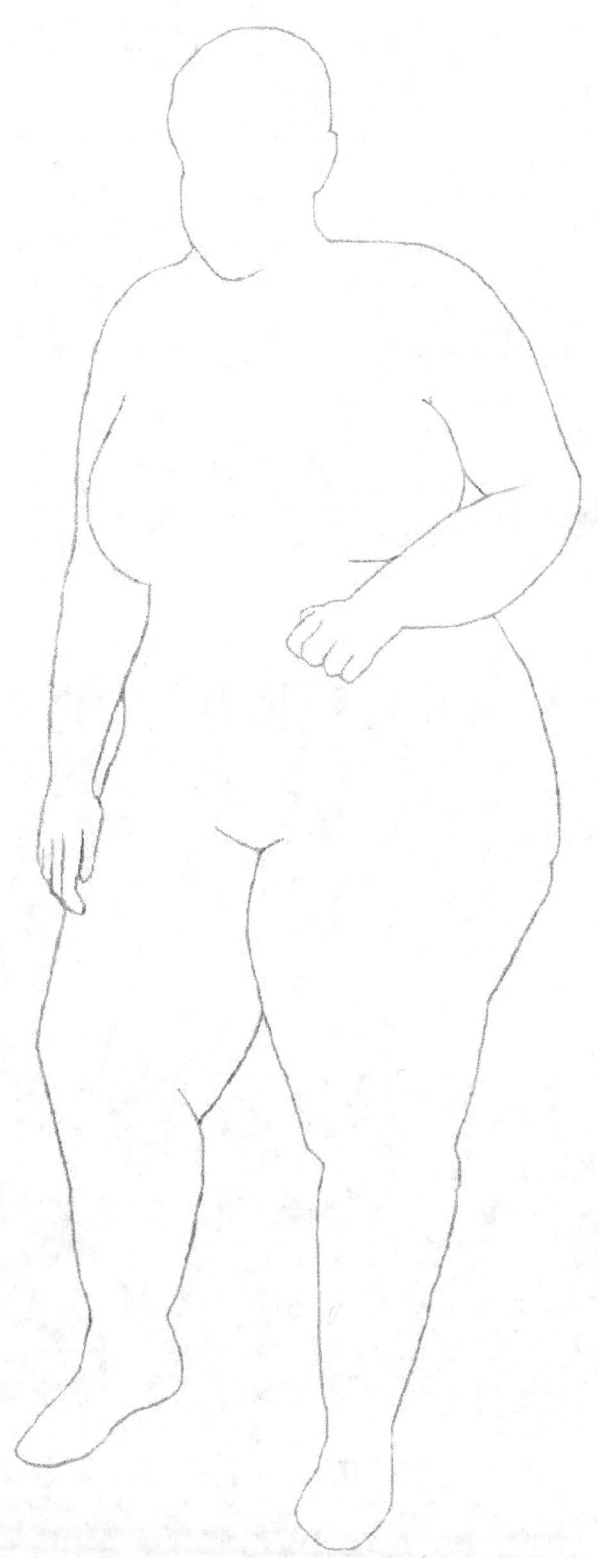

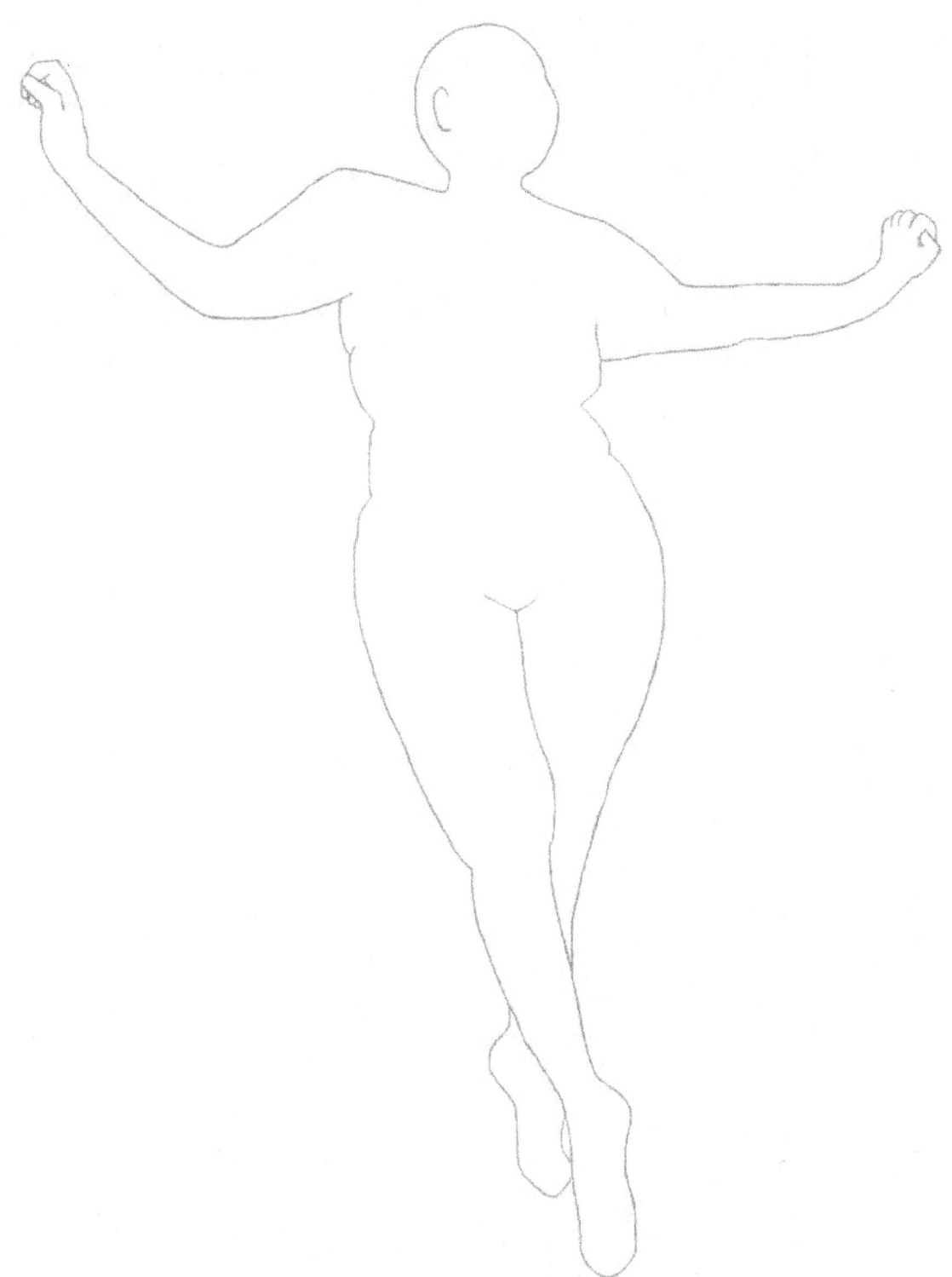

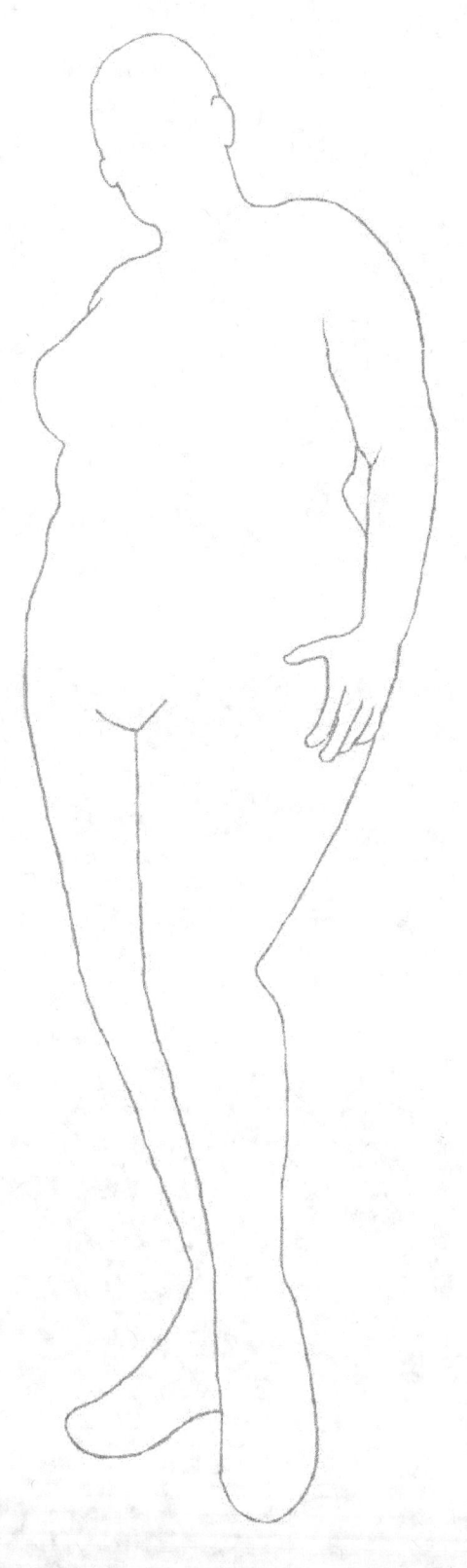

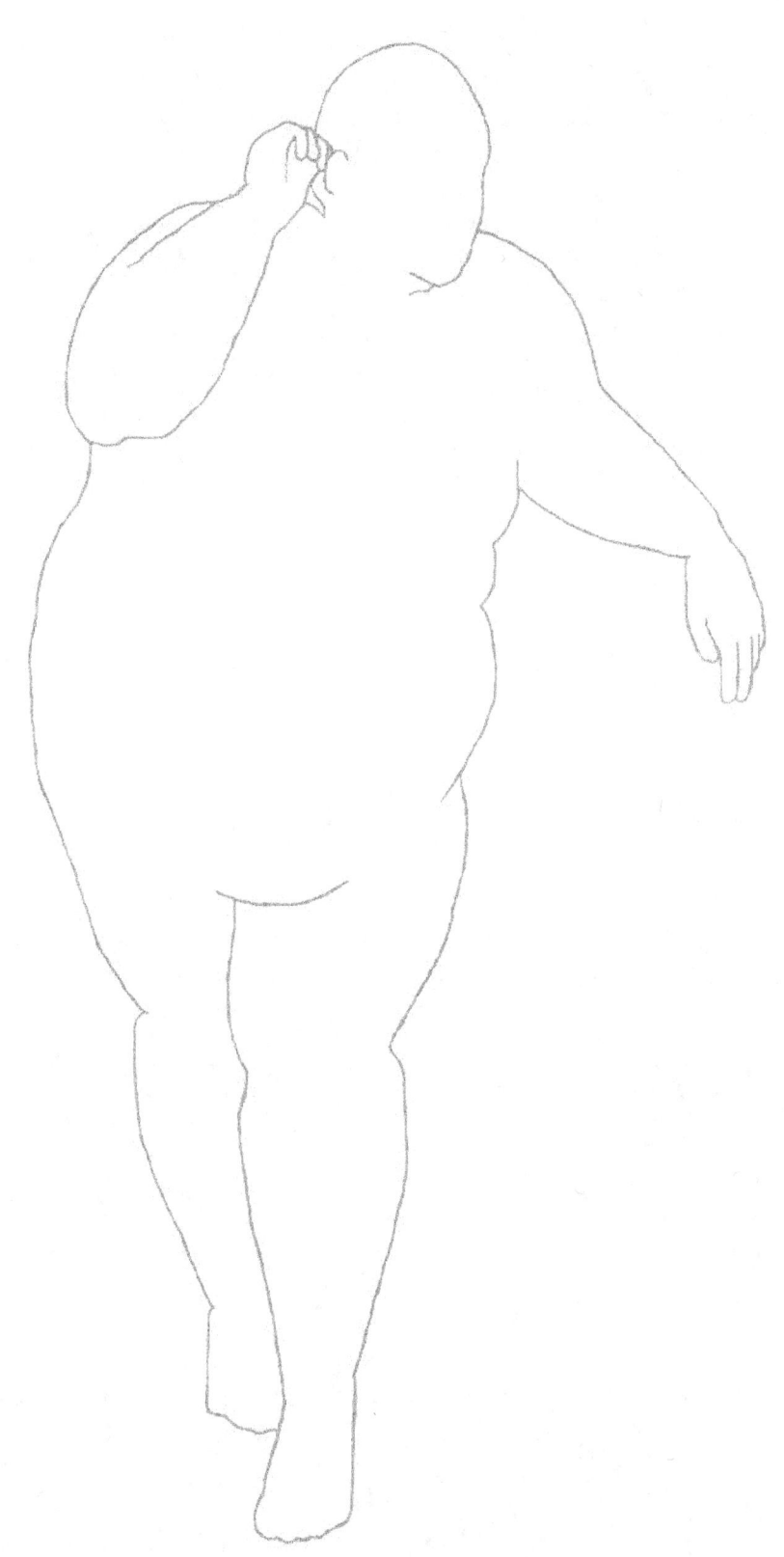

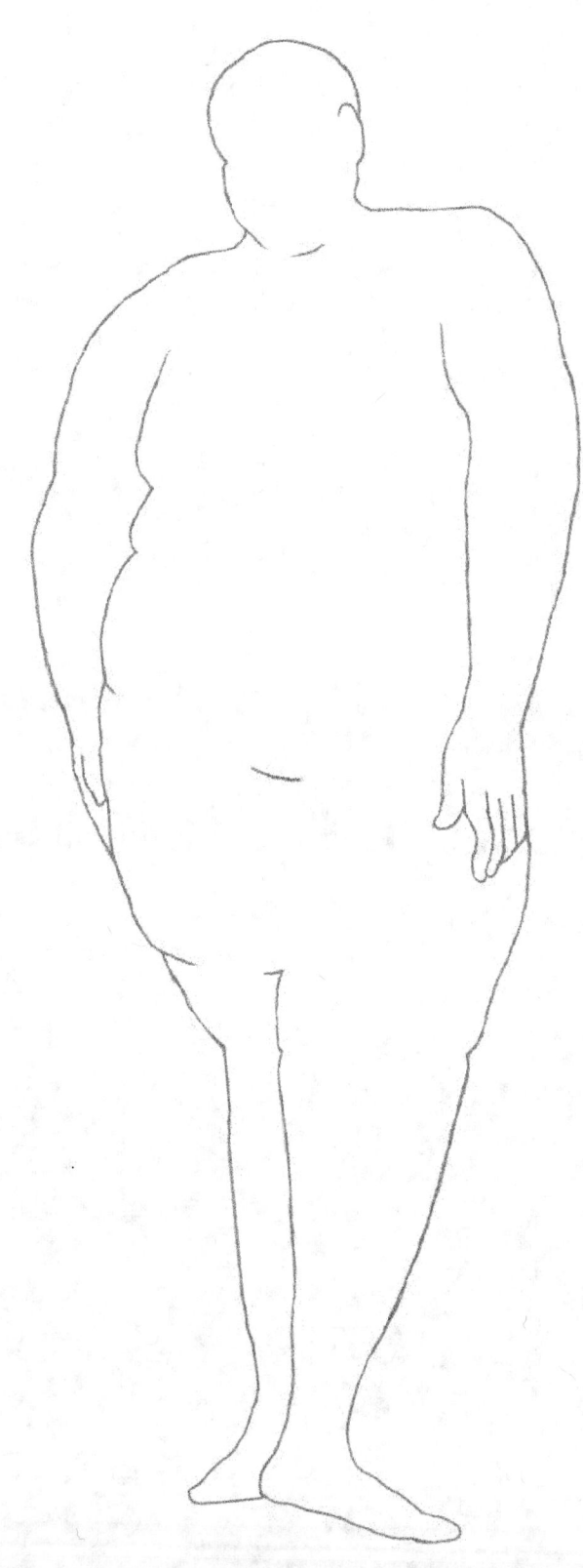

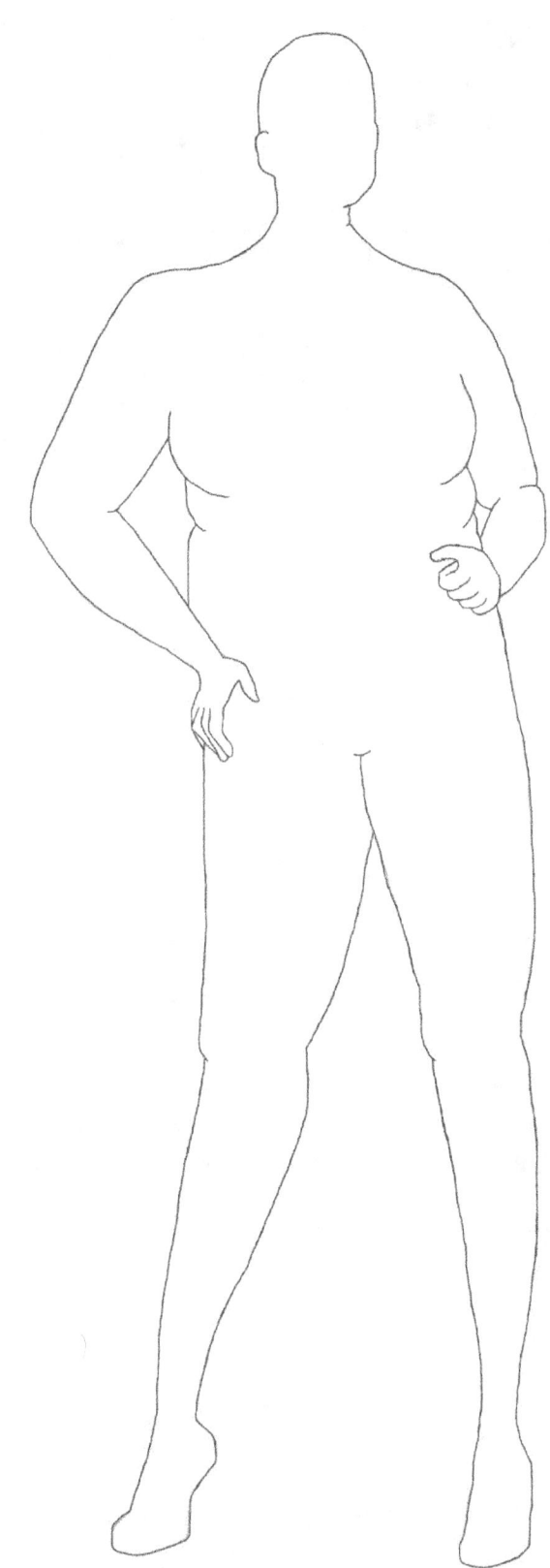

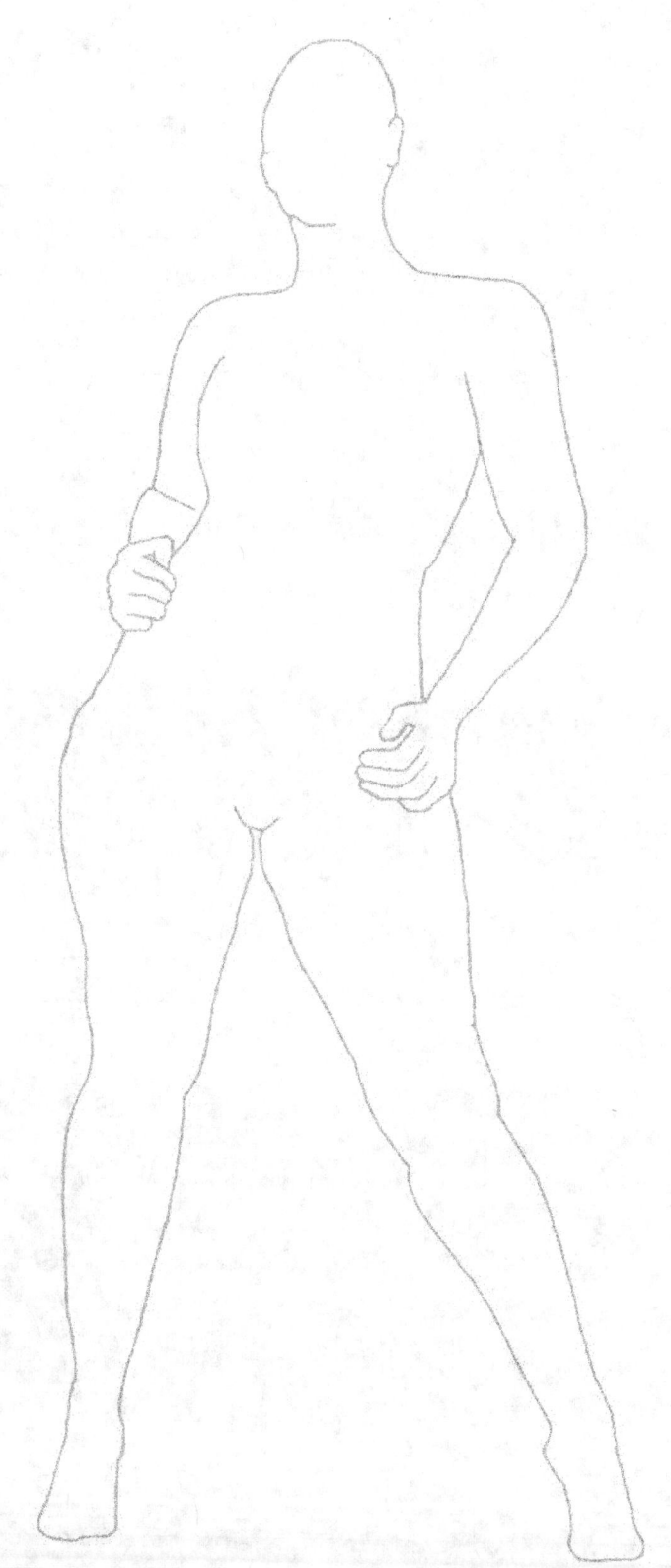

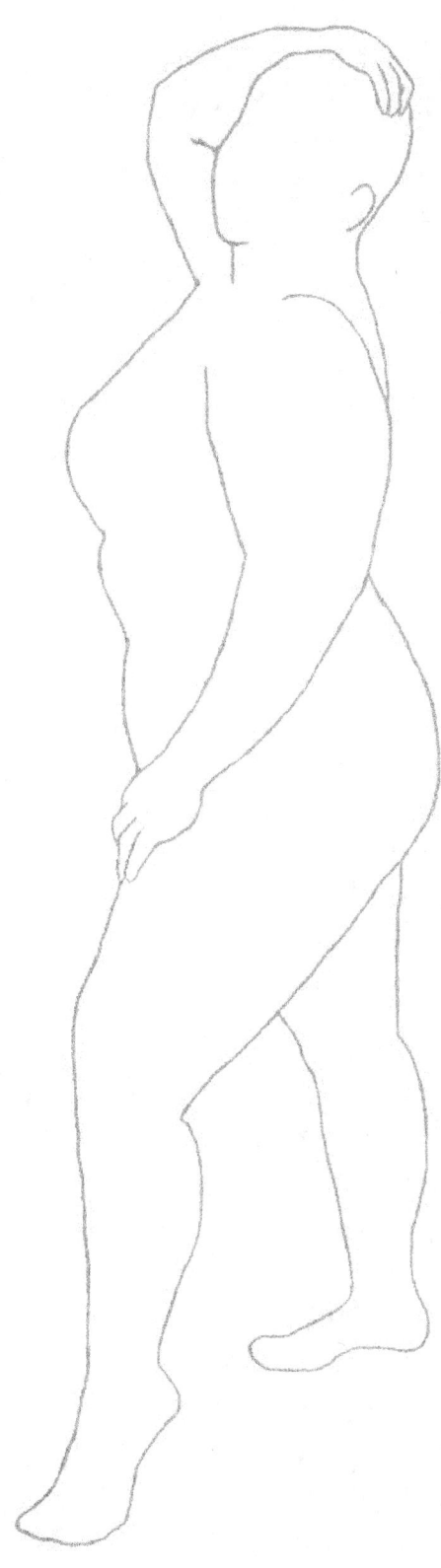

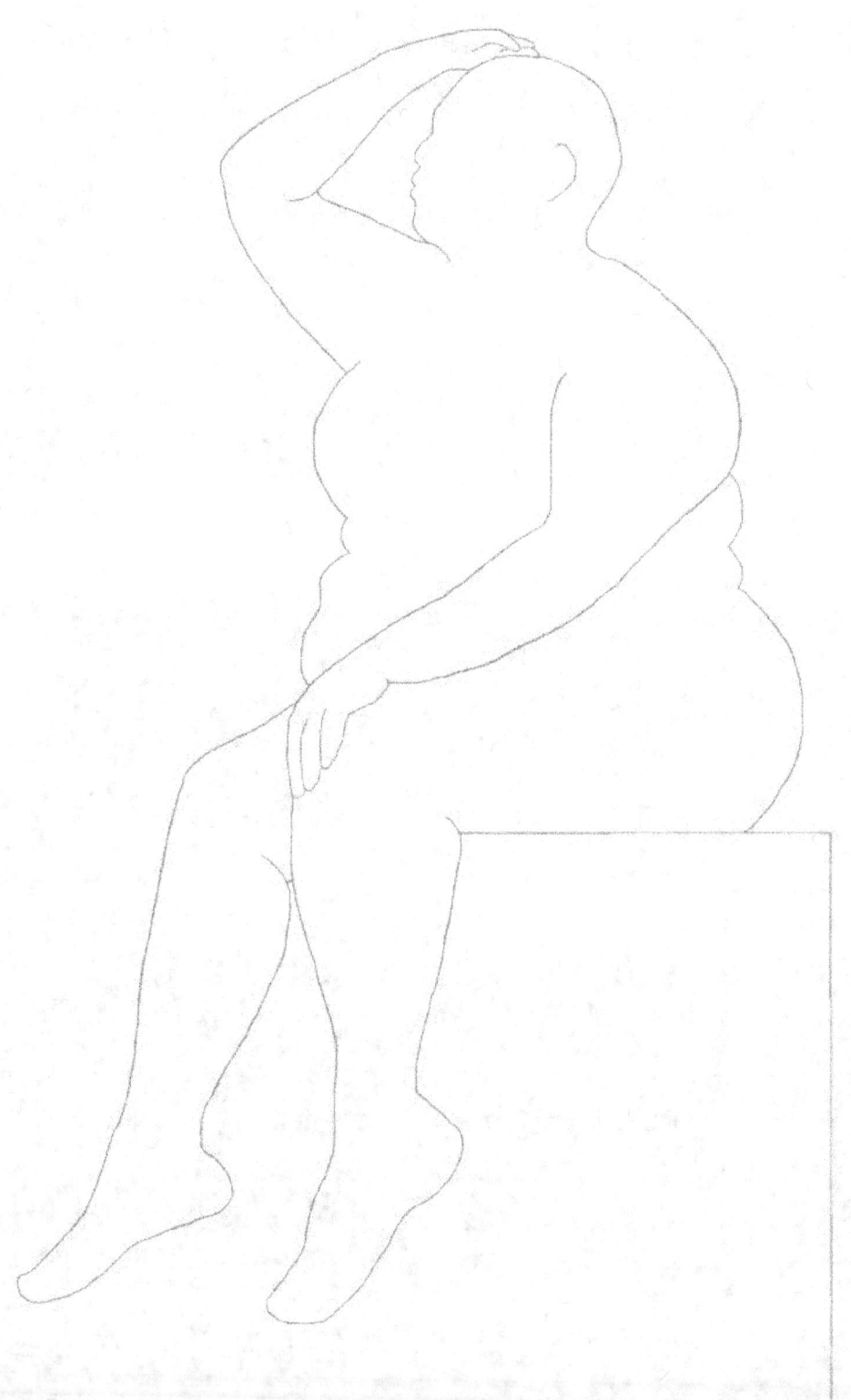

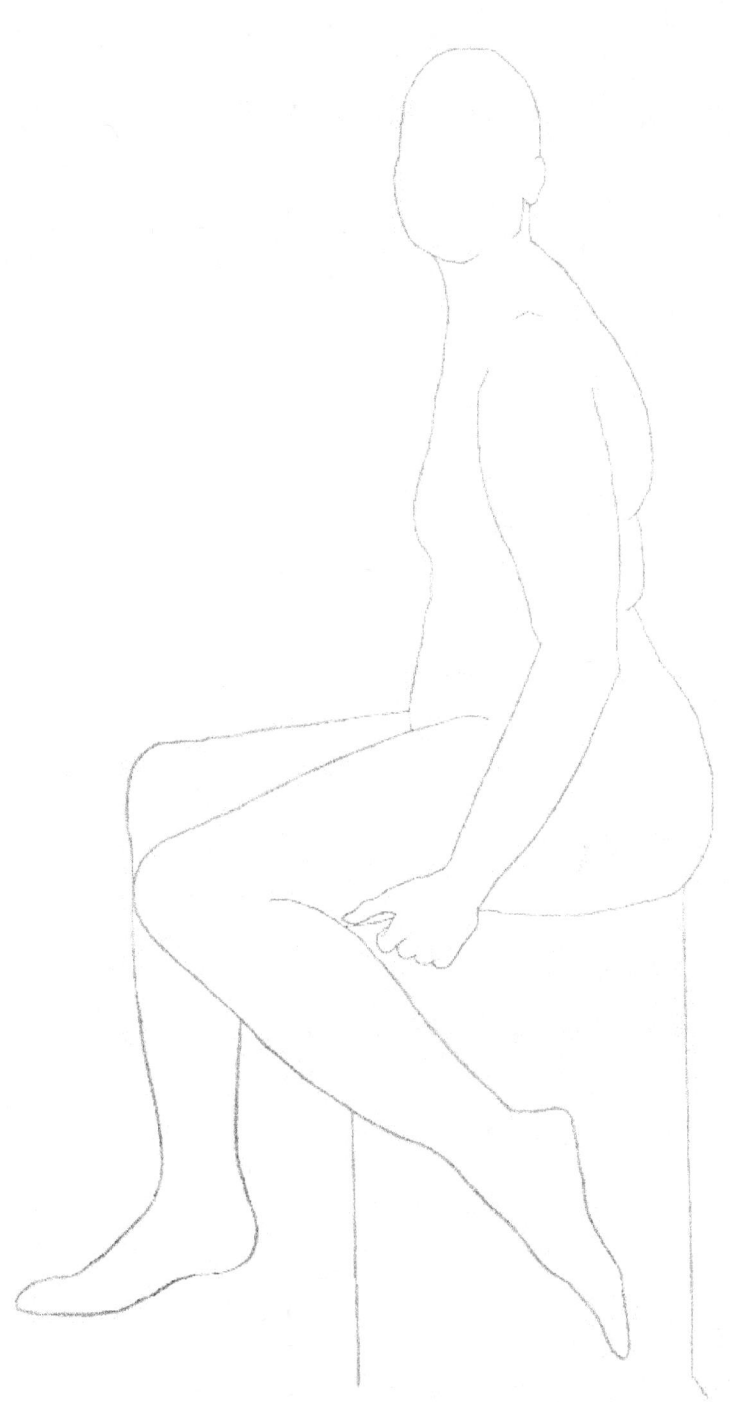

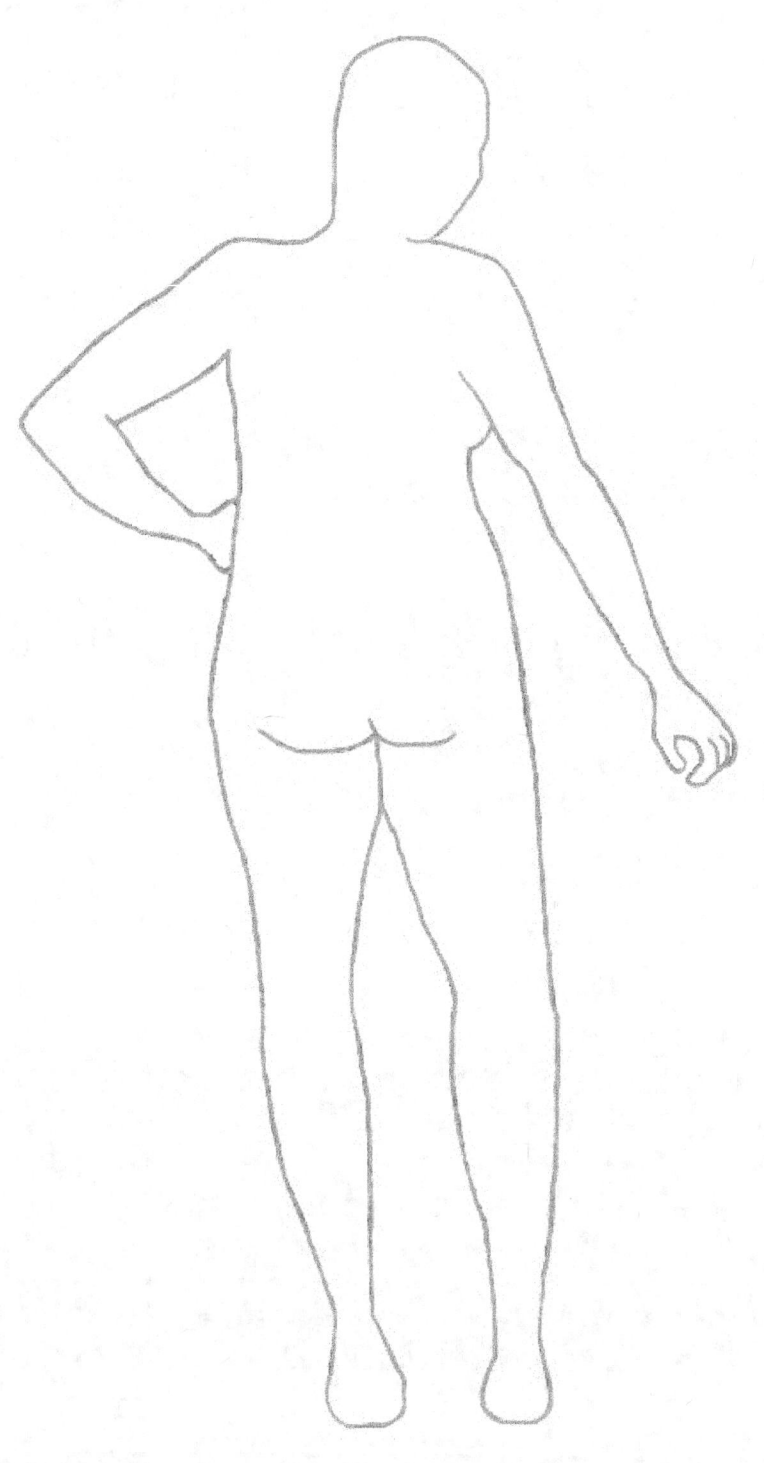

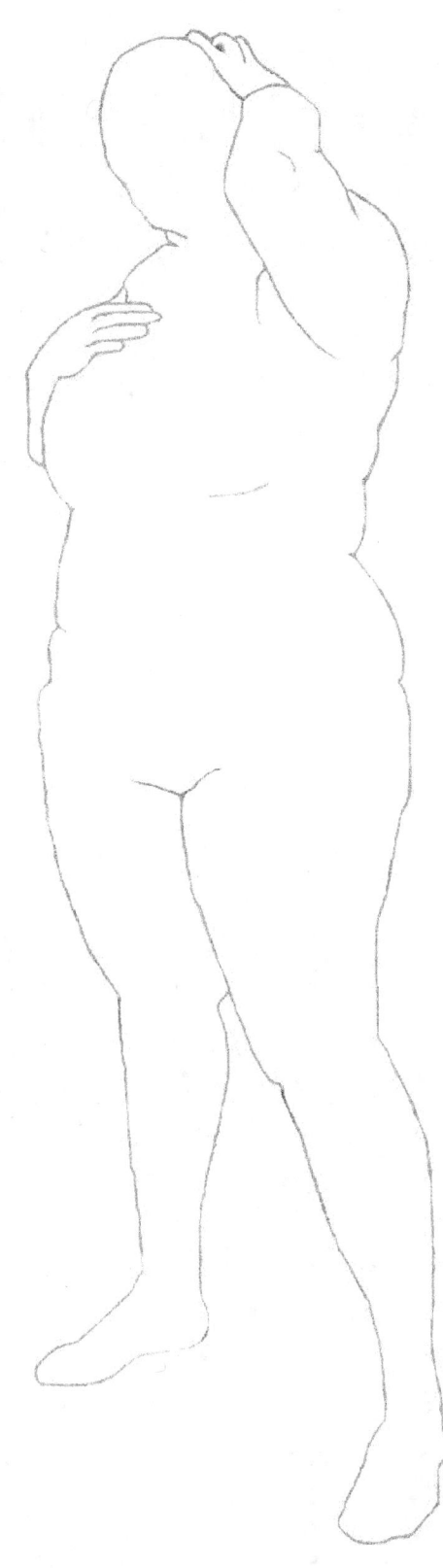

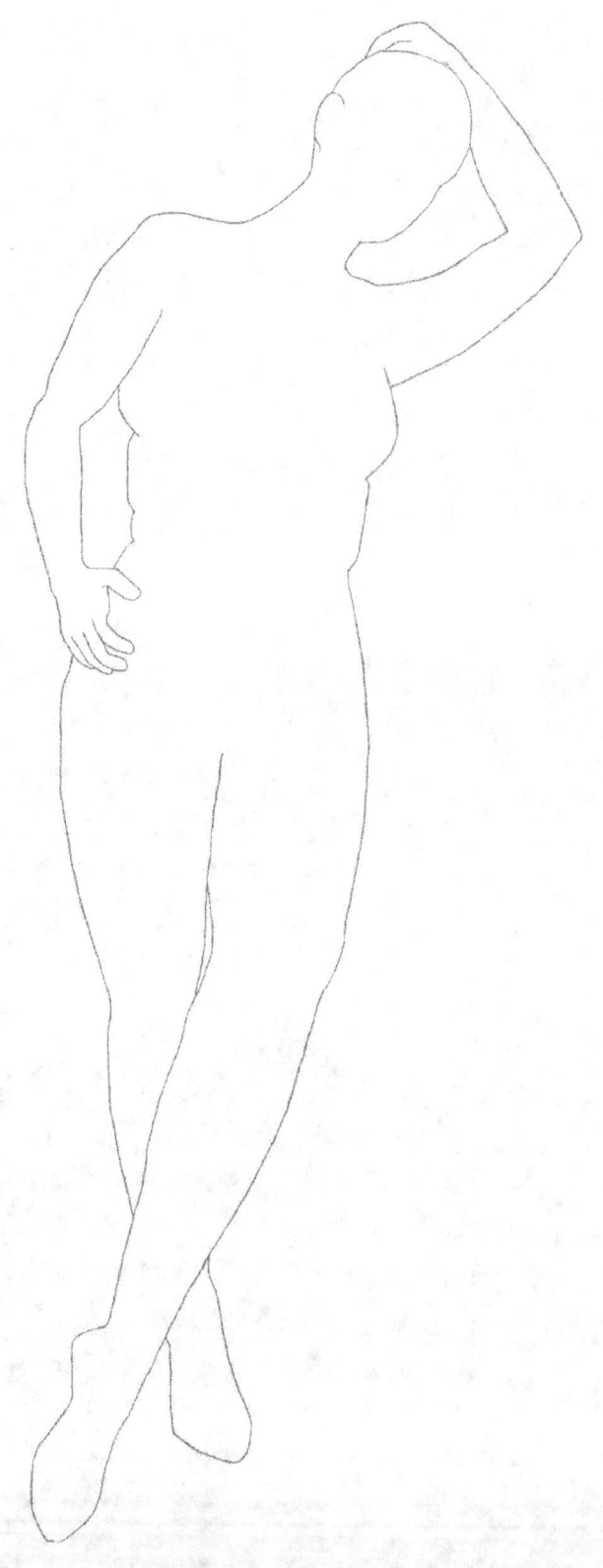

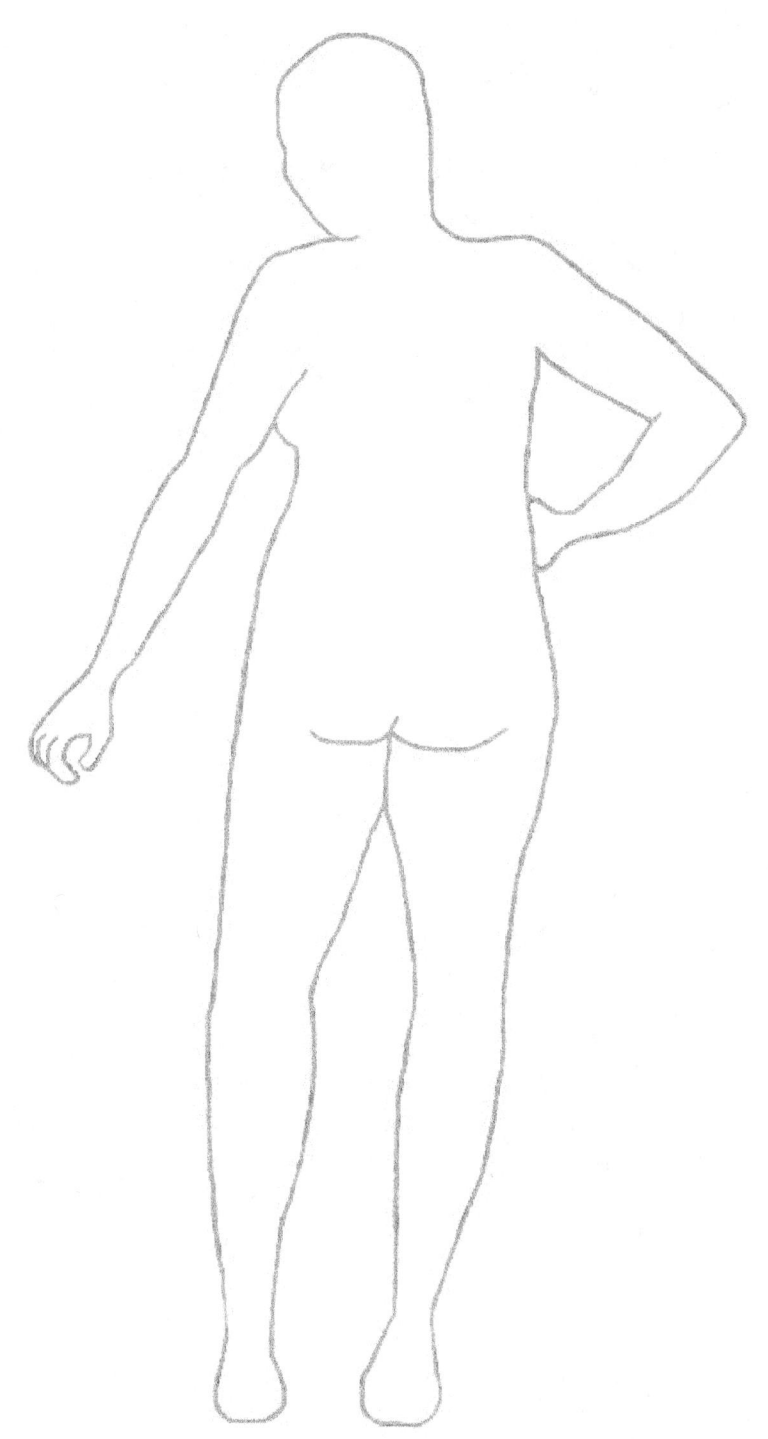

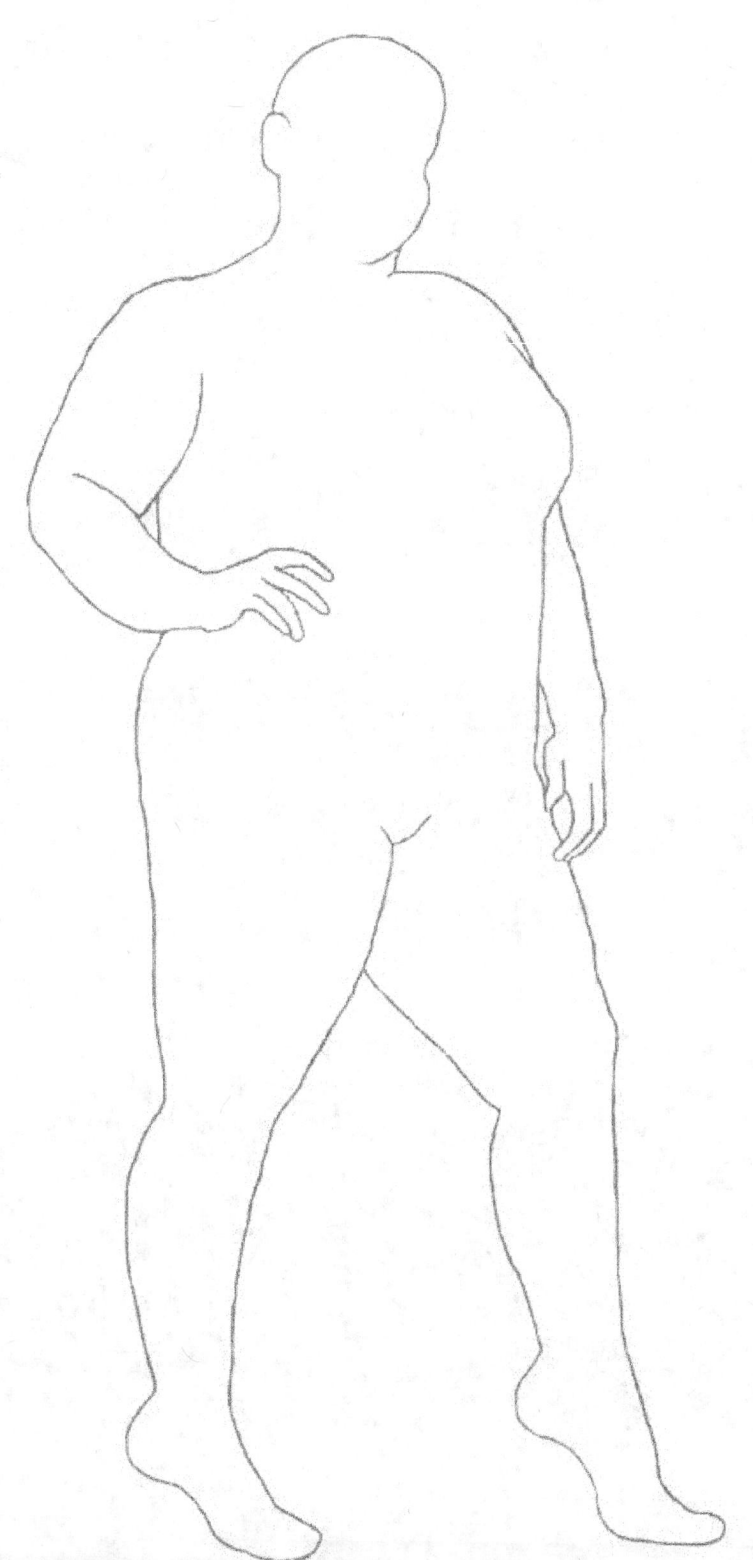

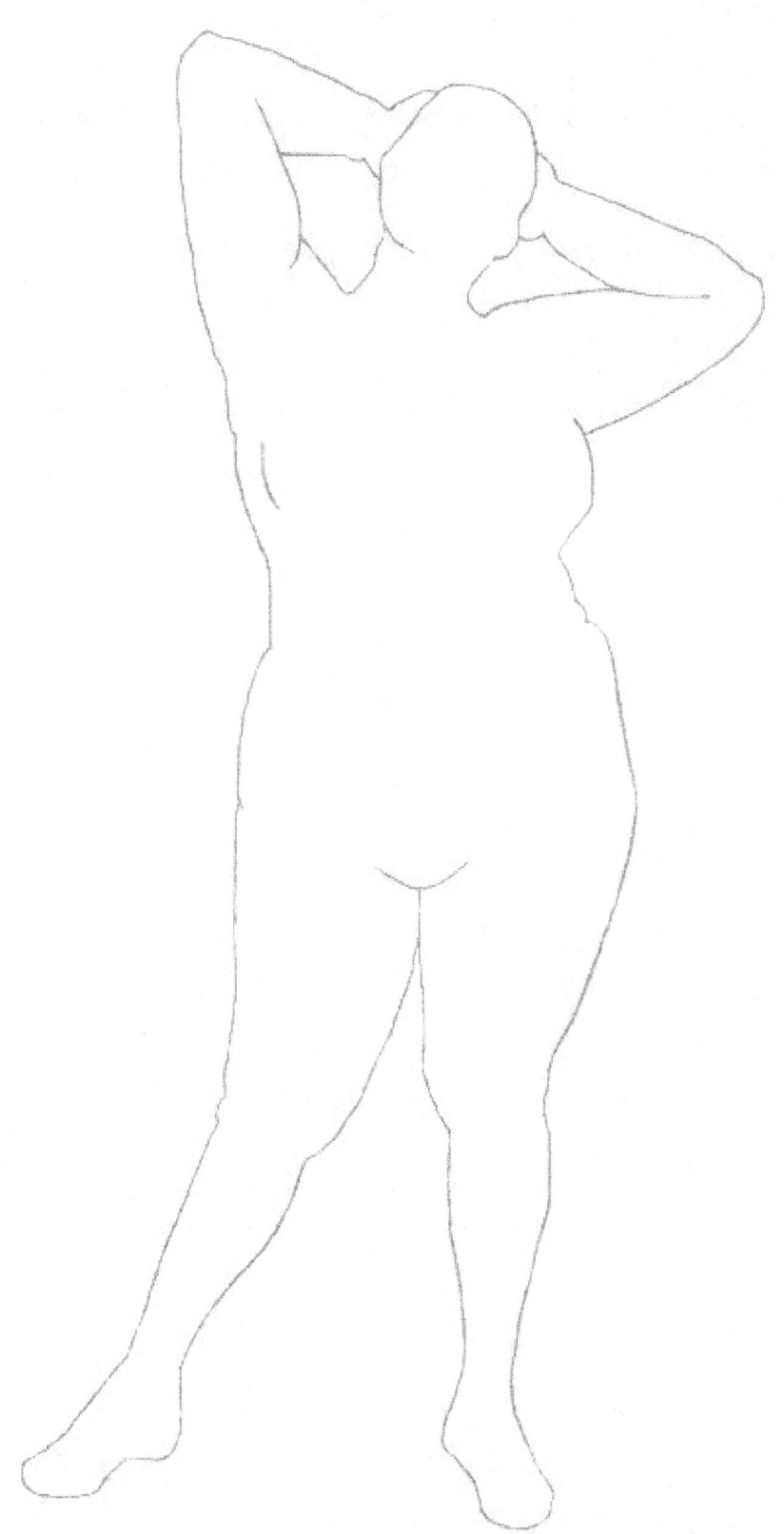

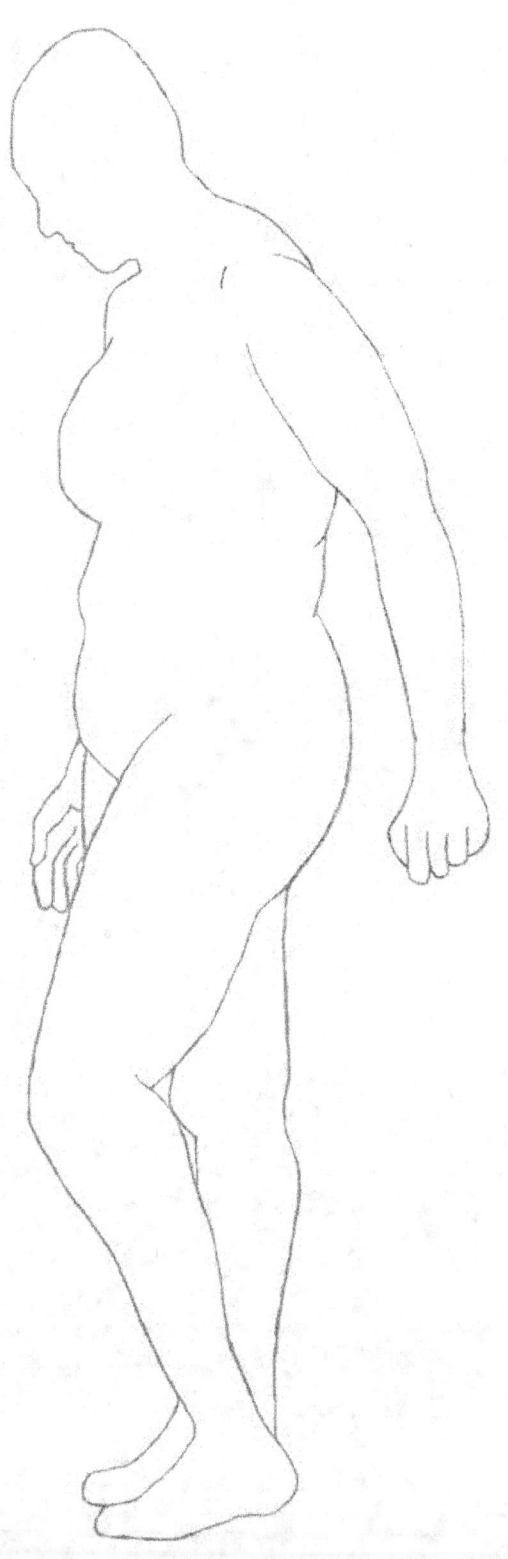

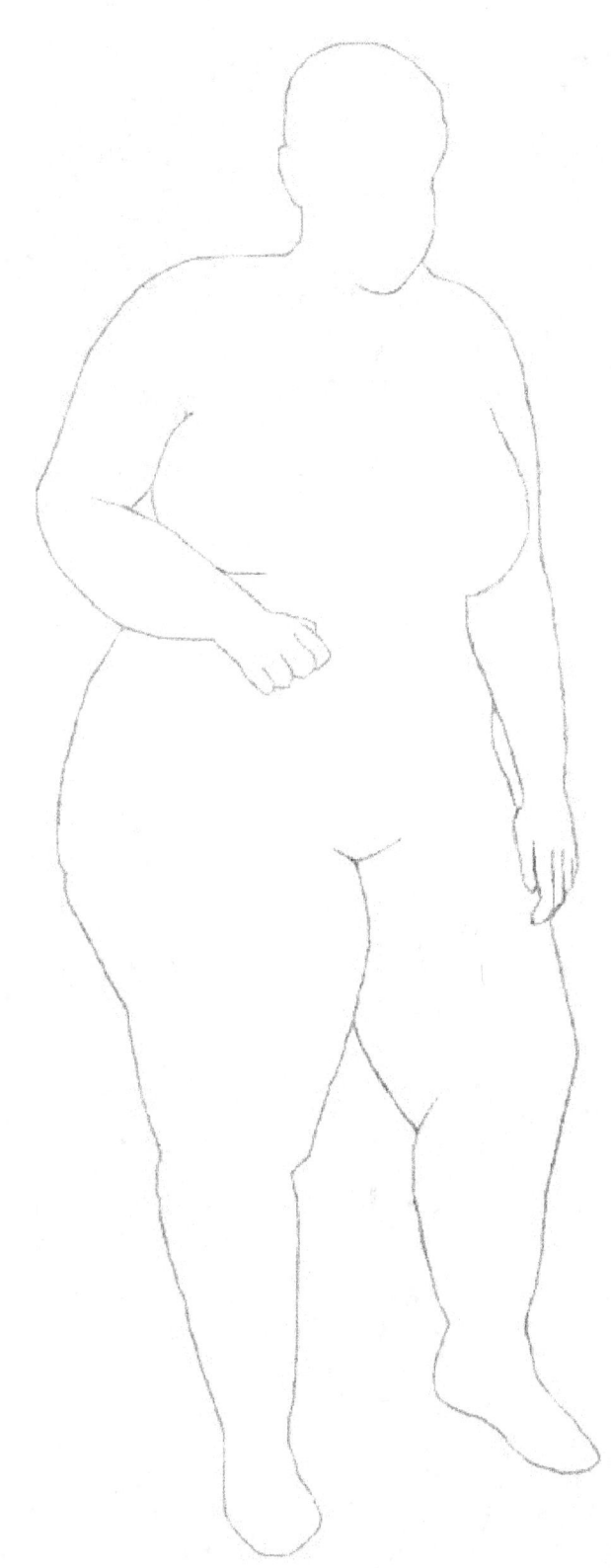

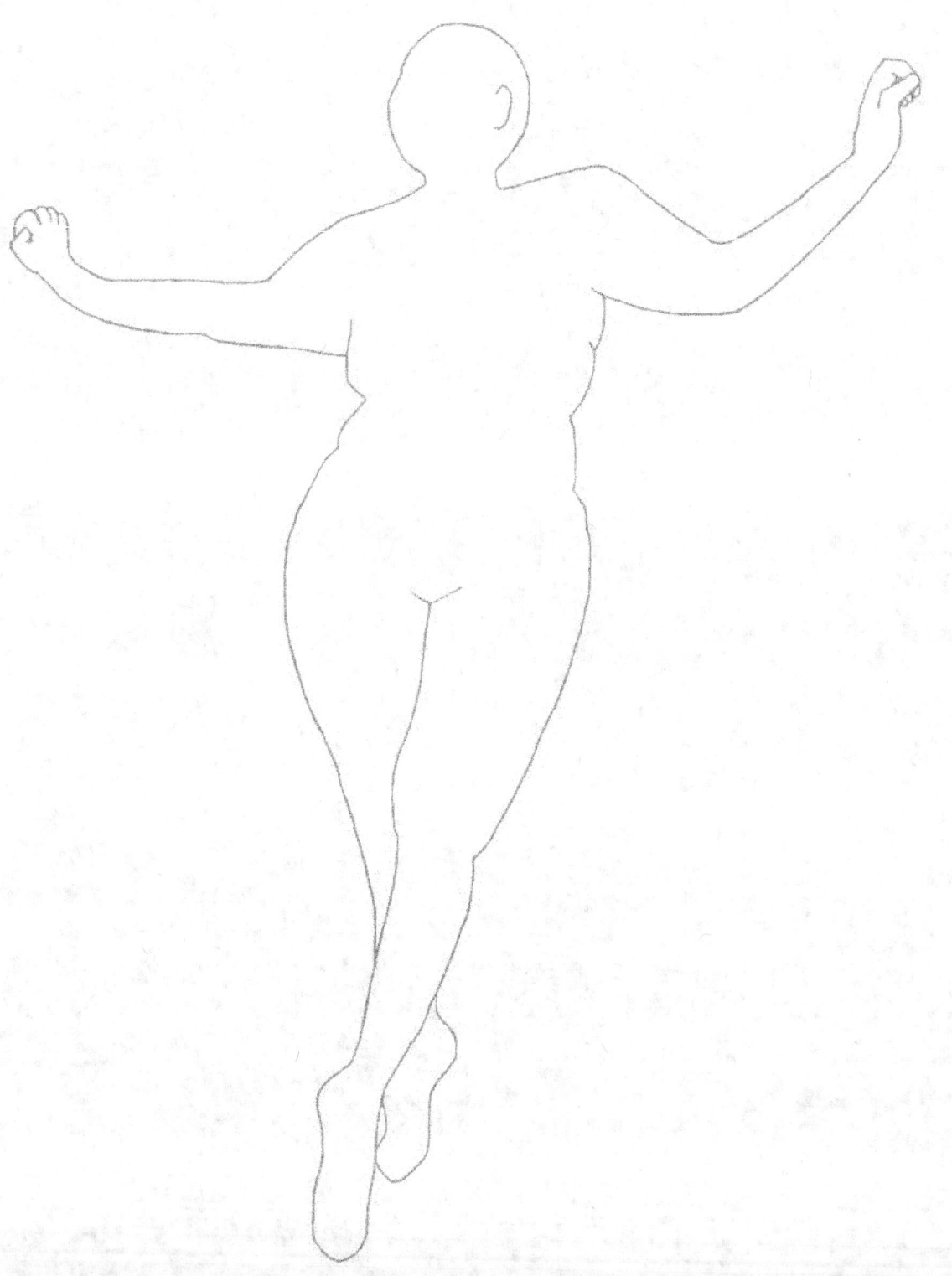

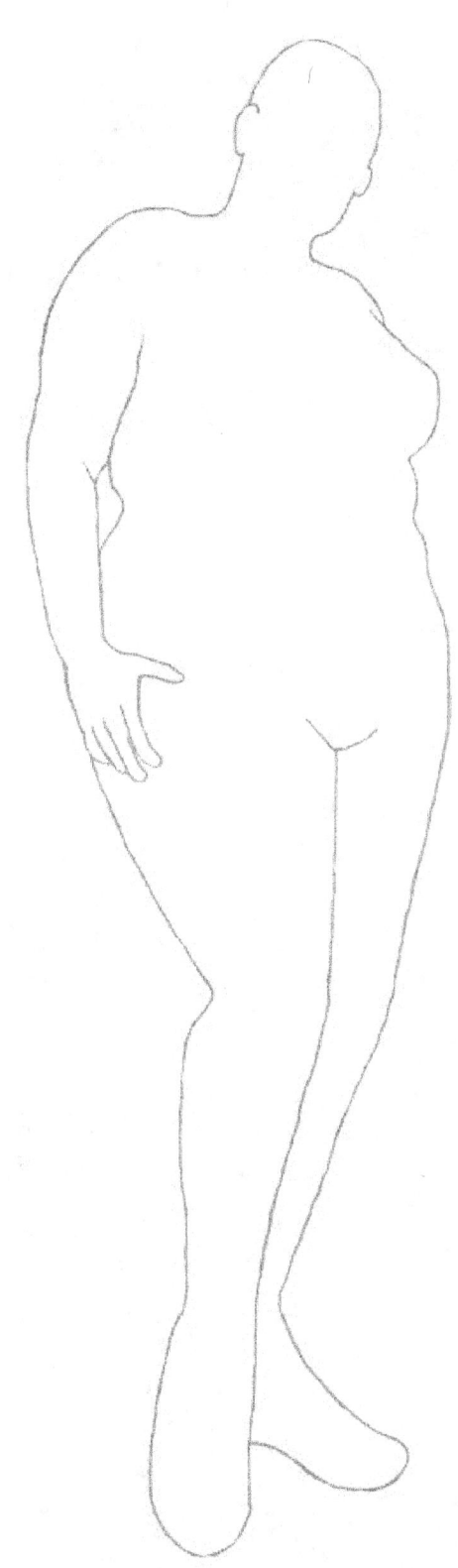

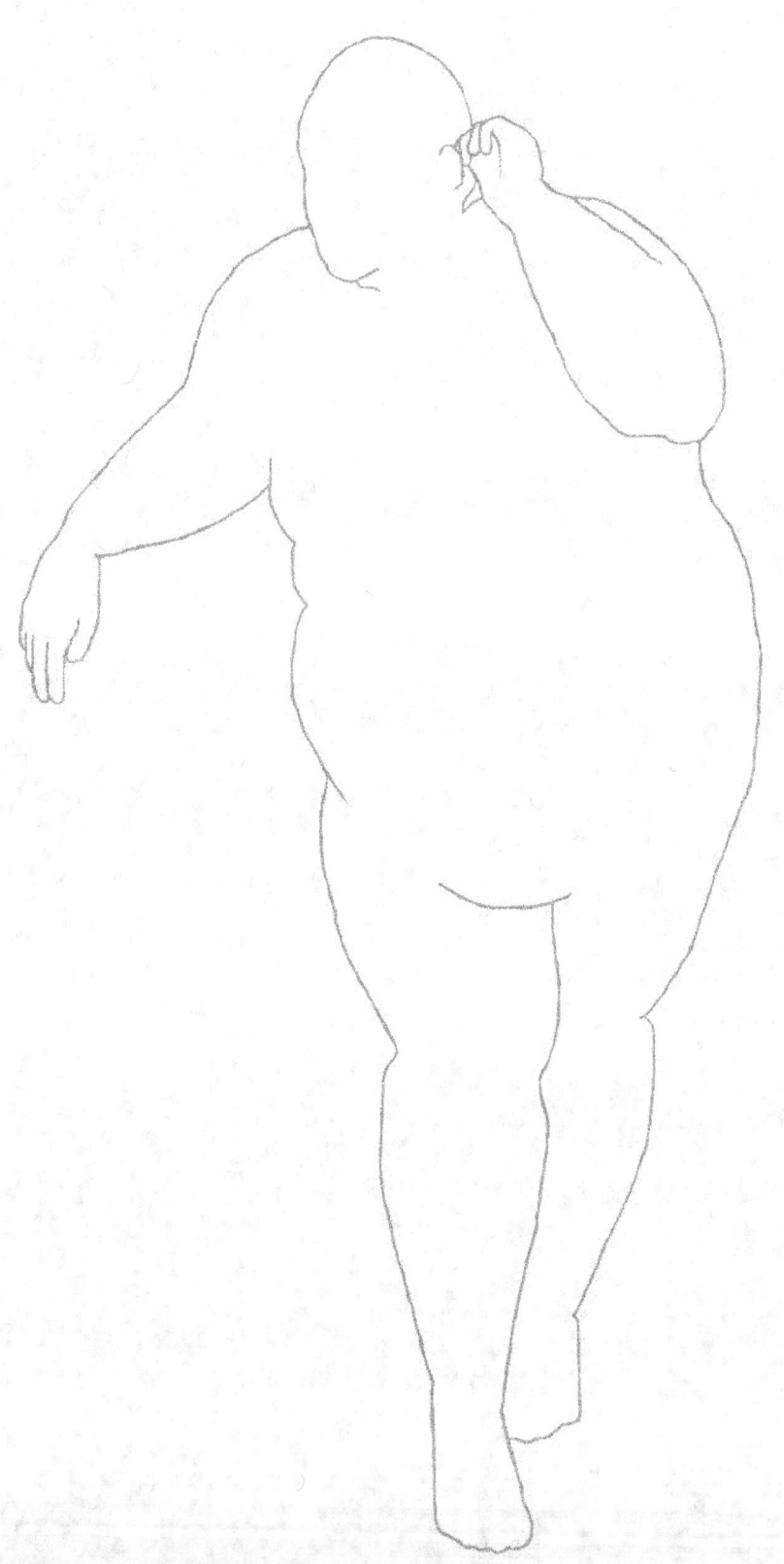

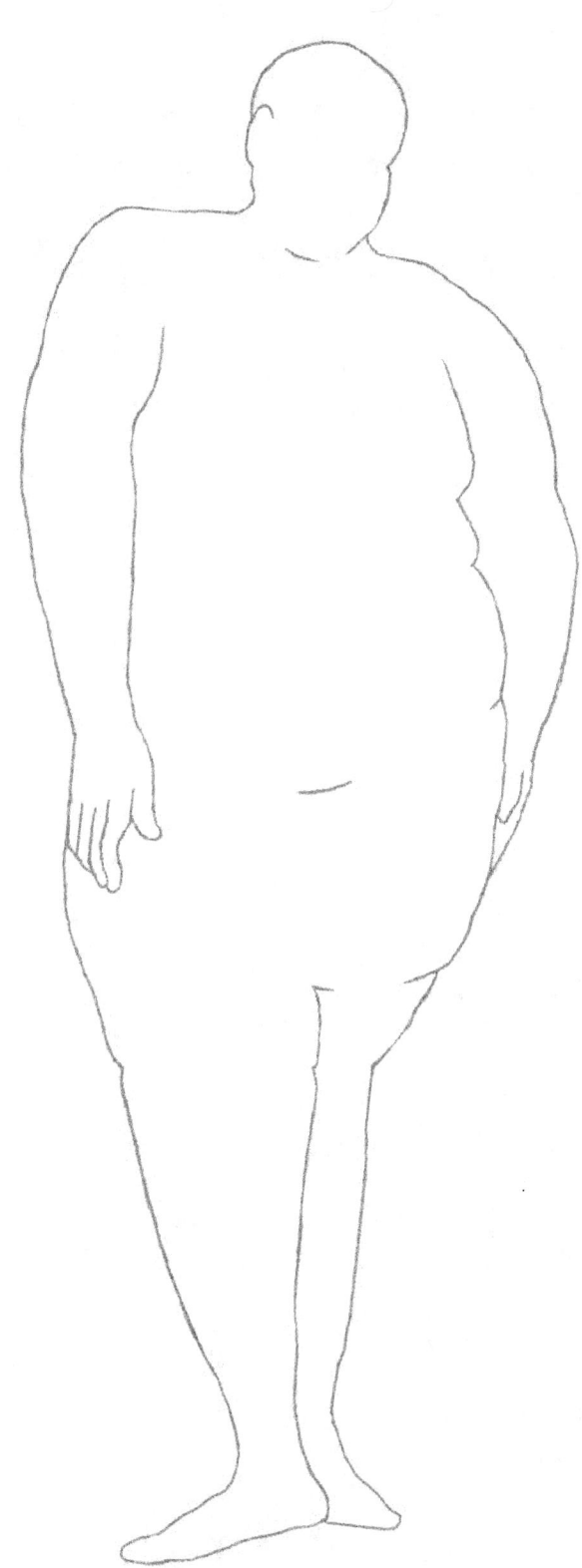

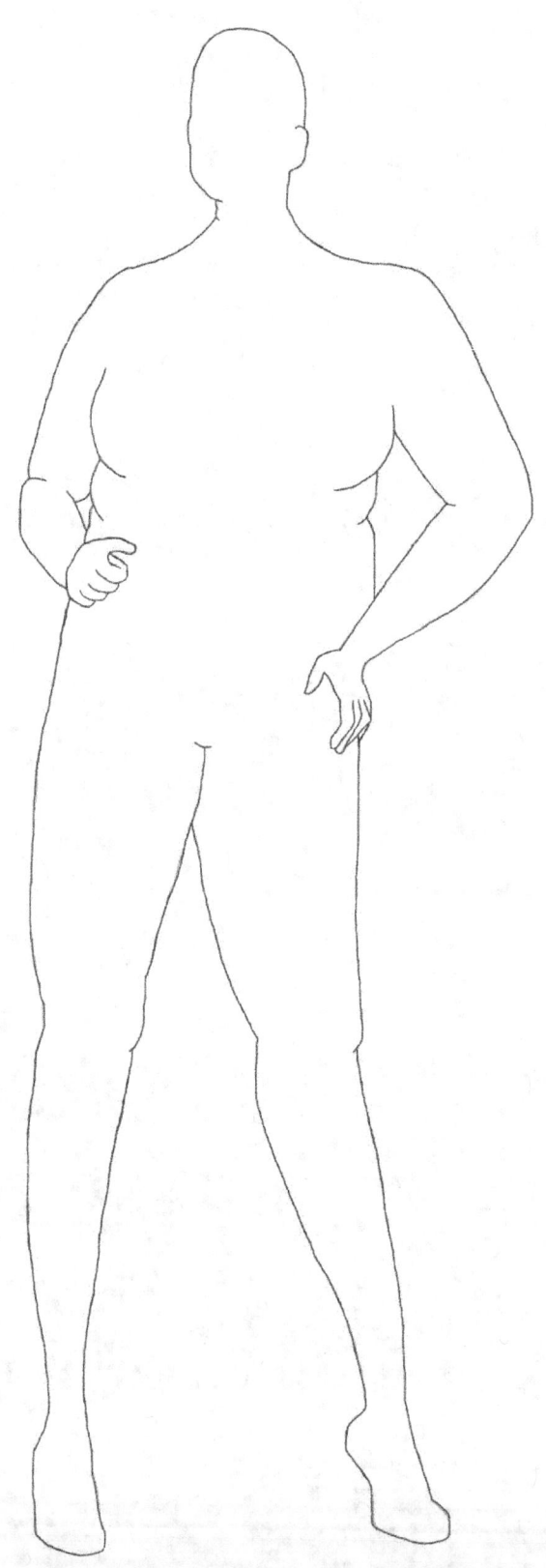

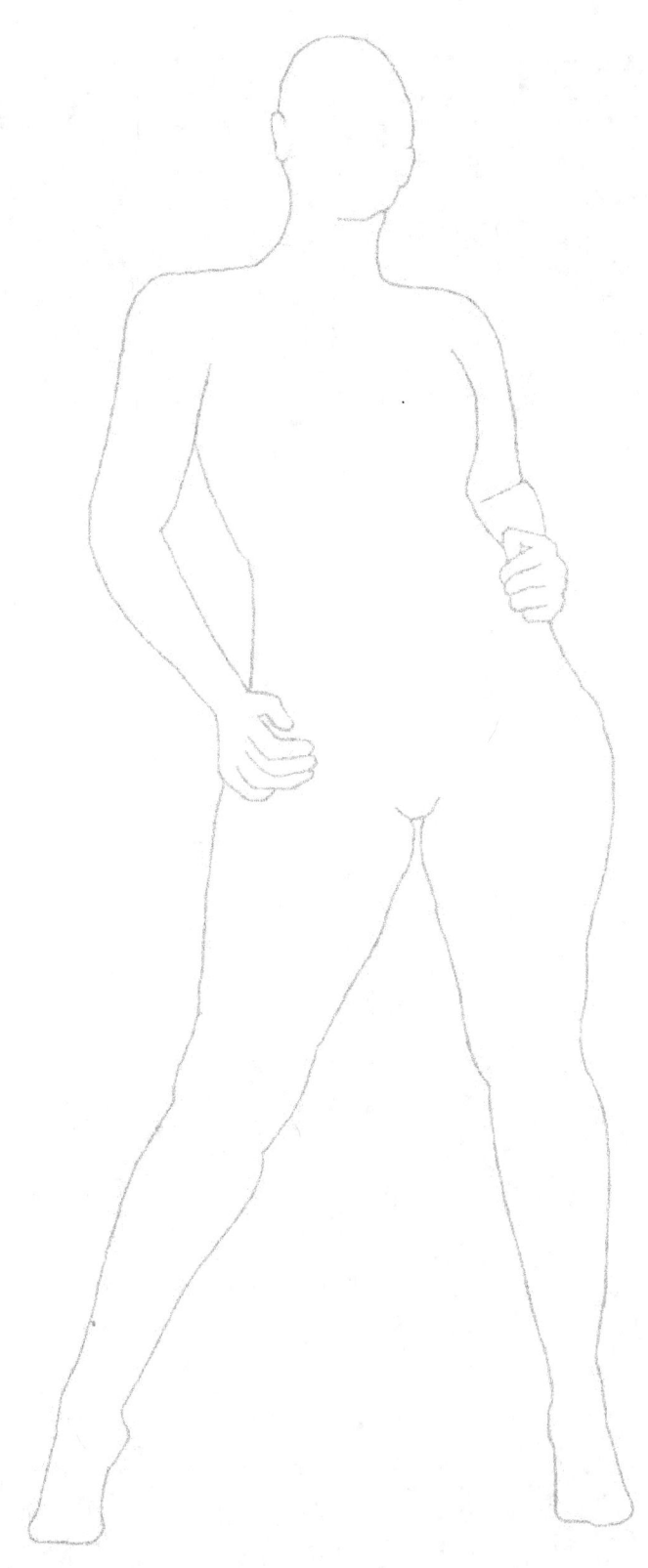

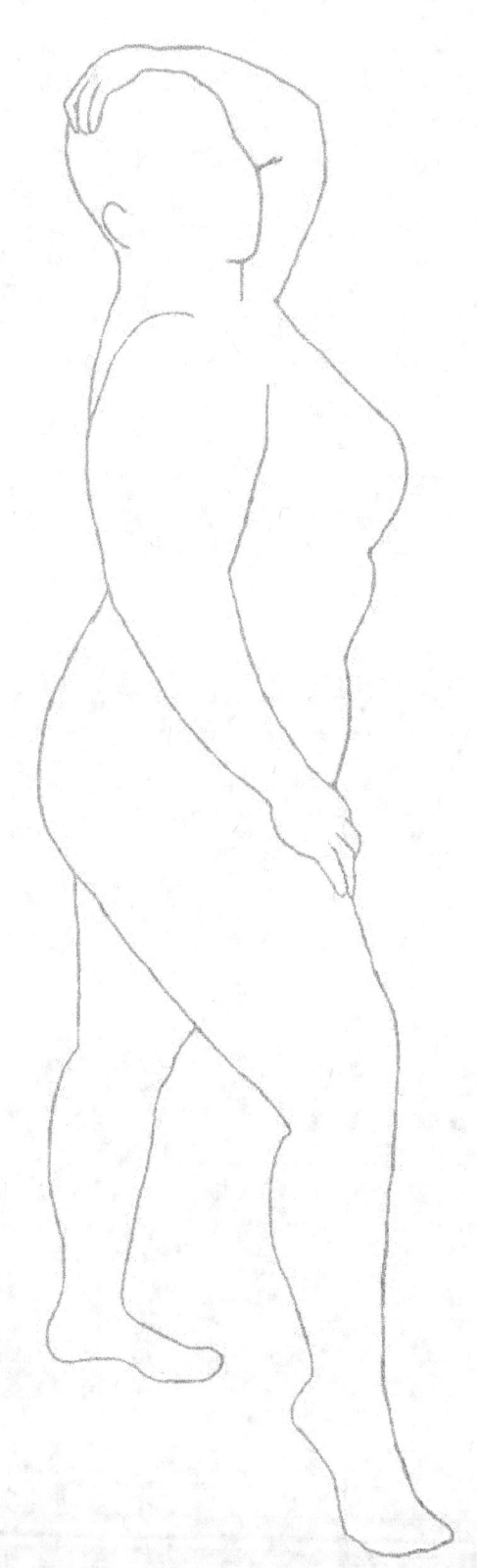

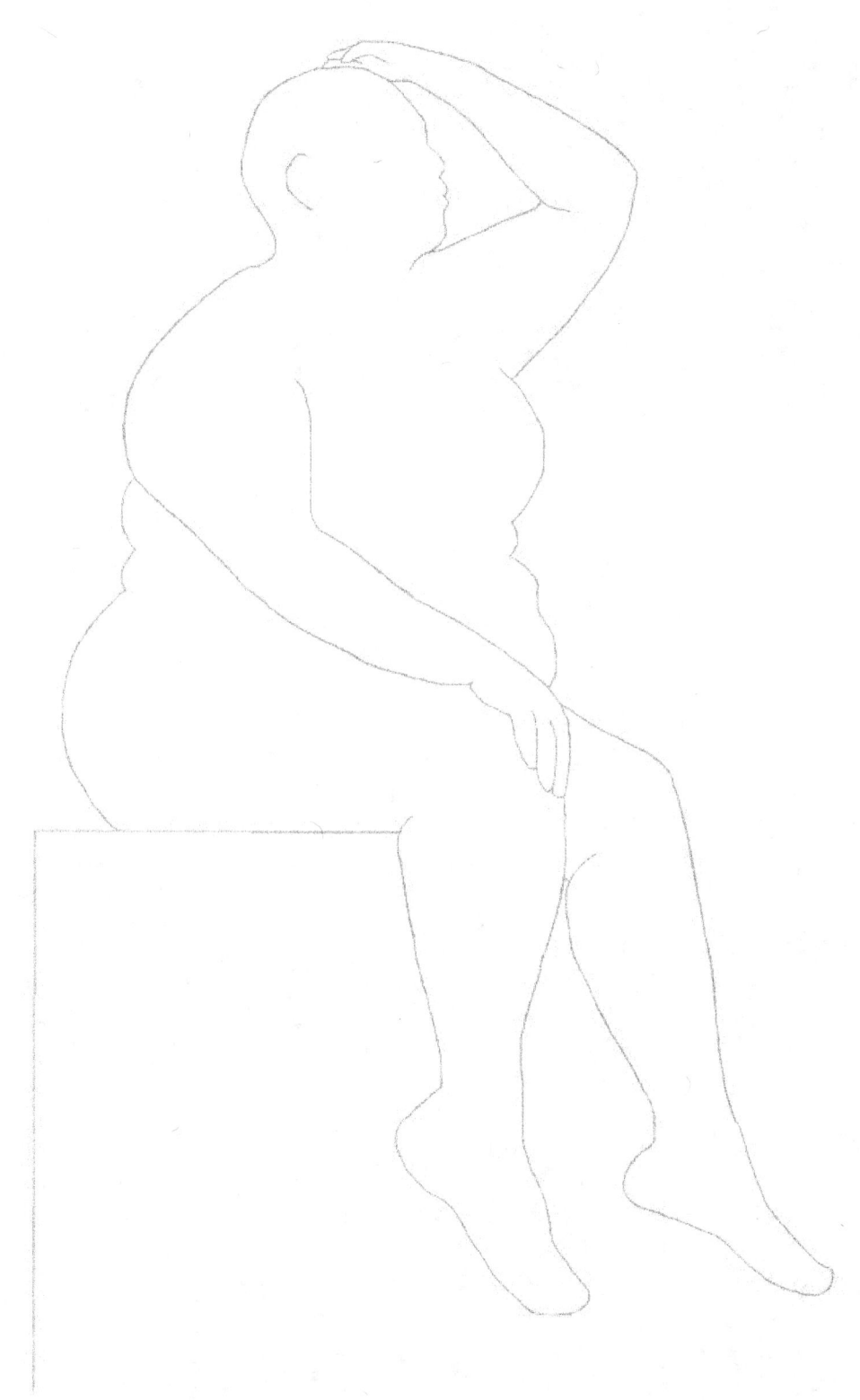

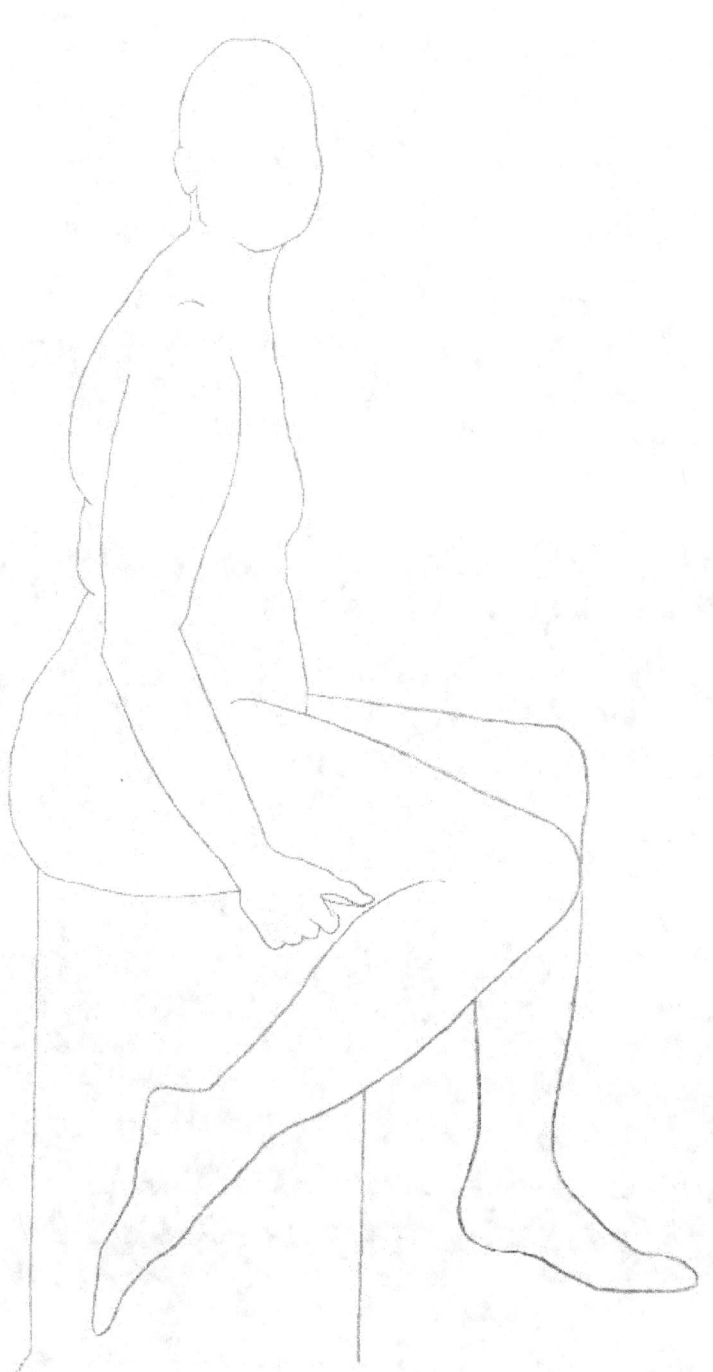

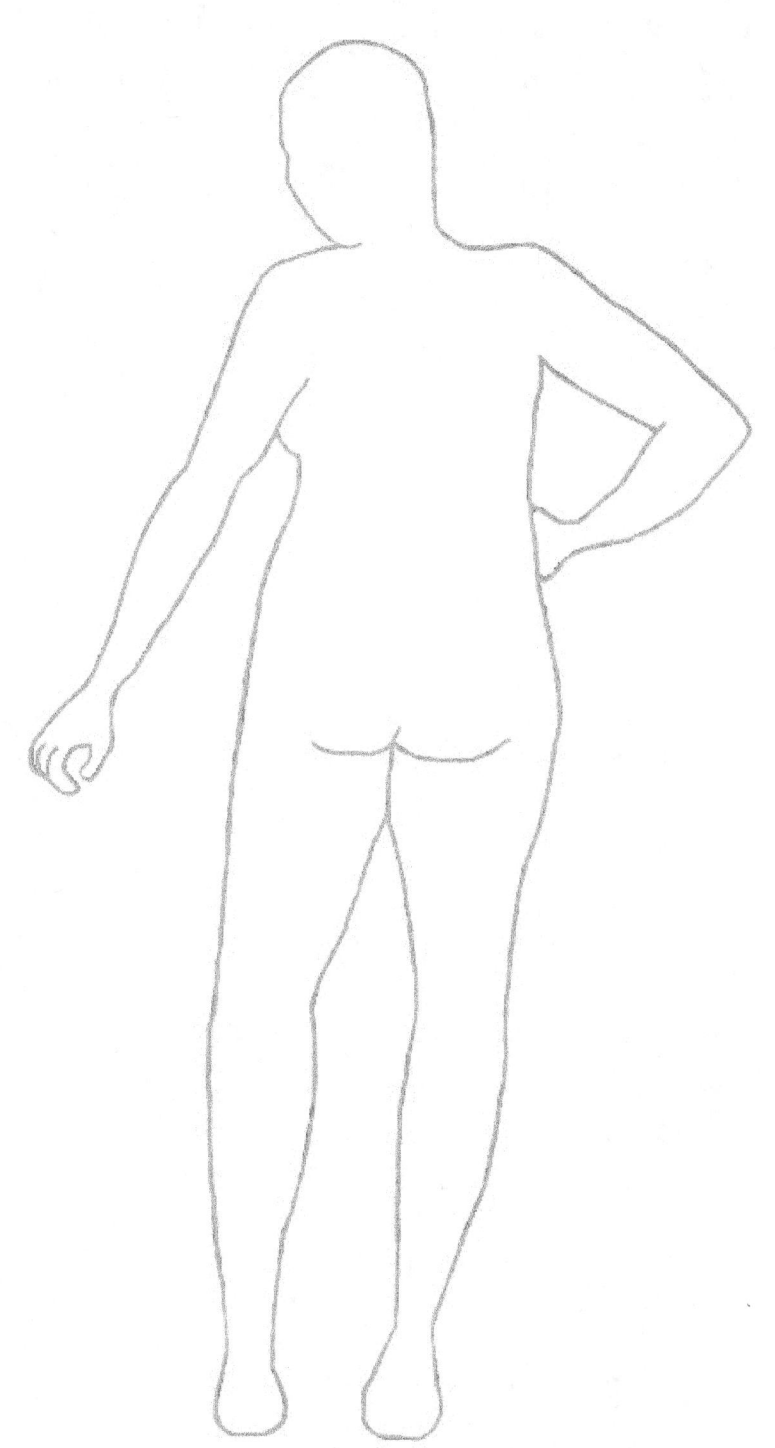

www.ingramcontent.com/pod-product-compliance
Lightning Source LLC
Chambersburg PA
CBHW081427220526
45466CB00008B/2290